SURPRISE!

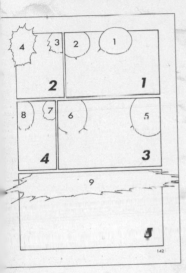

You may be reading the wrong way!

It's true: In keeping with the original Japanese comic format, this book reads from right to left—so action, sound effects, and word balloons are completely reversed. This preserves the orientation of the original artwork—plus, it's fun! Check out the diagram shown here to get the hang of things, and then turn to the other side of the book to get started!

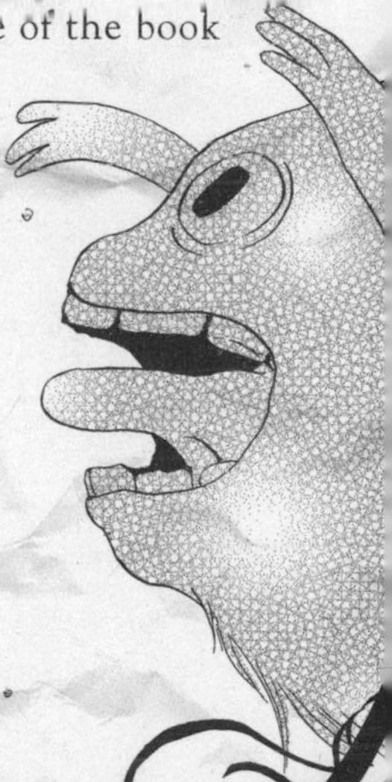

IDOL *dreams*

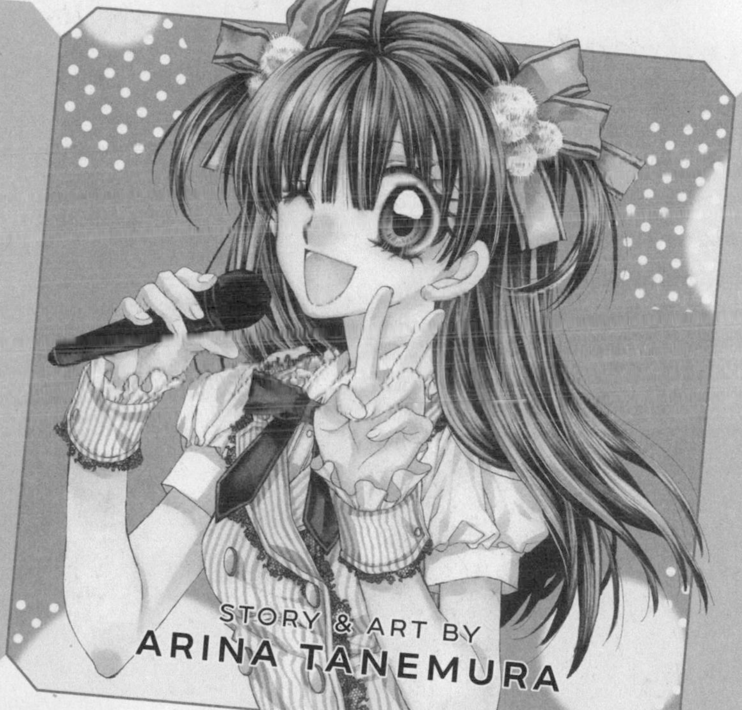

STORY & ART BY
ARINA TANEMURA

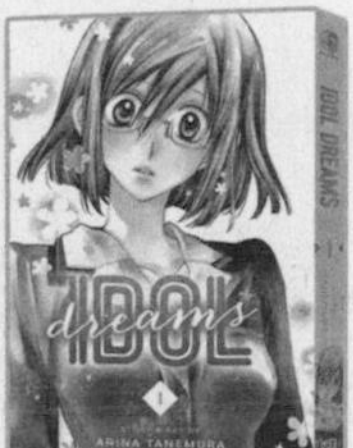
IDOL DREAMS
IDOL
dreams
1
ARINA TANEMURA

At age 31, office worker Chikage Deguchi feels she missed her chances at love and success. When word gets out that she's a virgin, Chikage is humiliated and wishes she could turn back time to when she was still young and popular. She takes an experimental drug that changes her appearance back to when she was 15. Now Chikage is determined to pursue everything she missed out on all those years ago—including becoming a star!

Shojo Beat VIZ RATED T TEEN

Snow White
with the Red Hair

Inspired
the anime!

STORY & ART BY
SORATA AKIDUKI

Shirayuki is an herbalist famous for her naturally bright-red hair, and the prince of Tanbarun wants her all to himself! Unwilling to become the prince's possession, she seeks shelter in the woods of the neighboring kingdom, where she gains an unlikely ally—the prince of that kingdom! He rescues her from her plight, and thus begins the love story between a lovestruck prince and an unusual herbalist.

NATSUME'S BOOK OF FRIENDS

Vol. 10
Shojo Beat Edition

STORY AND ART BY **Yuki Midorikawa**

Translation & Adaptation **Lillian Olsen**
Touch-up Art & Lettering **Sabrina Heep**
Design **Fawn Lau**
Editor **Pancha Diaz**

Natsume Yujincho by Yuki Midorikawa
© Yuki Midorikawa 2010
All rights reserved.
First published in Japan in 2010 by HAKUSENSHA, Inc., Tokyo.
English language translation rights arranged with HAKUSENSHA, Inc., Tokyo.

The stories, characters and incidents mentioned in this publication are entirely fictional.

Printed in Canada

Published by VIZ Media, LLC
P.O. Box 77010
San Francisco, CA 94107

10 9 8 7 6 5 4 3
First printing, December 2011
Third printing, February 2019

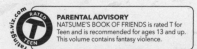

Yuki Midorikawa

is the creator of *Natsume's Book of Friends*, which was nominated for the Manga Taisho (Cartoon Grand Prize). Her other titles published in Japan include *Hotarubi no Mori e* (Into the Forest of Fireflies), *Hiiro no Isu* (The Scarlet Chair) and *Akaku Saku Koe* (The Voice That Blooms Red).

Natsume's
BOOK of FRIENDS

Shojo Beat

Natsume's BOOK of FRIENDS

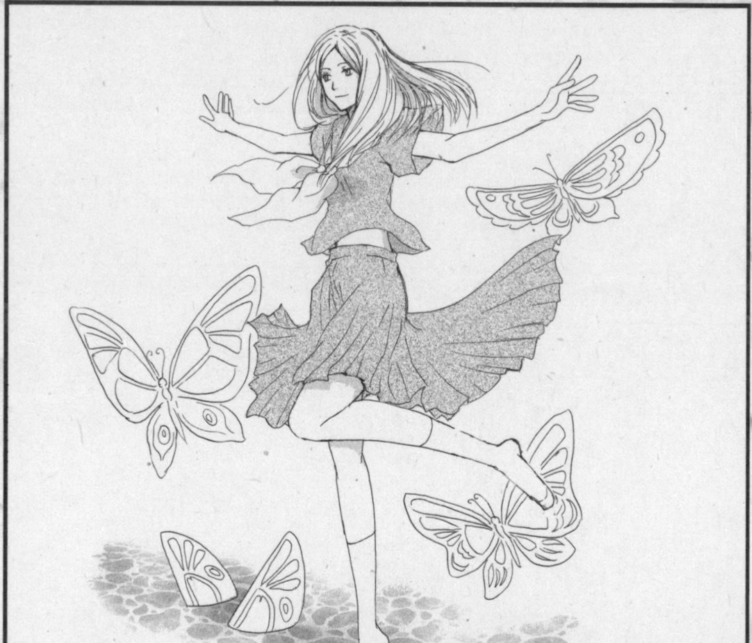

STORY and ART by
Yuki Midorikawa

VOLUME 10

Natsume's BOOK of FRIENDS
VOLUME 10 CONTENTS

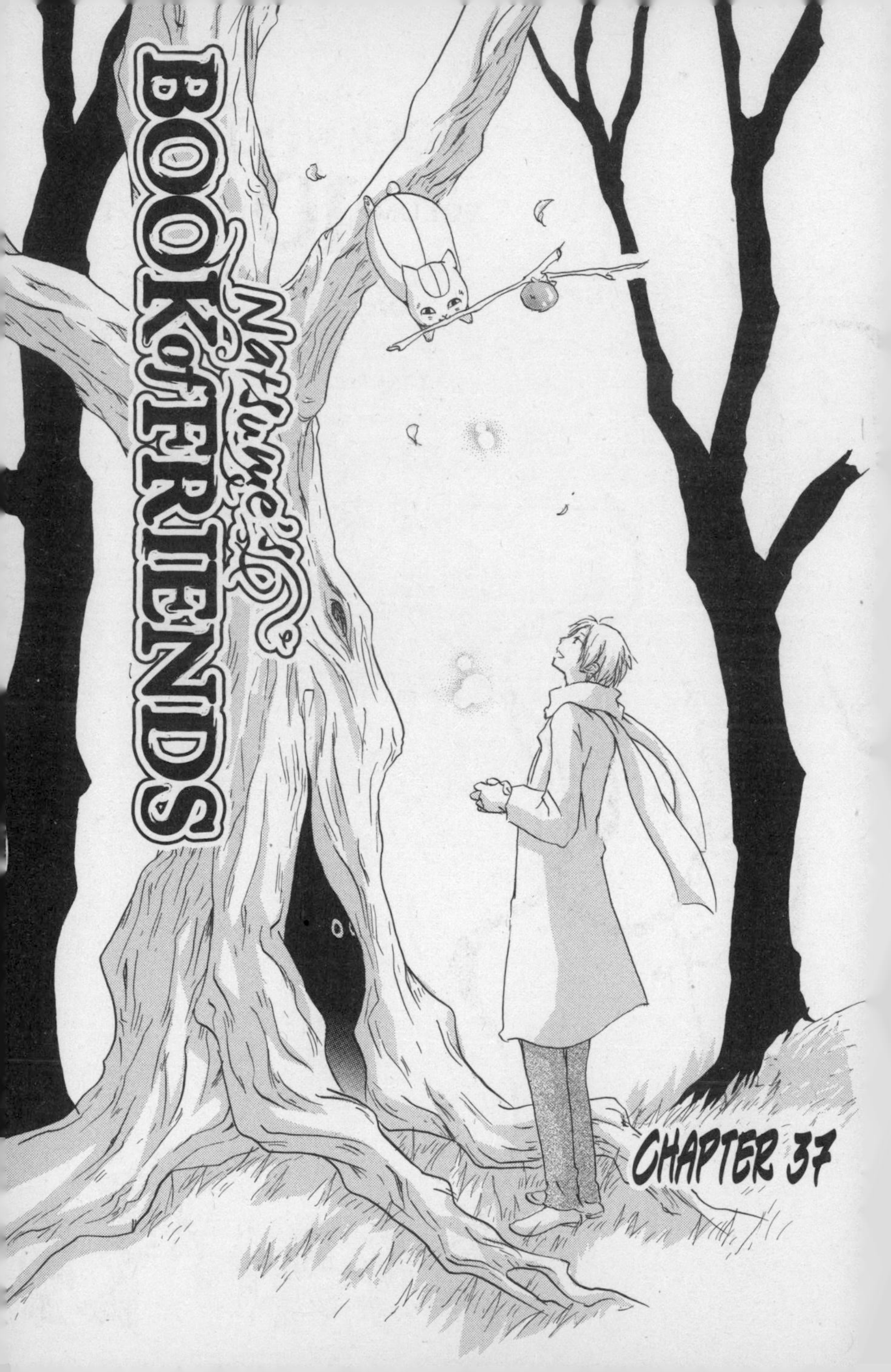
Natsume's
BOOK of FRIENDS
CHAPTER 37

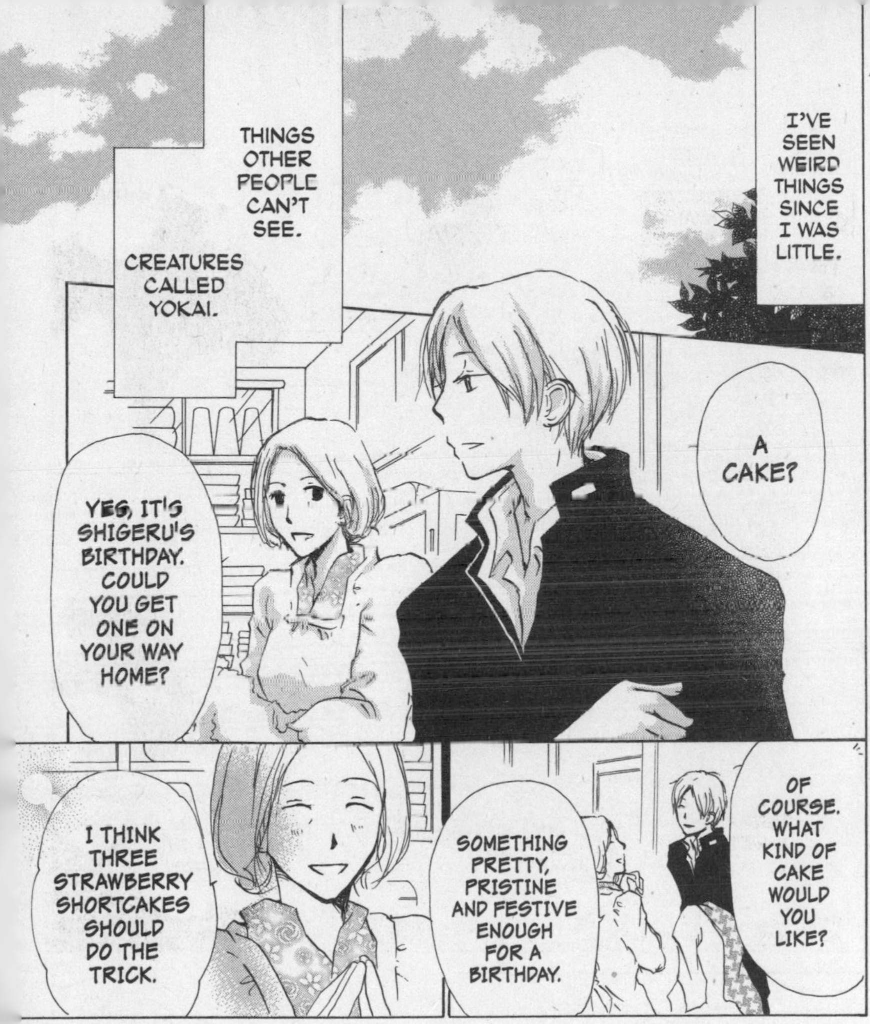
I'VE SEEN WEIRD THINGS SINCE I WAS LITTLE.
THINGS OTHER PEOPLE CAN'T SEE.
CREATURES CALLED YOKAI.
A CAKE?
YES, IT'S SHIGERU'S BIRTHDAY. COULD YOU GET ONE ON YOUR WAY HOME?
OF COURSE. WHAT KIND OF CAKE WOULD YOU LIKE?
SOMETHING PRETTY, PRISTINE AND FESTIVE ENOUGH FOR A BIRTHDAY.
I THINK THREE STRAWBERRY SHORTCAKES SHOULD DO THE TRICK.

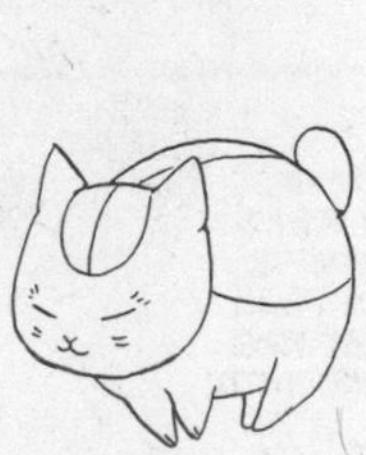

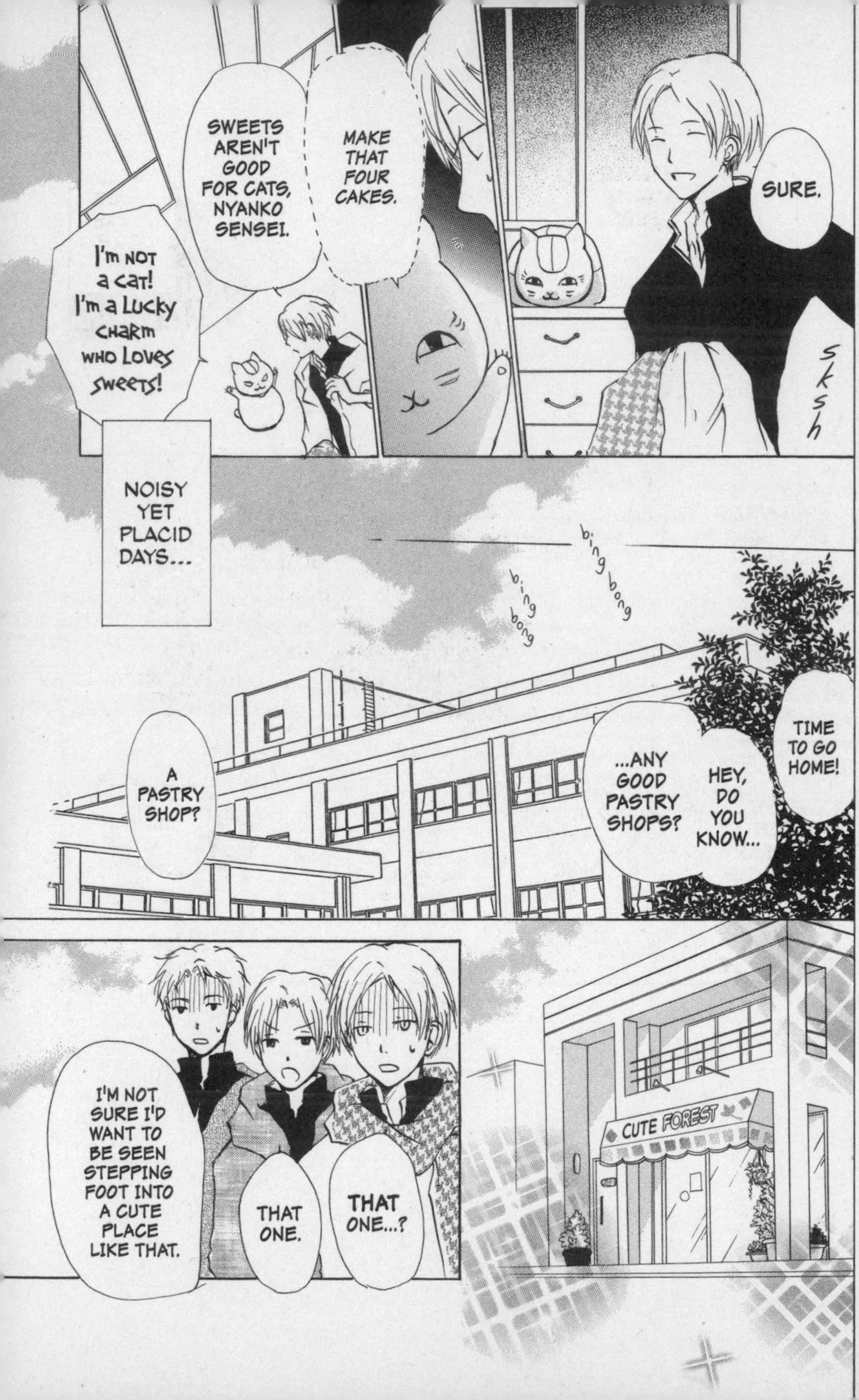
SURE.
sksh
MAKE THAT FOUR CAKES.
SWEETS AREN'T GOOD FOR CATS, NYANKO SENSEI.
I'm not a cat! I'm a lucky charm who loves sweets!
NOISY YET PLACID DAYS...
bing bong
bing bong
TIME TO GO HOME!
HEY, DO YOU KNOW...
...ANY GOOD PASTRY SHOPS?
A PASTRY SHOP?
CUTE FOREST
THAT ONE...?
THAT ONE.
I'M NOT SURE I'D WANT TO BE SEEN STEPPING FOOT INTO A CUTE PLACE LIKE THAT.

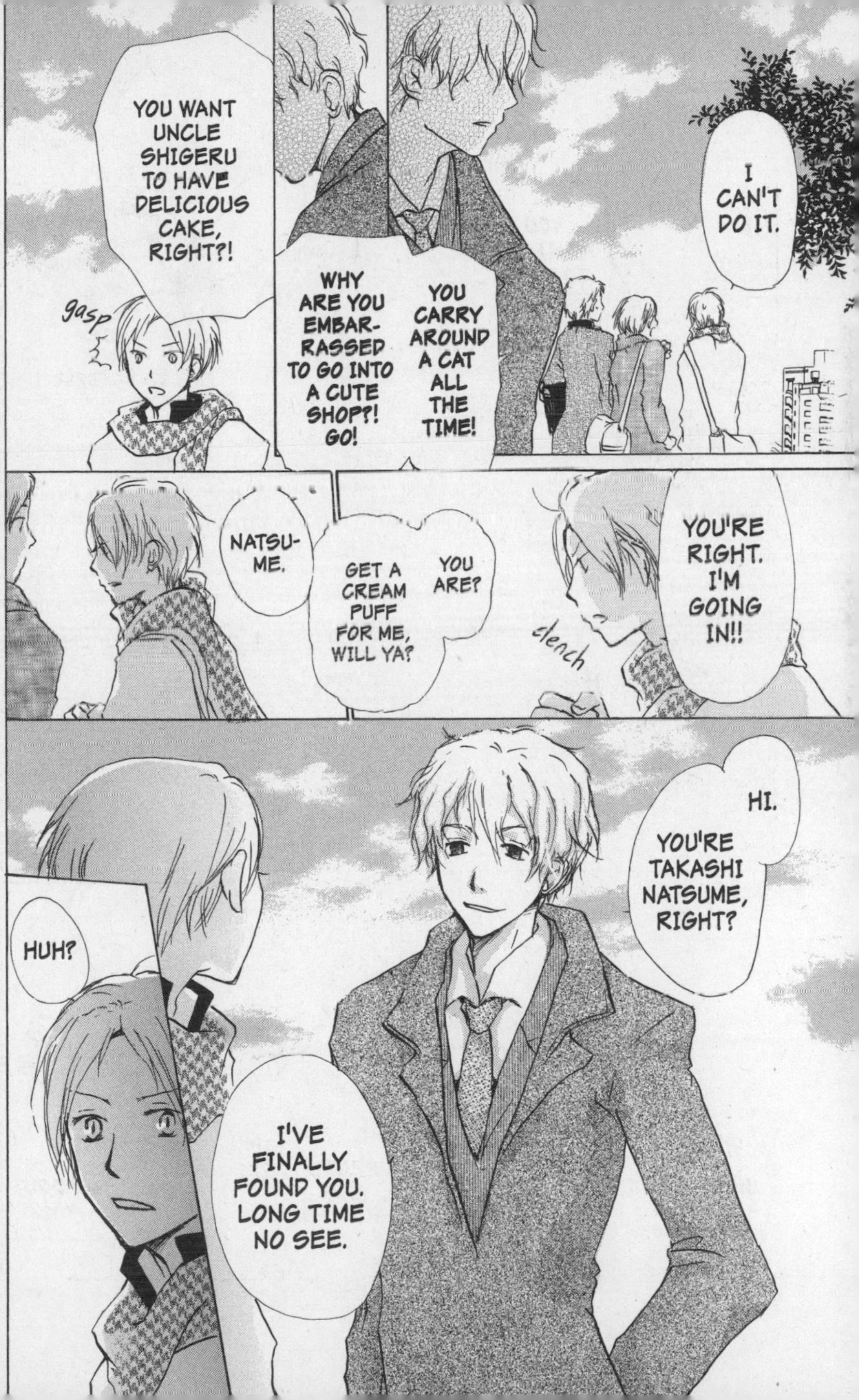
I CAN'T DO IT.
YOU CARRY AROUND A CAT ALL THE TIME!
WHY ARE YOU EMBARRASSED TO GO INTO A CUTE SHOP?! GO!
YOU WANT UNCLE SHIGERU TO HAVE DELICIOUS CAKE, RIGHT?!
gasp
YOU'RE RIGHT. I'M GOING IN!!
clench
YOU ARE?
NATSUME.
GET A CREAM PUFF FOR ME, WILL YA?
HI.
YOU'RE TAKASHI NATSUME, RIGHT?
I'VE FINALLY FOUND YOU. LONG TIME NO SEE.
HUH?

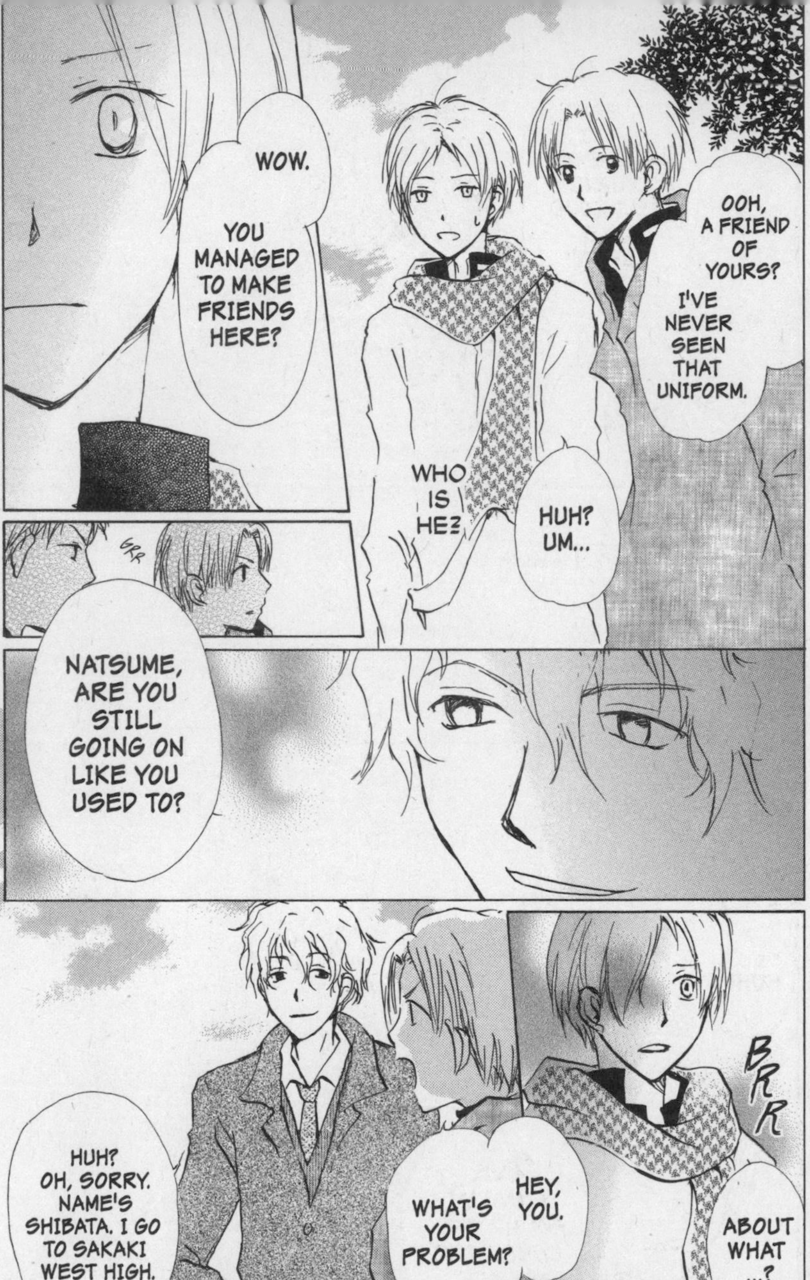
OOH, A FRIEND OF YOURS? I'VE NEVER SEEN THAT UNIFORM.
HUH? UM...
WHO IS HE?
WOW. YOU MANAGED TO MAKE FRIENDS HERE?
GRR
NATSUME, ARE YOU STILL GOING ON LIKE YOU USED TO?
BRR
ABOUT WHAT ...?
HEY, YOU. WHAT'S YOUR PROBLEM?
HUH? OH, SORRY. NAME'S SHIBATA. I GO TO SAKAKI WEST HIGH.

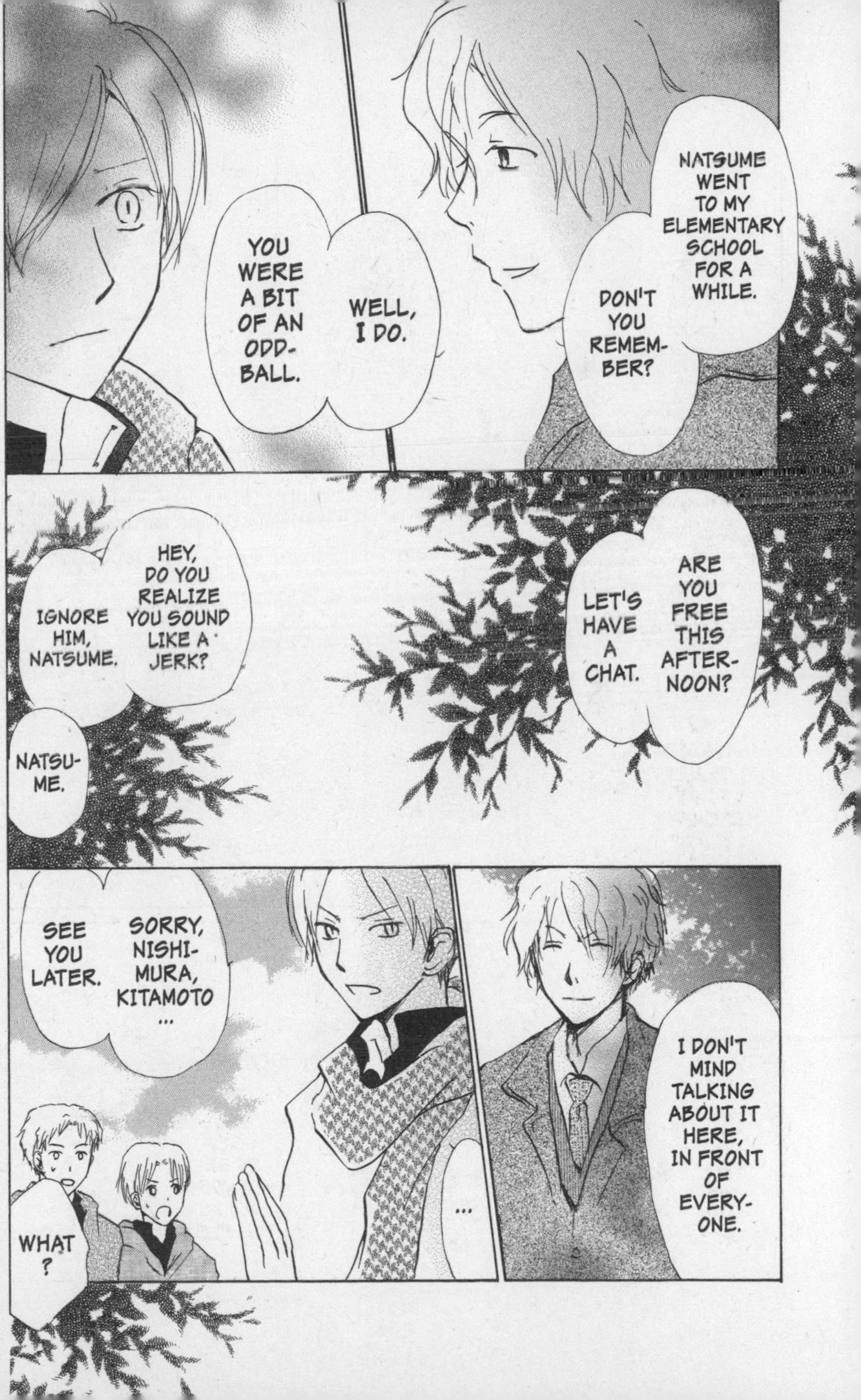
NATSUME WENT TO MY ELEMENTARY SCHOOL FOR A WHILE.
DON'T YOU REMEMBER?
WELL, I DO.
YOU WERE A BIT OF AN ODDBALL.
ARE YOU FREE THIS AFTERNOON?
LET'S HAVE A CHAT.
HEY, DO YOU REALIZE YOU SOUND LIKE A JERK?
IGNORE HIM, NATSUME.
NATSUME.
I DON'T MIND TALKING ABOUT IT HERE, IN FRONT OF EVERYONE.
...
SORRY, NISHIMURA, KITAMOTO...
SEE YOU LATER.
WHAT?

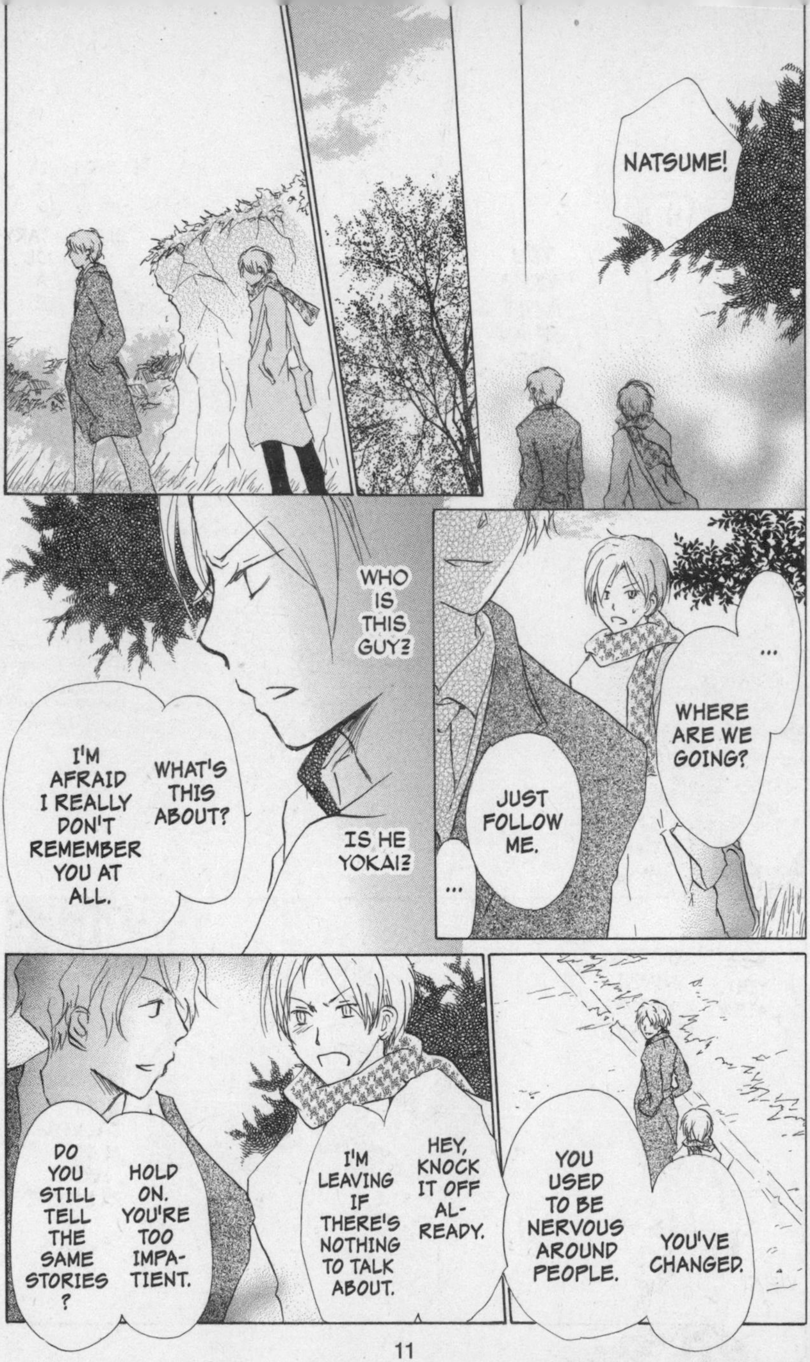
NATSUME!
...
WHERE ARE WE GOING?
JUST FOLLOW ME.
...
WHO IS THIS GUY?!
IS HE YOKAI?!
WHAT'S THIS ABOUT?
I'M AFRAID I REALLY DON'T REMEMBER YOU AT ALL.
YOU'VE CHANGED.
YOU USED TO BE NERVOUS AROUND PEOPLE.
HEY, KNOCK IT OFF AL-READY.
I'M LEAVING IF THERE'S NOTHING TO TALK ABOUT.
HOLD ON. YOU'RE TOO IMPA-TIENT.
DO YOU STILL TELL THE SAME STORIES?

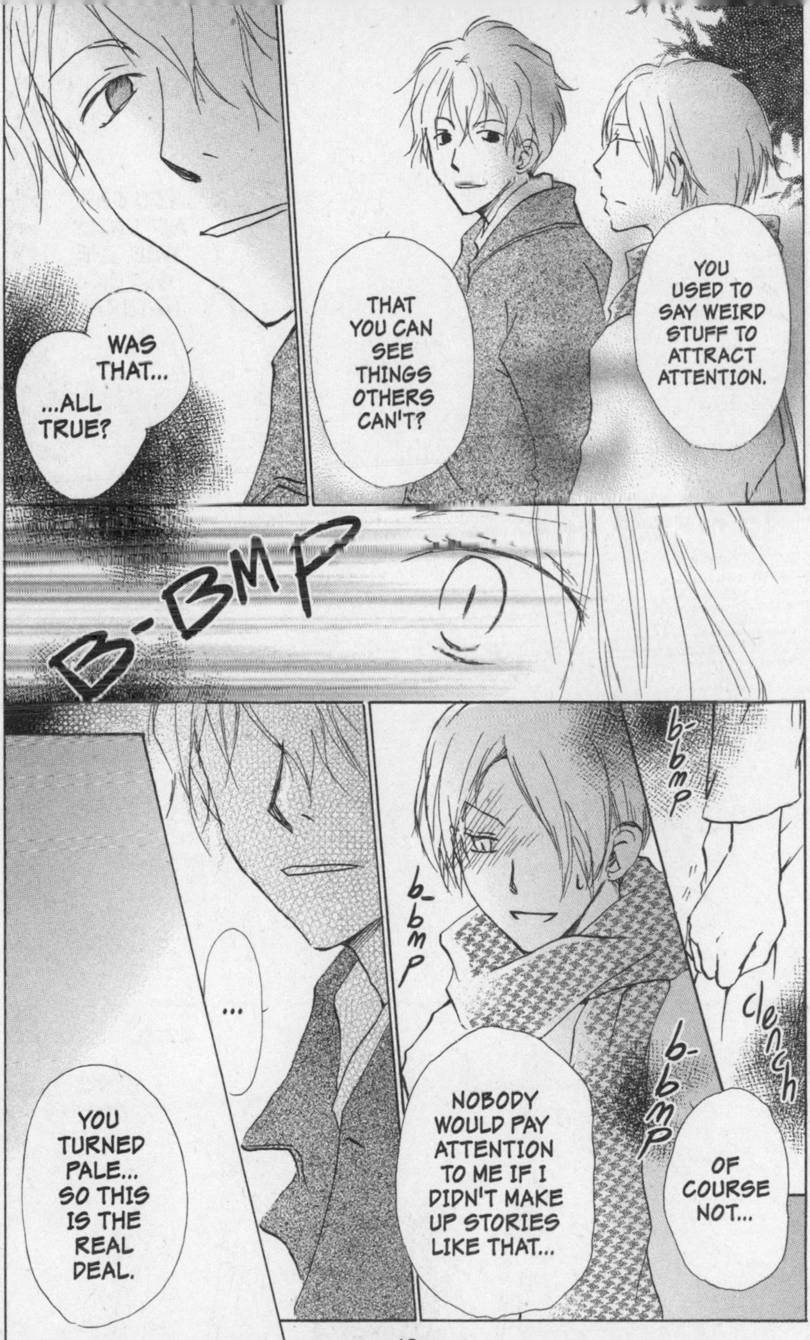
YOU USED TO SAY WEIRD STUFF TO ATTRACT ATTENTION.
THAT YOU CAN SEE THINGS OTHERS CAN'T?
WAS THAT...
...ALL TRUE?
B-BMP
b-bmp
clench
OF COURSE NOT...
b-bmp
NOBODY WOULD PAY ATTENTION TO ME IF I DIDN'T MAKE UP STORIES LIKE THAT...
b-bmp
...
YOU TURNED PALE... SO THIS IS THE REAL DEAL.

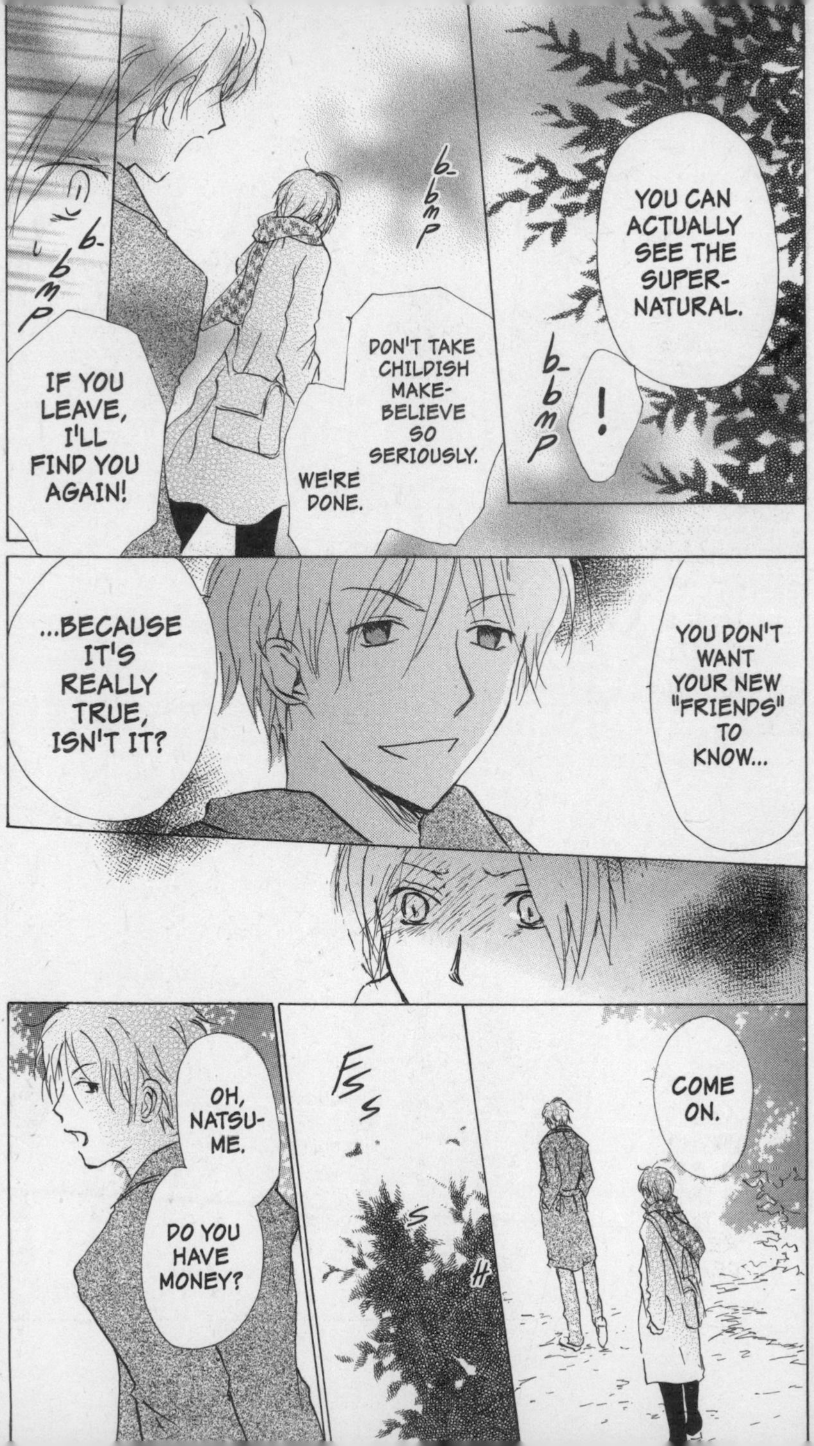
YOU CAN ACTUALLY SEE THE SUPER-NATURAL.
!
b-bmp
b-bmp
DON'T TAKE CHILDISH MAKE-BELIEVE SO SERIOUSLY.
WE'RE DONE.
IF YOU LEAVE, I'LL FIND YOU AGAIN!
b-bmp
YOU DON'T WANT YOUR NEW "FRIENDS" TO KNOW...
...BECAUSE IT'S REALLY TRUE, ISN'T IT?
COME ON.
FSS
OH, NATSU-ME.
DO YOU HAVE MONEY?

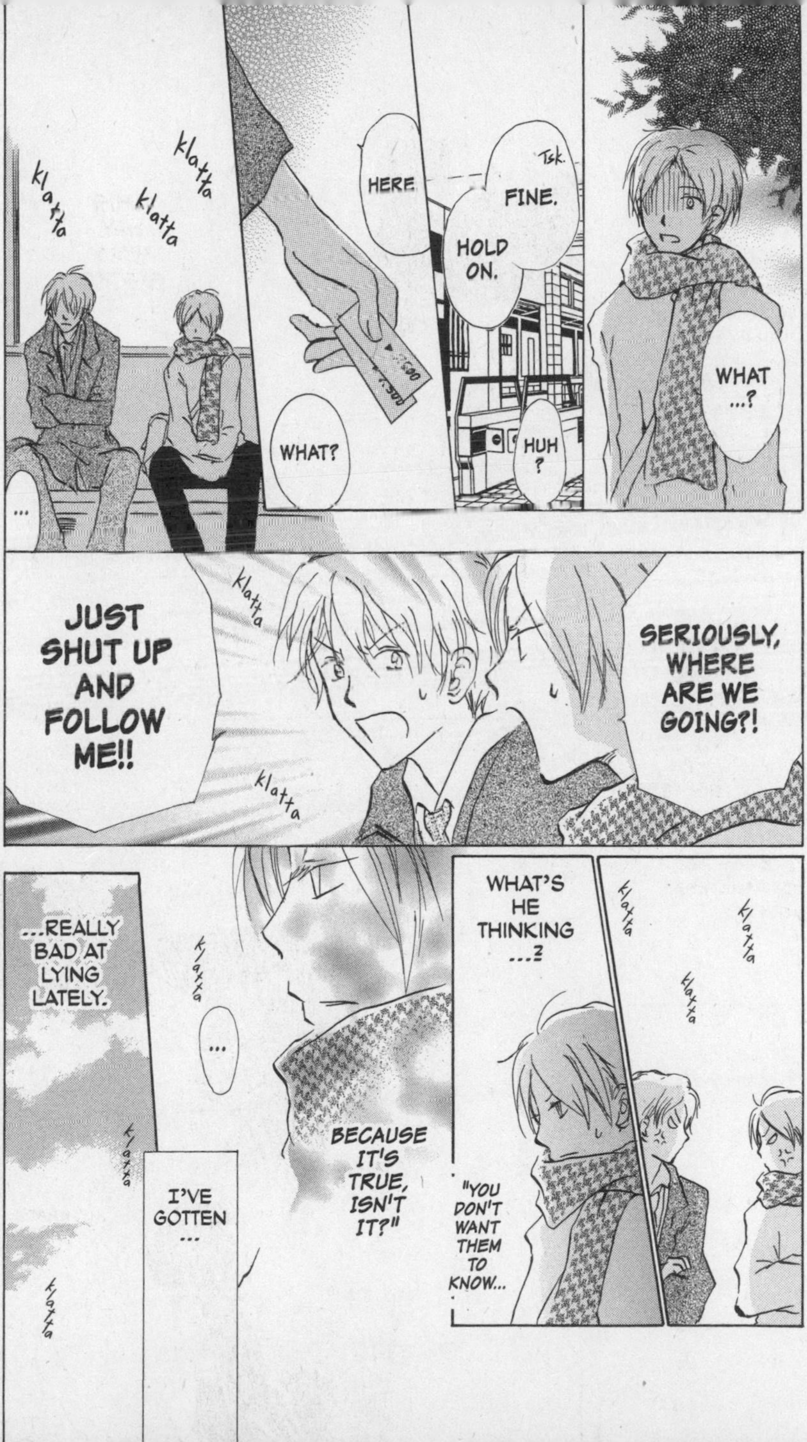
WHAT ...?
Tsk.
FINE.
HOLD ON.
HUH ?
HERE
WHAT?
klatta
klatta
klatta
...
SERIOUSLY, WHERE ARE WE GOING?!
klatta
JUST SHUT UP AND FOLLOW ME!!
klatta
klatta
klatta
klatta
WHAT'S HE THINKING ...?
"YOU DON'T WANT THEM TO KNOW...
BECAUSE IT'S TRUE, ISN'T IT?"
...
klatta
klatta
klatta
I'VE GOTTEN ...
...REALLY BAD AT LYING LATELY.

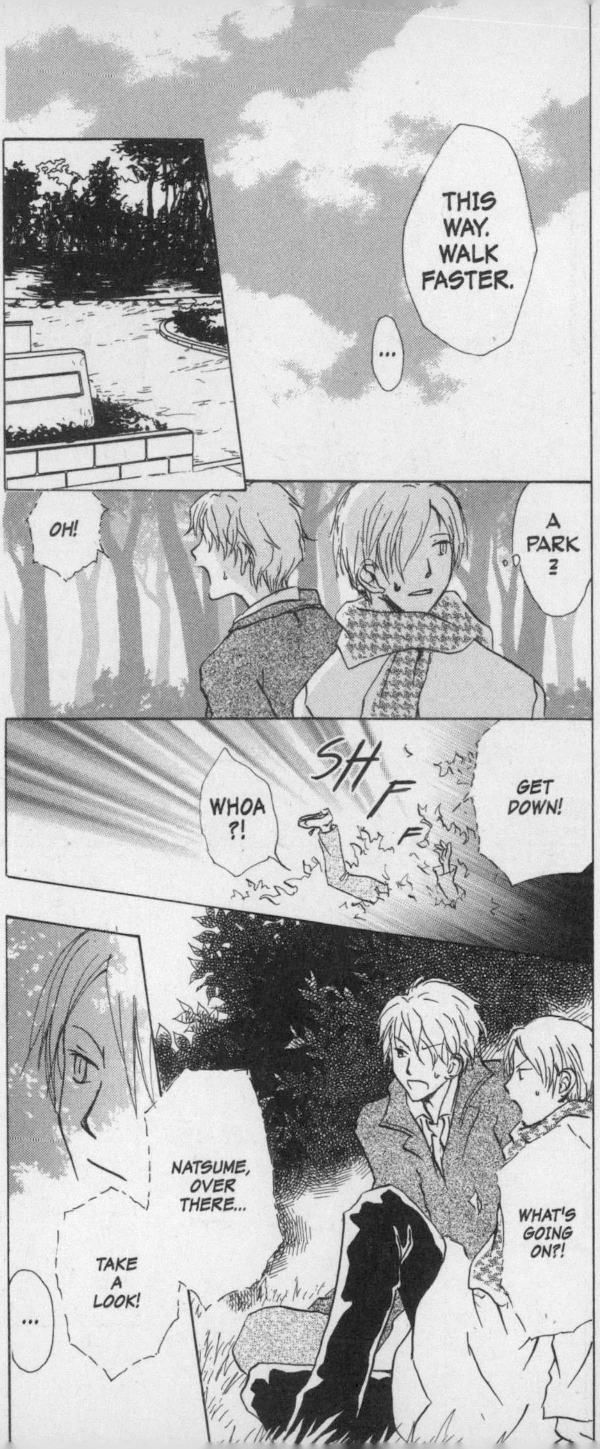
THIS WAY. WALK FASTER.
...
A PARK?
OH!
GET DOWN!
SHFF
WHOA?!
WHAT'S GOING ON?!
NATSUME, OVER THERE...
TAKE A LOOK!
...

01

Hello, I'm Midorikawa. This is my 18th total graphic novel, and the tenth for Natsume, thank you very much.

I'm savoring the joys of being able to keep working on characters and stories I've become attached to.

Thank you for picking this book up and starting a relationship with this series!

I'll keep working hard episode by episode, although I struggle sometimes, so please continue your support.

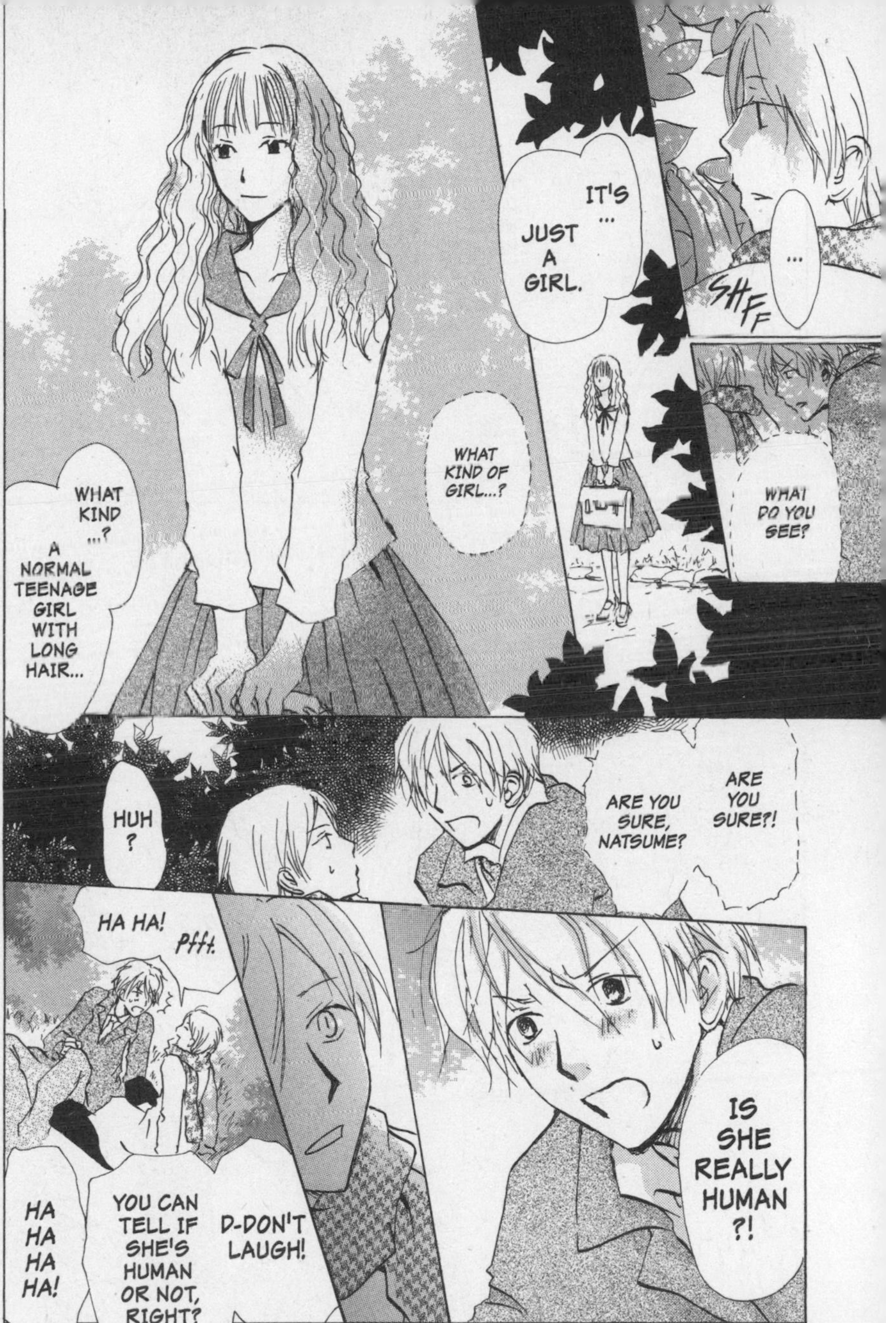

...
SHFF
WHAT DO YOU SEE?
IT'S ... JUST A GIRL.
WHAT KIND OF GIRL...?
WHAT KIND ...?
A NORMAL TEENAGE GIRL WITH LONG HAIR...
ARE YOU SURE?!
ARE YOU SURE, NATSUME?
HUH?
IS SHE REALLY HUMAN?!
Pfft.
HA HA!
D-DON'T LAUGH!
YOU CAN TELL IF SHE'S HUMAN OR NOT, RIGHT?
HA HA HA HA!

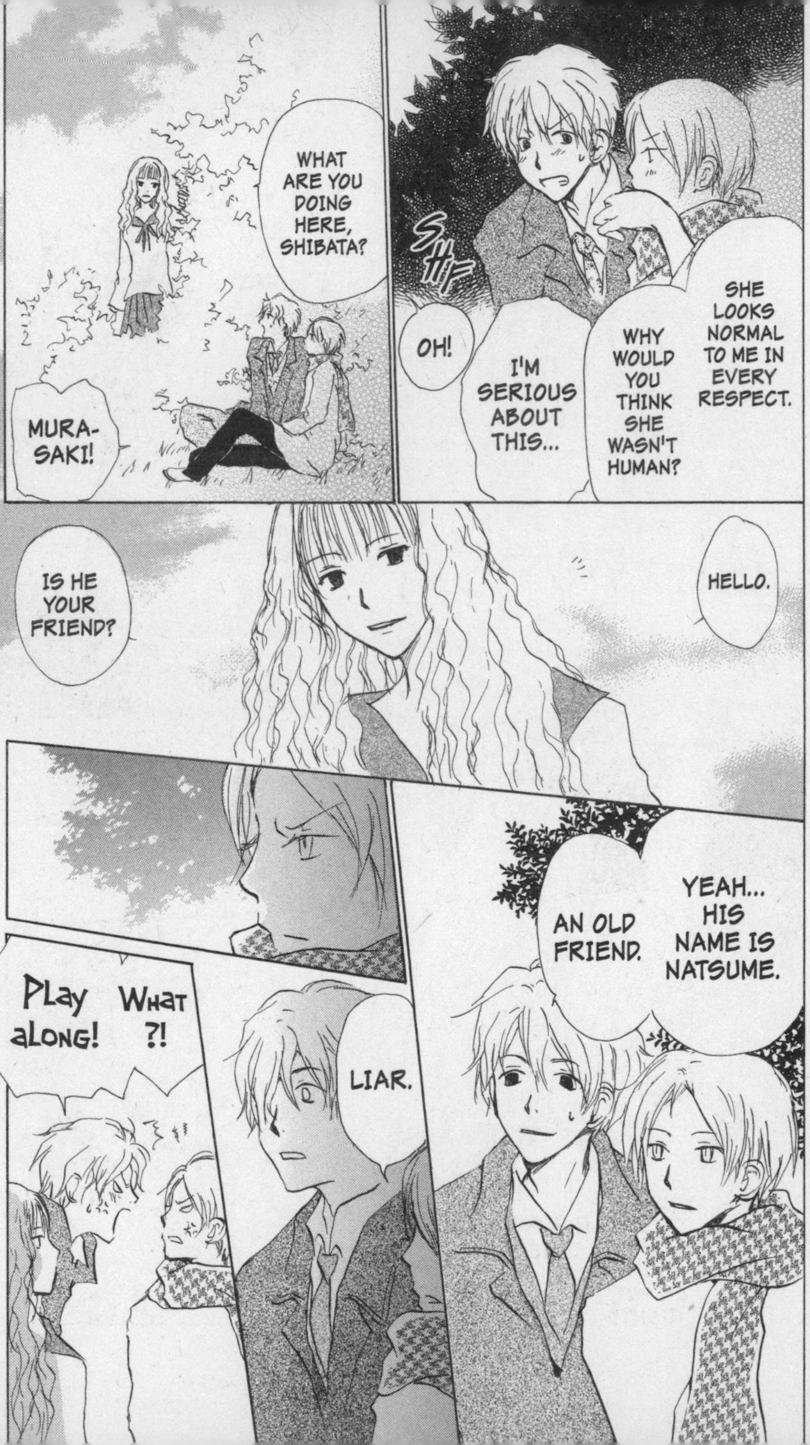
SHE LOOKS NORMAL TO ME IN EVERY RESPECT.
WHY WOULD YOU THINK SHE WASN'T HUMAN?
I'M SERIOUS ABOUT THIS...
OH!
SHF
WHAT ARE YOU DOING HERE, SHIBATA?
MURA-SAKI!
HELLO.
IS HE YOUR FRIEND?
YEAH... HIS NAME IS NATSUME.
AN OLD FRIEND.
LIAR.
WHAT ?!
PLAY ALONG!

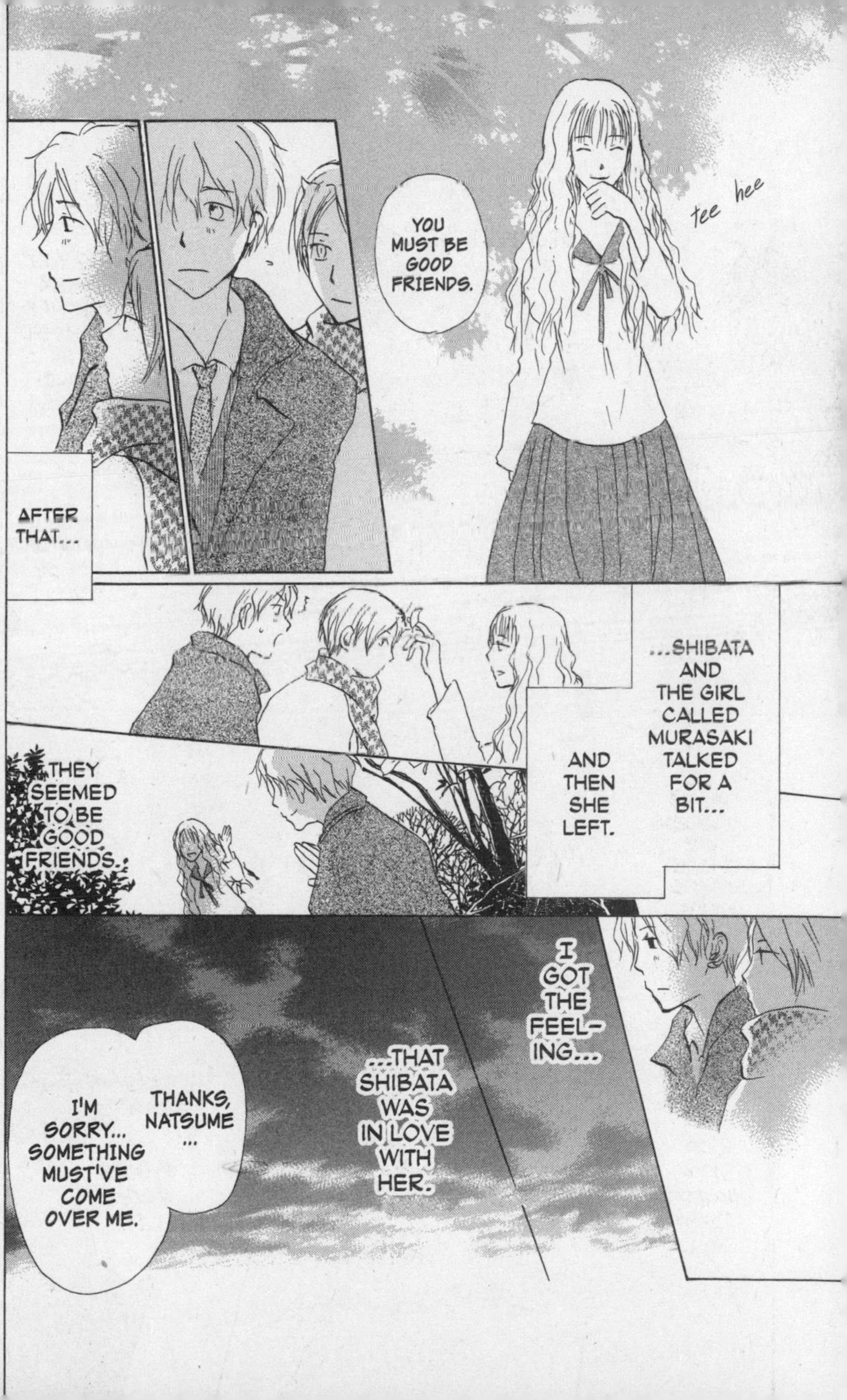
tee hee
YOU MUST BE GOOD FRIENDS.
AFTER THAT...
...SHIBATA AND THE GIRL CALLED MURASAKI TALKED FOR A BIT...
AND THEN SHE LEFT.
THEY SEEMED TO BE GOOD FRIENDS.
I GOT THE FEEL-ING...
...THAT SHIBATA WAS IN LOVE WITH HER.
THANKS, NATSUME ...
I'M SORRY... SOMETHING MUST'VE COME OVER ME.

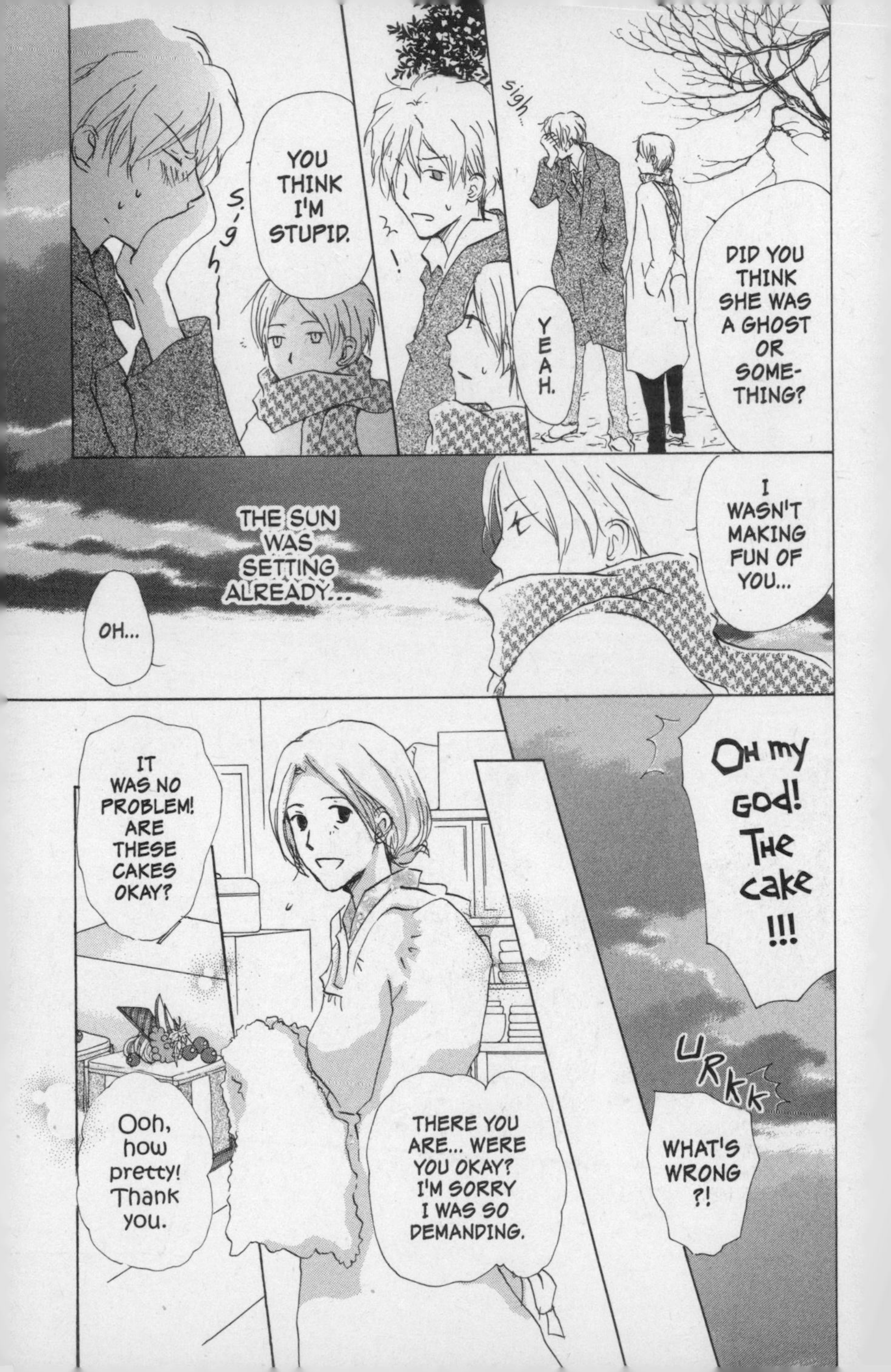
DID YOU THINK SHE WAS A GHOST OR SOMETHING?
sigh...
YEAH.
YOU THINK I'M STUPID.
!
Sigh
I WASN'T MAKING FUN OF YOU...
THE SUN WAS SETTING ALREADY...
OH...
OH my GOD! The cake!!!
URKK
WHAT'S WRONG?!
THERE YOU ARE... WERE YOU OKAY? I'M SORRY I WAS SO DEMANDING.
IT WAS NO PROBLEM! ARE THESE CAKES OKAY?
Ooh, how pretty! Thank you.

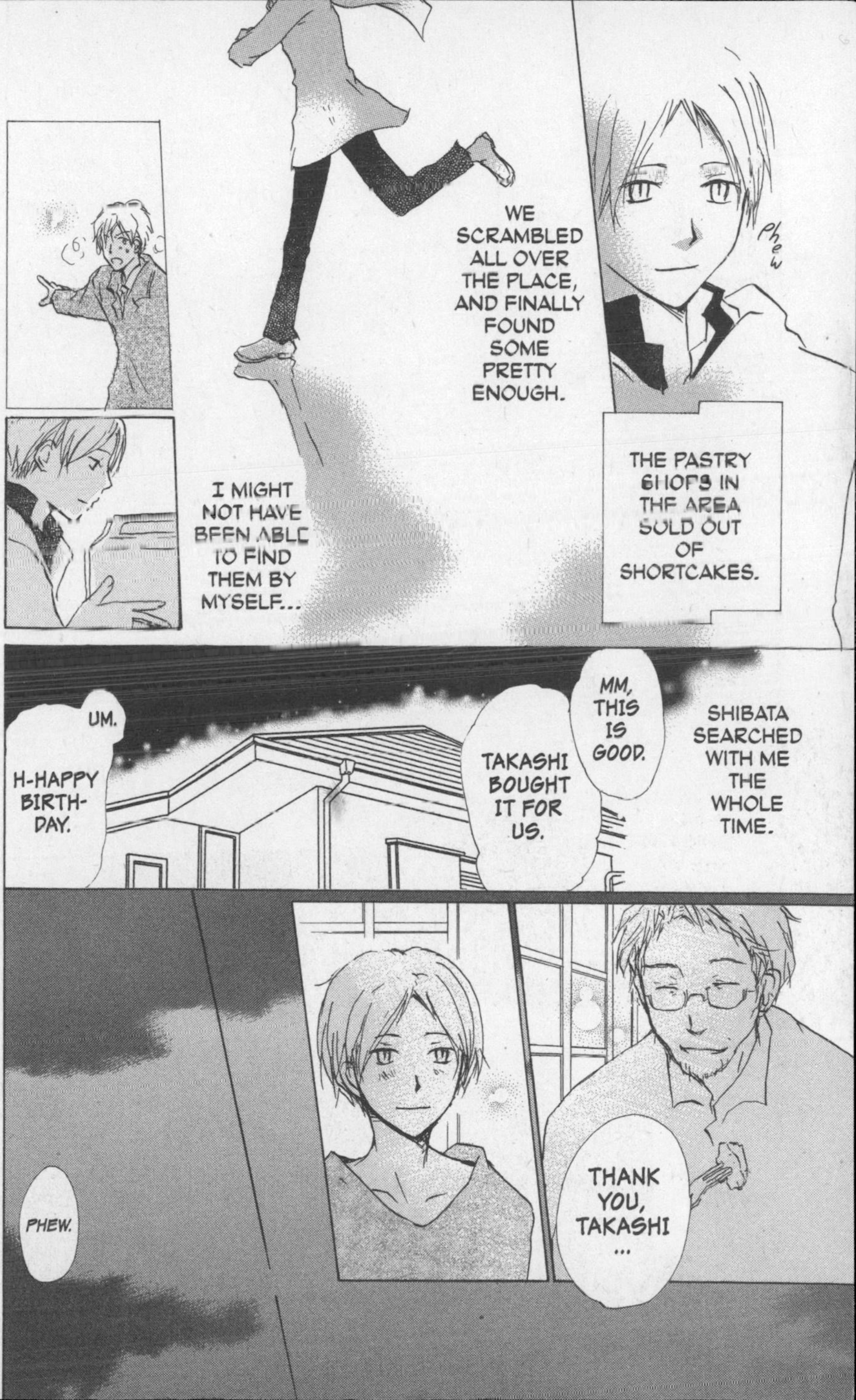

Phew
THE PASTRY SHOPS IN THE AREA SOLD OUT OF SHORTCAKES.
WE SCRAMBLED ALL OVER THE PLACE, AND FINALLY FOUND SOME PRETTY ENOUGH.
I MIGHT NOT HAVE BEEN ABLE TO FIND THEM BY MYSELF...
SHIBATA SEARCHED WITH ME THE WHOLE TIME.
MM, THIS IS GOOD.
TAKASHI BOUGHT IT FOR US.
UM.
H-HAPPY BIRTHDAY.
THANK YOU, TAKASHI ...
PHEW.

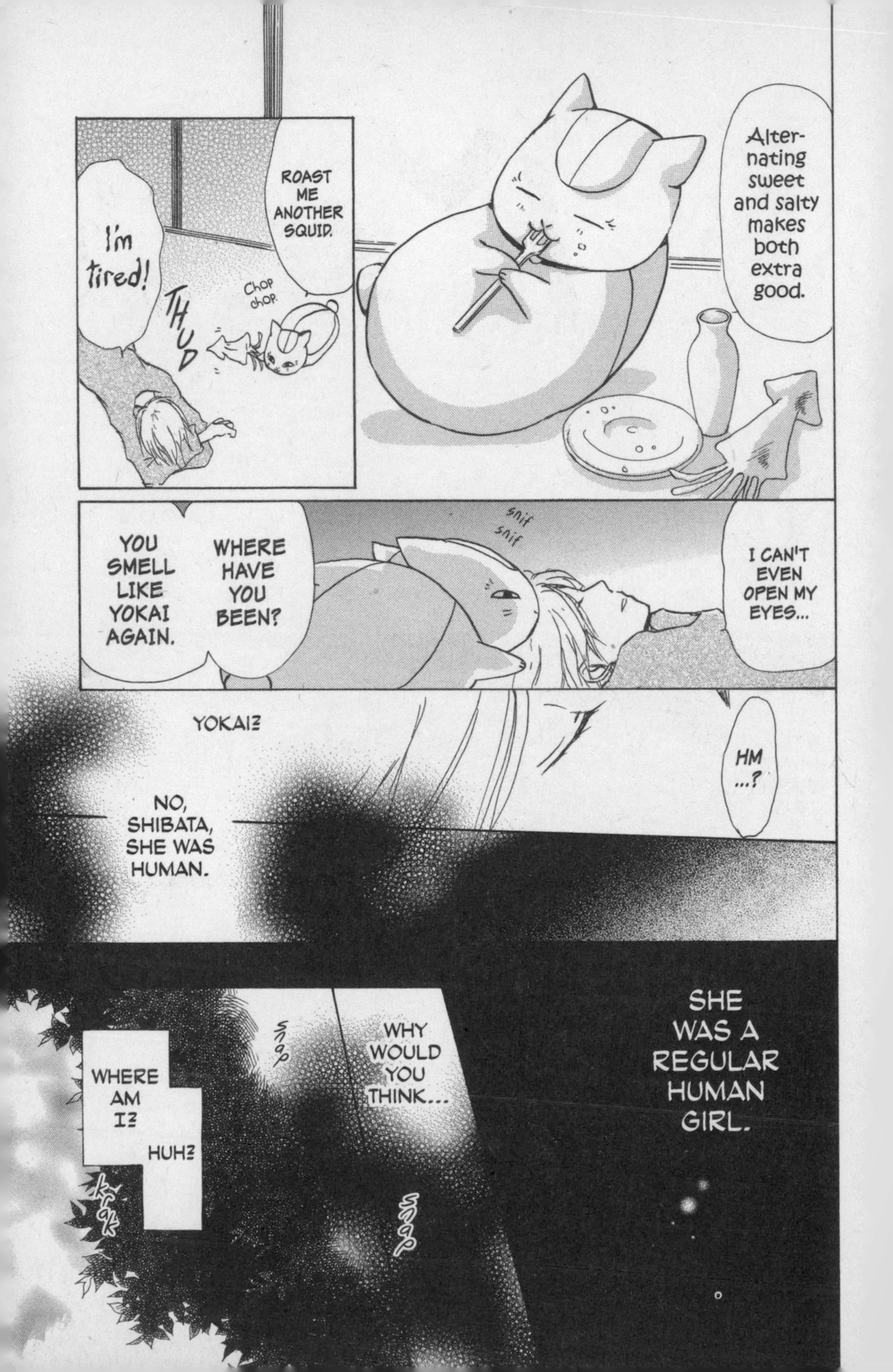
Alternating sweet and salty makes both extra good.
ROAST ME ANOTHER SQUID.
Chop chop.
THUD
I'm tired!
I CAN'T EVEN OPEN MY EYES...
snif snif
WHERE HAVE YOU BEEN?
YOU SMELL LIKE YOKAI AGAIN.
HM ...?
YOKAI?
NO, SHIBATA, SHE WAS HUMAN.
SHE WAS A REGULAR HUMAN GIRL.
WHY WOULD YOU THINK...
snap
snap
WHERE AM I?
HUH?
krak

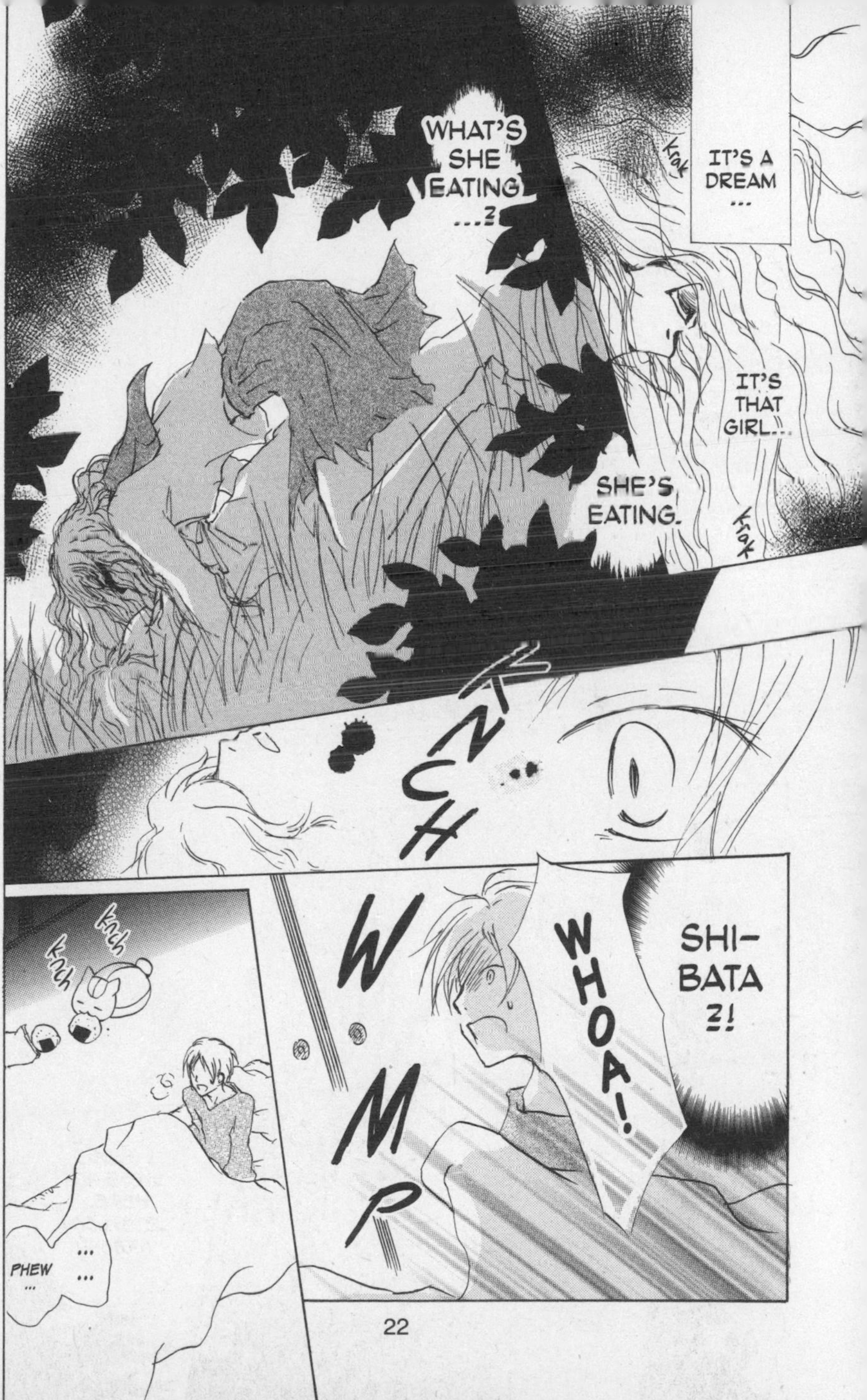
IT'S A DREAM ...
krak
WHAT'S SHE EATING ...?
IT'S THAT GIRL...
SHE'S EATING.
krak
NCH
SHI-BATA?!
WHOA!
WMP
knch
knch
...
...
PHEW ...

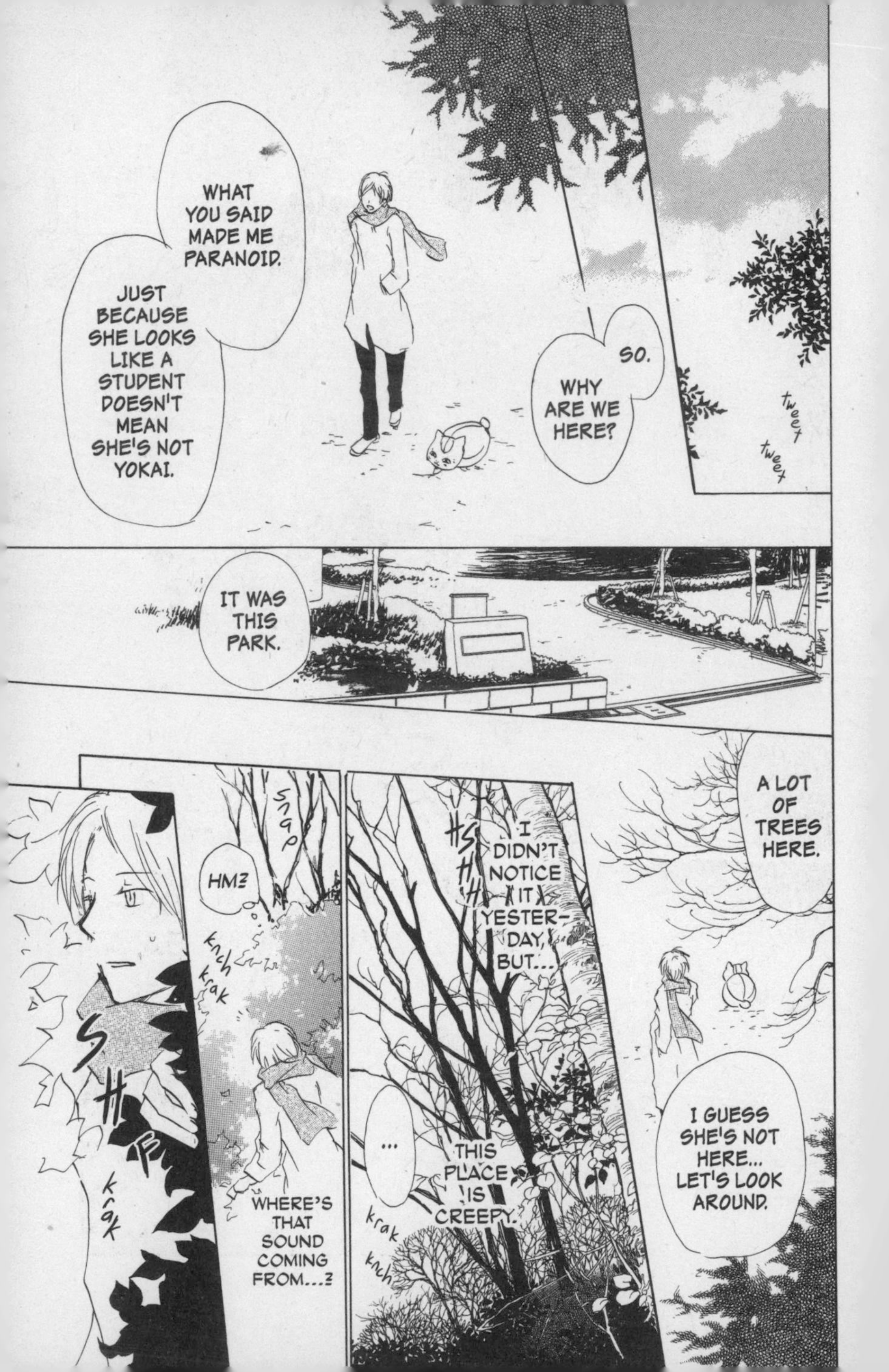
SO.
WHY ARE WE HERE?
tweet
tweet
WHAT YOU SAID MADE ME PARANOID.
JUST BECAUSE SHE LOOKS LIKE A STUDENT DOESN'T MEAN SHE'S NOT YOKAI.
IT WAS THIS PARK.
A LOT OF TREES HERE.
I GUESS SHE'S NOT HERE... LET'S LOOK AROUND.
I DIDN'T NOTICE IT YESTERDAY, BUT...
...
THIS PLACE IS CREEPY.
krak
knch
snap
HM?
knch
krak
WHERE'S THAT SOUND COMING FROM...?
krak

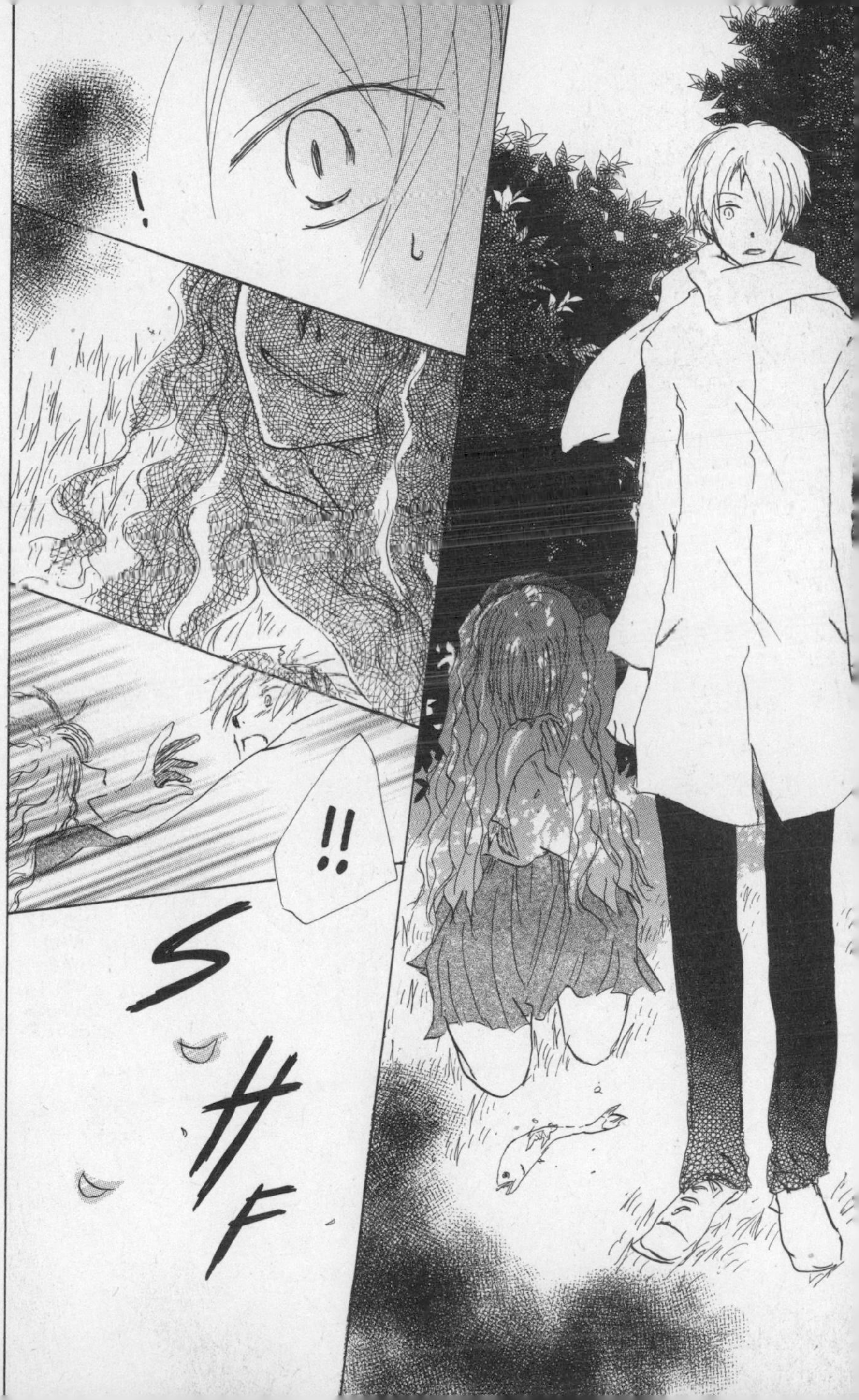
!
!!
SHFF

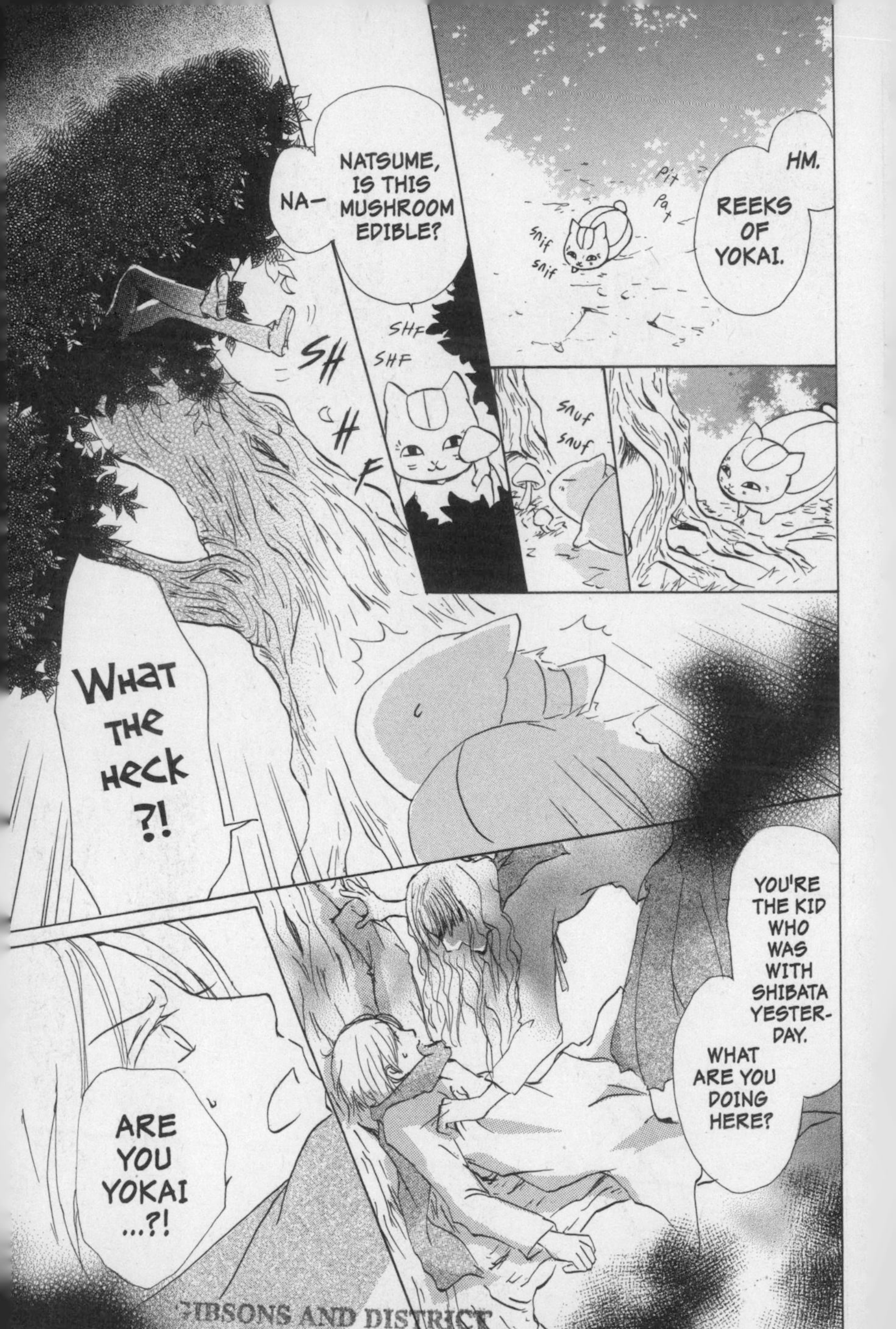
Pit
Pat
snif
snif
HM.
REEKS OF YOKAI.
snauf
snauf
SHF
SHF
NATSUME, IS THIS MUSHROOM EDIBLE?
NA–
SHHF
WHAT THE HECK ?!
YOU'RE THE KID WHO WAS WITH SHIBATA YESTER-DAY.
WHAT ARE YOU DOING HERE?
ARE YOU YOKAI ...?!

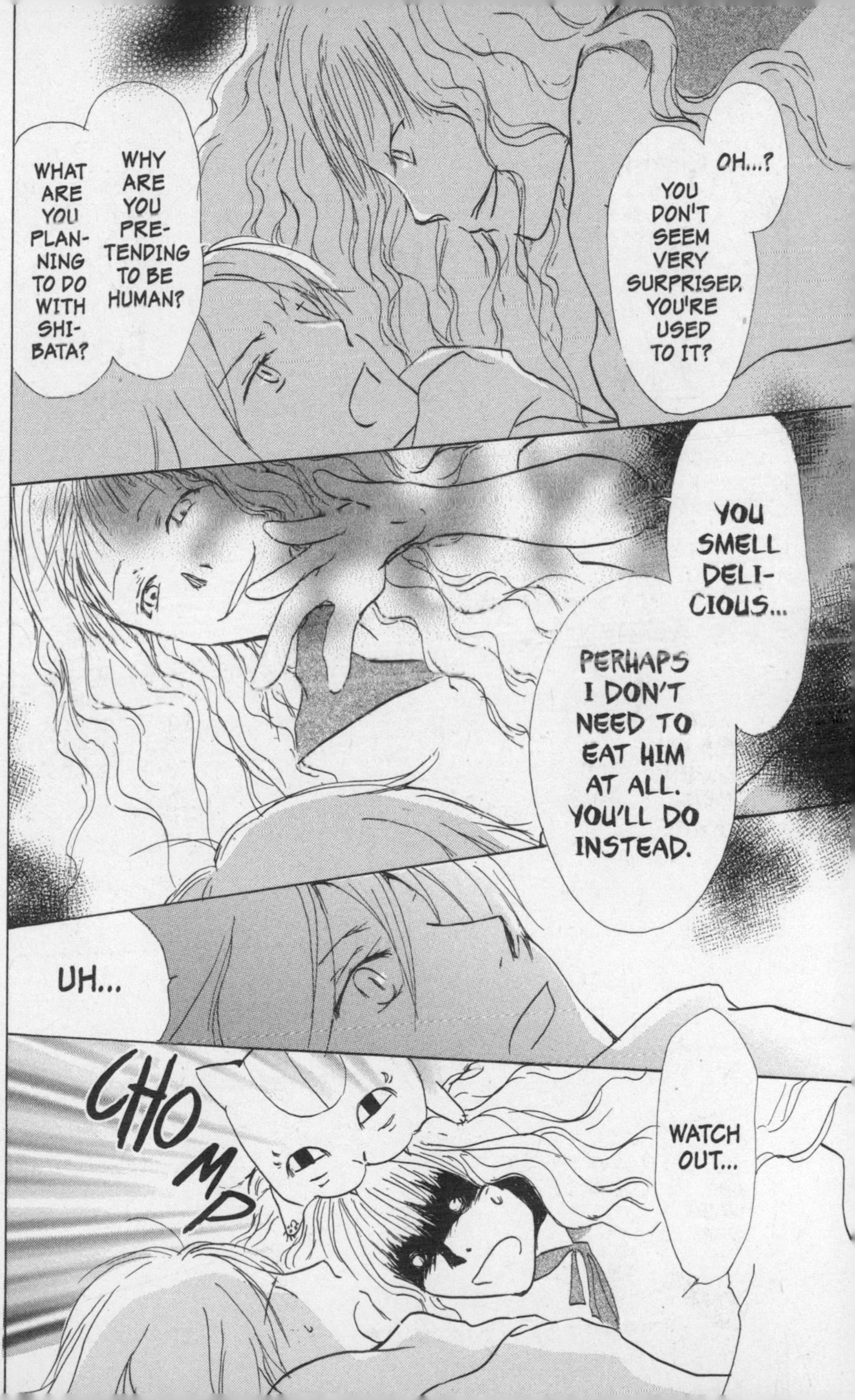
OH...? YOU DON'T SEEM VERY SURPRISED. YOU'RE USED TO IT?
WHY ARE YOU PRETENDING TO BE HUMAN?
WHAT ARE YOU PLANNING TO DO WITH SHIBATA?
YOU SMELL DELICIOUS...
PERHAPS I DON'T NEED TO EAT HIM AT ALL. YOU'LL DO INSTEAD.
UH...
WATCH OUT...
CHOMP

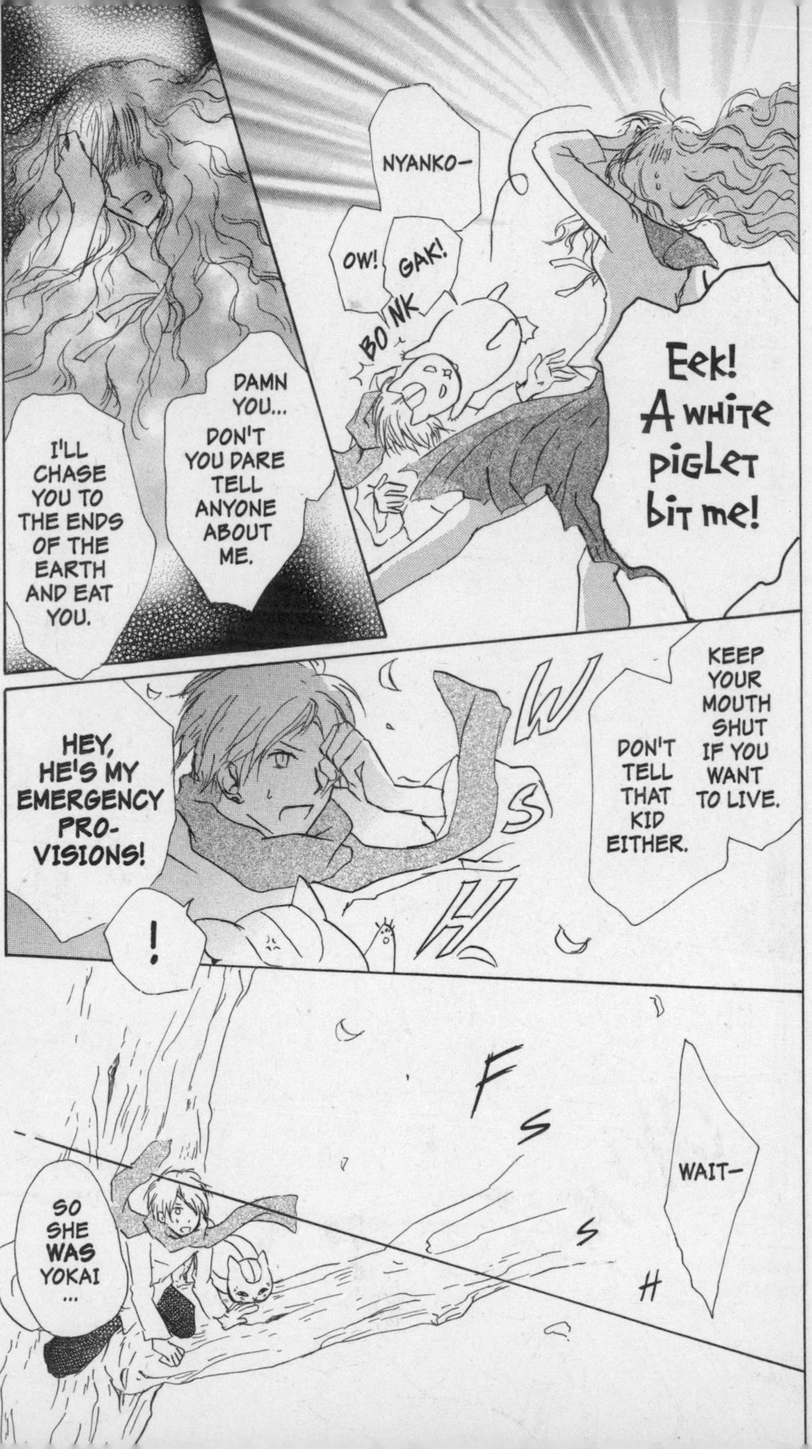
NYANKO—
GAK!
OW!
Eek! A white piglet bit me!
BONK
DAMN YOU... DON'T YOU DARE TELL ANYONE ABOUT ME.
I'LL CHASE YOU TO THE ENDS OF THE EARTH AND EAT YOU.
KEEP YOUR MOUTH SHUT IF YOU WANT TO LIVE.
DON'T TELL THAT KID EITHER.
WSH
HEY, HE'S MY EMERGENCY PRO-VISIONS!
!
WAIT—
FSSH
SO SHE WAS YOKAI ...

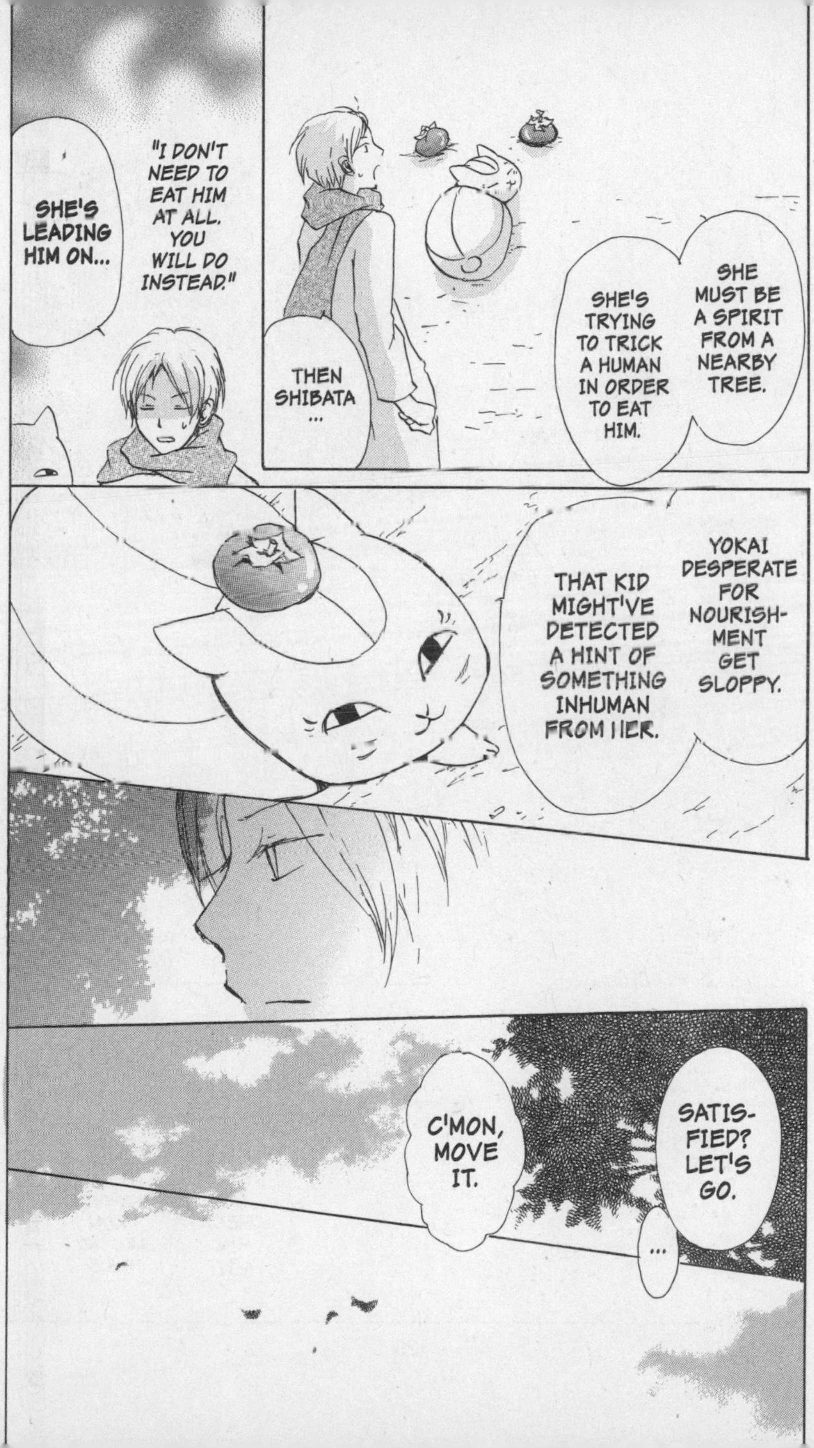
SHE MUST BE A SPIRIT FROM A NEARBY TREE.
SHE'S TRYING TO TRICK A HUMAN IN ORDER TO EAT HIM.
THEN SHIBATA ...
"I DON'T NEED TO EAT HIM AT ALL. YOU WILL DO INSTEAD."
SHE'S LEADING HIM ON...
YOKAI DESPERATE FOR NOURISH-MENT GET SLOPPY.
THAT KID MIGHT'VE DETECTED A HINT OF SOMETHING INHUMAN FROM HER.
SATIS-FIED? LET'S GO.
...
C'MON, MOVE IT.

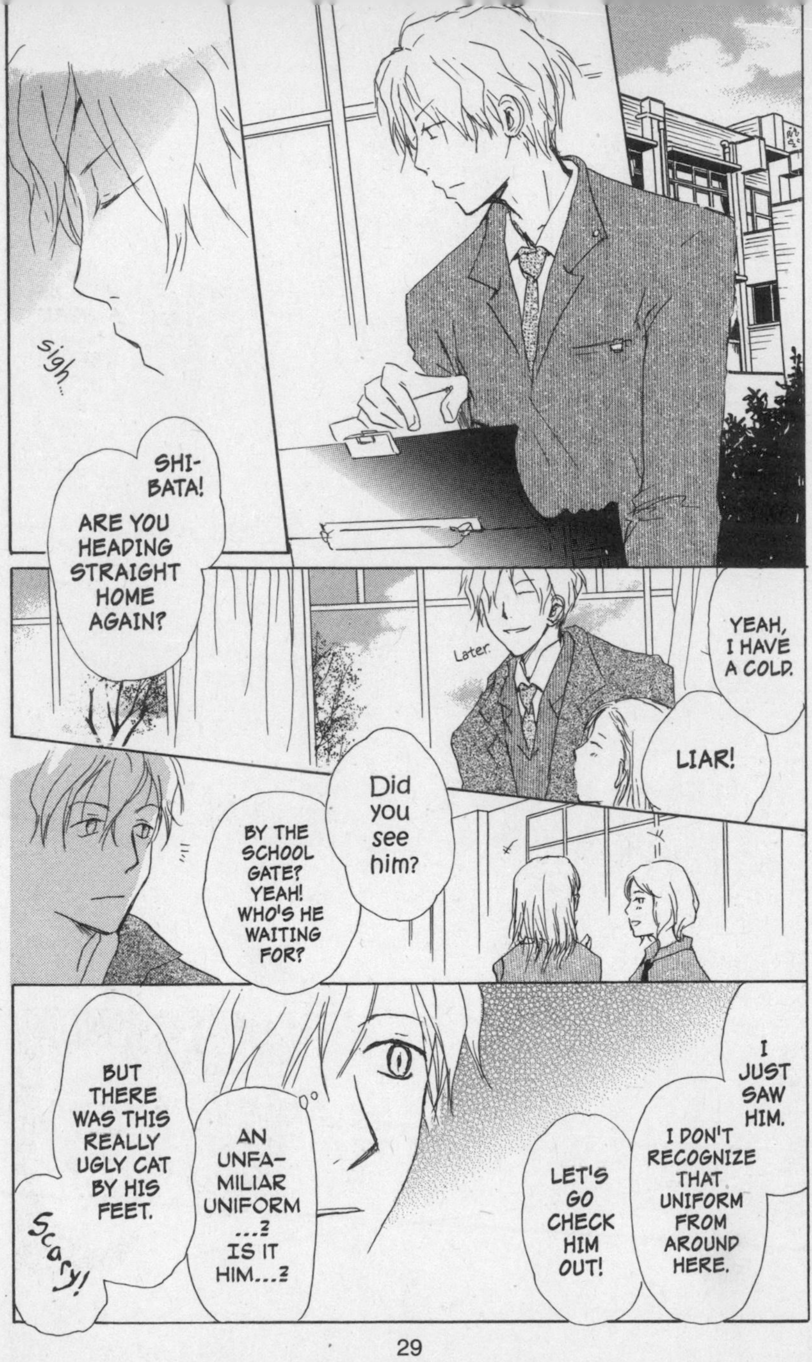
sigh...
SHI-BATA! ARE YOU HEADING STRAIGHT HOME AGAIN?
YEAH, I HAVE A COLD.
LIAR!
Later.
Did you see him?
BY THE SCHOOL GATE? YEAH! WHO'S HE WAITING FOR?
I JUST SAW HIM.
I DON'T RECOGNIZE THAT UNIFORM FROM AROUND HERE.
LET'S GO CHECK HIM OUT!
AN UNFA-MILIAR UNIFORM ...? IS IT HIM...?
BUT THERE WAS THIS REALLY UGLY CAT BY HIS FEET.
Scary!

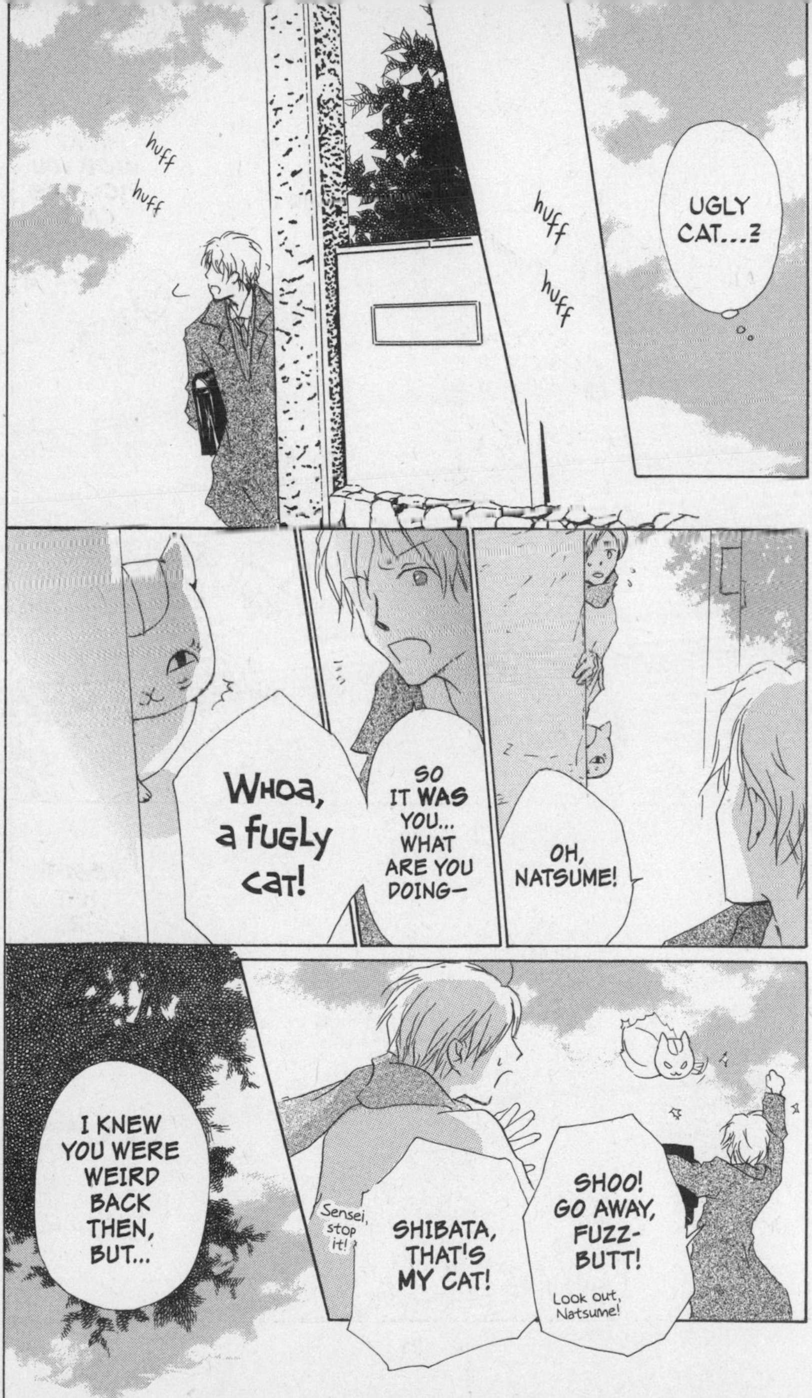
UGLY CAT...?
huff
huff
huff
huff
OH, NATSUME!
SO IT WAS YOU... WHAT ARE YOU DOING—
Whoa, a fugly cat!
SHOO! GO AWAY, FUZZ-BUTT!
Look out, Natsume!
SHIBATA, THAT'S MY CAT!
Sensei, stop it!
I KNEW YOU WERE WEIRD BACK THEN, BUT...

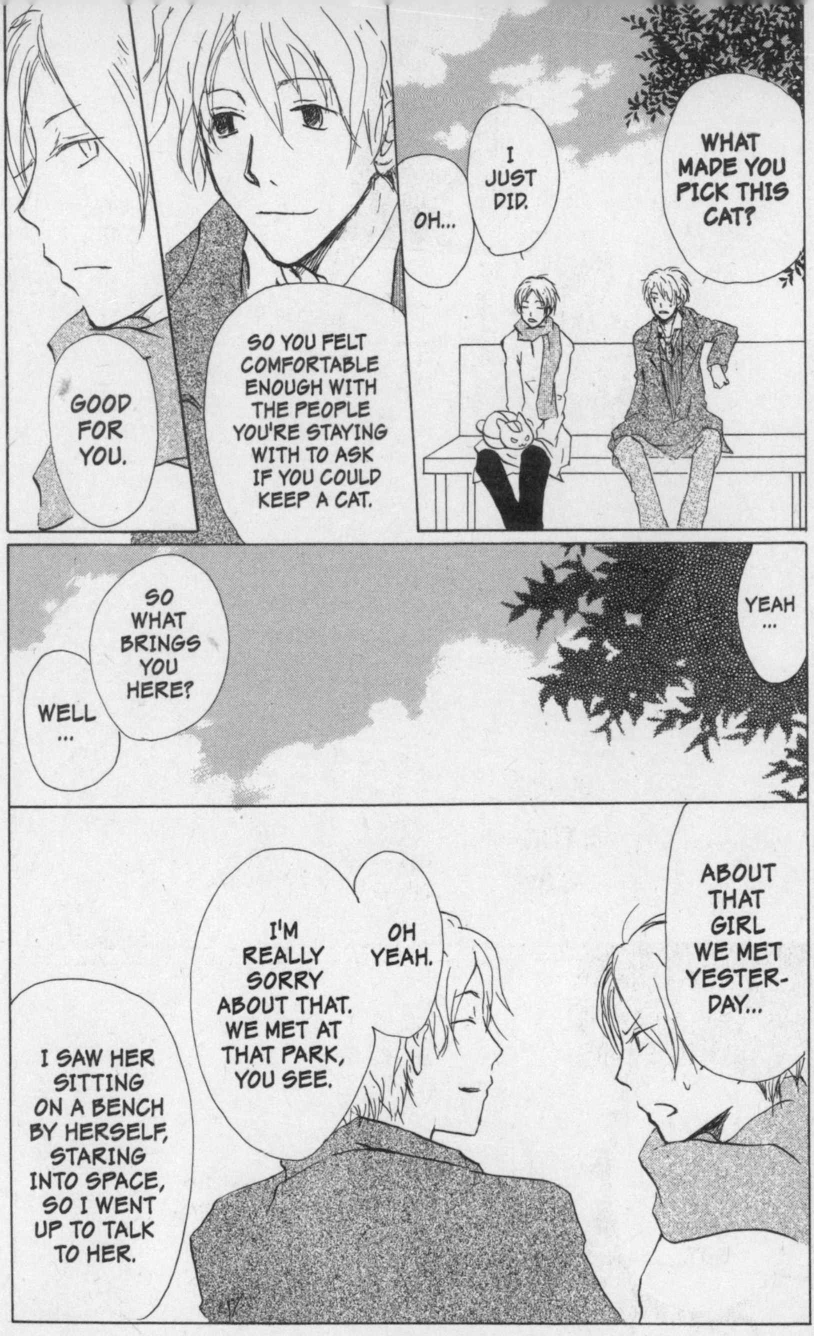
WHAT MADE YOU PICK THIS CAT?
I JUST DID.
OH...
SO YOU FELT COMFORTABLE ENOUGH WITH THE PEOPLE YOU'RE STAYING WITH TO ASK IF YOU COULD KEEP A CAT.
GOOD FOR YOU.
YEAH ...
SO WHAT BRINGS YOU HERE?
WELL ...
ABOUT THAT GIRL WE MET YESTER-DAY...
OH YEAH.
I'M REALLY SORRY ABOUT THAT. WE MET AT THAT PARK, YOU SEE.
I SAW HER SITTING ON A BENCH BY HERSELF, STARING INTO SPACE, SO I WENT UP TO TALK TO HER.

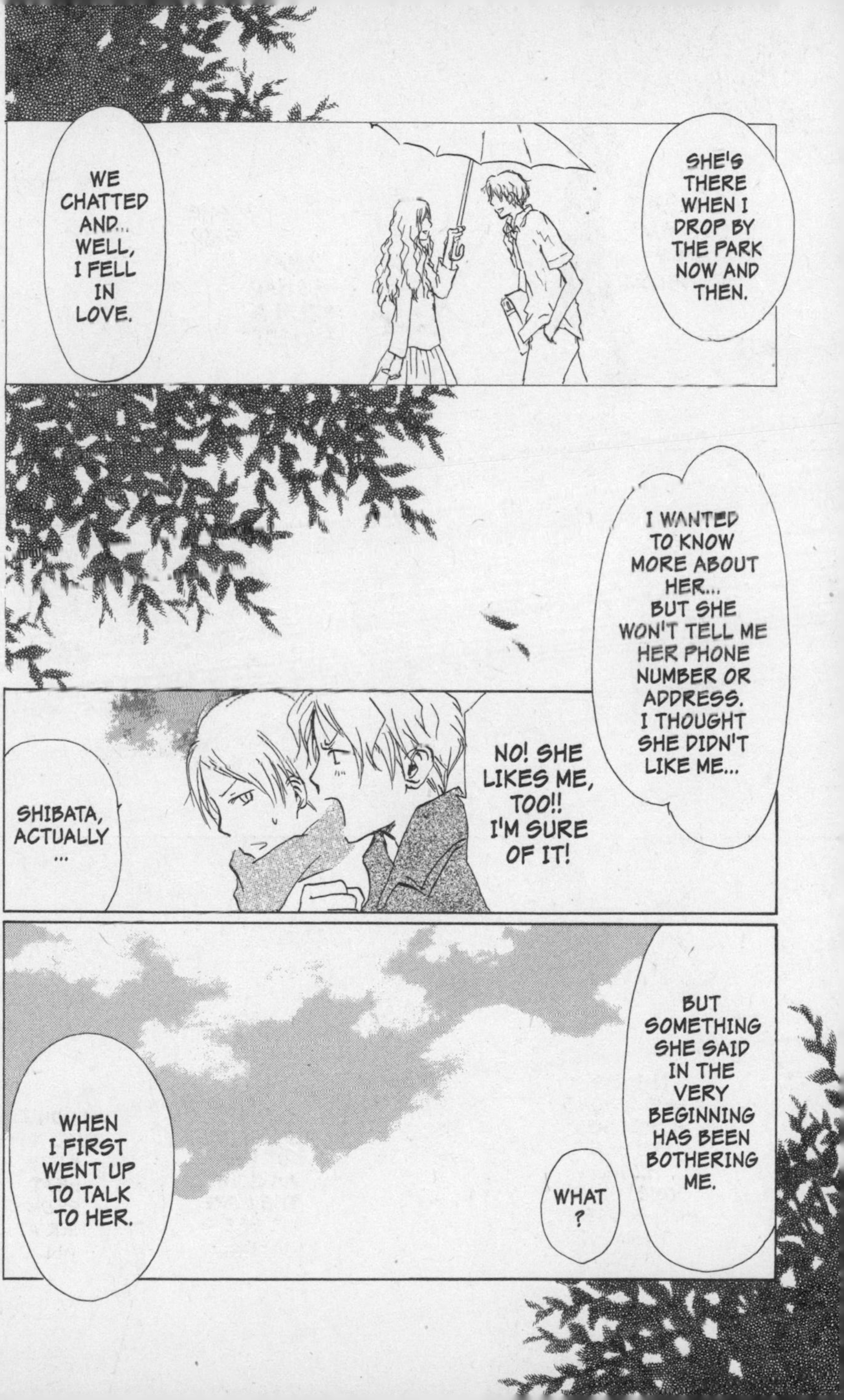
SHE'S THERE WHEN I DROP BY THE PARK NOW AND THEN.
WE CHATTED AND... WELL, I FELL IN LOVE.
I WANTED TO KNOW MORE ABOUT HER... BUT SHE WON'T TELL ME HER PHONE NUMBER OR ADDRESS. I THOUGHT SHE DIDN'T LIKE ME...
NO! SHE LIKES ME, TOO!! I'M SURE OF IT!
SHIBATA, ACTUALLY ...
BUT SOMETHING SHE SAID IN THE VERY BEGINNING HAS BEEN BOTHERING ME.
WHAT ?
WHEN I FIRST WENT UP TO TALK TO HER.

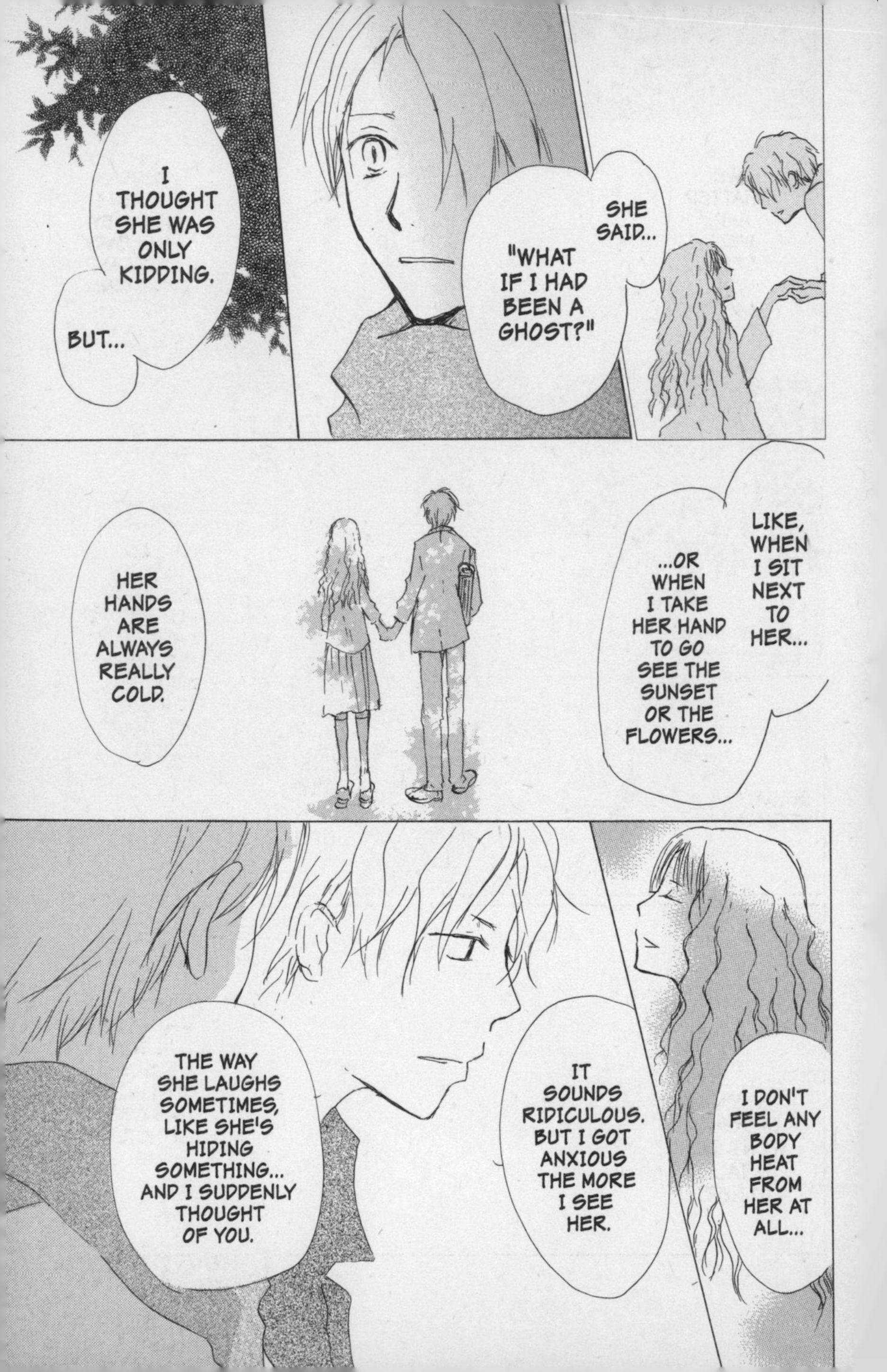
SHE SAID...
"WHAT IF I HAD BEEN A GHOST?"
I THOUGHT SHE WAS ONLY KIDDING.
BUT...
LIKE, WHEN I SIT NEXT TO HER...
...OR WHEN I TAKE HER HAND TO GO SEE THE SUNSET OR THE FLOWERS...
HER HANDS ARE ALWAYS REALLY COLD.
I DON'T FEEL ANY BODY HEAT FROM HER AT ALL...
IT SOUNDS RIDICULOUS. BUT I GOT ANXIOUS THE MORE I SEE HER.
THE WAY SHE LAUGHS SOMETIMES, LIKE SHE'S HIDING SOMETHING... AND I SUDDENLY THOUGHT OF YOU.

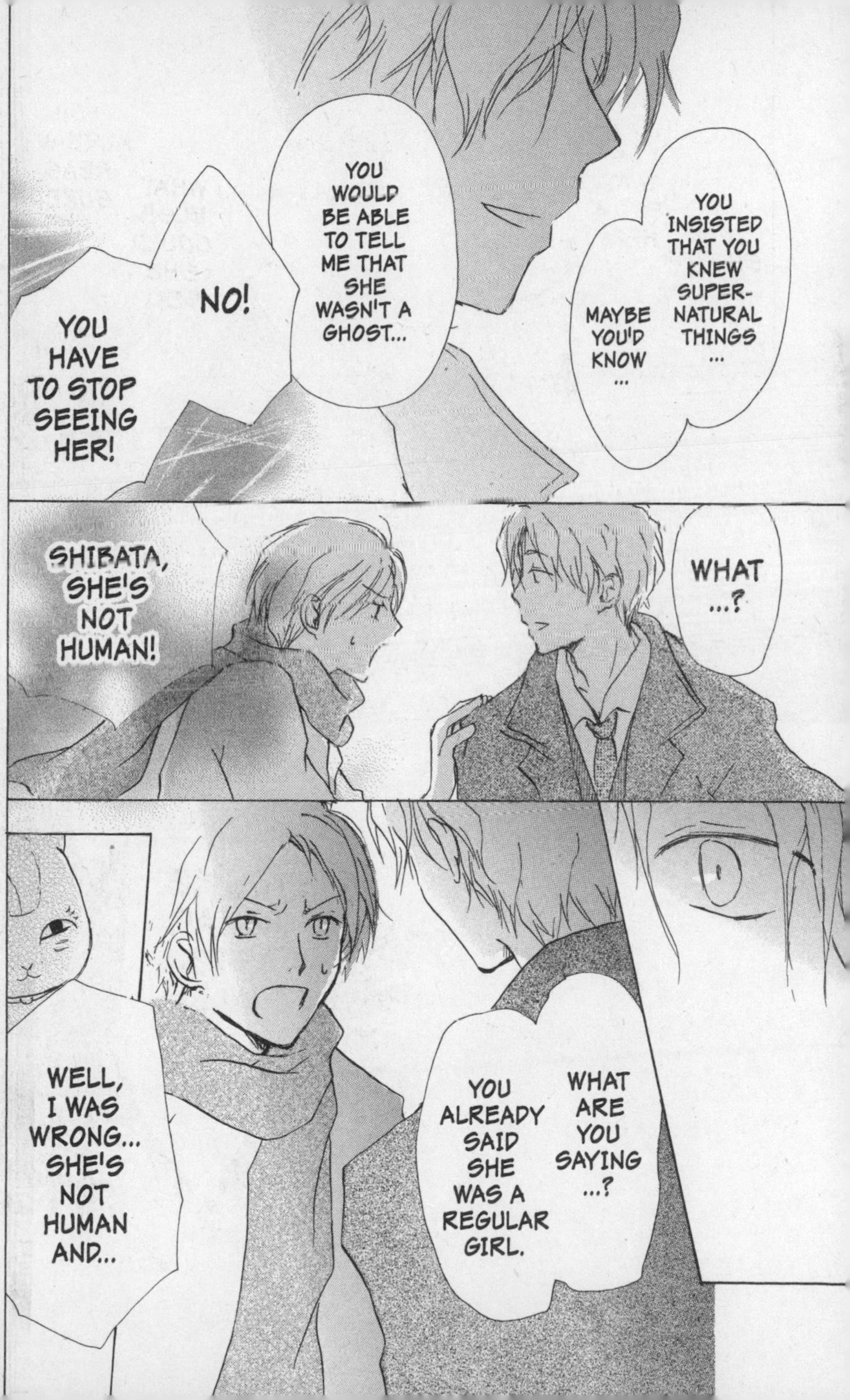
YOU INSISTED THAT YOU KNEW SUPER-NATURAL THINGS...
MAYBE YOU'D KNOW...
YOU WOULD BE ABLE TO TELL ME THAT SHE WASN'T A GHOST...
NO!
YOU HAVE TO STOP SEEING HER!
WHAT...?
SHIBATA, SHE'S NOT HUMAN!
WHAT ARE YOU SAYING...?
YOU ALREADY SAID SHE WAS A REGULAR GIRL.
WELL, I WAS WRONG... SHE'S NOT HUMAN AND...

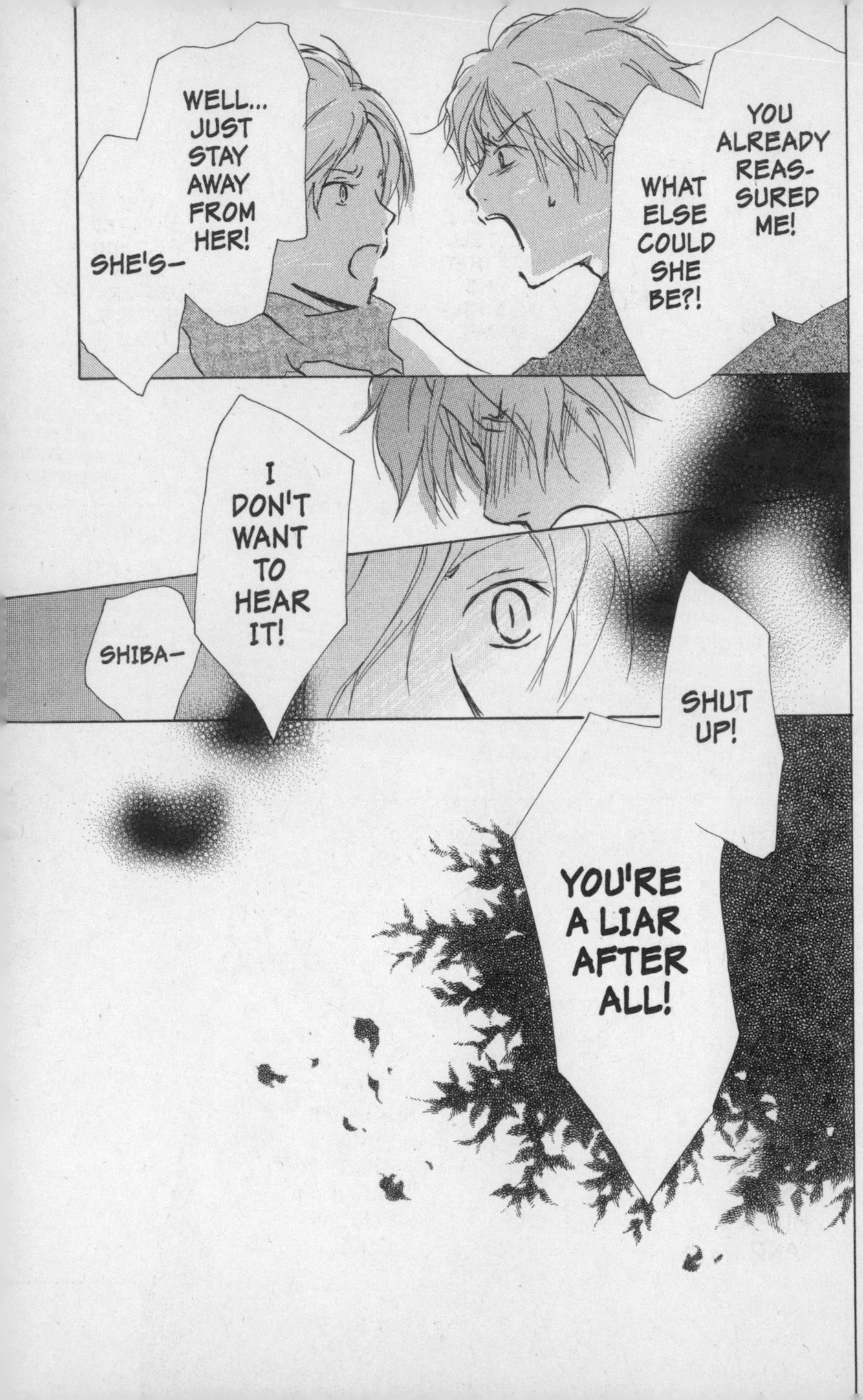
YOU ALREADY REAS-SURED ME!
WHAT ELSE COULD SHE BE?!
WELL... JUST STAY AWAY FROM HER!
SHE'S-
I DON'T WANT TO HEAR IT!
SHIBA-
SHUT UP!
YOU'RE A LIAR AFTER ALL!

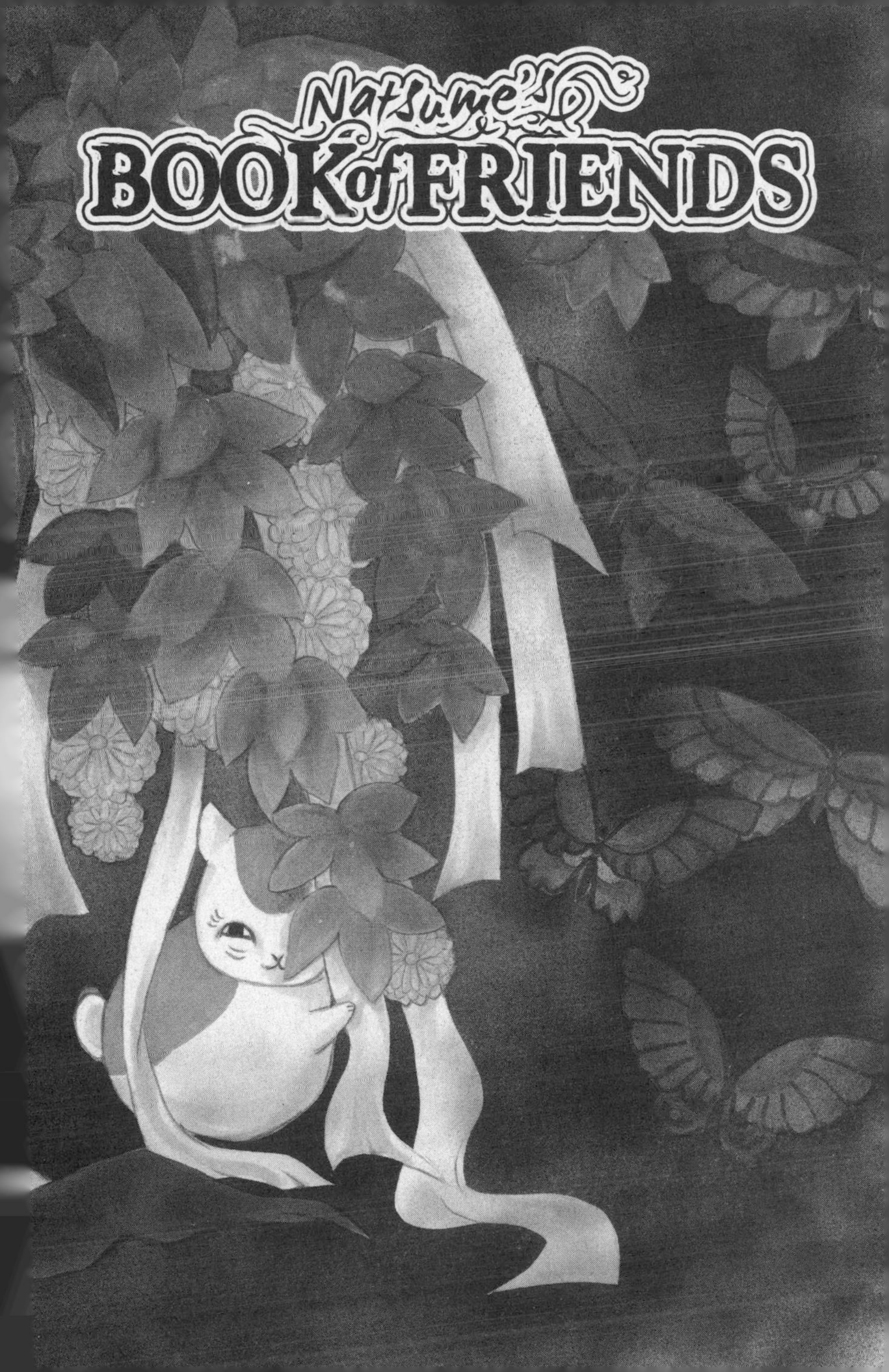
Natsume's
BOOK of FRIENDS

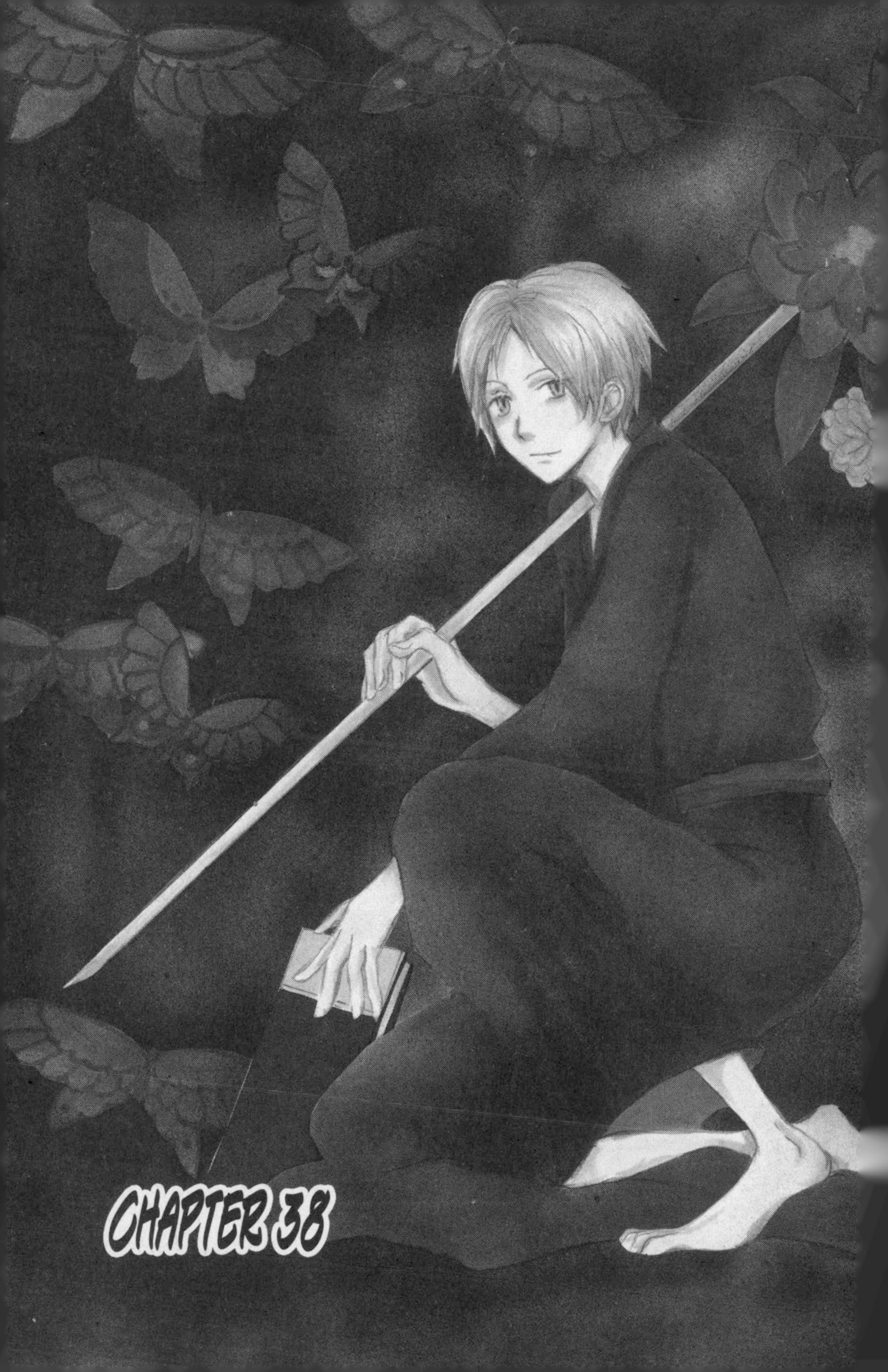
CHAPTER 38

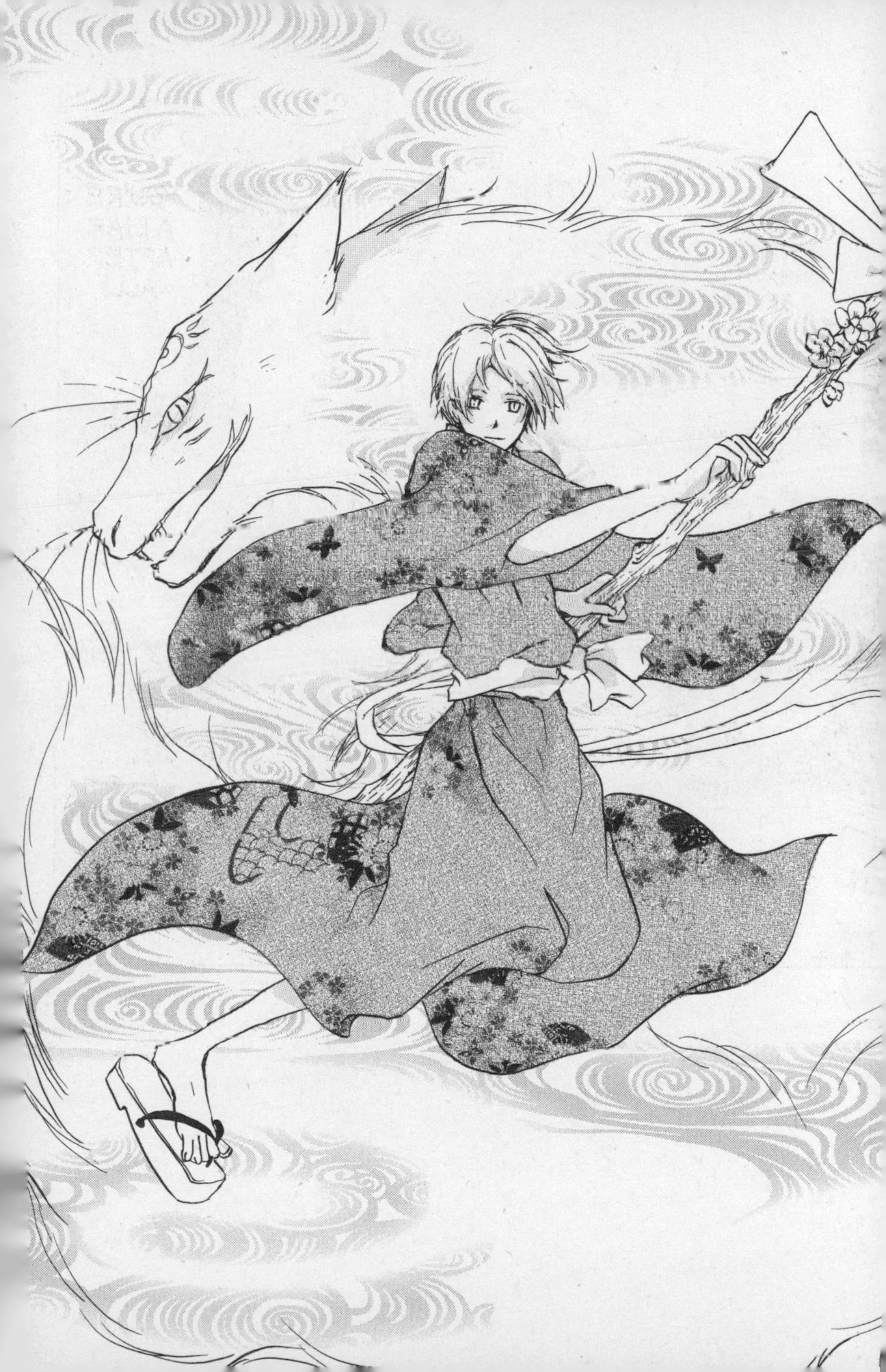

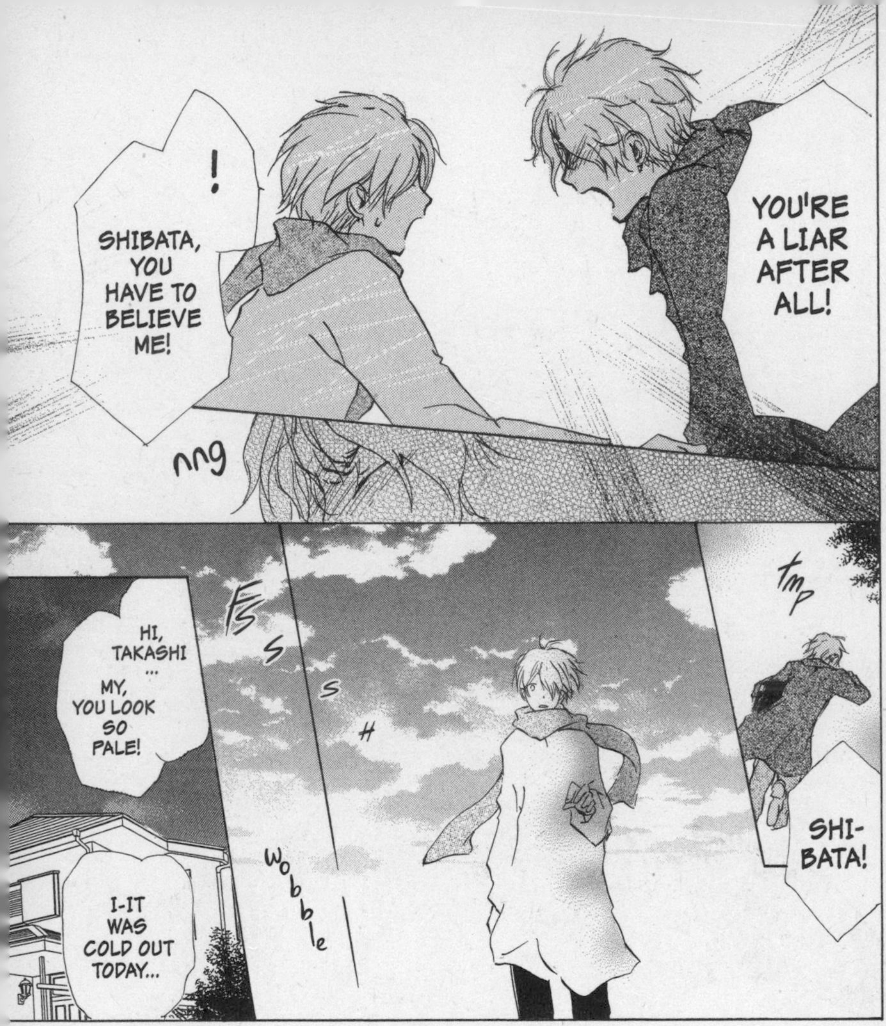
YOU'RE A LIAR AFTER ALL!
!
SHIBATA, YOU HAVE TO BELIEVE ME!
nng
tmp
SHI-BATA!
FSSSH
wobble
HI, TAKASHI...
MY, YOU LOOK SO PALE!
I-IT WAS COLD OUT TODAY...

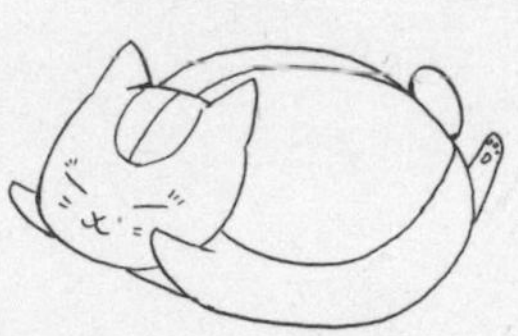

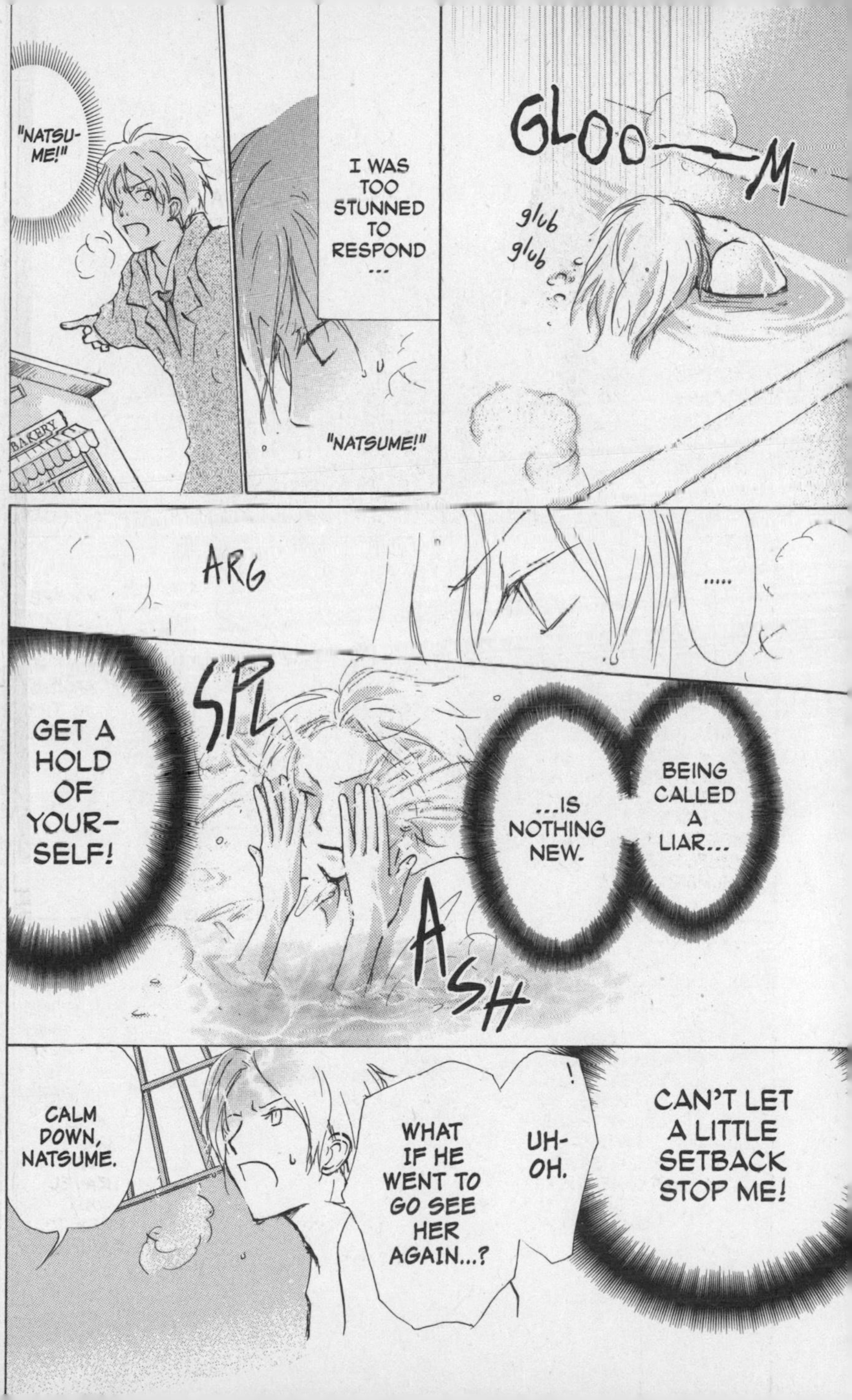
GLOO—M
glub glub
I WAS TOO STUNNED TO RESPOND...
"NATSUME!"
"NATSU-ME!"
BAKERY
.....
ARG
BEING CALLED A LIAR...
...IS NOTHING NEW.
SPLASH
GET A HOLD OF YOURSELF!
CAN'T LET A LITTLE SETBACK STOP ME!
!
UH-OH.
WHAT IF HE WENT TO GO SEE HER AGAIN...?
CALM DOWN, NATSUME.

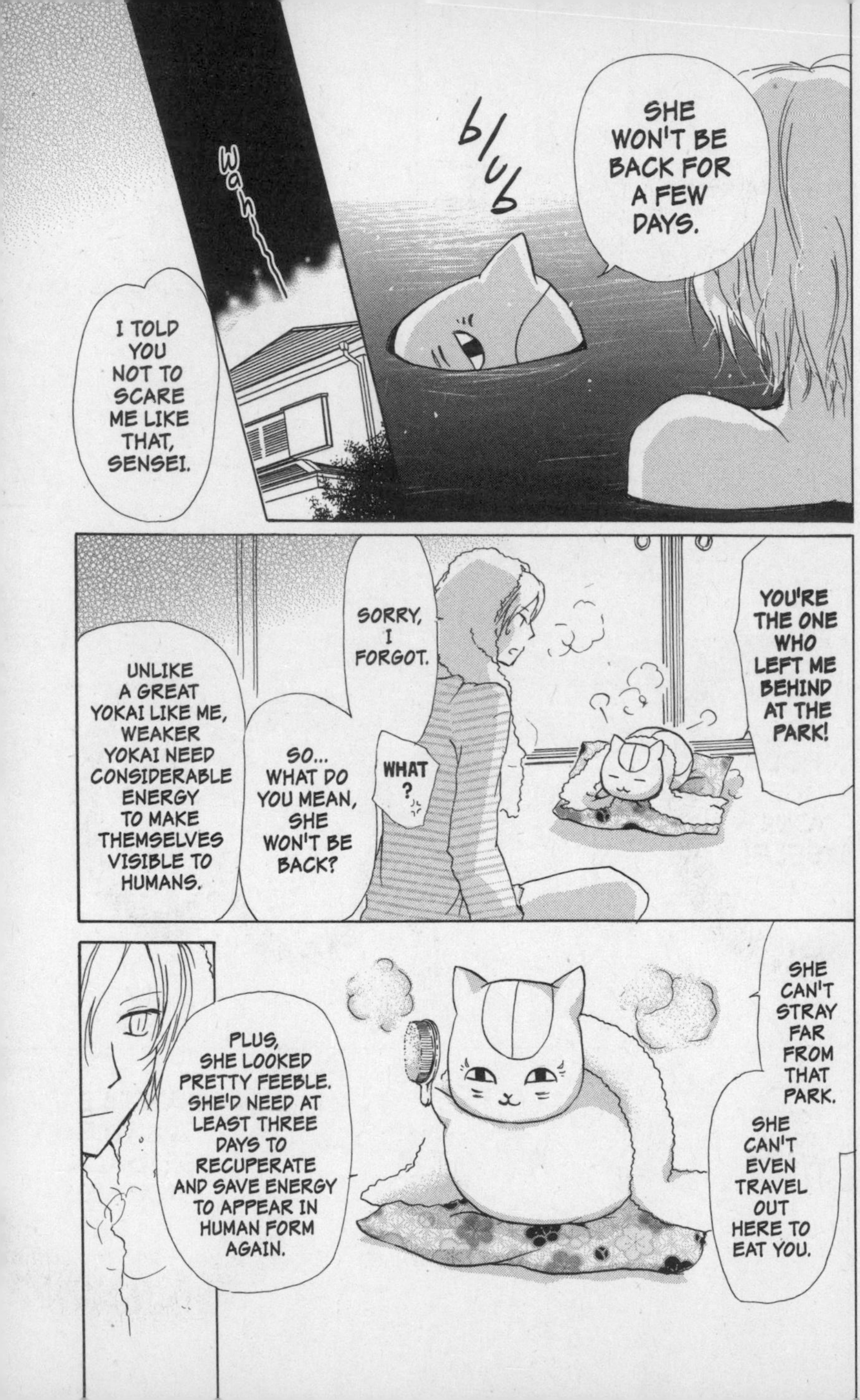

SHE WON'T BE BACK FOR A FEW DAYS.
blub
Wah
I TOLD YOU NOT TO SCARE ME LIKE THAT, SENSEI.
YOU'RE THE ONE WHO LEFT ME BEHIND AT THE PARK!
SORRY, I FORGOT.
WHAT?
SO... WHAT DO YOU MEAN, SHE WON'T BE BACK?
UNLIKE A GREAT YOKAI LIKE ME, WEAKER YOKAI NEED CONSIDERABLE ENERGY TO MAKE THEMSELVES VISIBLE TO HUMANS.
SHE CAN'T STRAY FAR FROM THAT PARK.
SHE CAN'T EVEN TRAVEL OUT HERE TO EAT YOU.
PLUS, SHE LOOKED PRETTY FEEBLE. SHE'D NEED AT LEAST THREE DAYS TO RECUPERATE AND SAVE ENERGY TO APPEAR IN HUMAN FORM AGAIN.

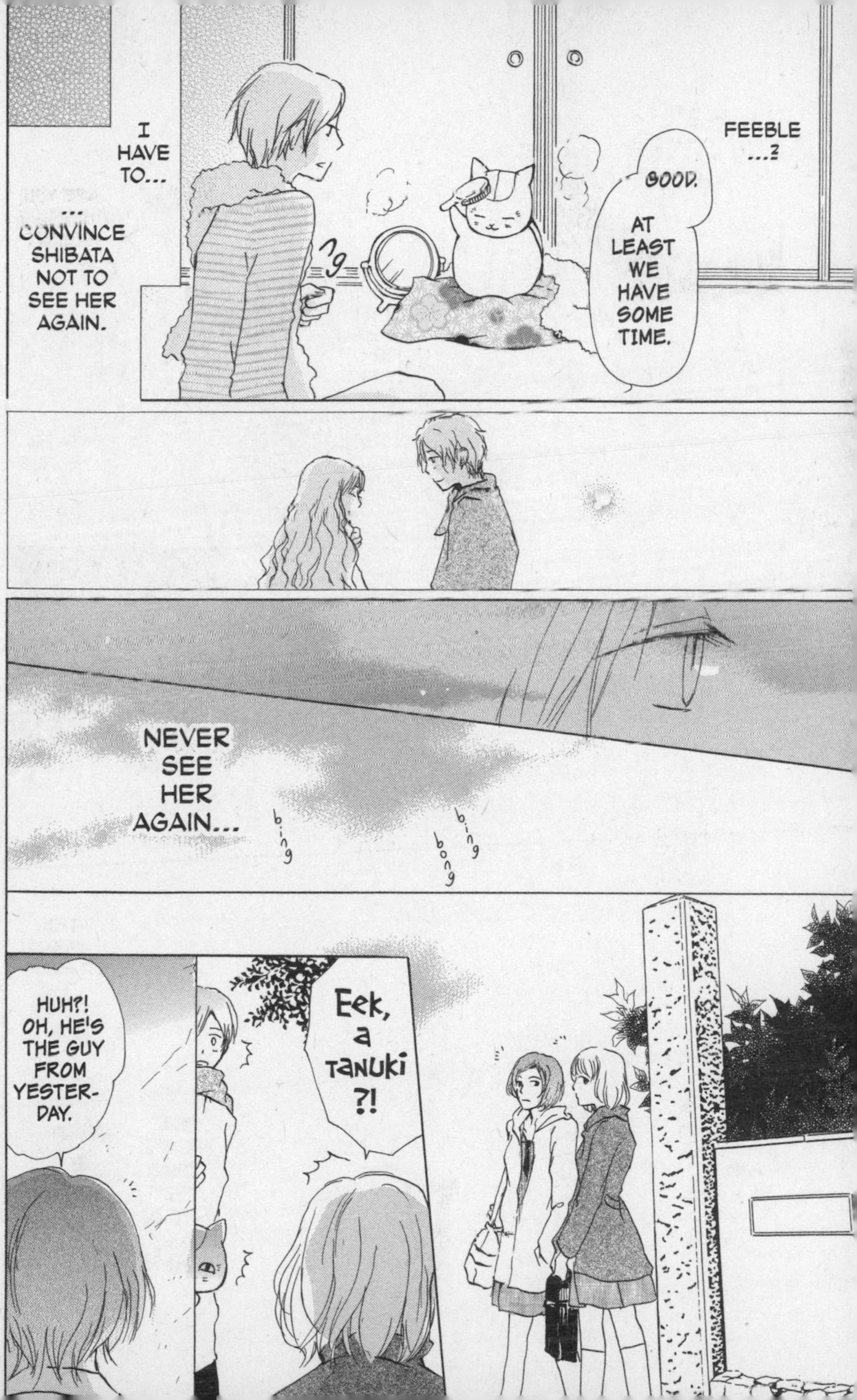
FEEBLE ...?
GOOD.
AT LEAST WE HAVE SOME TIME.
ng
I HAVE TO...
...CONVINCE SHIBATA NOT TO SEE HER AGAIN.
NEVER SEE HER AGAIN...
bing bong
bing
Eek, a tanuki?!
HUH?! OH, HE'S THE GUY FROM YESTER-DAY.

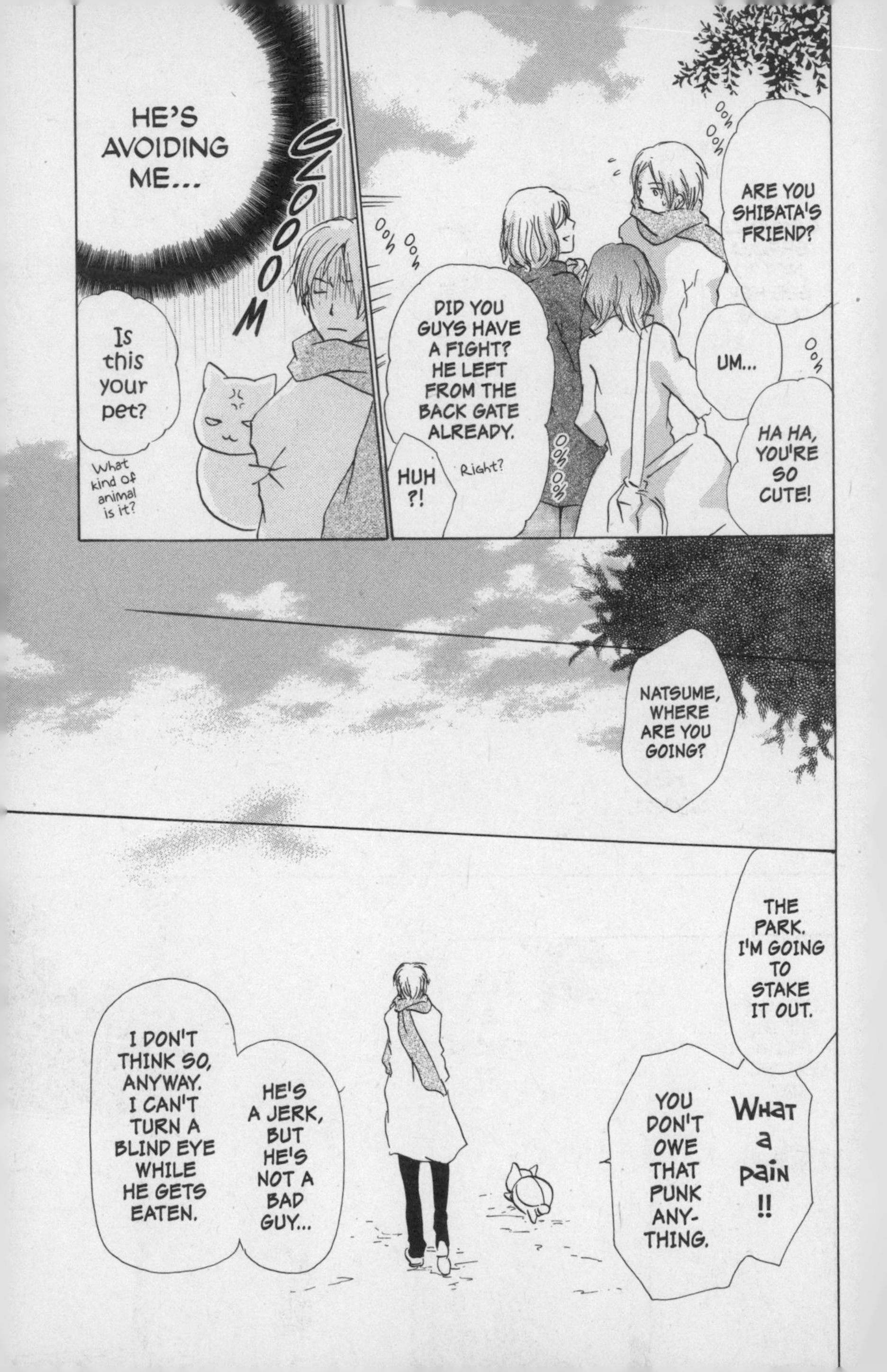
ARE YOU SHIBATA'S FRIEND?
UM...
HA HA, YOU'RE SO CUTE!
DID YOU GUYS HAVE A FIGHT? HE LEFT FROM THE BACK GATE ALREADY.
Right?
HUH?!
HE'S AVOIDING ME...
GLOOOOM
Is this your pet?
What kind of animal is it?
NATSUME, WHERE ARE YOU GOING?
THE PARK. I'M GOING TO STAKE IT OUT.
YOU DON'T OWE THAT PUNK ANY-THING.
What a pain!!
HE'S A JERK, BUT HE'S NOT A BAD GUY...
I DON'T THINK SO, ANYWAY. I CAN'T TURN A BLIND EYE WHILE HE GETS EATEN.

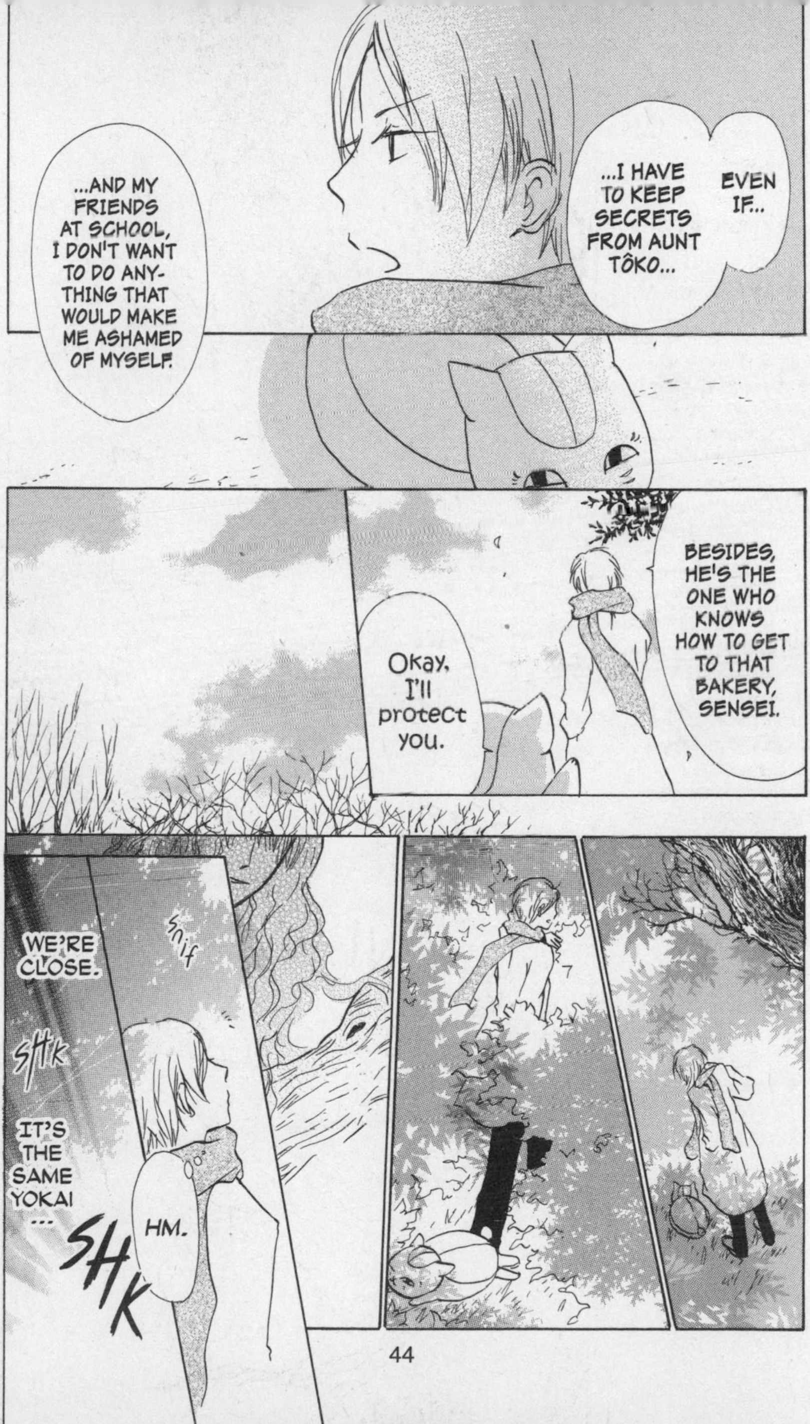
EVEN IF...
...I HAVE TO KEEP SECRETS FROM AUNT TÔKO...
...AND MY FRIENDS AT SCHOOL, I DON'T WANT TO DO ANY-THING THAT WOULD MAKE ME ASHAMED OF MYSELF.
BESIDES, HE'S THE ONE WHO KNOWS HOW TO GET TO THAT BAKERY, SENSEI.
Okay, I'll protect you.
Snif
WE'RE CLOSE.
SHK
IT'S THE SAME YOKAI ...
HM.
SHK

02

❋Preview ads

Preview ads are illustrations that preview the episode that will run in the next issue of the magazine. They're pretty hard to do for Natsume. Most of the time, I haven't decided on what the guest character or the yokai looks like, or haven't definitively finished the plot yet. Only Natsume and Nyanko Sensei will absolutely show up, so unfortunately I haven't been able to draw other characters or the yokai in color. I wish I could finish the planning earlier so that I could draw some other characters in color.

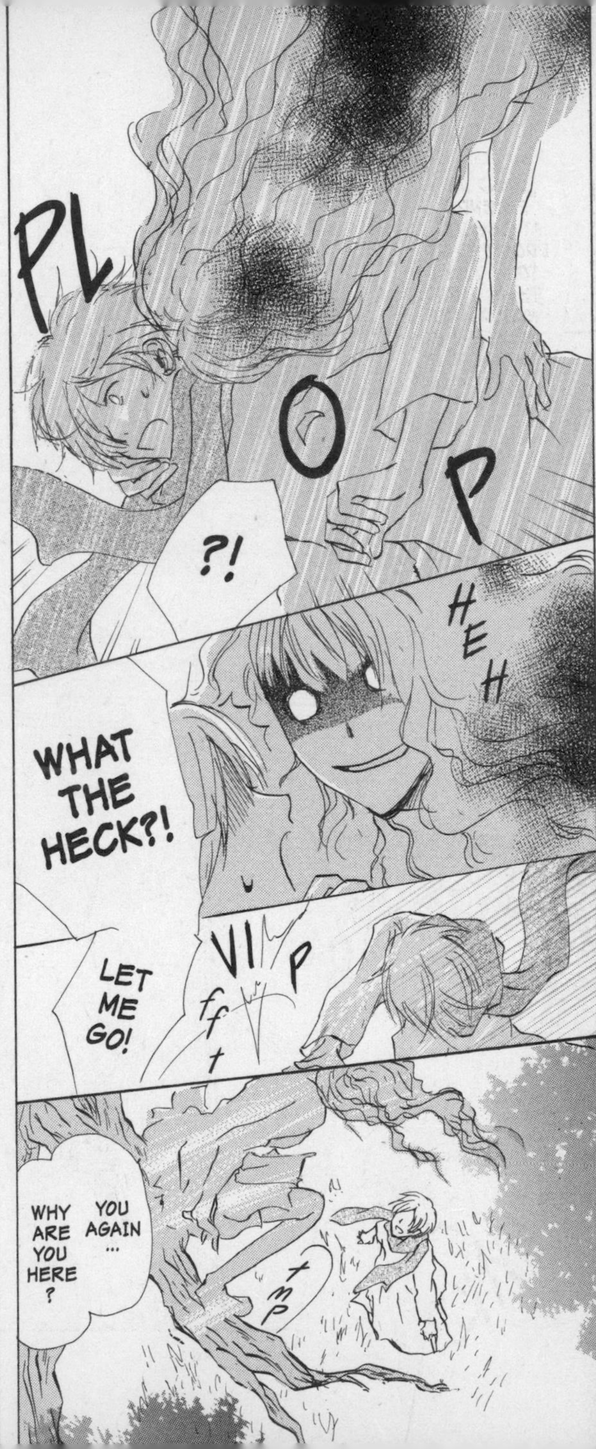
PLOP
?!
HEH
WHAT THE HECK?!
VIP
fft
LET ME GO!
YOU AGAIN ...
WHY ARE YOU HERE ?
tmp

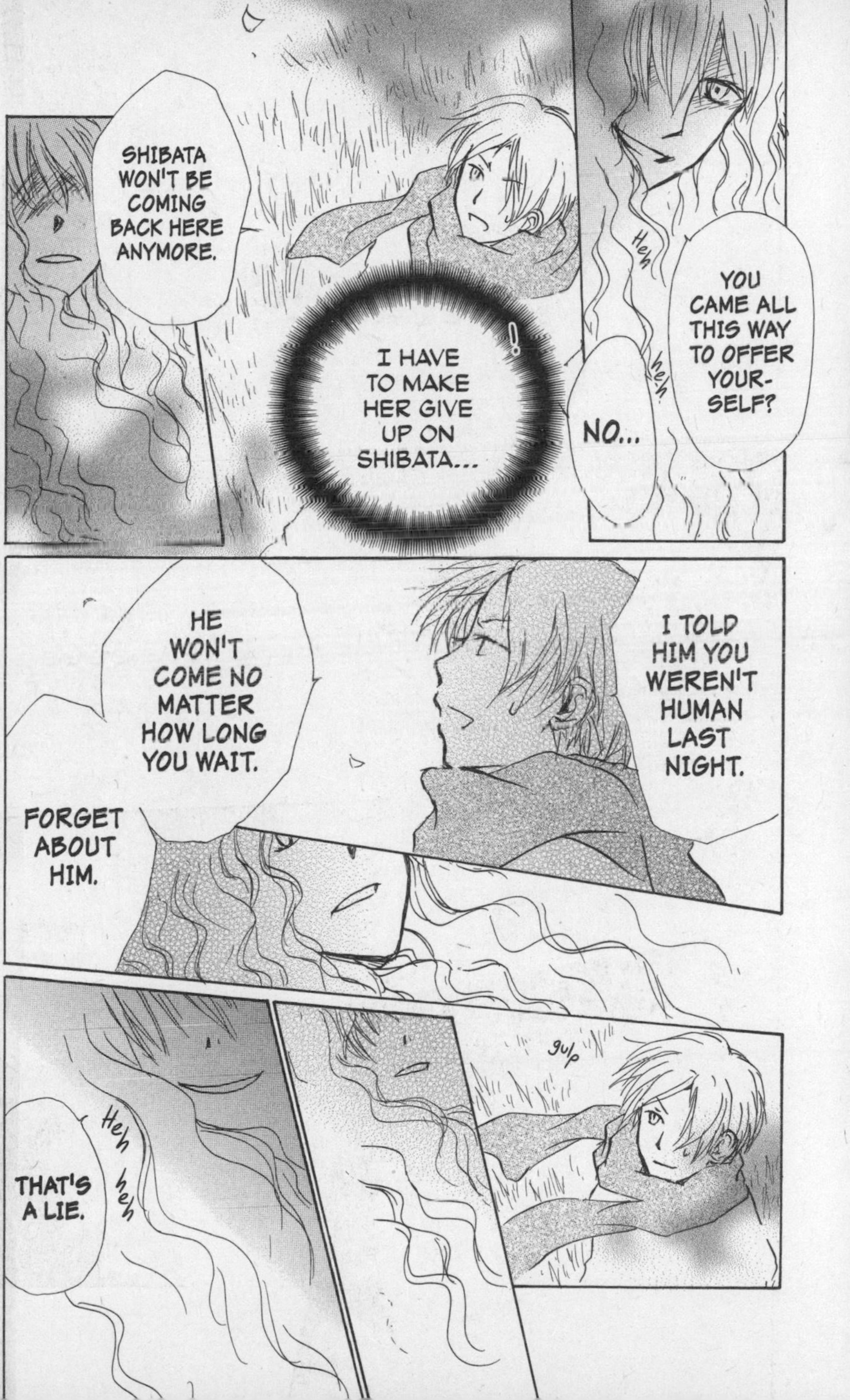
Heh heh
YOU CAME ALL THIS WAY TO OFFER YOUR-SELF?
NO...
!
I HAVE TO MAKE HER GIVE UP ON SHIBATA...
SHIBATA WON'T BE COMING BACK HERE ANYMORE.
I TOLD HIM YOU WEREN'T HUMAN LAST NIGHT.
HE WON'T COME NO MATTER HOW LONG YOU WAIT.
FORGET ABOUT HIM.
gulp
Heh heh
THAT'S A LIE.

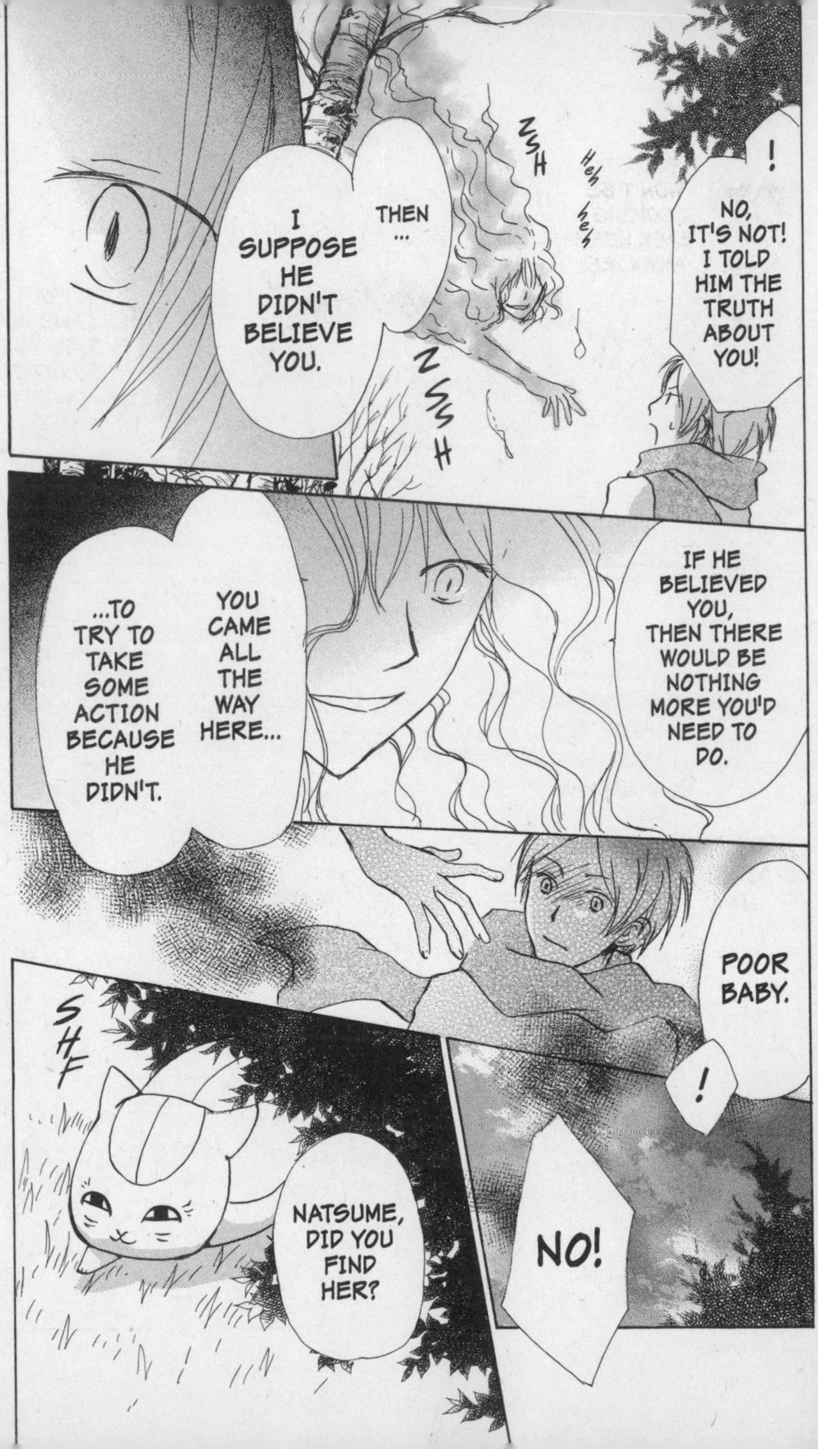
!
NO, IT'S NOT! I TOLD HIM THE TRUTH ABOUT YOU!
ZSH
Heh heh
THEN...
I SUPPOSE HE DIDN'T BELIEVE YOU.
ZSSH
IF HE BELIEVED YOU, THEN THERE WOULD BE NOTHING MORE YOU'D NEED TO DO.
YOU CAME ALL THE WAY HERE...
...TO TRY TO TAKE SOME ACTION BECAUSE HE DIDN'T.
POOR BABY.
!
NO!
SHF
NATSUME, DID YOU FIND HER?

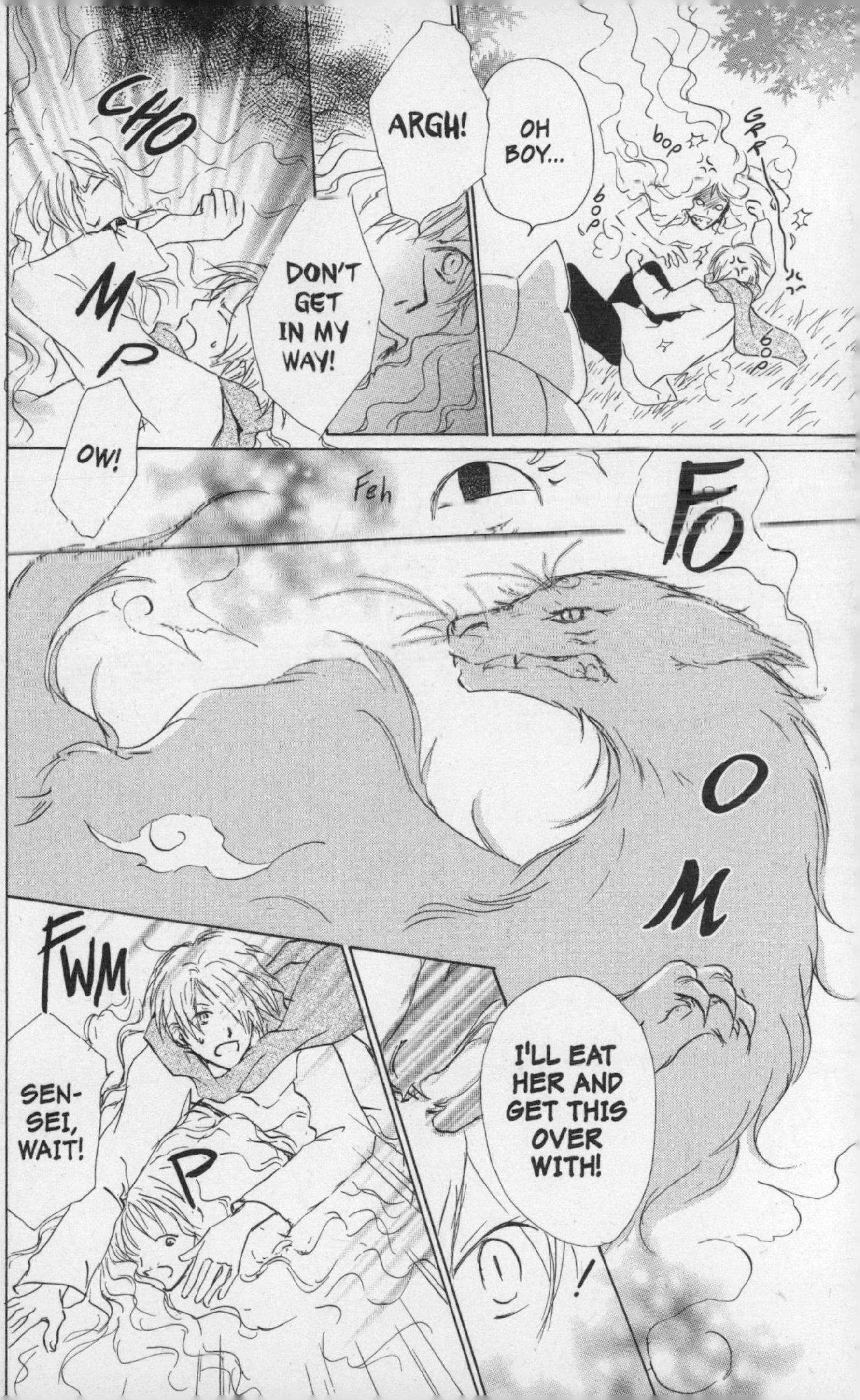
GRR
bop
bop
bop
OH BOY...
ARGH!
DON'T GET IN MY WAY!
CHOMP
OW!
Feh
FOOM
I'LL EAT HER AND GET THIS OVER WITH!
!
FWMP
SEN-SEI, WAIT!

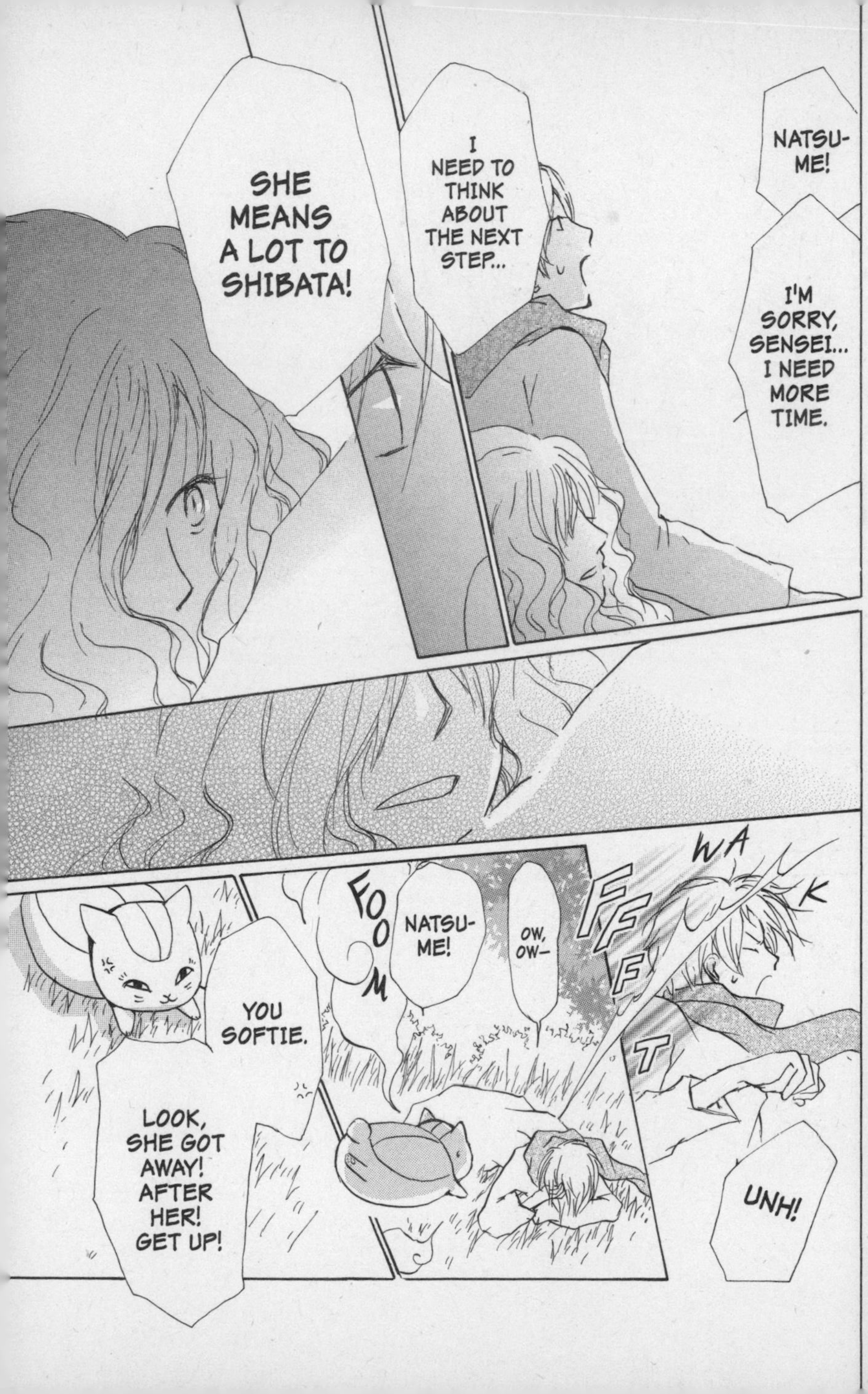

NATSU-ME!
I NEED TO THINK ABOUT THE NEXT STEP...
I'M SORRY, SENSEI... I NEED MORE TIME.
SHE MEANS A LOT TO SHIBATA!
WAKK
FFFFT
UNH!
OW, OW–
NATSU-ME!
FOOM
YOU SOFTIE.
LOOK, SHE GOT AWAY! AFTER HER! GET UP!

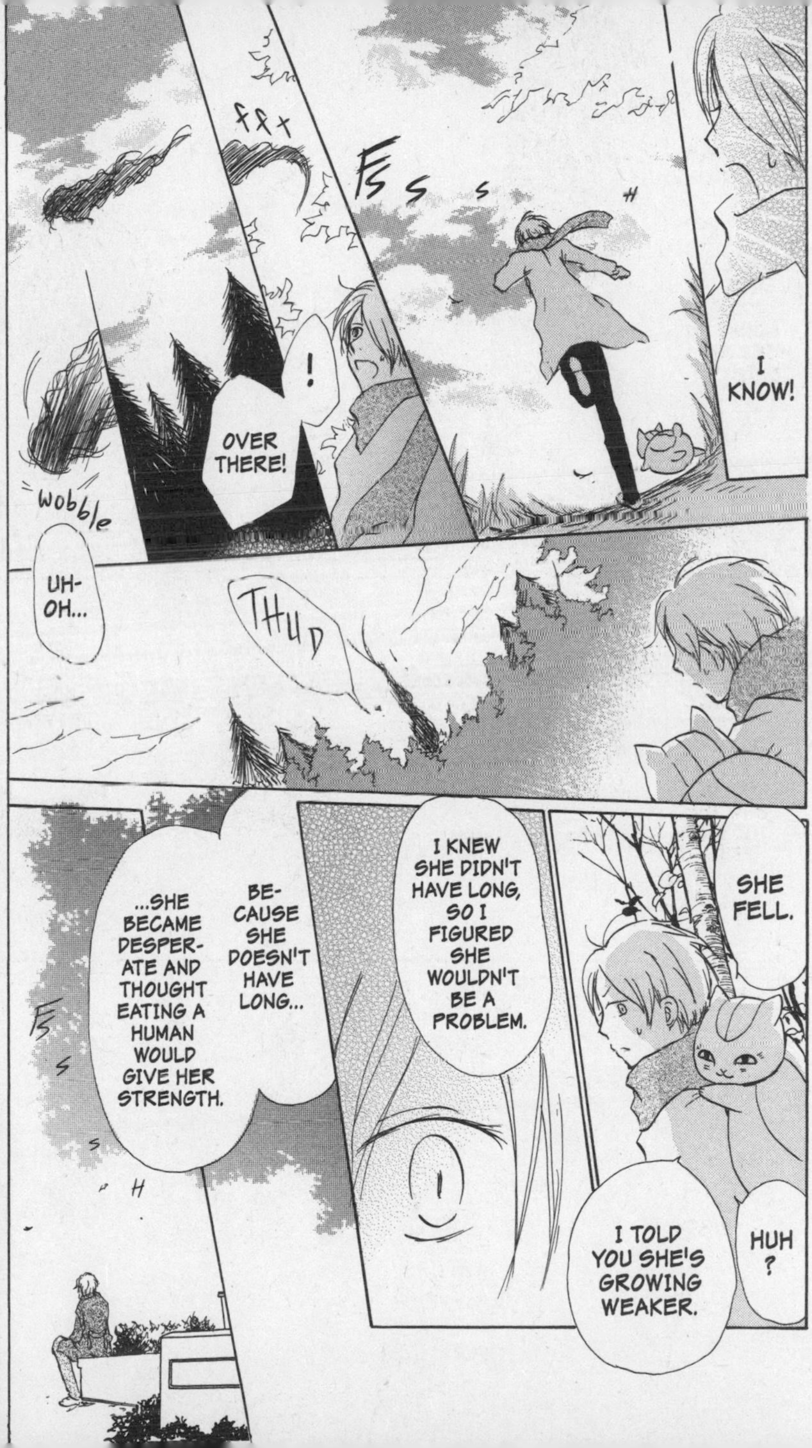
I KNOW!
FSSSH
fft
!
OVER THERE!
wobble
UH-OH...
THUD
SHE FELL.
HUH?
I TOLD YOU SHE'S GROWING WEAKER.
I KNEW SHE DIDN'T HAVE LONG, SO I FIGURED SHE WOULDN'T BE A PROBLEM.
BECAUSE SHE DOESN'T HAVE LONG...
...SHE BECAME DESPERATE AND THOUGHT EATING A HUMAN WOULD GIVE HER STRENGTH.
FSSSH

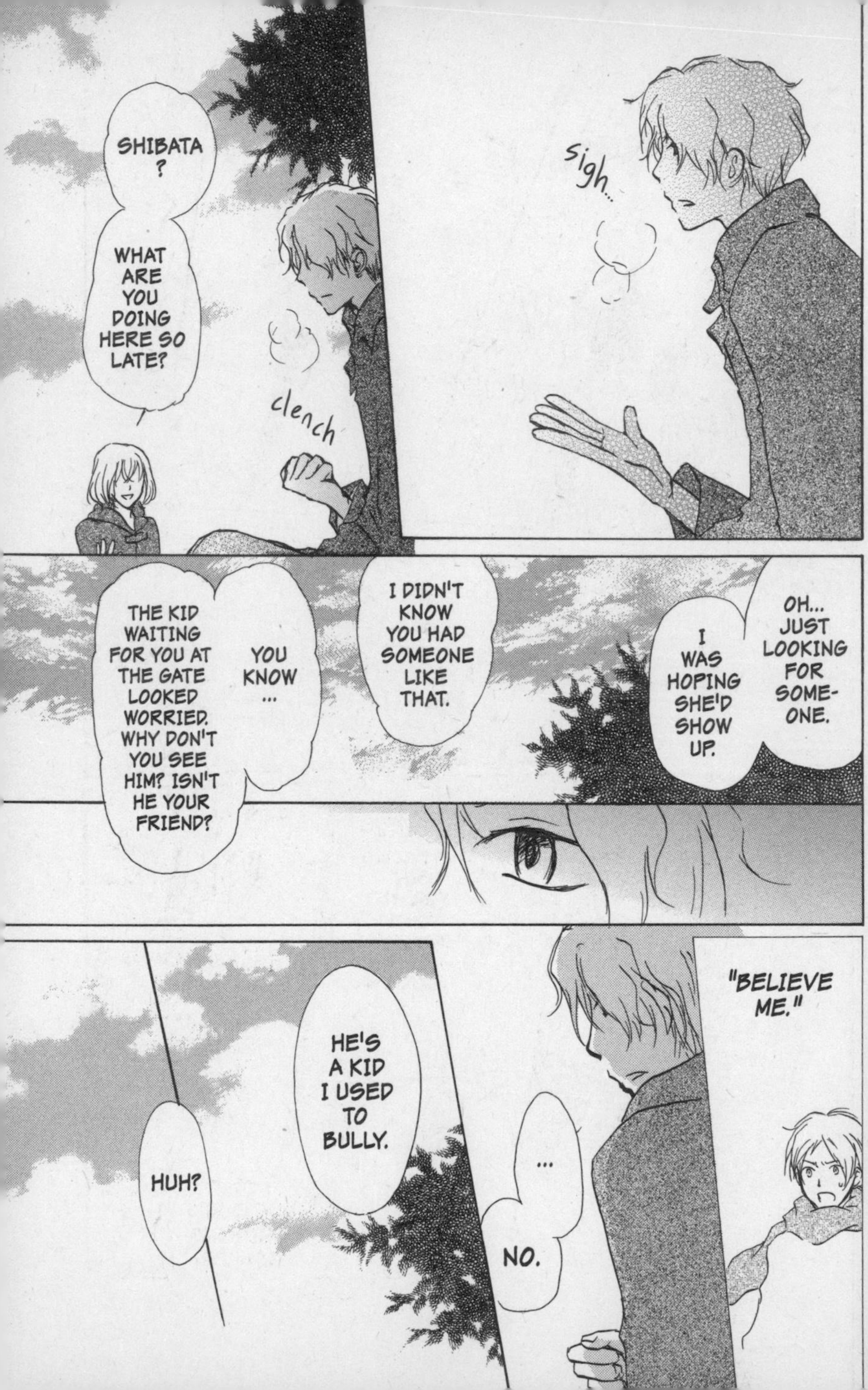
sigh...
SHIBATA?
WHAT ARE YOU DOING HERE SO LATE?
clench
OH... JUST LOOKING FOR SOME-ONE.
I WAS HOPING SHE'D SHOW UP.
I DIDN'T KNOW YOU HAD SOMEONE LIKE THAT.
YOU KNOW ...
THE KID WAITING FOR YOU AT THE GATE LOOKED WORRIED. WHY DON'T YOU SEE HIM? ISN'T HE YOUR FRIEND?
"BELIEVE ME."
...
NO.
HE'S A KID I USED TO BULLY.
HUH?

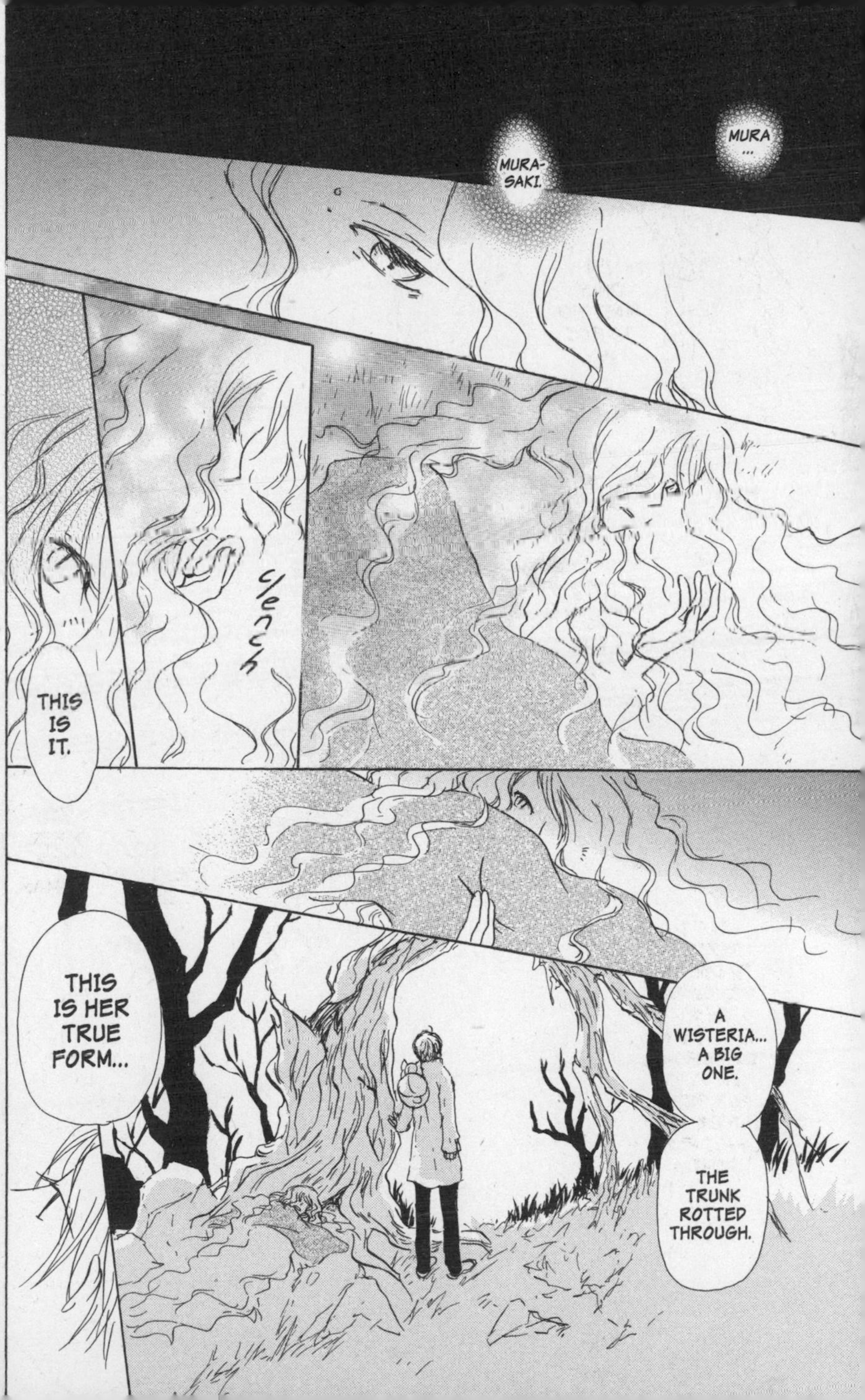
MURA...
MURA-SAKI.
clench
THIS IS IT.
A WISTERIA... A BIG ONE.
THE TRUNK ROTTED THROUGH.
THIS IS HER TRUE FORM...

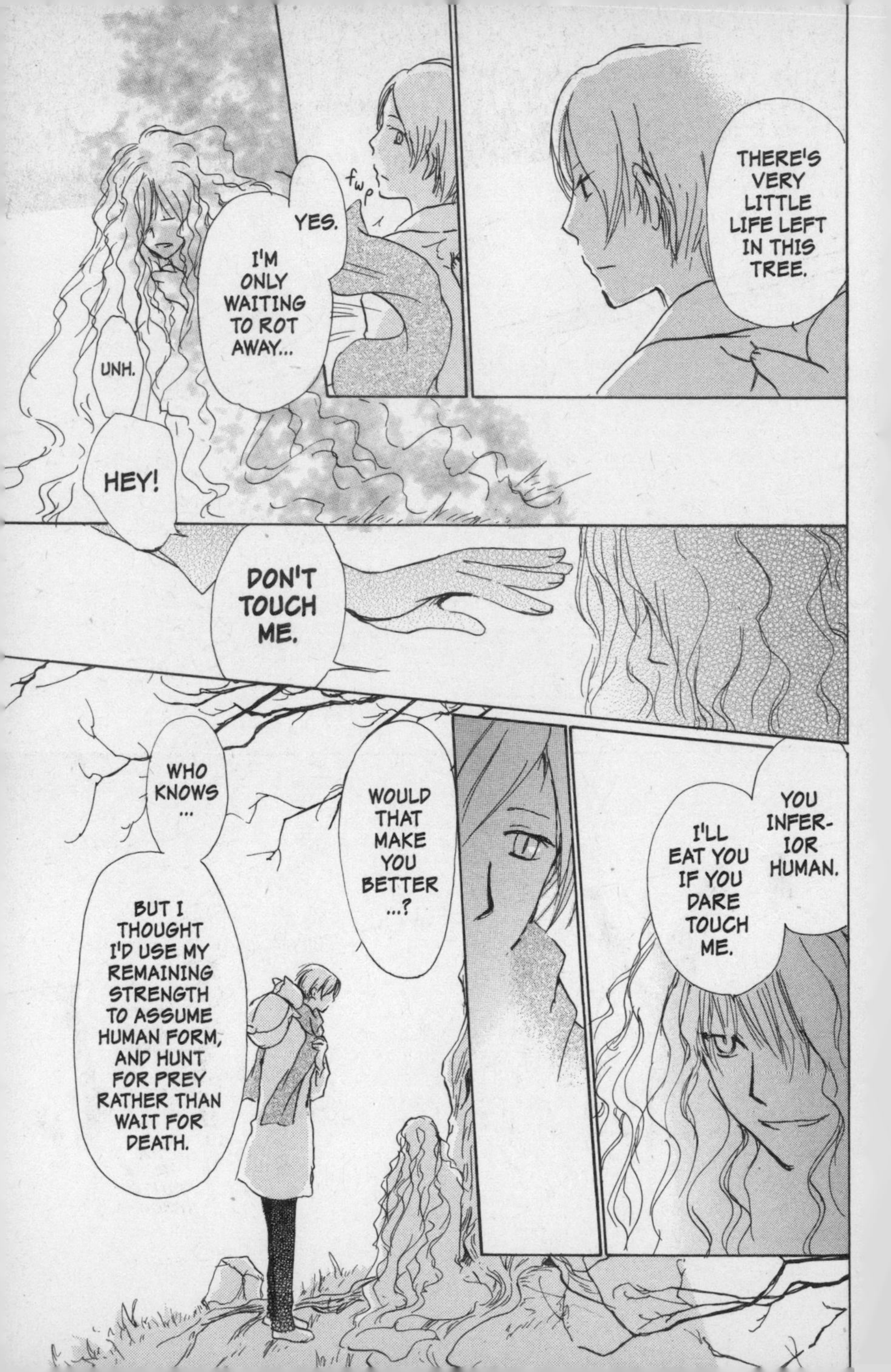
THERE'S VERY LITTLE LIFE LEFT IN THIS TREE.
YES.
fwp
I'M ONLY WAITING TO ROT AWAY...
UNH.
HEY!
DON'T TOUCH ME.
YOU INFERIOR HUMAN.
I'LL EAT YOU IF YOU DARE TOUCH ME.
WOULD THAT MAKE YOU BETTER ...?
WHO KNOWS ...
BUT I THOUGHT I'D USE MY REMAINING STRENGTH TO ASSUME HUMAN FORM, AND HUNT FOR PREY RATHER THAN WAIT FOR DEATH.

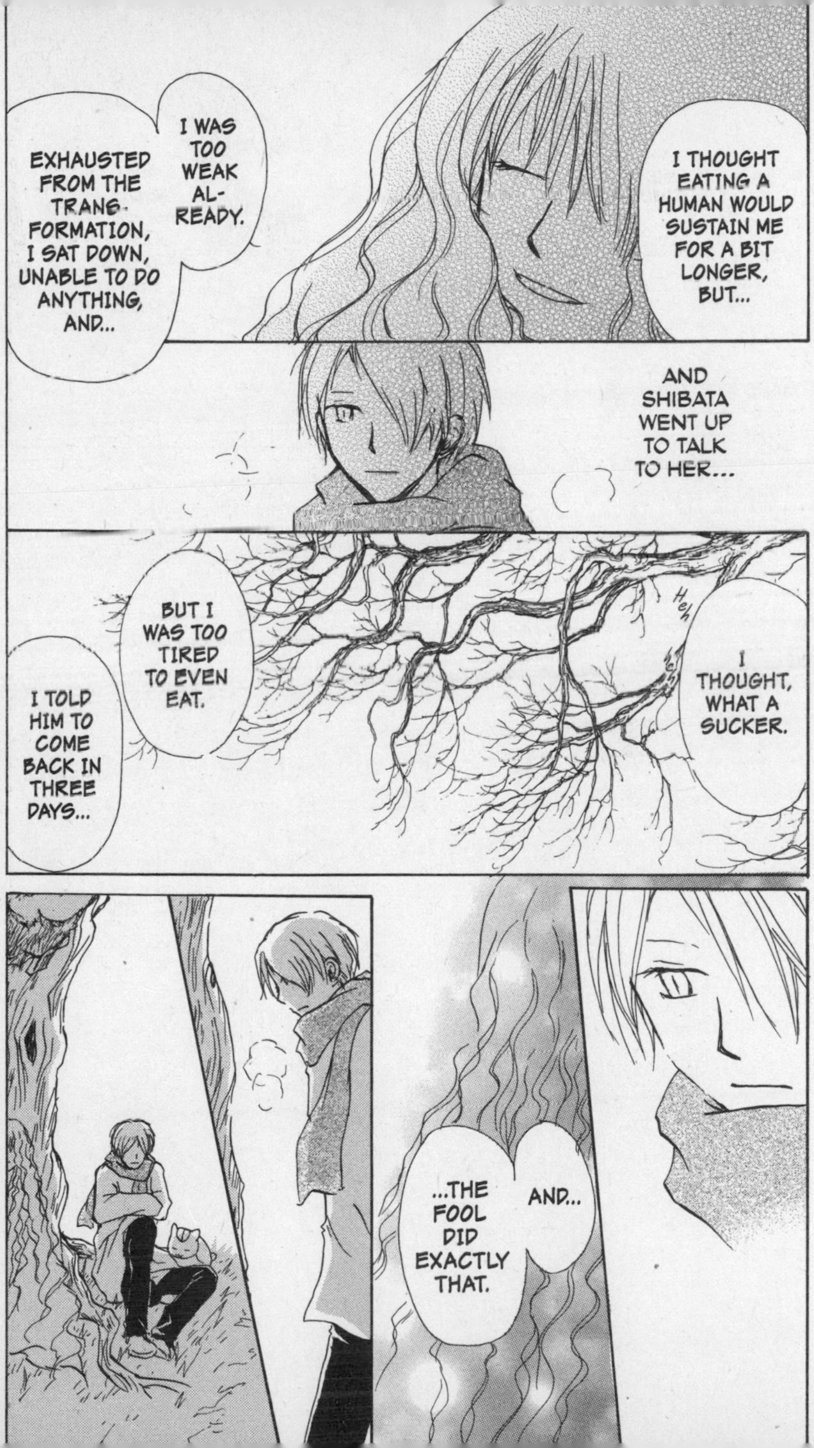
I THOUGHT EATING A HUMAN WOULD SUSTAIN ME FOR A BIT LONGER, BUT...
I WAS TOO WEAK AL-READY.
EXHAUSTED FROM THE TRANS-FORMATION, I SAT DOWN, UNABLE TO DO ANYTHING, AND...
AND SHIBATA WENT UP TO TALK TO HER...
Heh heh
I THOUGHT, WHAT A SUCKER.
BUT I WAS TOO TIRED TO EVEN EAT.
I TOLD HIM TO COME BACK IN THREE DAYS...
AND...
...THE FOOL DID EXACTLY THAT.

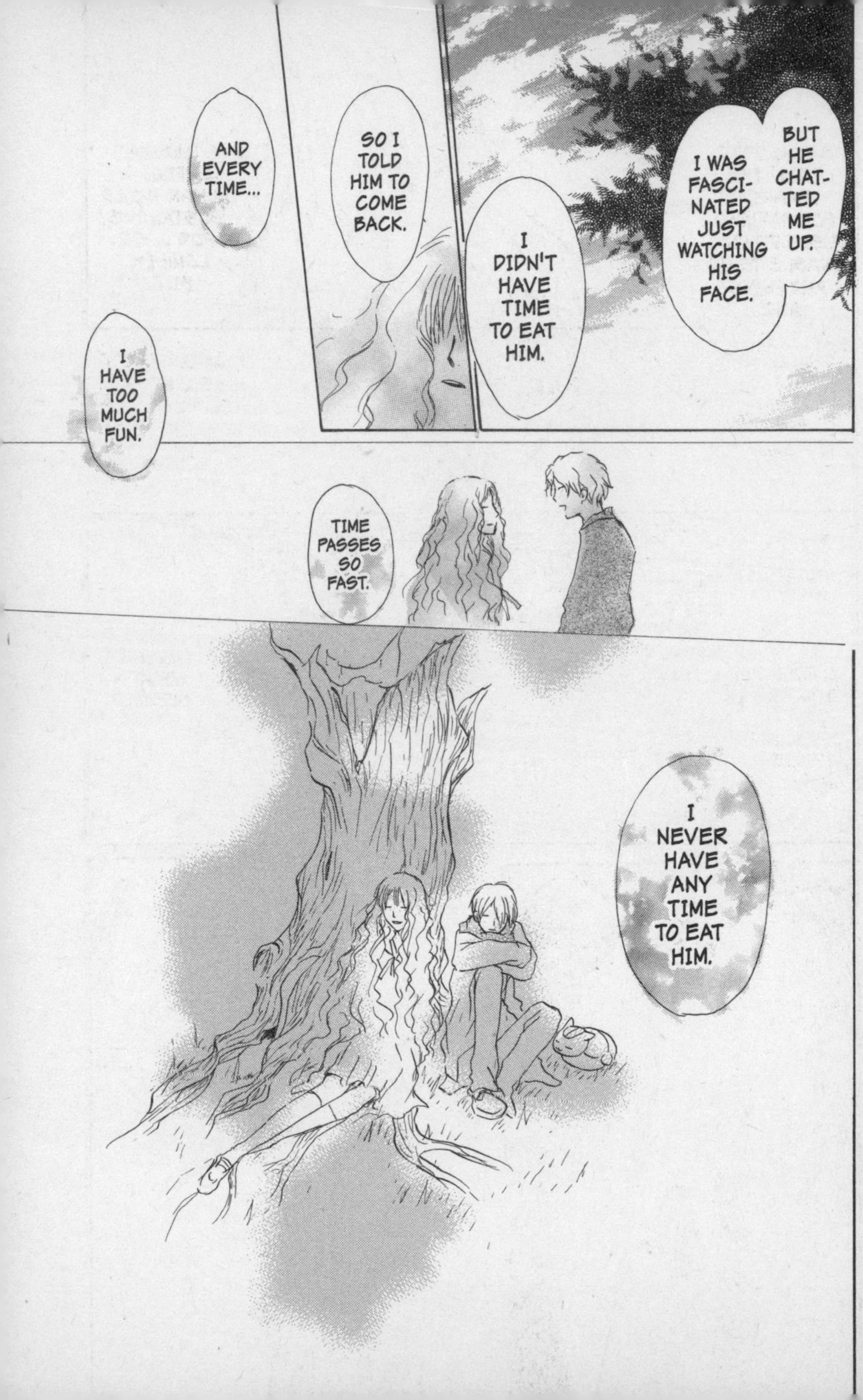
BUT HE CHAT-TED ME UP.
I WAS FASCI-NATED JUST WATCHING HIS FACE.
I DIDN'T HAVE TIME TO EAT HIM.
SO I TOLD HIM TO COME BACK.
AND EVERY TIME...
I HAVE TOO MUCH FUN.
TIME PASSES SO FAST.
I NEVER HAVE ANY TIME TO EAT HIM.

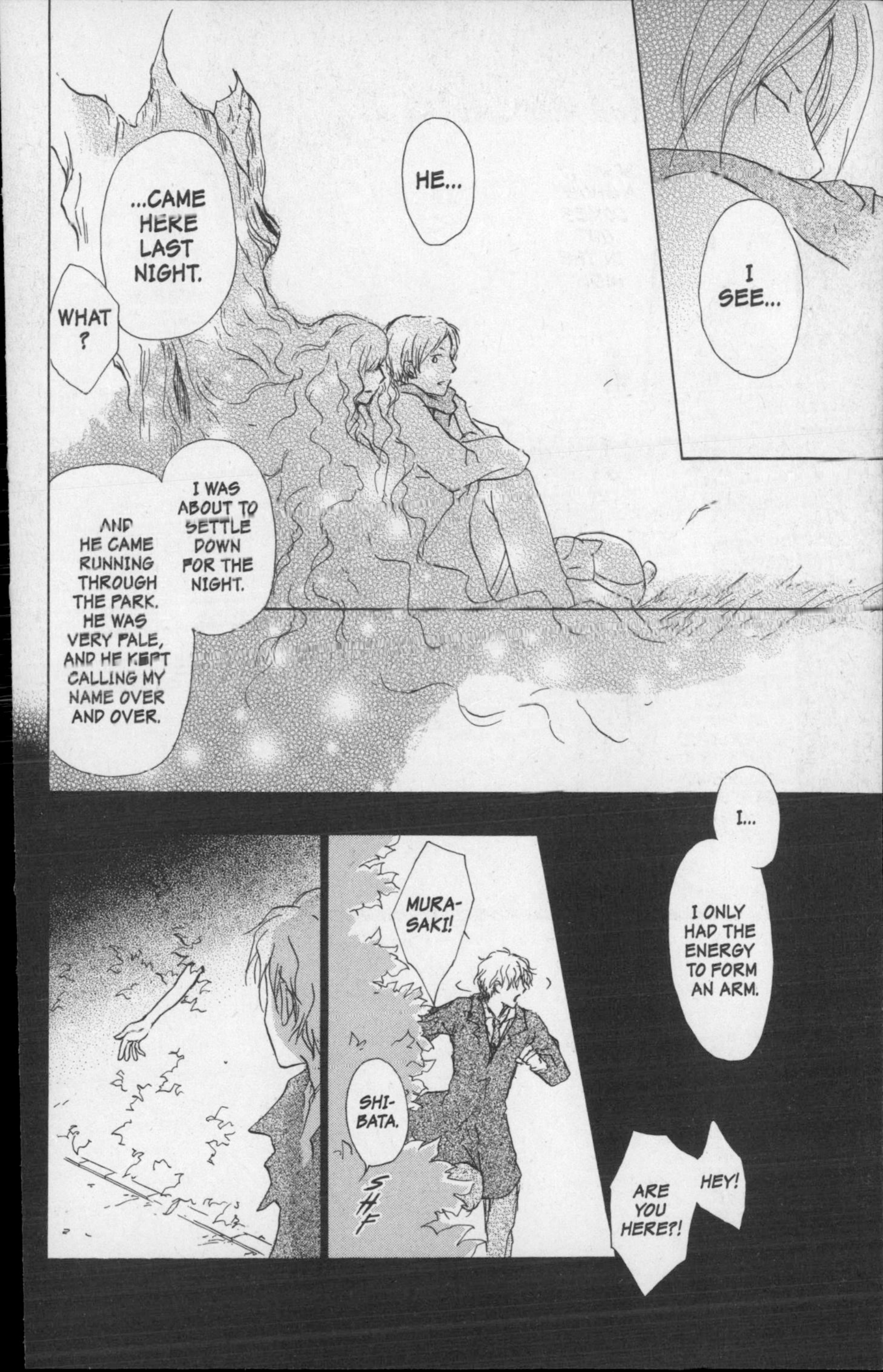
I SEE...
HE...
...CAME HERE LAST NIGHT.
WHAT?
I WAS ABOUT TO SETTLE DOWN FOR THE NIGHT.
AND HE CAME RUNNING THROUGH THE PARK. HE WAS VERY PALE, AND HE KEPT CALLING MY NAME OVER AND OVER.
I...
I ONLY HAD THE ENERGY TO FORM AN ARM.
HEY!
ARE YOU HERE?!
MURA-SAKI!
SHI-BATA.
SHF

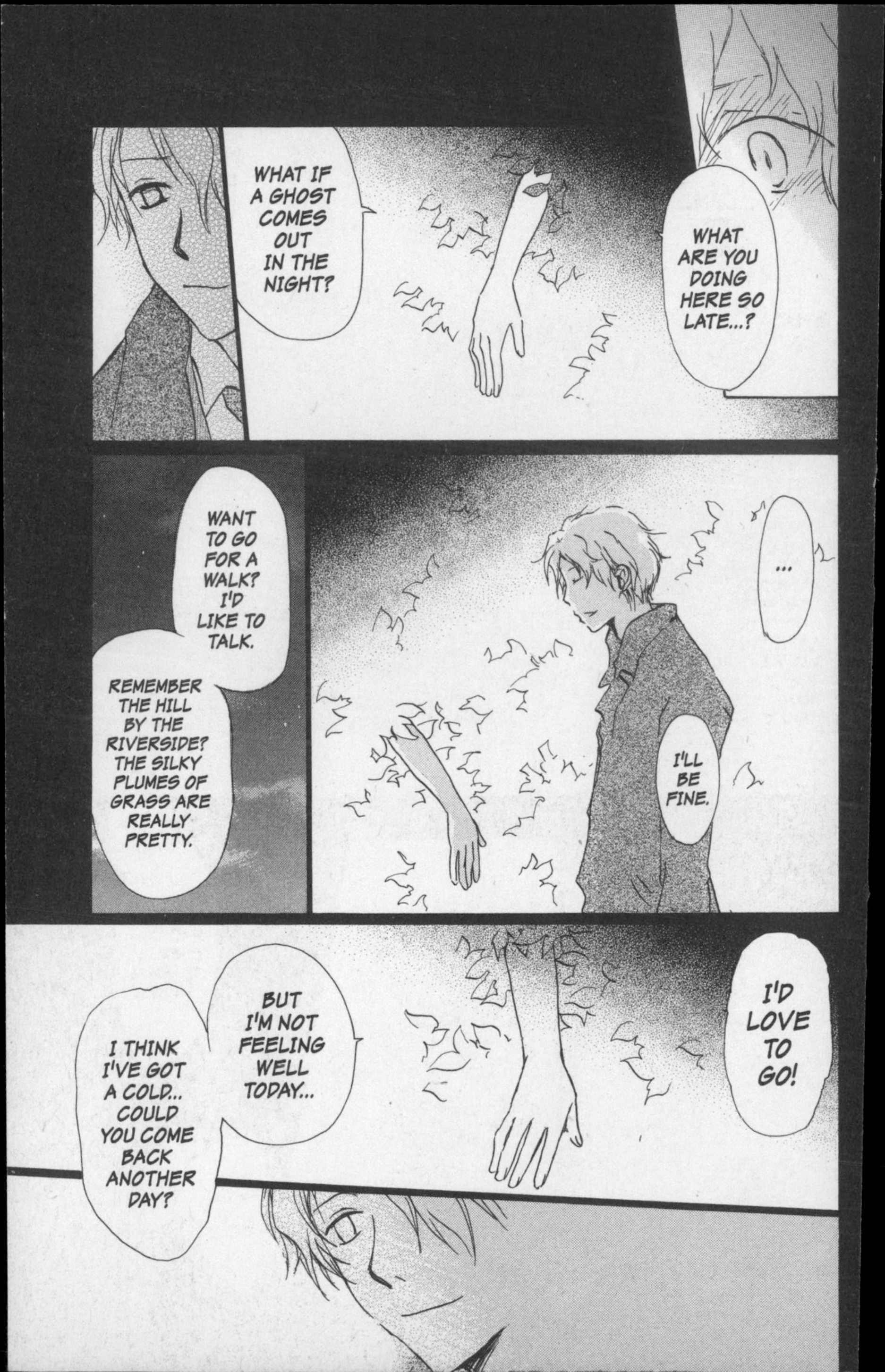
WHAT ARE YOU DOING HERE SO LATE...?
WHAT IF A GHOST COMES OUT IN THE NIGHT?
...
I'LL BE FINE.
WANT TO GO FOR A WALK? I'D LIKE TO TALK.
REMEMBER THE HILL BY THE RIVERSIDE? THE SILKY PLUMES OF GRASS ARE REALLY PRETTY.
I'D LOVE TO GO!
BUT I'M NOT FEELING WELL TODAY...
I THINK I'VE GOT A COLD... COULD YOU COME BACK ANOTHER DAY?

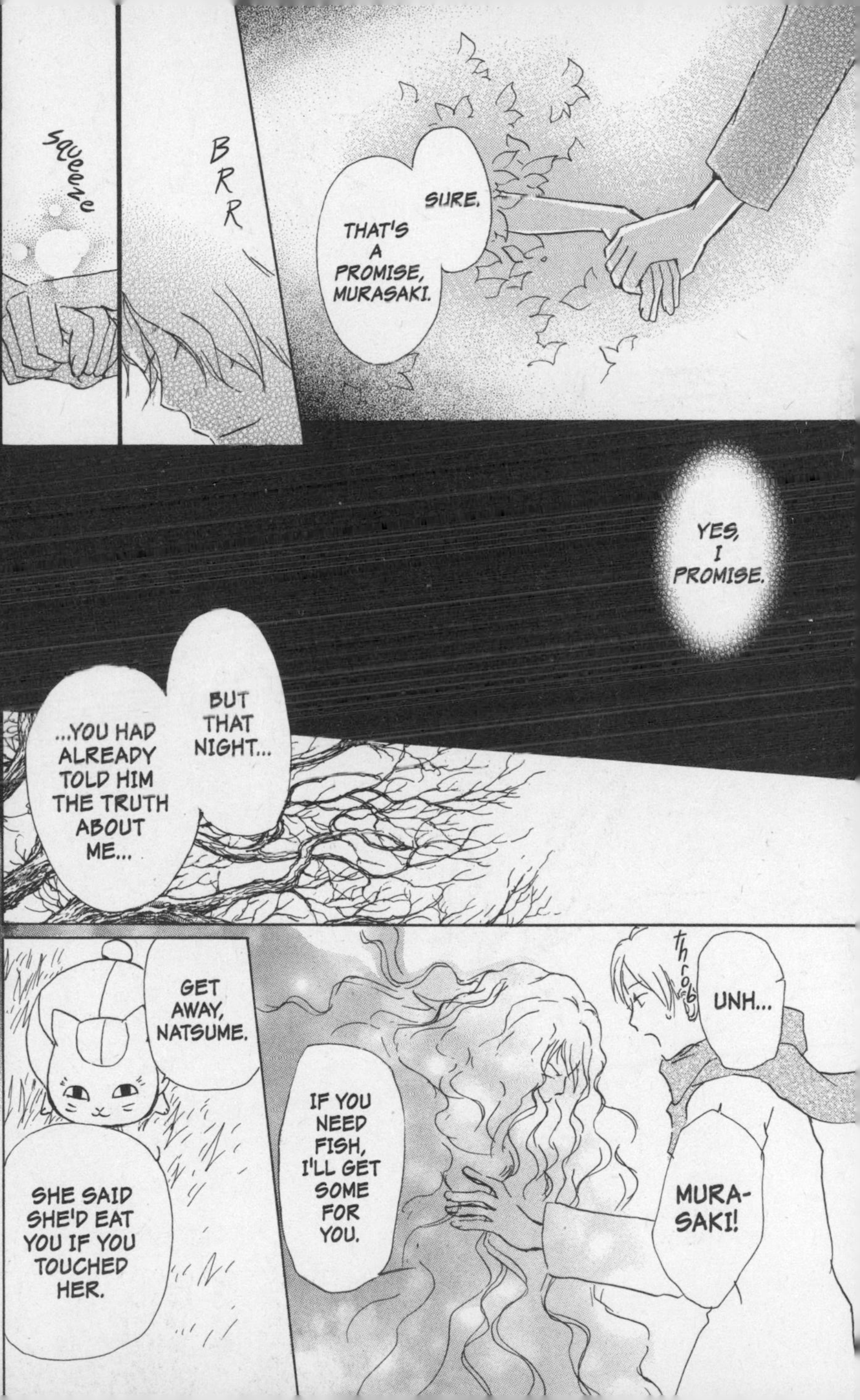
SURE. THAT'S A PROMISE, MURASAKI.
BRR
squeeze
YES, I PROMISE.
BUT THAT NIGHT...
...YOU HAD ALREADY TOLD HIM THE TRUTH ABOUT ME...
throb
UNH...
MURA-SAKI!
IF YOU NEED FISH, I'LL GET SOME FOR YOU.
GET AWAY, NATSUME.
SHE SAID SHE'D EAT YOU IF YOU TOUCHED HER.

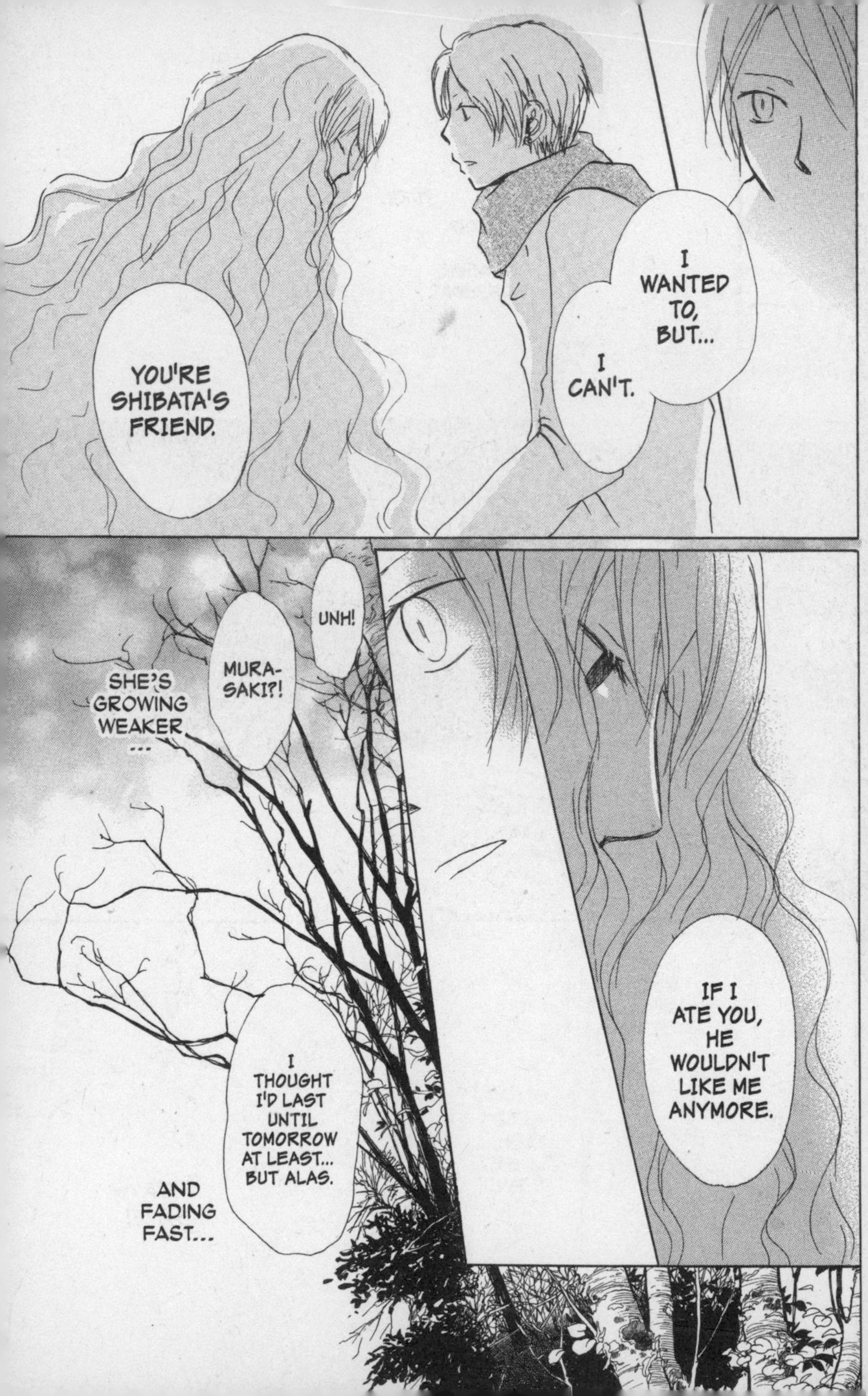
I WANTED TO, BUT...
I CAN'T.
YOU'RE SHIBATA'S FRIEND.
IF I ATE YOU, HE WOULDN'T LIKE ME ANYMORE.
UNH!
MURA-SAKI?!
SHE'S GROWING WEAKER...
I THOUGHT I'D LAST UNTIL TOMORROW AT LEAST... BUT ALAS.
AND FADING FAST...

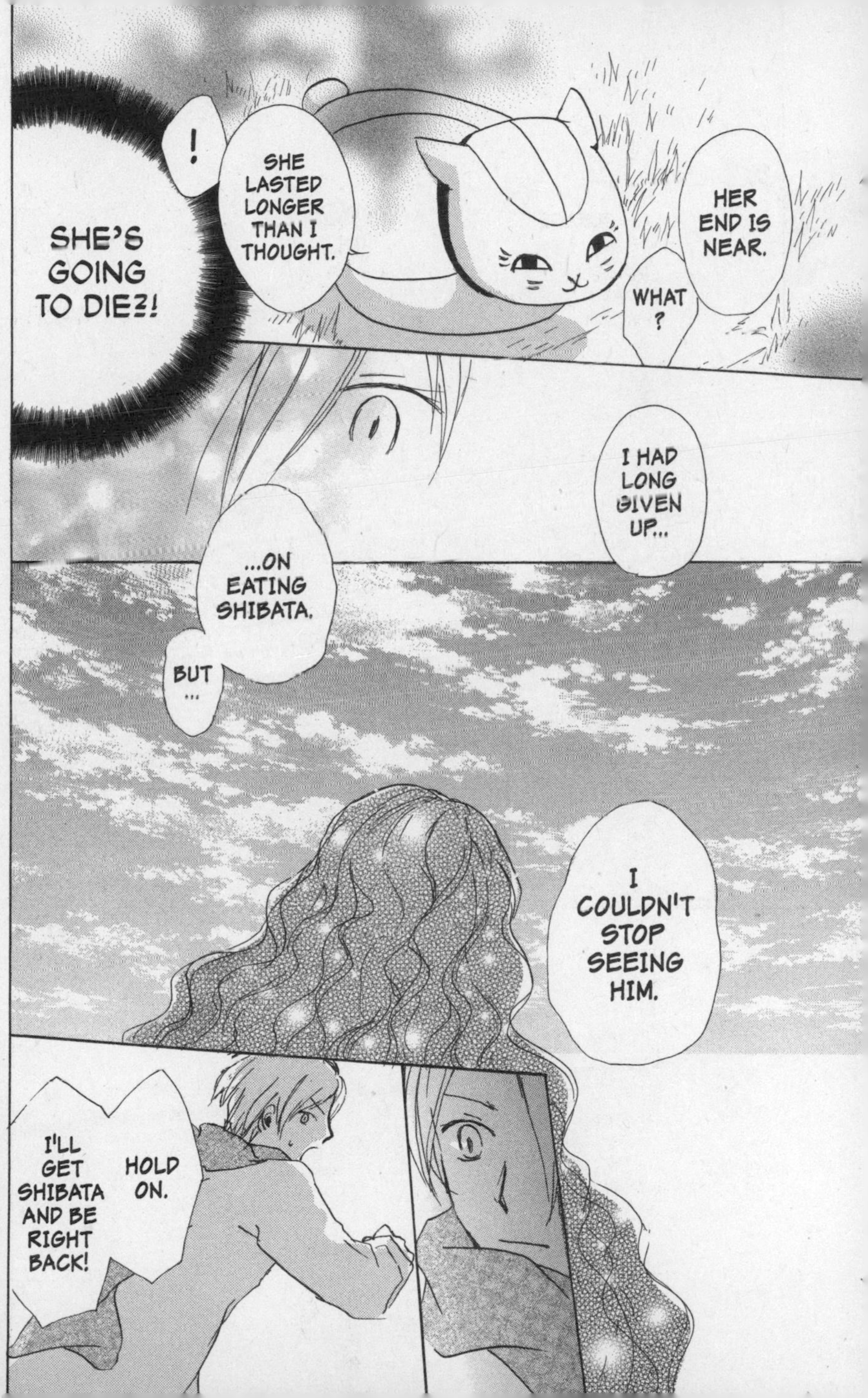
HER END IS NEAR.
WHAT?
SHE LASTED LONGER THAN I THOUGHT.
!
SHE'S GOING TO DIE?!
I HAD LONG GIVEN UP...
...ON EATING SHIBATA.
BUT...
I COULDN'T STOP SEEING HIM.
HOLD ON.
I'LL GET SHIBATA AND BE RIGHT BACK!

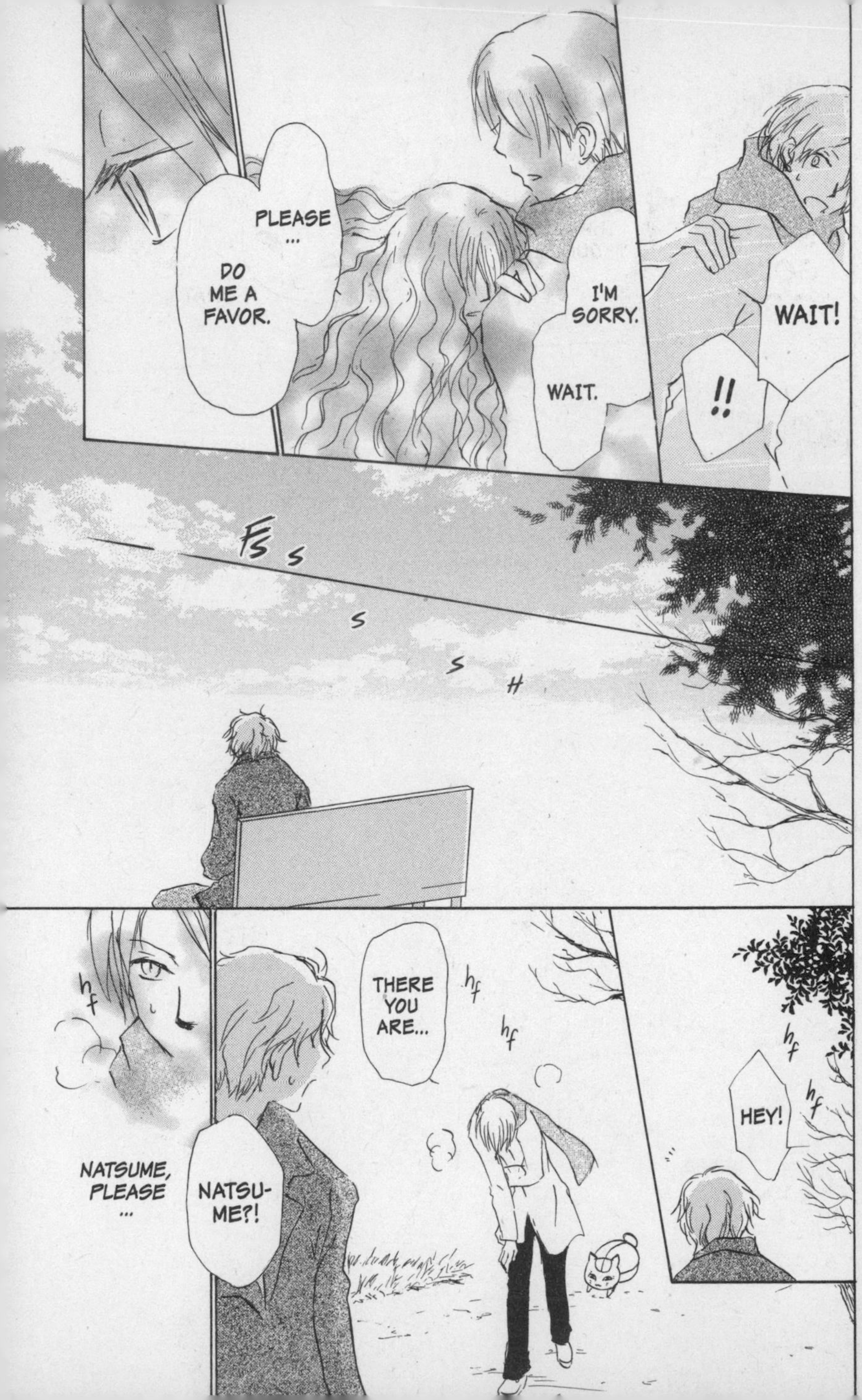
WAIT!
!!
I'M SORRY.
WAIT.
PLEASE ...
DO ME A FAVOR.
FSSSH
HEY!
hf
hf
THERE YOU ARE...
hf
hf
NATSU-ME?!
NATSUME, PLEASE ...
hf

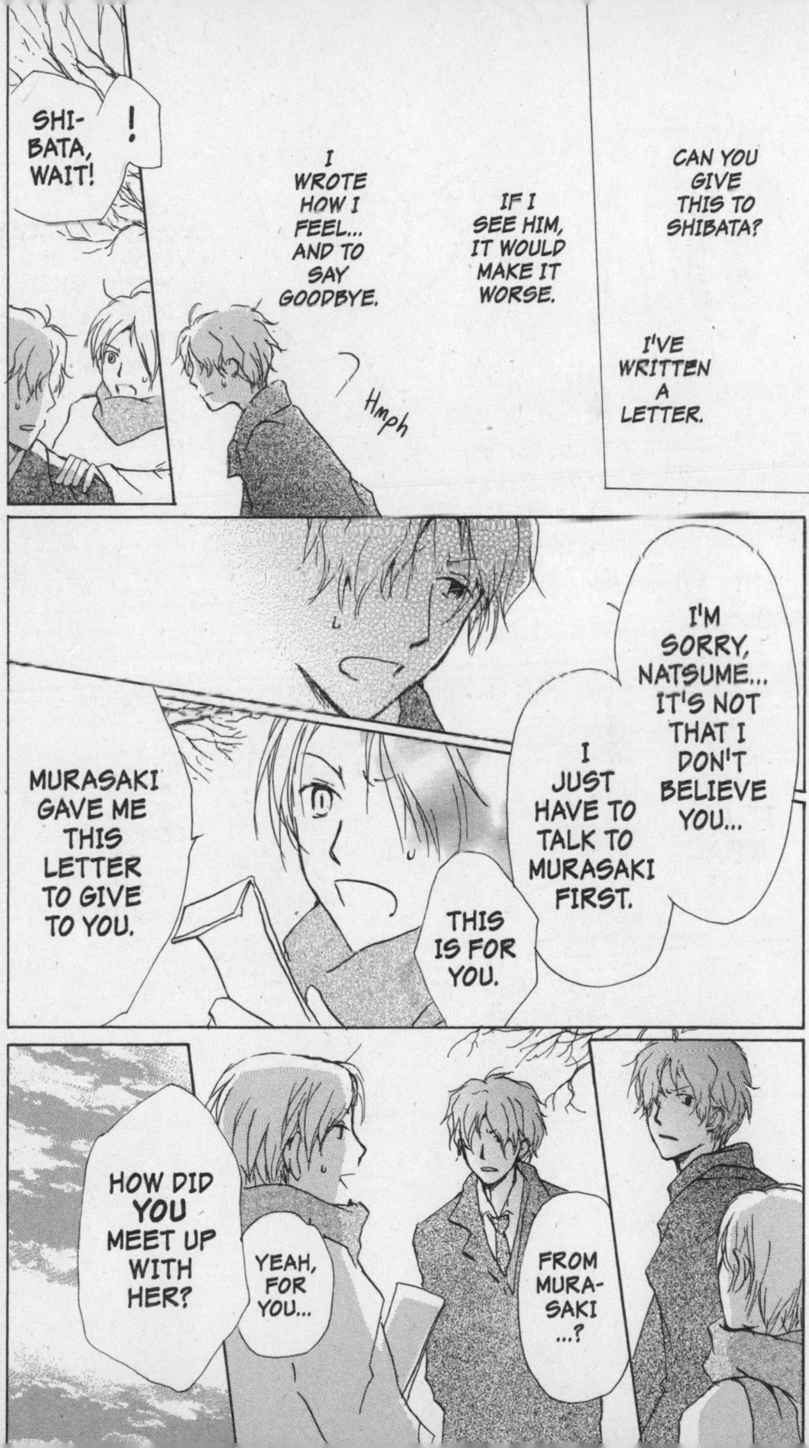
CAN YOU GIVE THIS TO SHIBATA?
I'VE WRITTEN A LETTER.
IF I SEE HIM, IT WOULD MAKE IT WORSE.
I WROTE HOW I FEEL... AND TO SAY GOODBYE.
Hmph
!
SHI-BATA, WAIT!
I'M SORRY, NATSUME... IT'S NOT THAT I DON'T BELIEVE YOU...
I JUST HAVE TO TALK TO MURASAKI FIRST.
THIS IS FOR YOU.
MURASAKI GAVE ME THIS LETTER TO GIVE TO YOU.
FROM MURA-SAKI ...?
YEAH, FOR YOU...
HOW DID YOU MEET UP WITH HER?

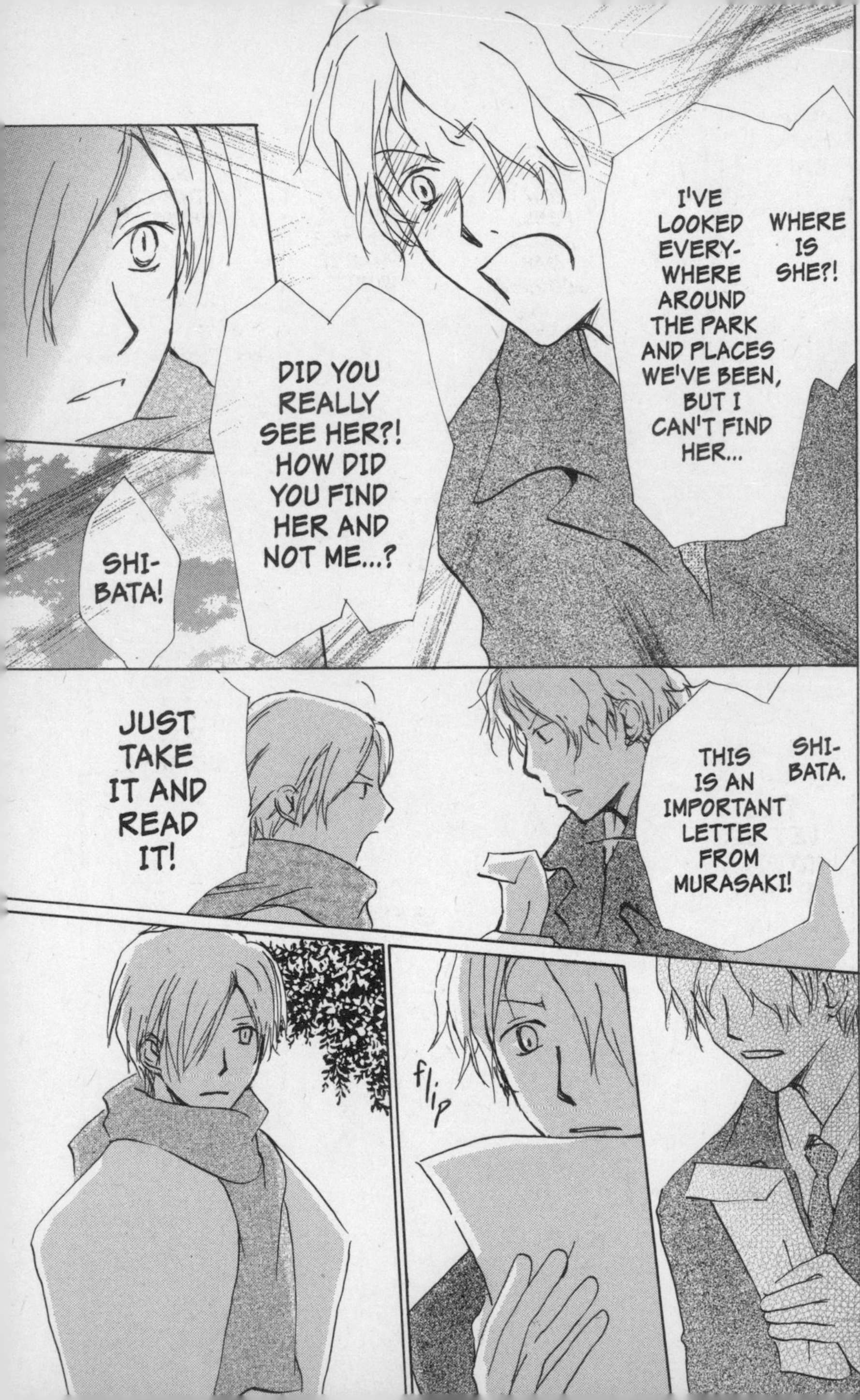
WHERE IS SHE?!
I'VE LOOKED EVERY-WHERE AROUND THE PARK AND PLACES WE'VE BEEN, BUT I CAN'T FIND HER...
DID YOU REALLY SEE HER?! HOW DID YOU FIND HER AND NOT ME...?
SHI-BATA!
SHI-BATA.
THIS IS AN IMPORTANT LETTER FROM MURASAKI!
JUST TAKE IT AND READ IT!
flip

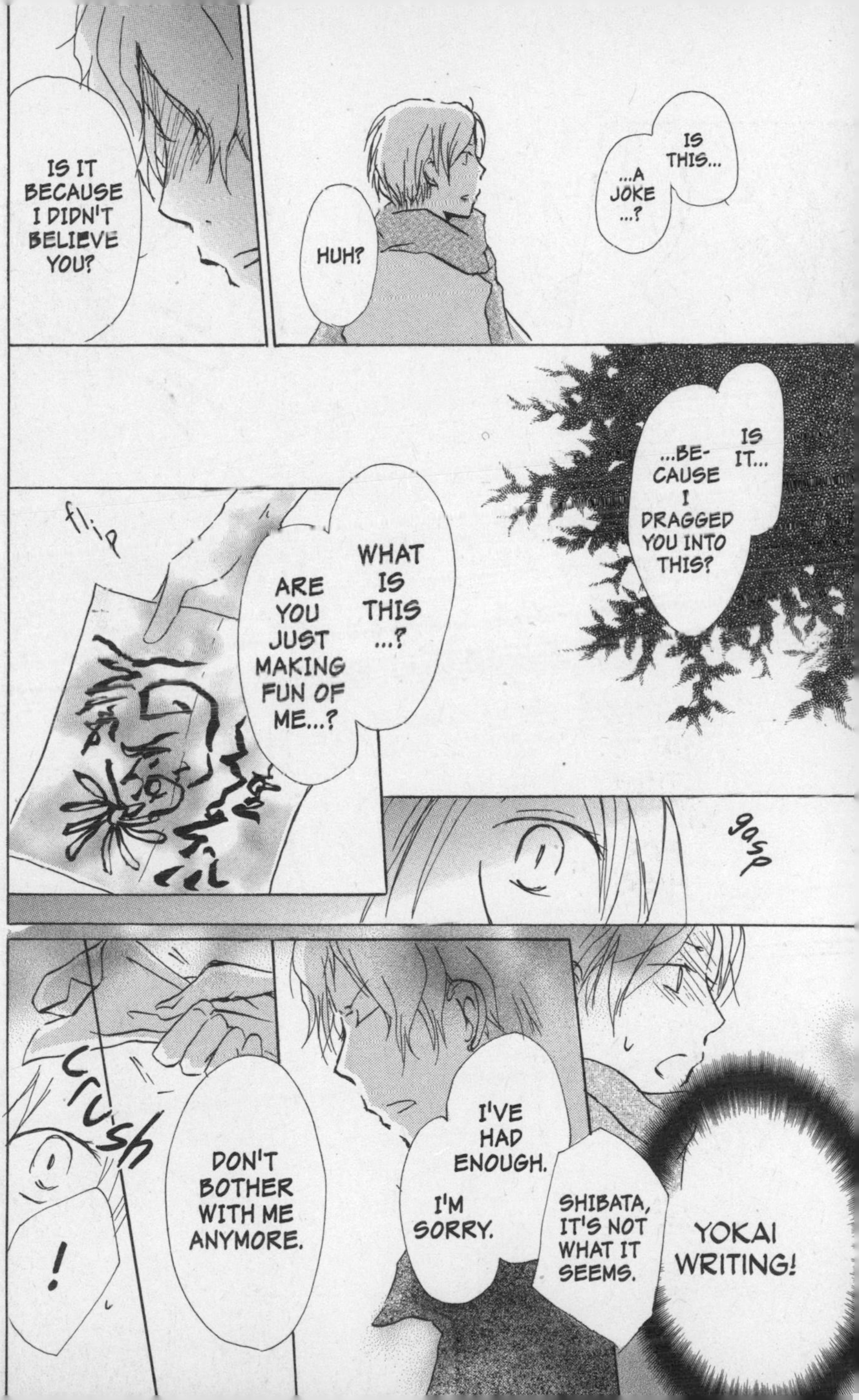
IS THIS... ...A JOKE ...?
HUH?
IS IT BECAUSE I DIDN'T BELIEVE YOU?
IS IT... ...BECAUSE I DRAGGED YOU INTO THIS?
flip
WHAT IS THIS ...?
ARE YOU JUST MAKING FUN OF ME...?
gasp
YOKAI WRITING!
SHIBATA, IT'S NOT WHAT IT SEEMS.
I'VE HAD ENOUGH.
I'M SORRY.
DON'T BOTHER WITH ME ANYMORE.
crush
!

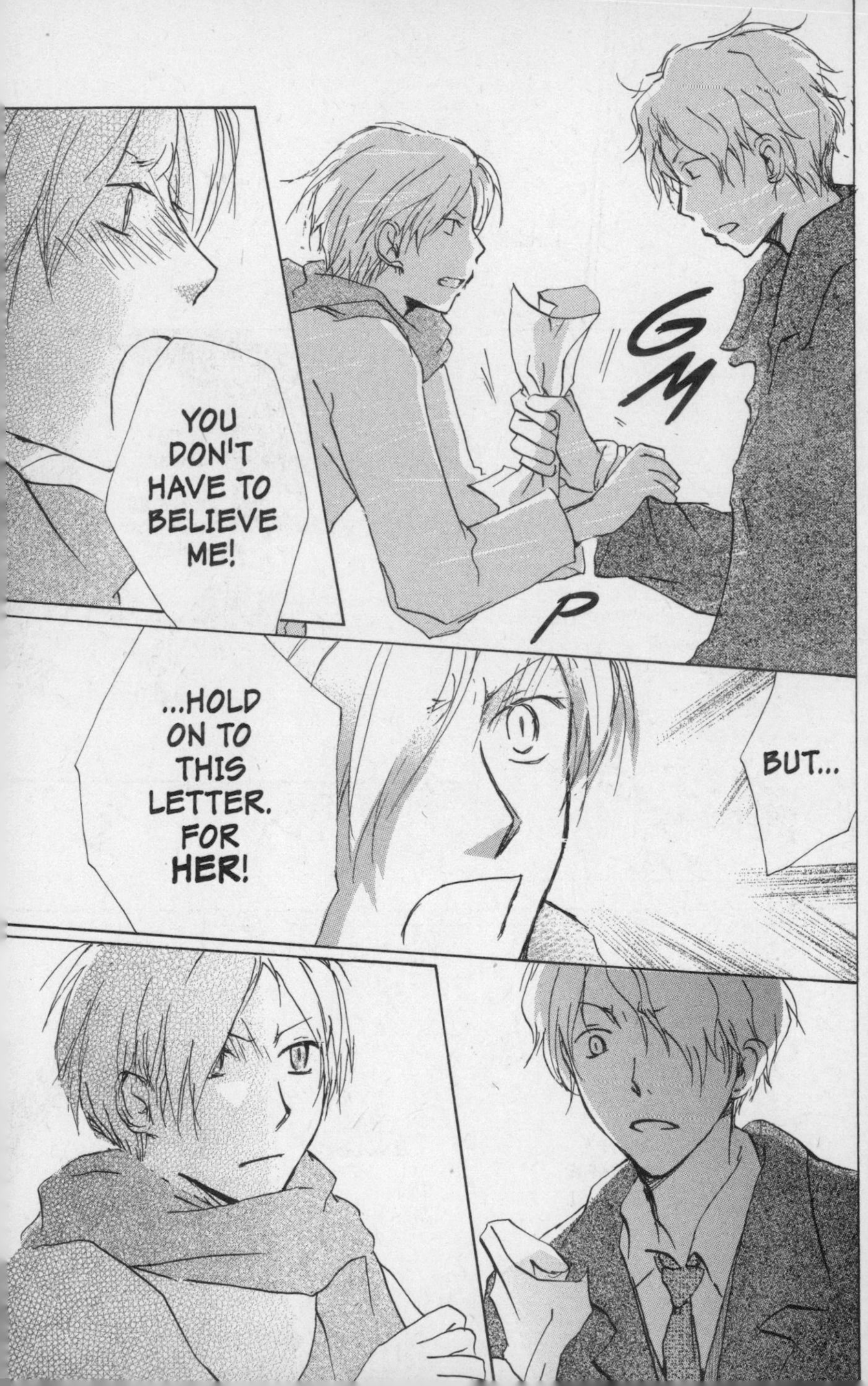
GMP
YOU DON'T HAVE TO BELIEVE ME!
BUT...
...HOLD ON TO THIS LETTER. FOR HER!

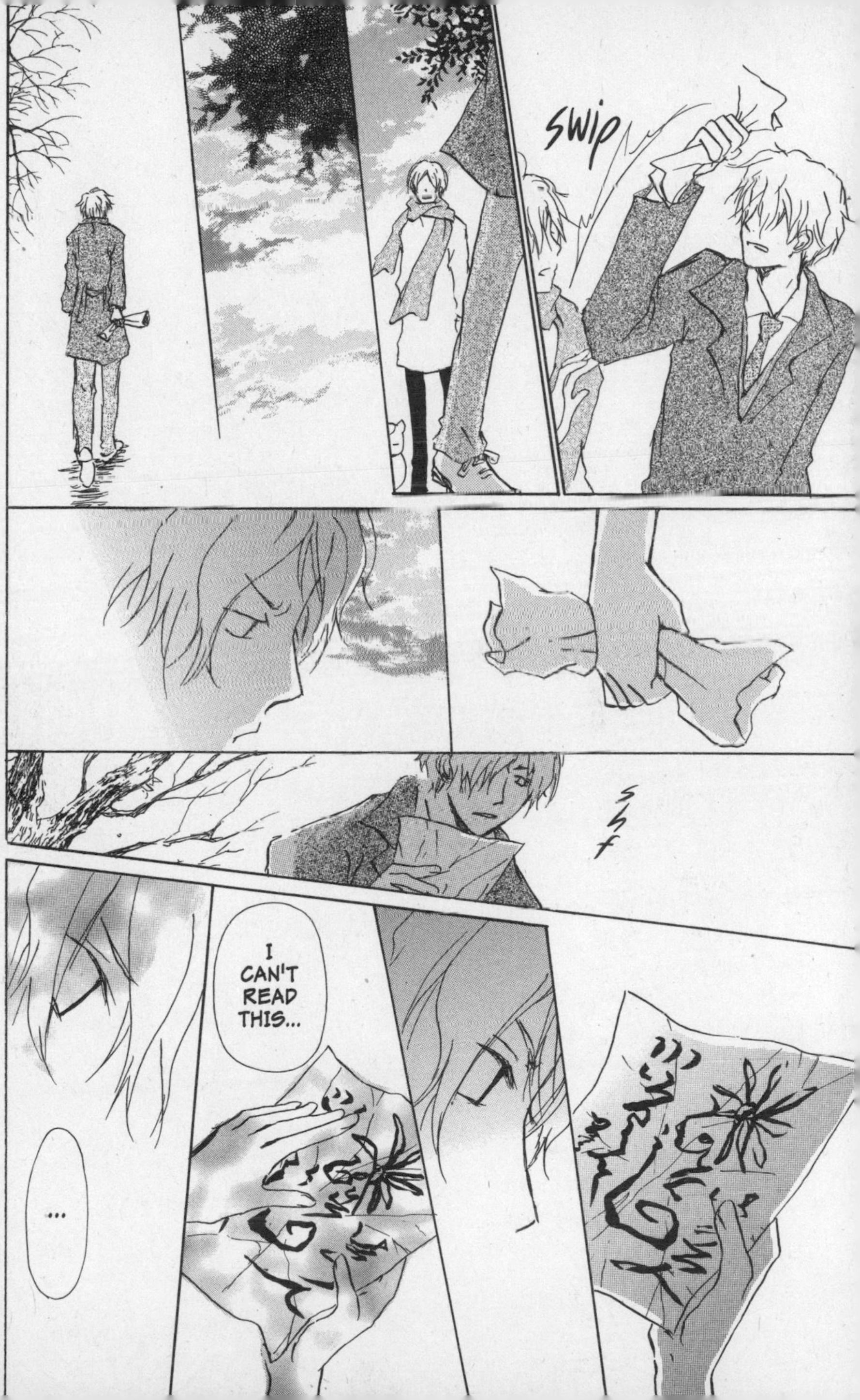
swip
shf
I CAN'T READ THIS...
...

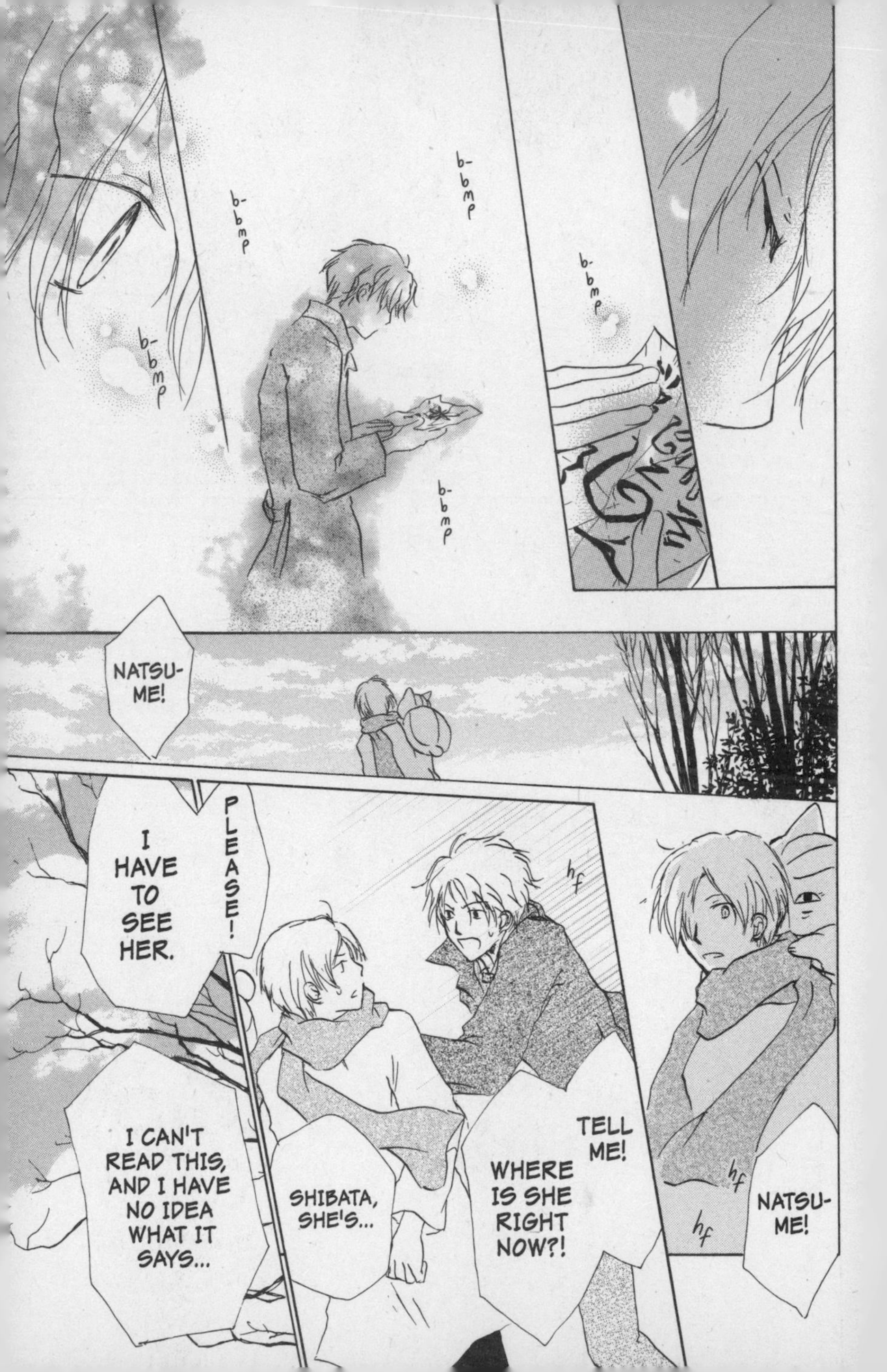
b-bmp
b-bmp
b-bmp
b-bmp
b-bmp
NATSU-ME!
NATSU-ME!
hf
hf
hf
TELL ME!
WHERE IS SHE RIGHT NOW?!
PLEASE!
I HAVE TO SEE HER.
SHIBATA, SHE'S...
I CAN'T READ THIS, AND I HAVE NO IDEA WHAT IT SAYS...

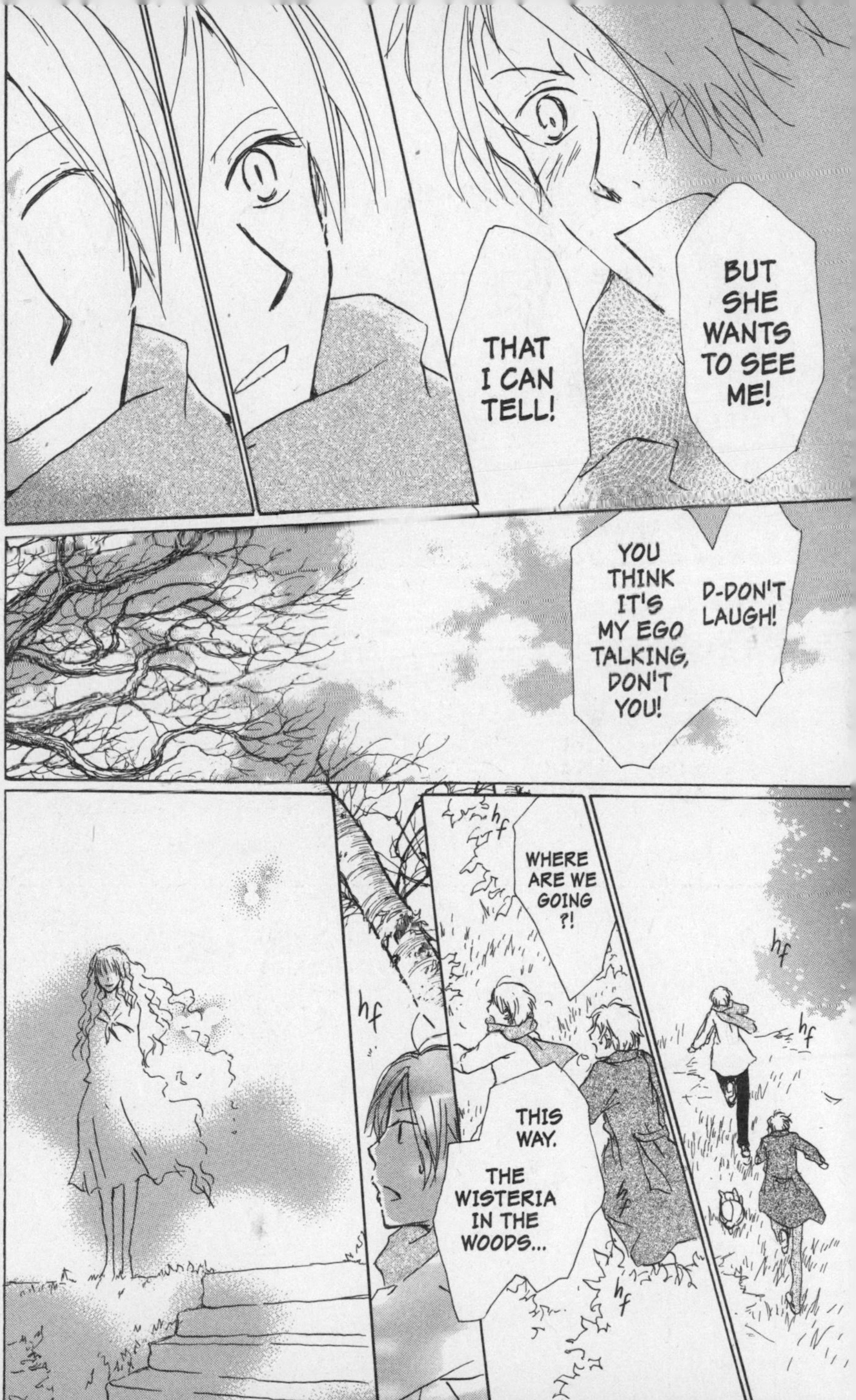
BUT SHE WANTS TO SEE ME!
THAT I CAN TELL!
D-DON'T LAUGH!
YOU THINK IT'S MY EGO TALKING, DON'T YOU!
hf
hf
hf
WHERE ARE WE GOING ?!
hf
THIS WAY.
THE WISTERIA IN THE WOODS...
hf
hf

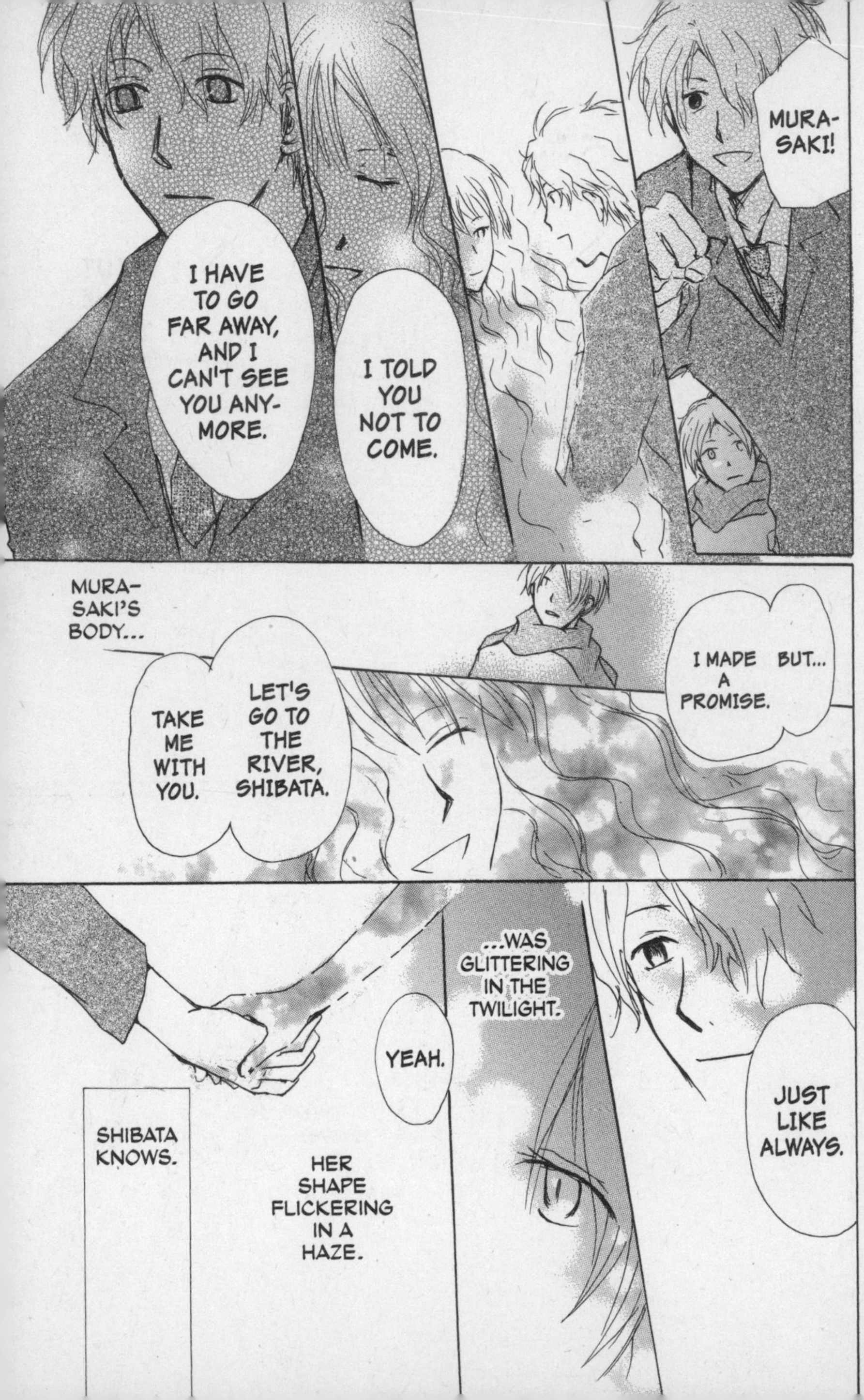
MURA-SAKI!
I TOLD YOU NOT TO COME.
I HAVE TO GO FAR AWAY, AND I CAN'T SEE YOU ANY-MORE.
I MADE A PROMISE. BUT...
MURA-SAKI'S BODY...
TAKE ME WITH YOU. LET'S GO TO THE RIVER, SHIBATA.
JUST LIKE ALWAYS.
...WAS GLITTERING IN THE TWILIGHT.
YEAH.
HER SHAPE FLICKERING IN A HAZE.
SHIBATA KNOWS.

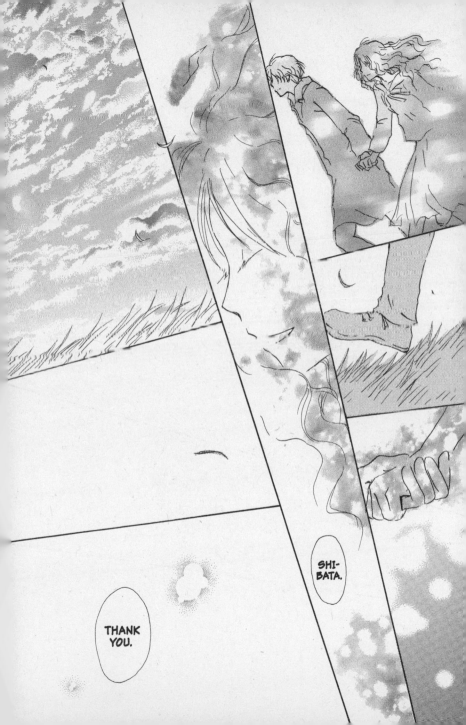

SHI-
BATA.

THANK
YOU.

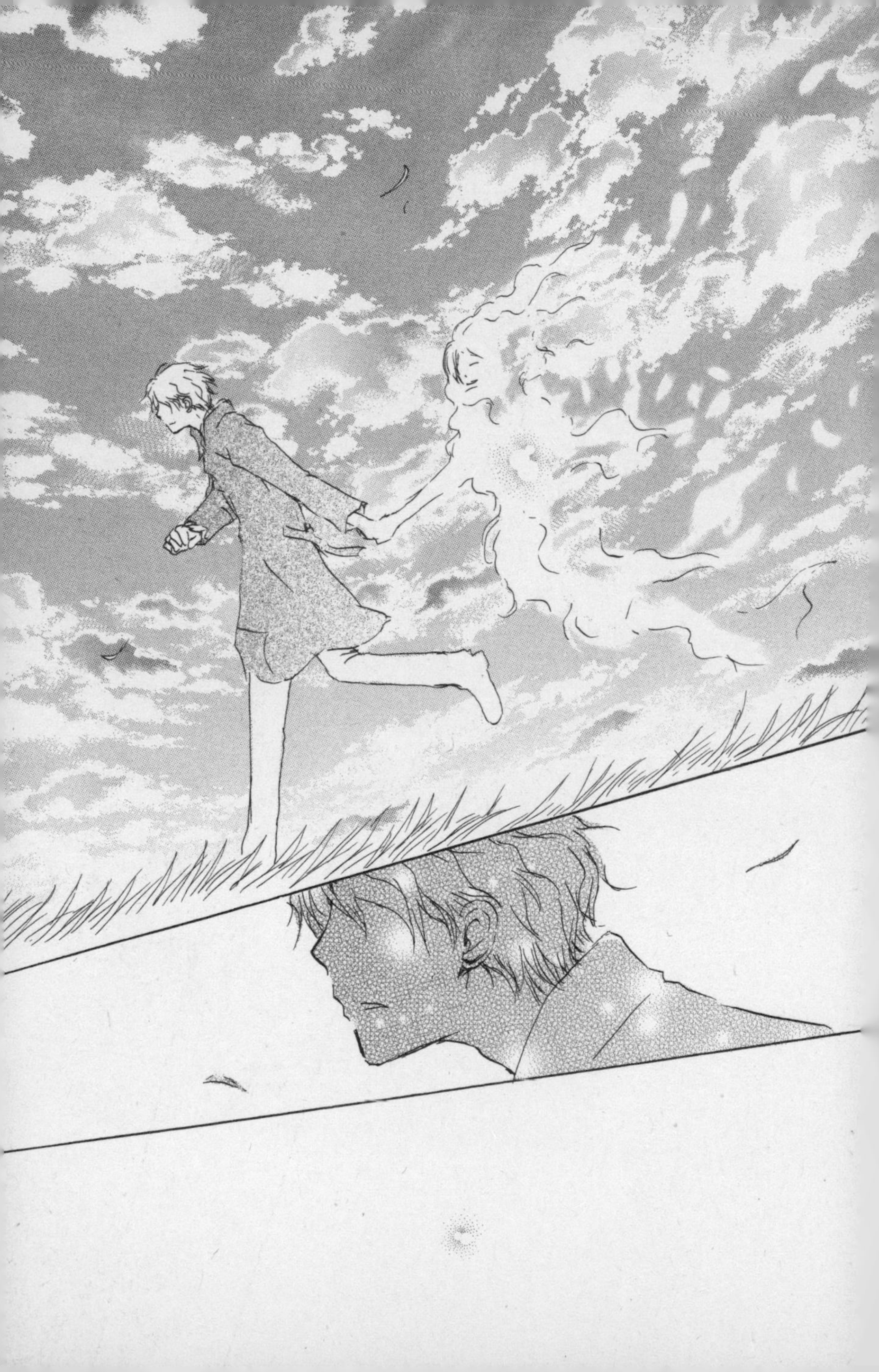

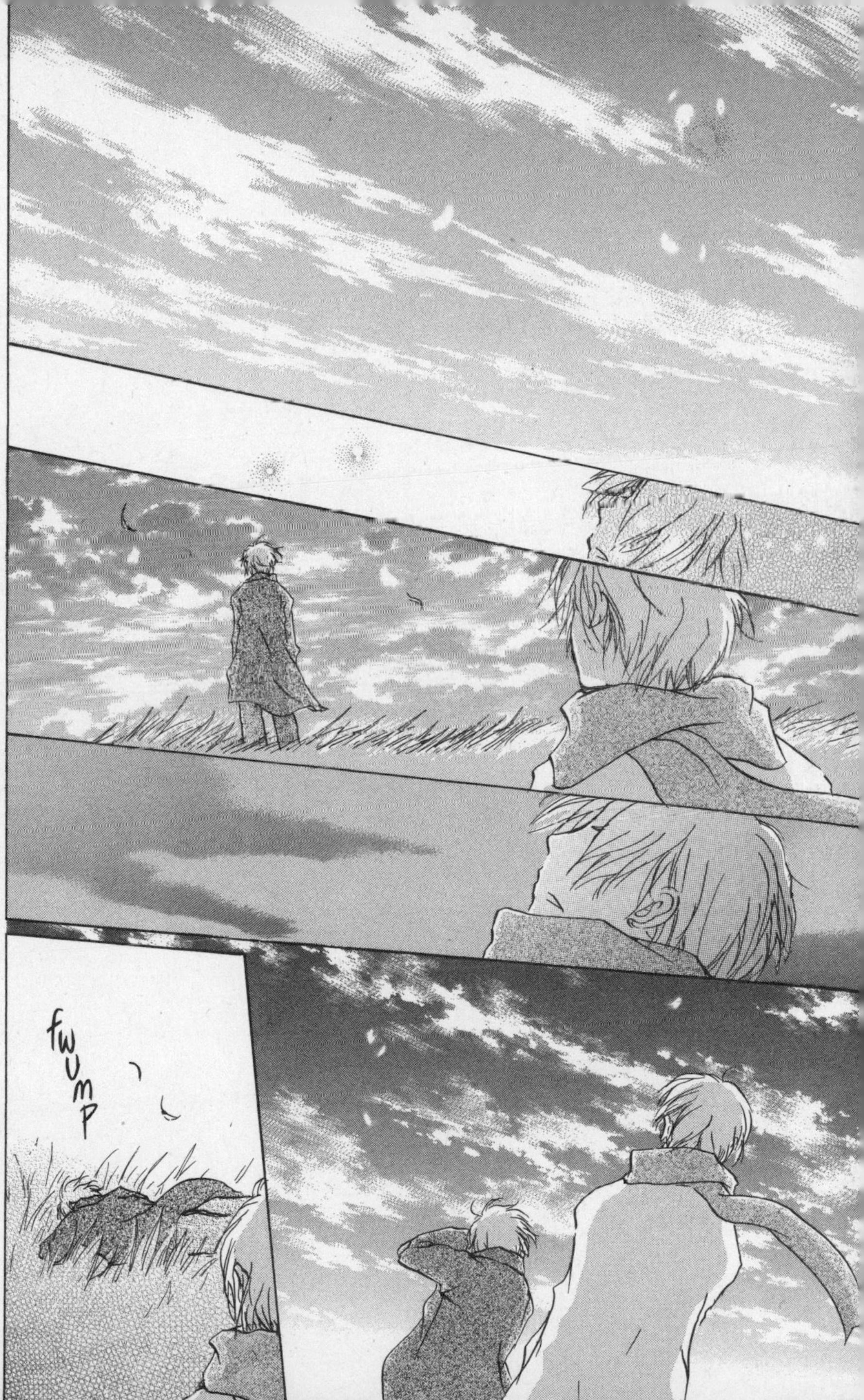
fwump

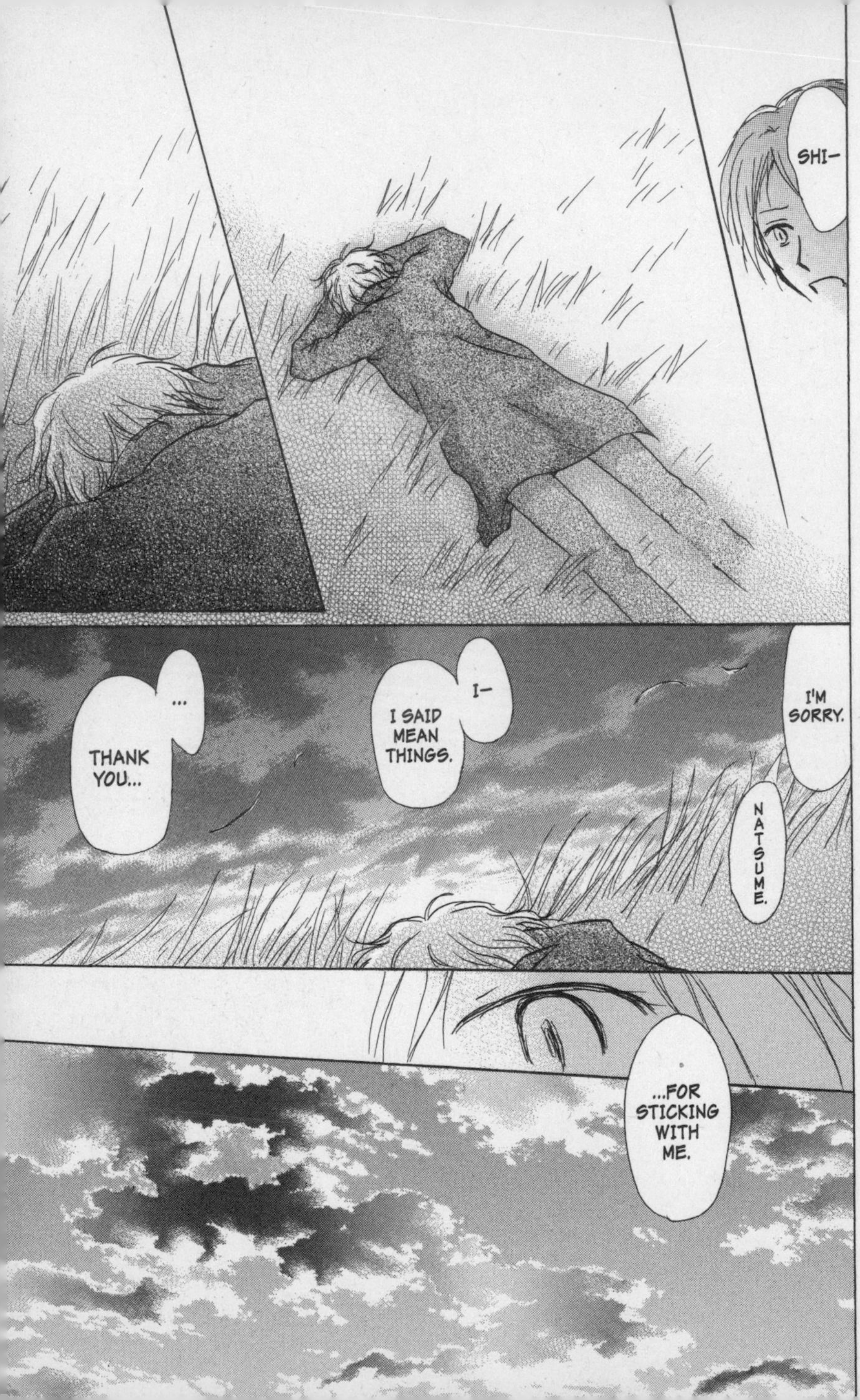
SHI—
I'M SORRY.
NATSUME.
I—
I SAID MEAN THINGS.
...
THANK YOU...
...FOR STICKING WITH ME.

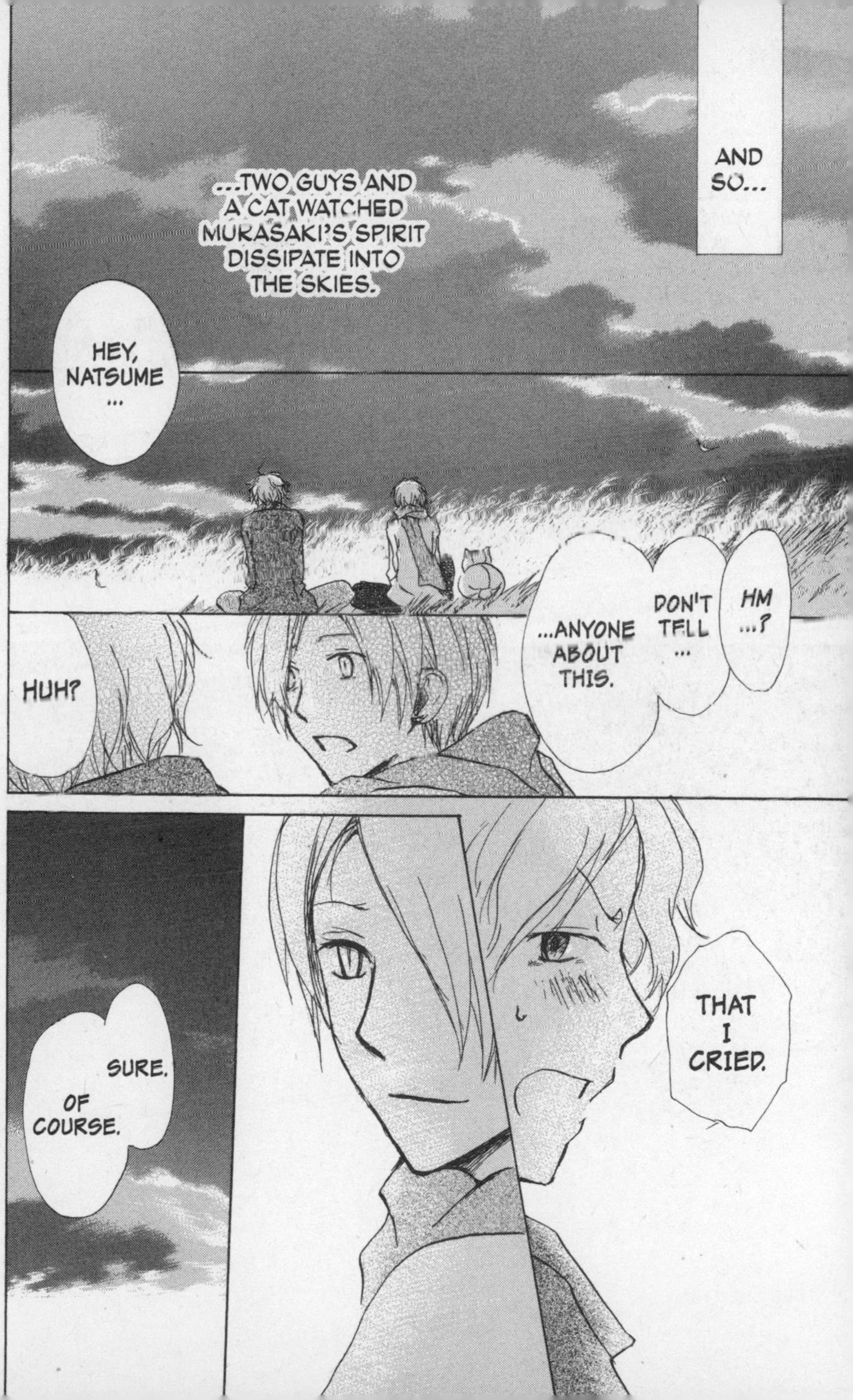
AND SO...
...TWO GUYS AND A CAT WATCHED MURASAKI'S SPIRIT DISSIPATE INTO THE SKIES.
HEY, NATSUME ...
HM ...?
DON'T TELL ...
...ANYONE ABOUT THIS.
HUH?
THAT I CRIED.
SURE.
OF COURSE.

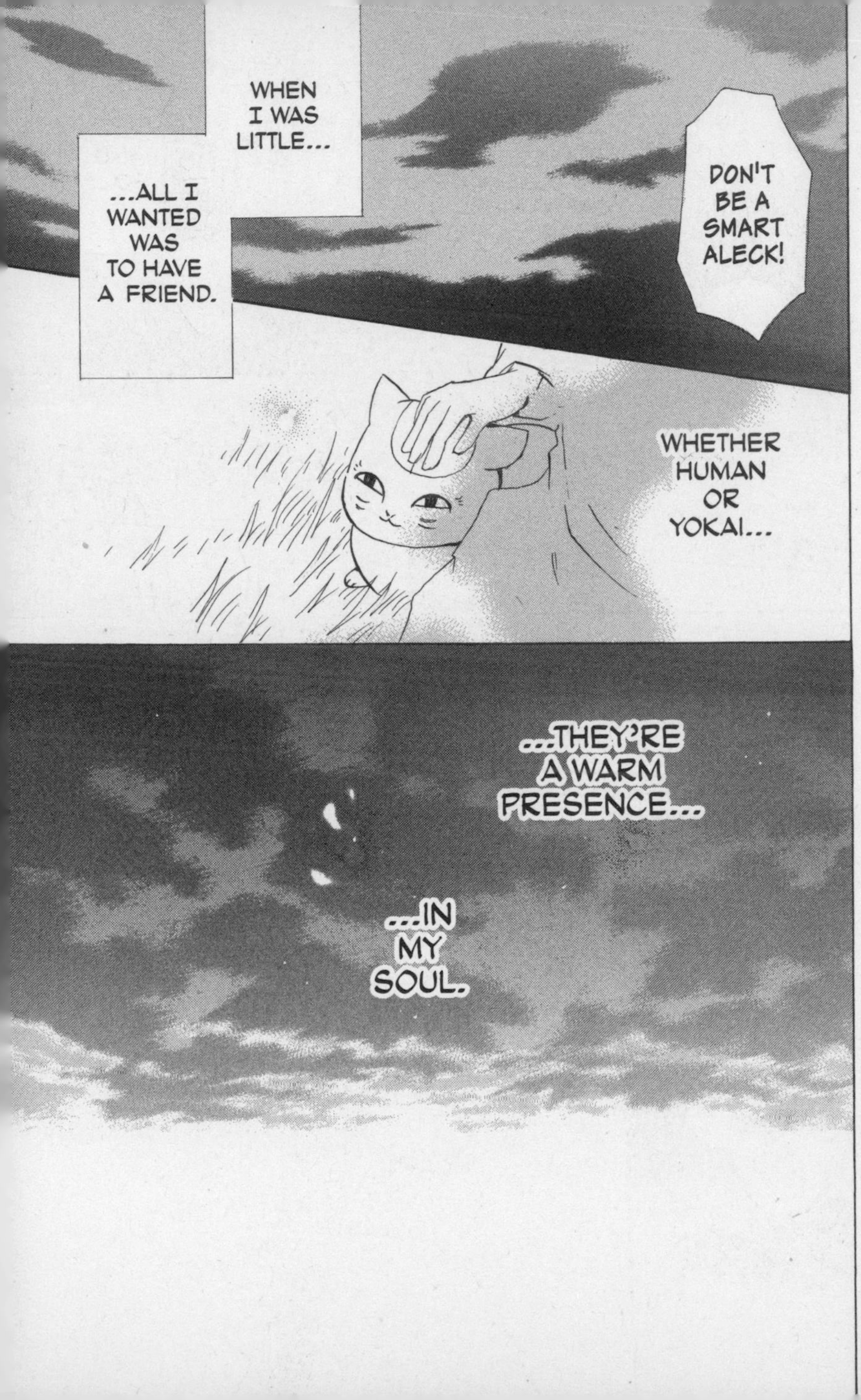
DON'T BE A SMART ALECK!
WHEN I WAS LITTLE...
...ALL I WANTED WAS TO HAVE A FRIEND.
WHETHER HUMAN OR YOKAI...
...THEY'RE A WARM PRESENCE...
...IN MY SOUL.

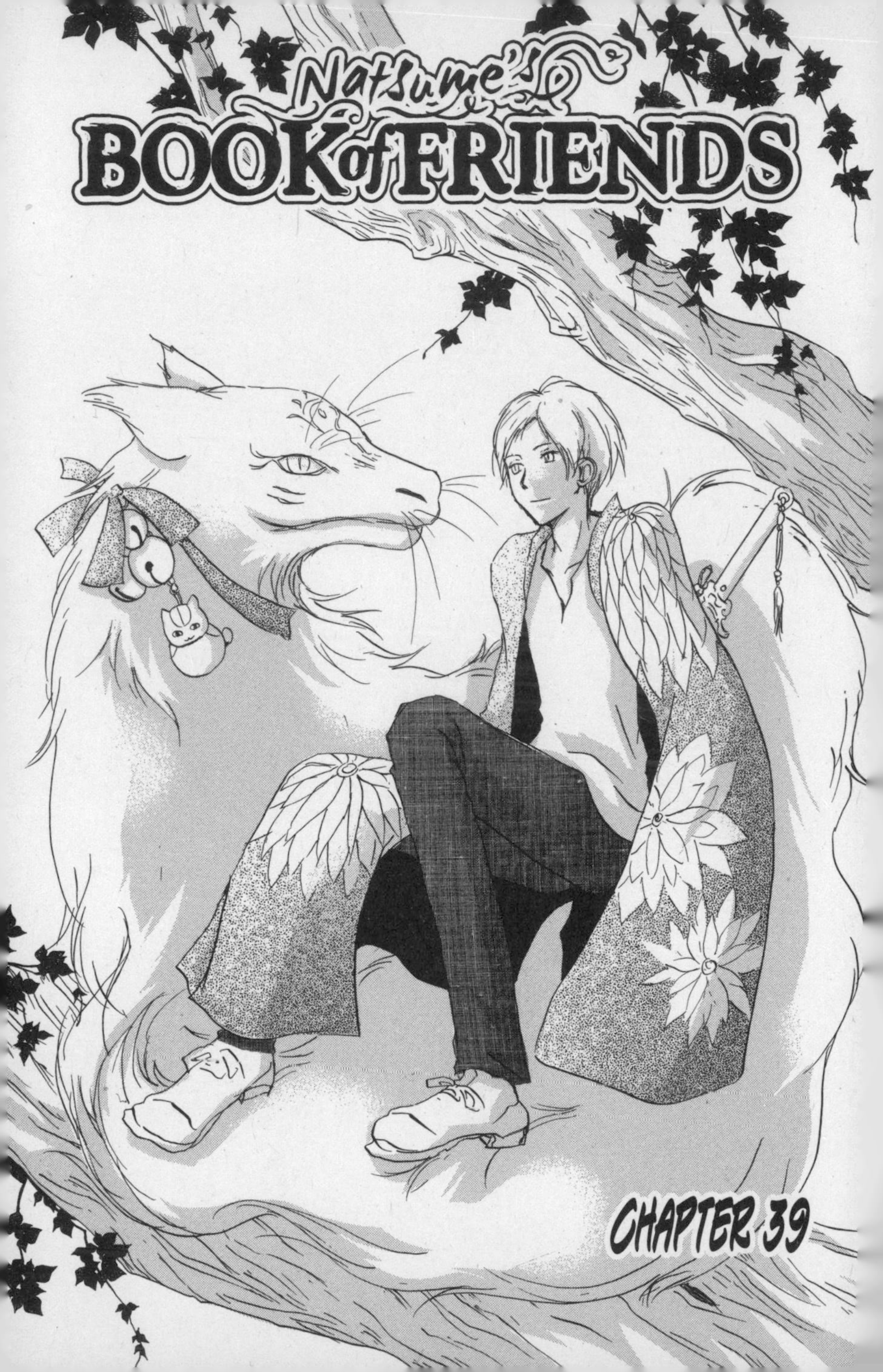
Natsume's BOOK of FRIENDS
CHAPTER 39

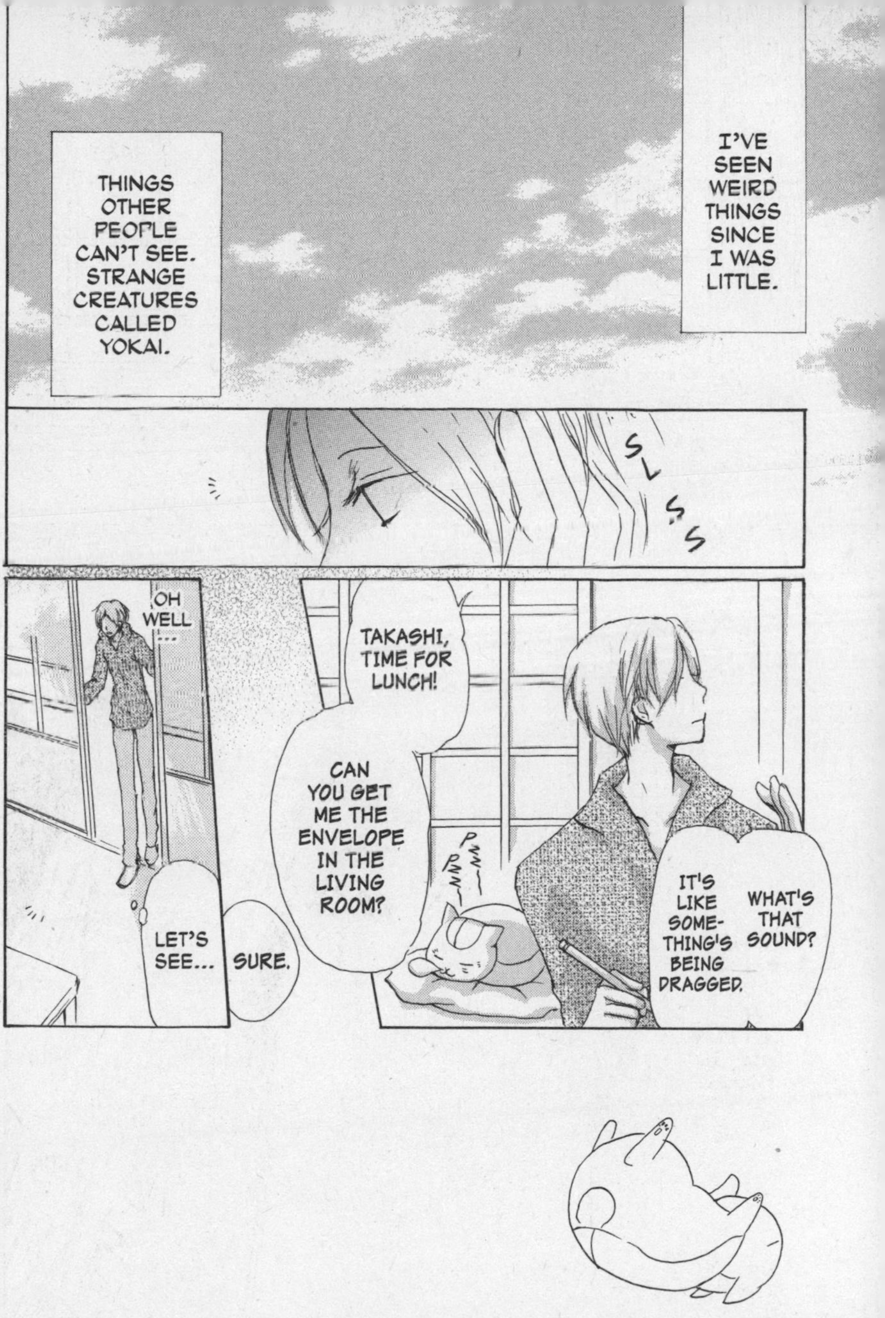

I'VE SEEN WEIRD THINGS SINCE I WAS LITTLE.
THINGS OTHER PEOPLE CAN'T SEE. STRANGE CREATURES CALLED YOKAI.
SLSS
WHAT'S THAT SOUND?
IT'S LIKE SOME-THING'S BEING DRAGGED.
TAKASHI, TIME FOR LUNCH!
CAN YOU GET ME THE ENVELOPE IN THE LIVING ROOM?
PZZ PZZ
SURE.
OH WELL...
LET'S SEE...

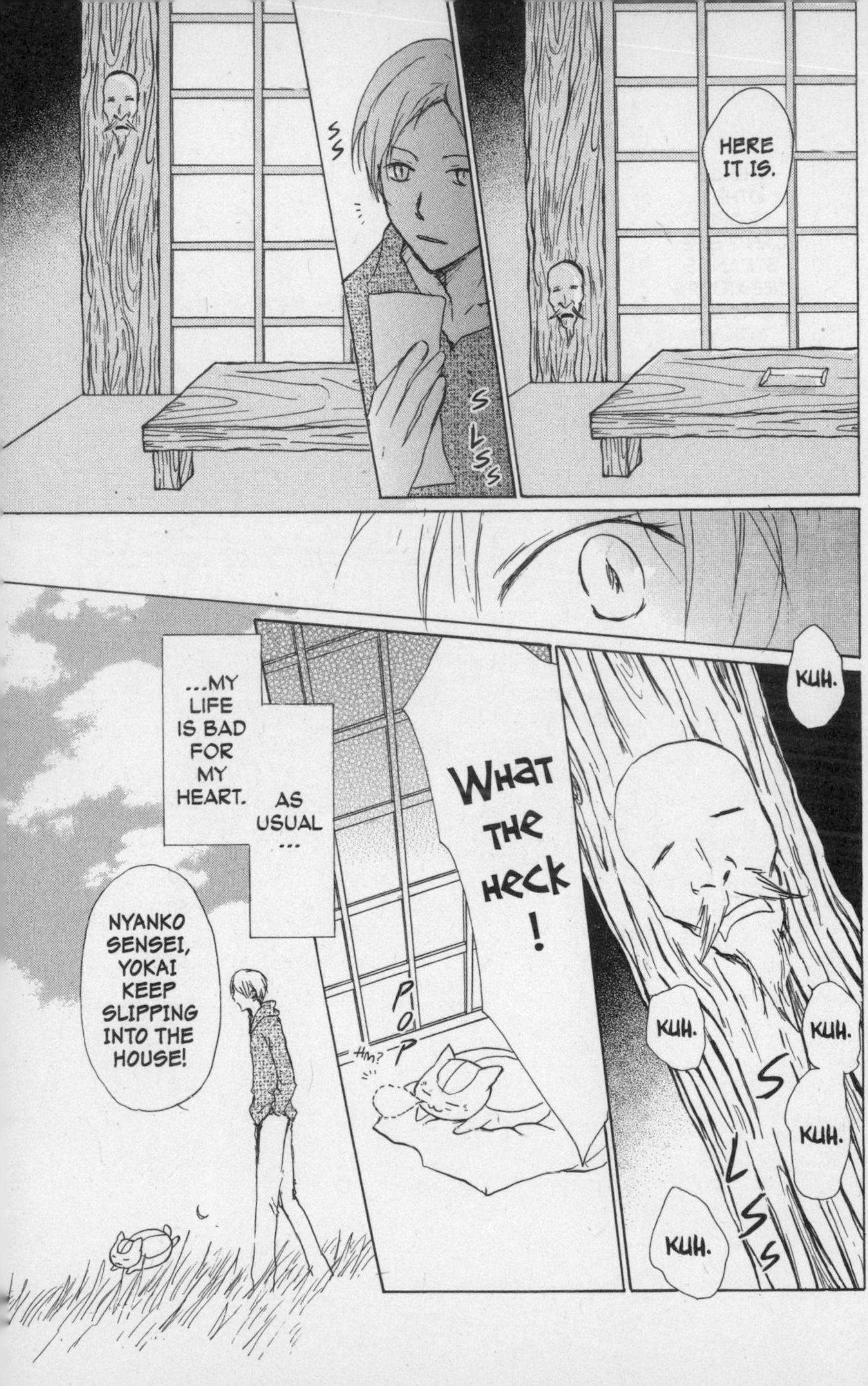
HERE IT IS.
SS
SLSS
KUH.
KUH.
KUH.
KUH.
KUH.
SLSS
WHAT THE HECK!
POP
Hm?
AS USUAL ...
...MY LIFE IS BAD FOR MY HEART.
NYANKO SENSEI, YOKAI KEEP SLIPPING INTO THE HOUSE!

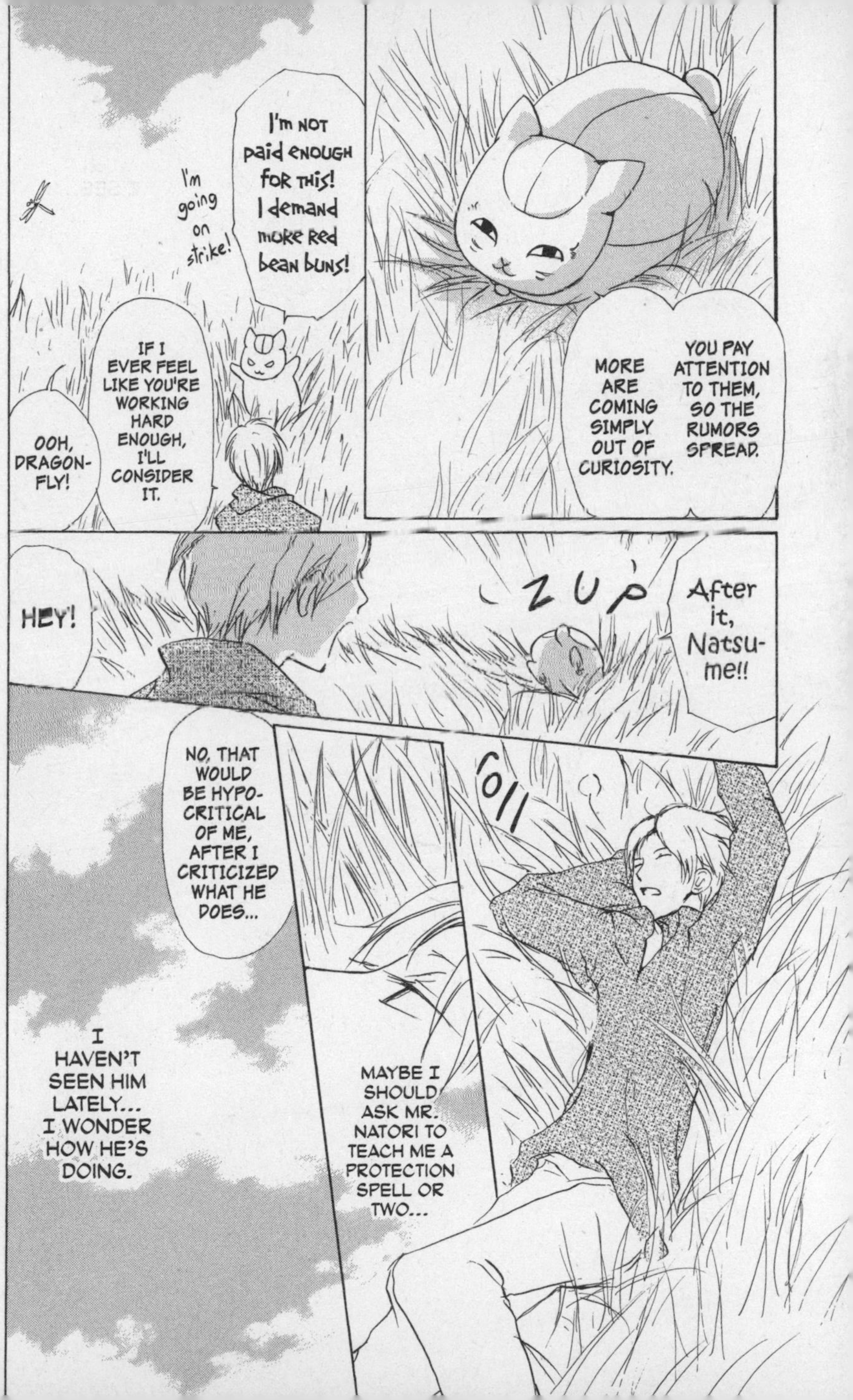
YOU PAY ATTENTION TO THEM, SO THE RUMORS SPREAD.
MORE ARE COMING SIMPLY OUT OF CURIOSITY.
I'm NOT paid ENOUGH FOR THIS! I demand more red bean buns!
I'm going on strike!
IF I EVER FEEL LIKE YOU'RE WORKING HARD ENOUGH, I'LL CONSIDER IT.
OOH, DRAGON-FLY!
After it, Natsu-me!!
ZUP
HEY!
roll
MAYBE I SHOULD ASK MR. NATORI TO TEACH ME A PROTECTION SPELL OR TWO...
NO, THAT WOULD BE HYPO-CRITICAL OF ME, AFTER I CRITICIZED WHAT HE DOES...
I HAVEN'T SEEN HIM LATELY... I WONDER HOW HE'S DOING.

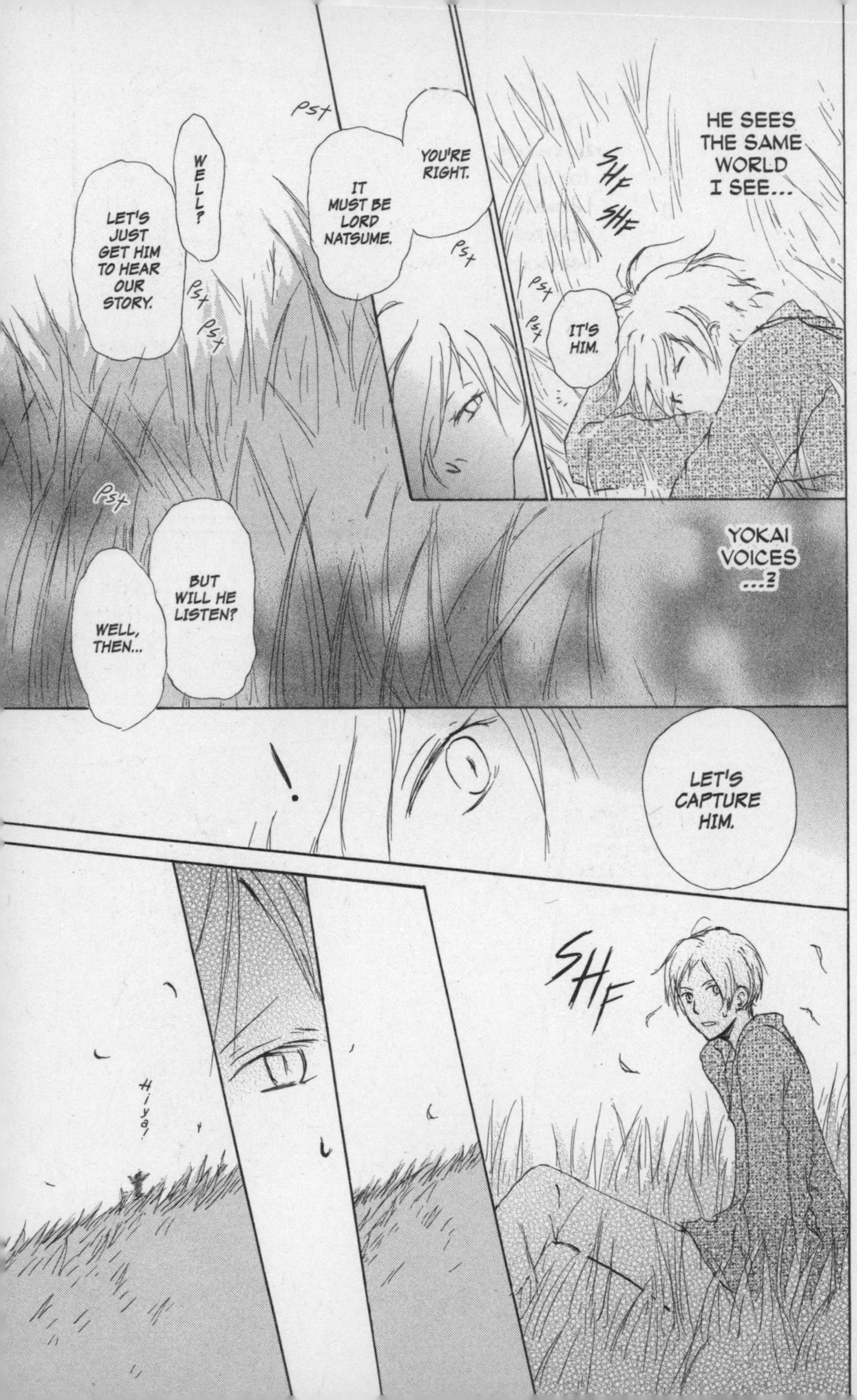
HE SEES THE SAME WORLD I SEE...
SHF SHF
pst
pst
IT'S HIM.
pst
YOU'RE RIGHT.
IT MUST BE LORD NATSUME.
pst
pst
WELL?
LET'S JUST GET HIM TO HEAR OUR STORY.
pst
pst
YOKAI VOICES ...?
BUT WILL HE LISTEN?
WELL, THEN...
Pst
LET'S CAPTURE HIM.
!
SHF
Hiya!

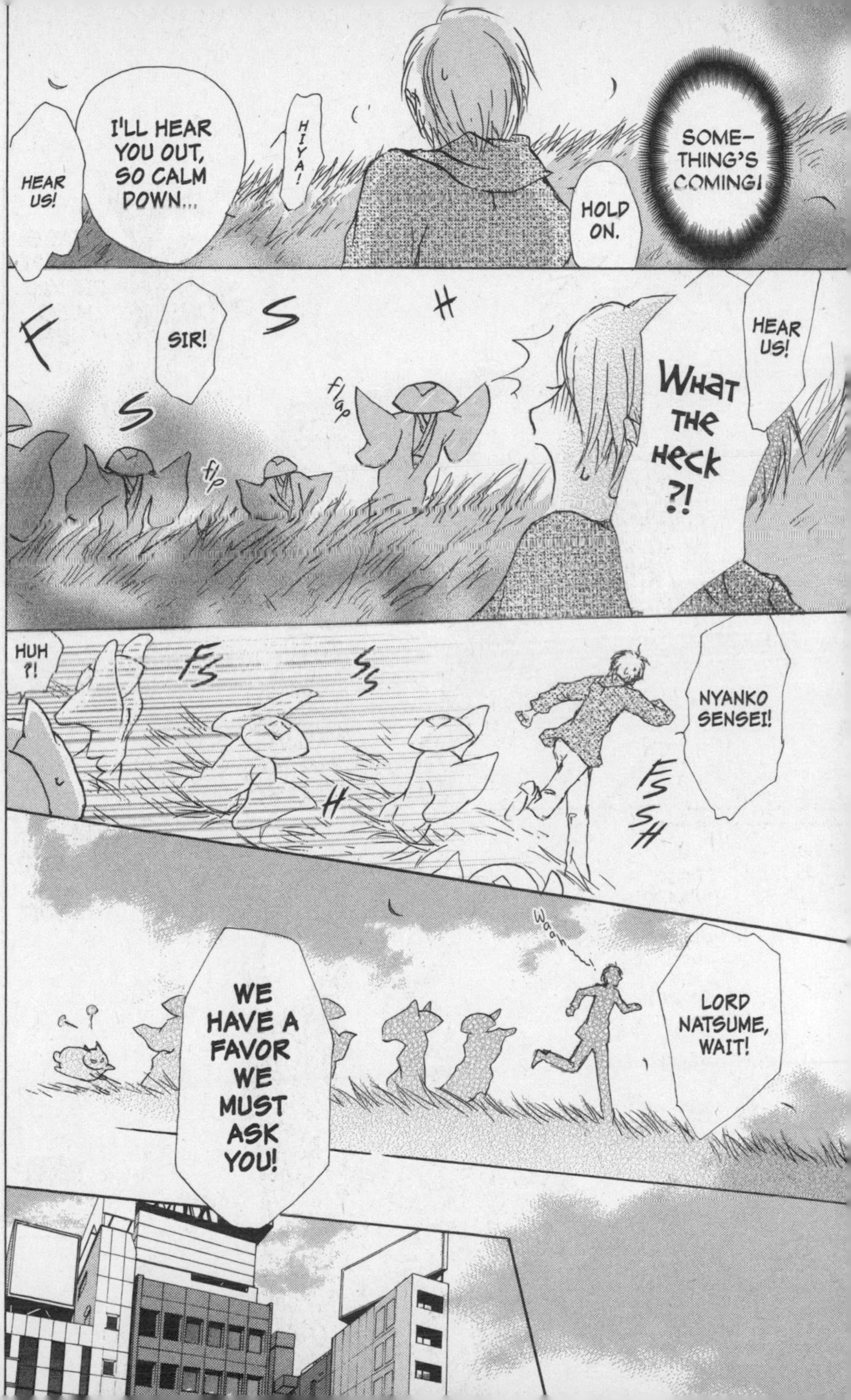
SOME-THING'S COMING!
HOLD ON.
HIYA!
I'LL HEAR YOU OUT, SO CALM DOWN...
HEAR US!
HEAR US!
WHAT THE HECK?!
H
flap
S
SIR!
F
S
flp
NYANKO SENSEI!
FSSH
SS
FS
H
HUH?!
LORD NATSUME, WAIT!
Waa
WE HAVE A FAVOR WE MUST ASK YOU!

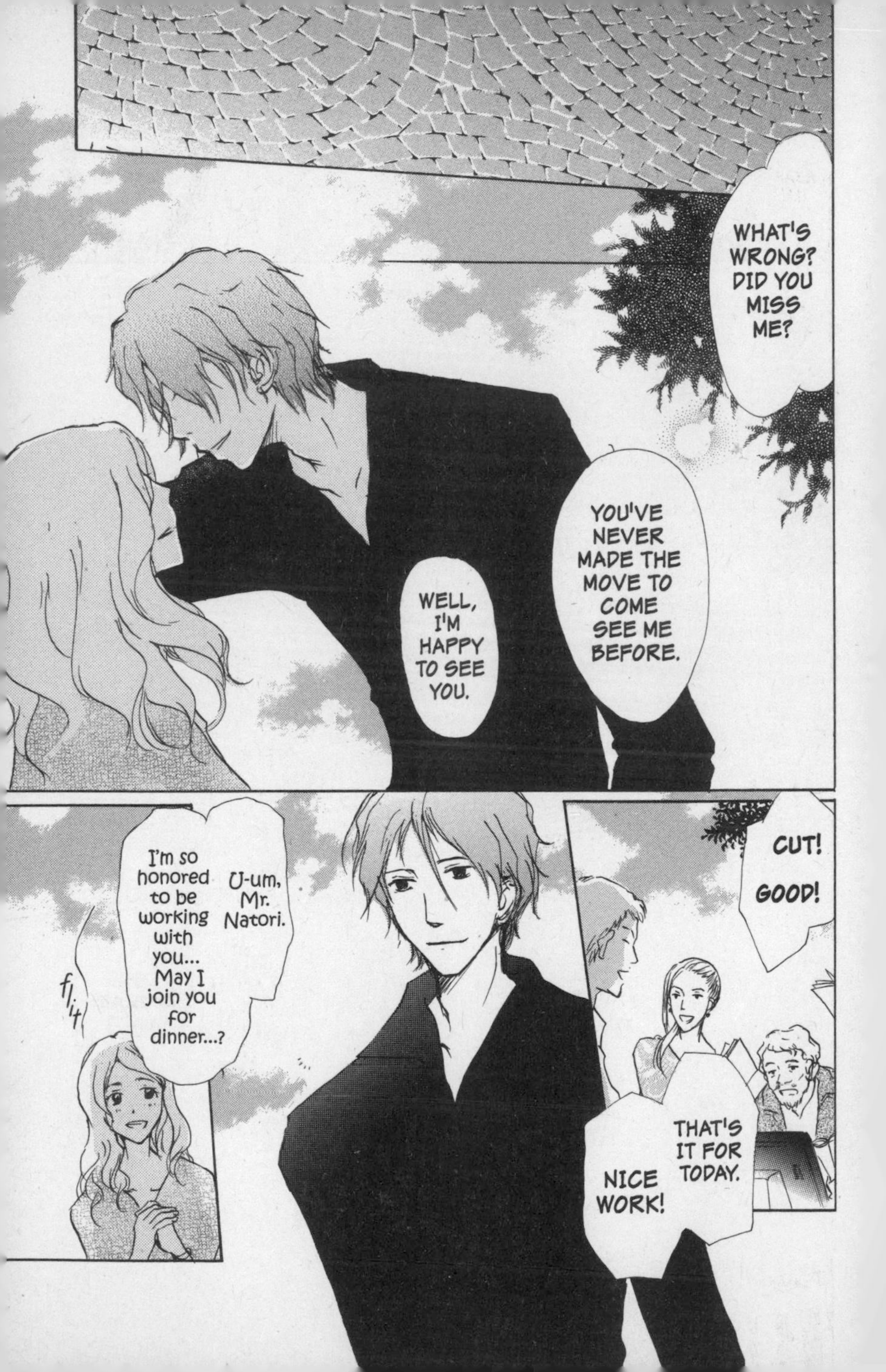
WHAT'S WRONG? DID YOU MISS ME?
YOU'VE NEVER MADE THE MOVE TO COME SEE ME BEFORE.
WELL, I'M HAPPY TO SEE YOU.
CUT!
GOOD!
THAT'S IT FOR TODAY.
NICE WORK!
U-um, Mr. Natori.
I'm so honored to be working with you... May I join you for dinner...?
flit

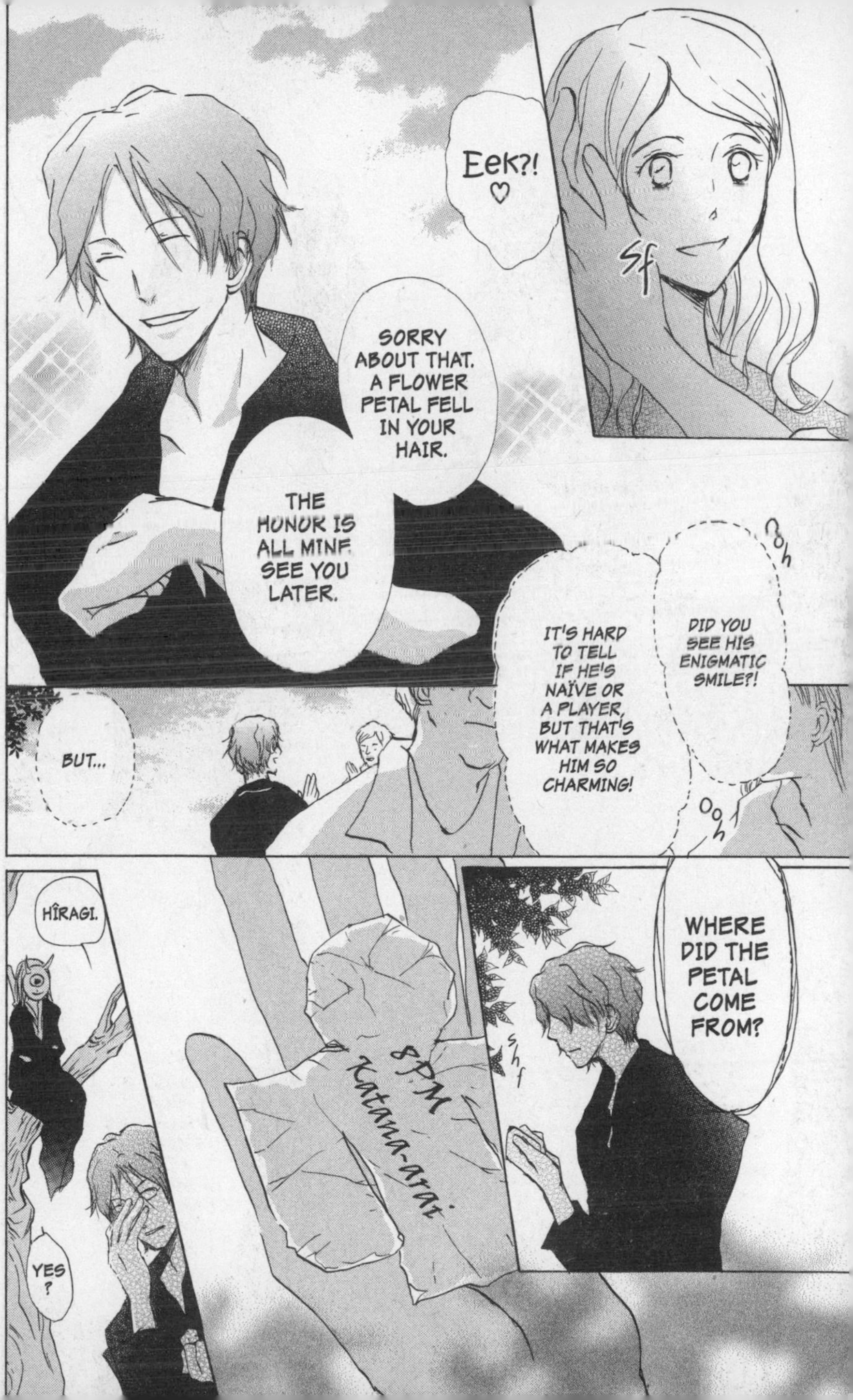
Eek?! ♡
Sf
SORRY ABOUT THAT. A FLOWER PETAL FELL IN YOUR HAIR.
THE HONOR IS ALL MINE. SEE YOU LATER.
Ooh
DID YOU SEE HIS ENIGMATIC SMILE?!
IT'S HARD TO TELL IF HE'S NAÏVE OR A PLAYER, BUT THAT'S WHAT MAKES HIM SO CHARMING!
Ooh
BUT...
WHERE DID THE PETAL COME FROM?
shf
8 P.M. Katana-arai
HÎRAGI.
YES?

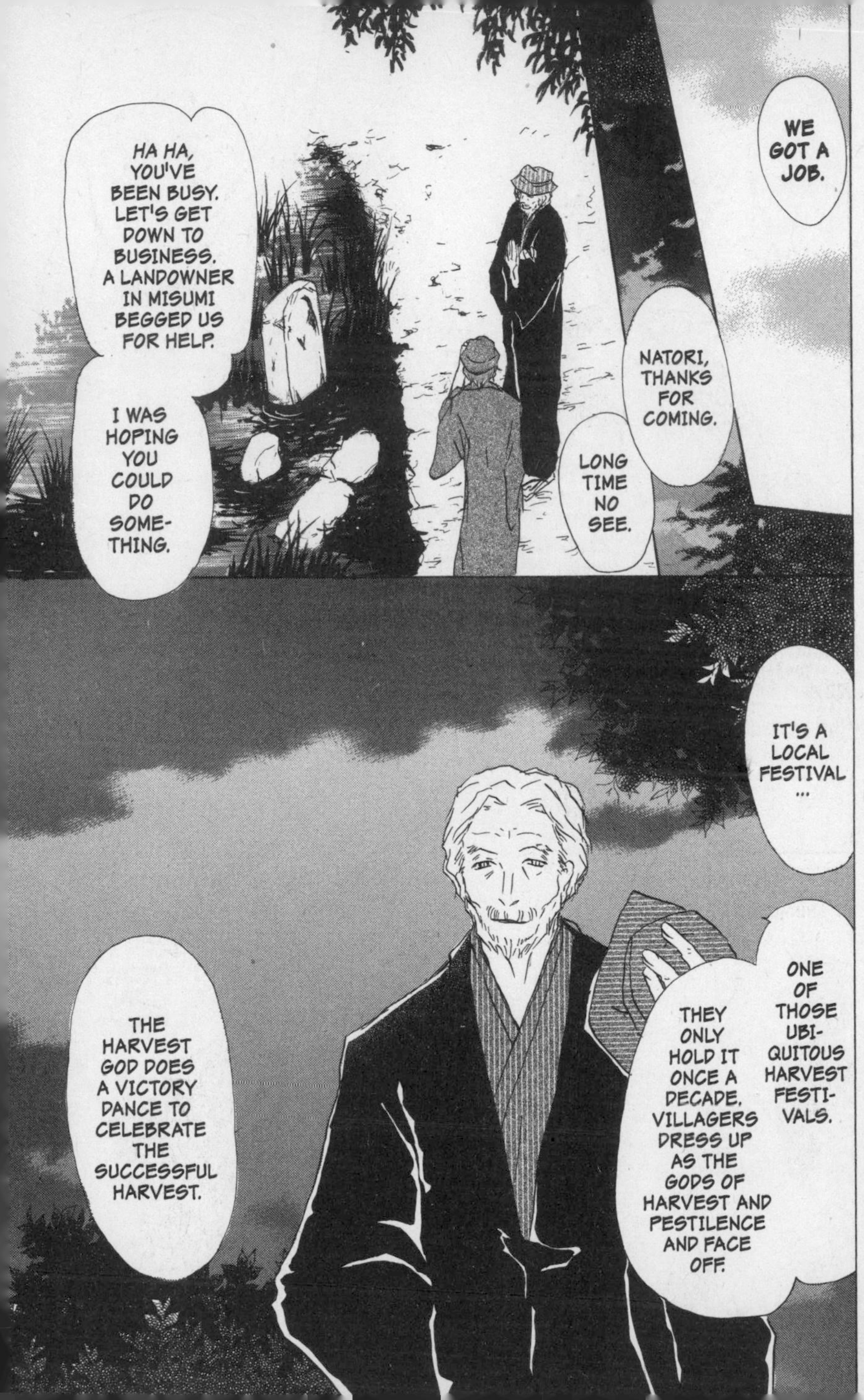
WE GOT A JOB.
NATORI, THANKS FOR COMING.
LONG TIME NO SEE.
HA HA, YOU'VE BEEN BUSY. LET'S GET DOWN TO BUSINESS. A LANDOWNER IN MISUMI BEGGED US FOR HELP.
I WAS HOPING YOU COULD DO SOME-THING.
IT'S A LOCAL FESTIVAL ...
ONE OF THOSE UBI-QUITOUS HARVEST FESTI-VALS.
THEY ONLY HOLD IT ONCE A DECADE. VILLAGERS DRESS UP AS THE GODS OF HARVEST AND PESTILENCE AND FACE OFF.
THE HARVEST GOD DOES A VICTORY DANCE TO CELEBRATE THE SUCCESSFUL HARVEST.

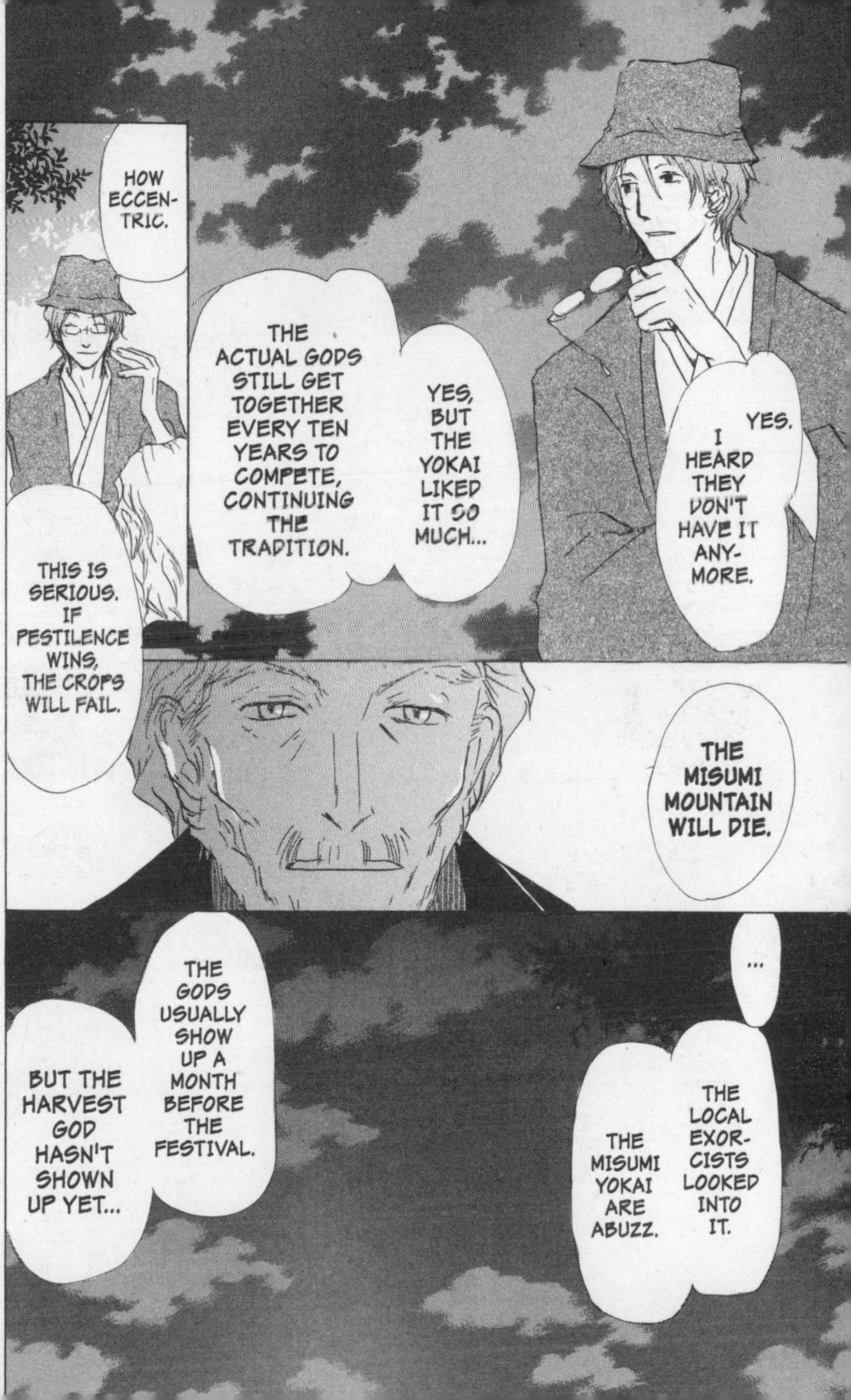
YES. I HEARD THEY DON'T HAVE IT ANYMORE.
YES, BUT THE YOKAI LIKED IT SO MUCH...
THE ACTUAL GODS STILL GET TOGETHER EVERY TEN YEARS TO COMPETE, CONTINUING THE TRADITION.
HOW ECCENTRIC.
THIS IS SERIOUS. IF PESTILENCE WINS, THE CROPS WILL FAIL.
THE MISUMI MOUNTAIN WILL DIE.
...
THE LOCAL EXORCISTS LOOKED INTO IT.
THE MISUMI YOKAI ARE ABUZZ.
THE GODS USUALLY SHOW UP A MONTH BEFORE THE FESTIVAL.
BUT THE HARVEST GOD HASN'T SHOWN UP YET...

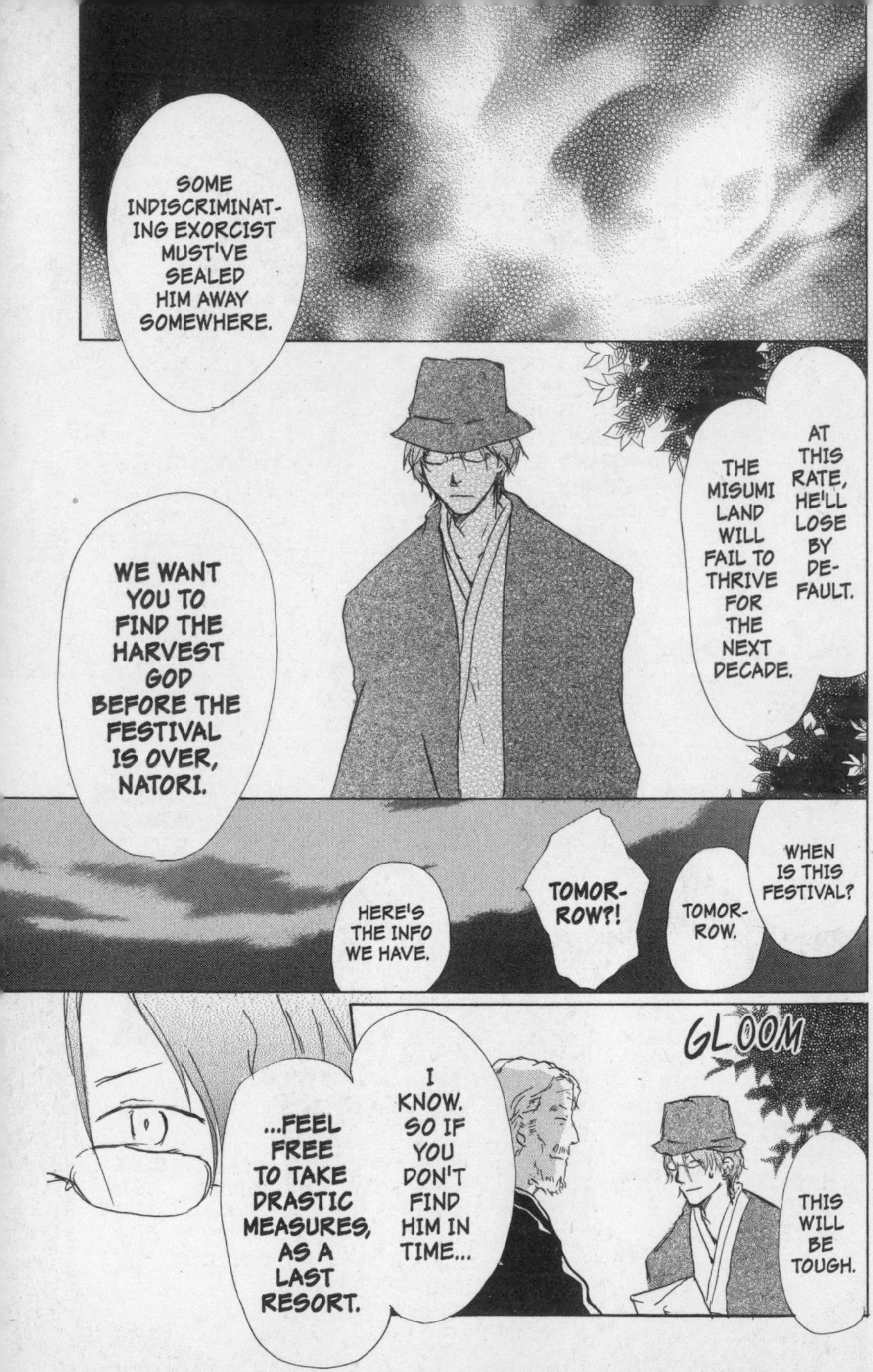
SOME INDISCRIMINATING EXORCIST MUST'VE SEALED HIM AWAY SOMEWHERE.
AT THIS RATE, HE'LL LOSE BY DEFAULT.
THE MISUMI LAND WILL FAIL TO THRIVE FOR THE NEXT DECADE.
WE WANT YOU TO FIND THE HARVEST GOD BEFORE THE FESTIVAL IS OVER, NATORI.
WHEN IS THIS FESTIVAL?
TOMORROW.
TOMORROW?!
HERE'S THE INFO WE HAVE.
GLOOM
THIS WILL BE TOUGH.
I KNOW. SO IF YOU DON'T FIND HIM IN TIME...
...FEEL FREE TO TAKE DRASTIC MEASURES, AS A LAST RESORT.

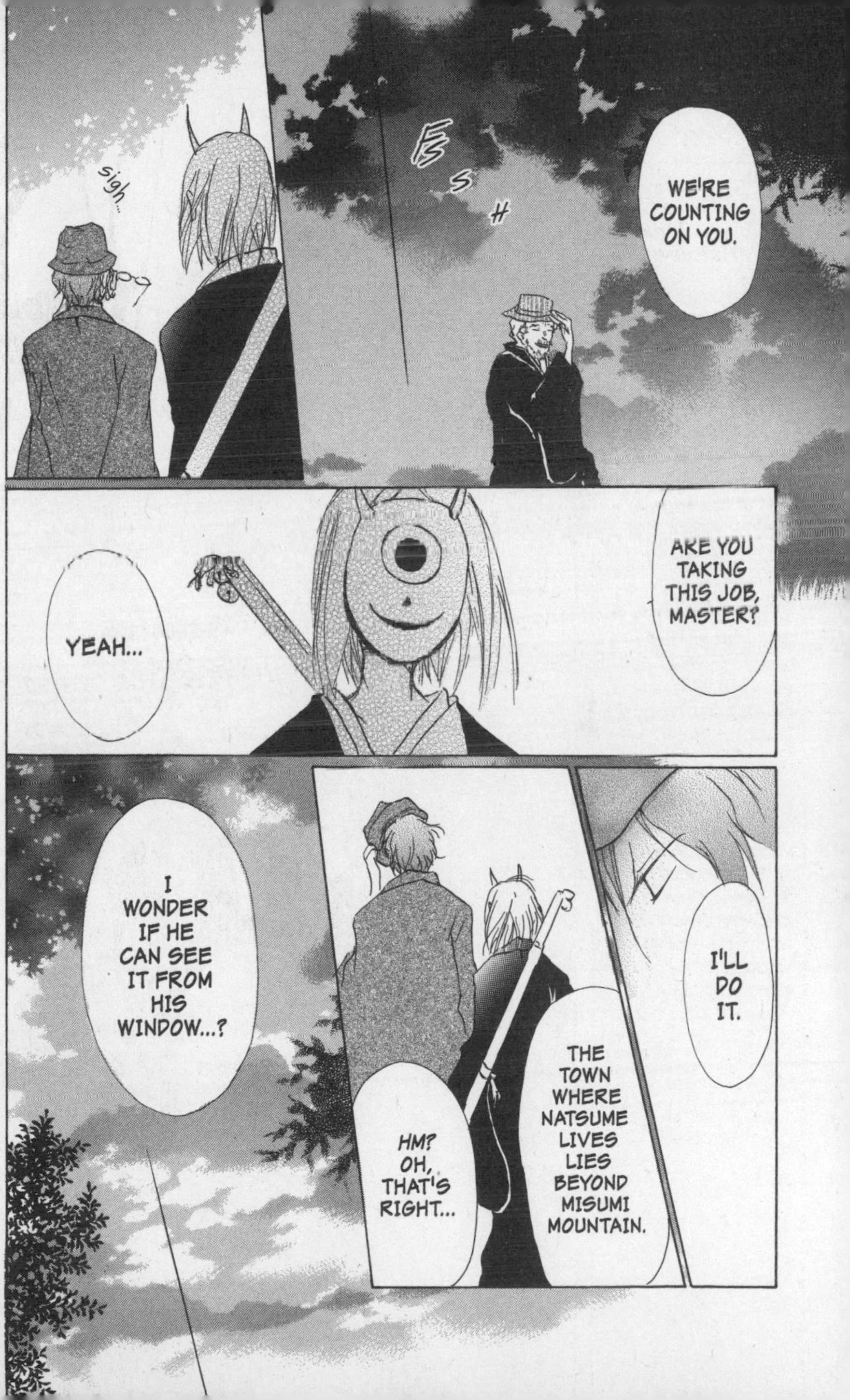
FSSH
WE'RE COUNTING ON YOU.
sigh...
ARE YOU TAKING THIS JOB, MASTER?
YEAH...
I'LL DO IT.
THE TOWN WHERE NATSUME LIVES LIES BEYOND MISUMI MOUNTAIN.
HM? OH, THAT'S RIGHT...
I WONDER IF HE CAN SEE IT FROM HIS WINDOW...?

03

❋Three Dimensional Natsume

I'm happy to report that they're going to make a figurine of Takashi Natsume. It's based on the poster art they used for the first season of the anime, of Natsume sitting on an old log by the water with a dangling Nyanko Sensei. I already feel so awed that they made so much merchandise for Nyanko Sensei, and after the washcloth with Takashi on it, now there's a figurine. I'm so happy I can hardly sit still.

They've recreated the surface of the water, the sharp blades of grass extending from it, and the pretty wood grain. It's beautiful enough to be a decorative ornament. Please check it out.

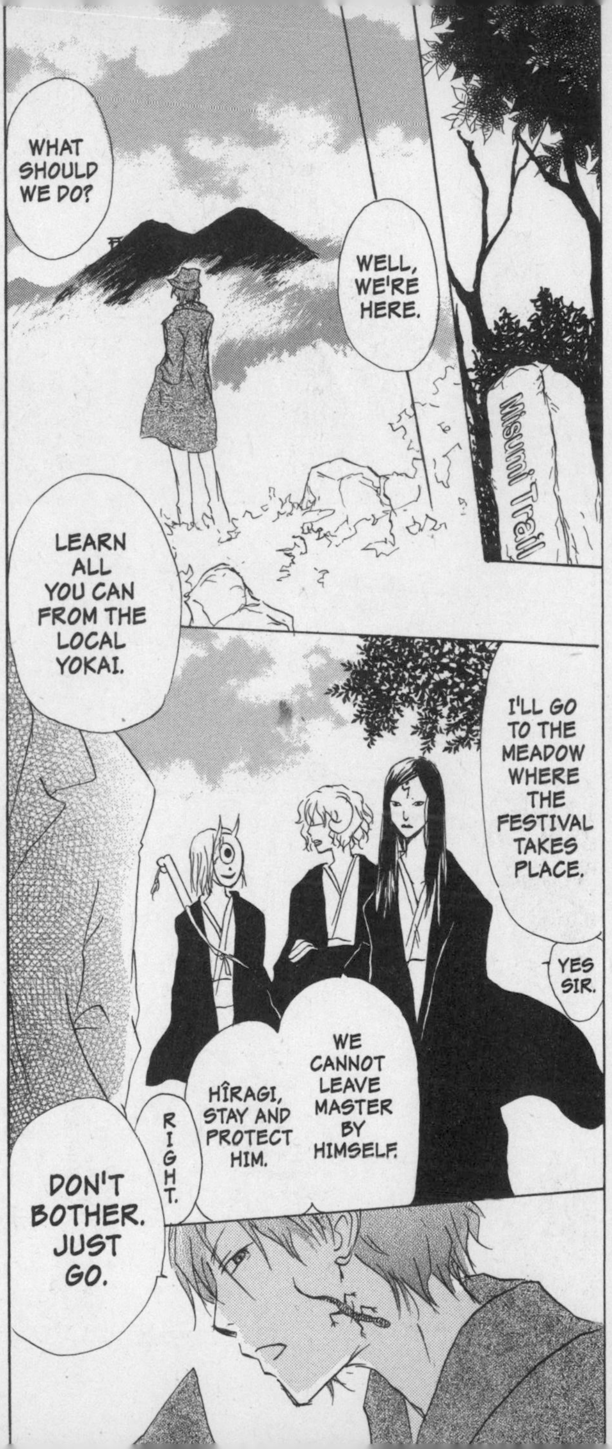
Misumi Trail
WELL, WE'RE HERE.
WHAT SHOULD WE DO?
LEARN ALL YOU CAN FROM THE LOCAL YOKAI.
I'LL GO TO THE MEADOW WHERE THE FESTIVAL TAKES PLACE.
YES SIR.
WE CANNOT LEAVE MASTER BY HIMSELF.
HÎRAGI, STAY AND PROTECT HIM.
RIGHT.
DON'T BOTHER. JUST GO.

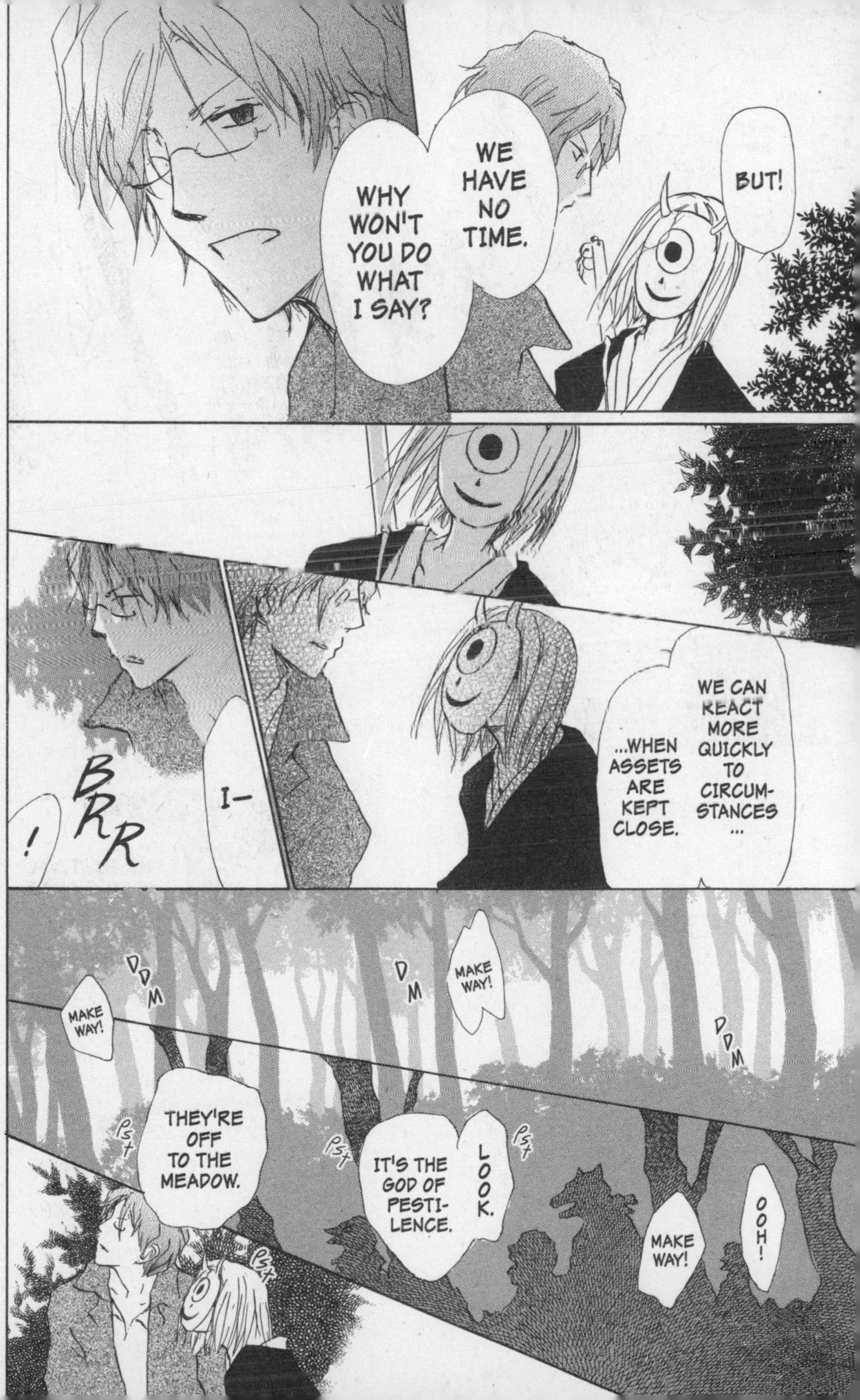
BUT!
WE HAVE NO TIME.
WHY WON'T YOU DO WHAT I SAY?
WE CAN REACT MORE QUICKLY TO CIRCUM- STANCES ...
...WHEN ASSETS ARE KEPT CLOSE.
I—
BRR
!
DDM
MAKE WAY!
DM
DDM
MAKE WAY!
OOH!
MAKE WAY!
Pst
LOOK.
IT'S THE GOD OF PESTI- LENCE.
Pst
THEY'RE OFF TO THE MEADOW.
Pst
Pst

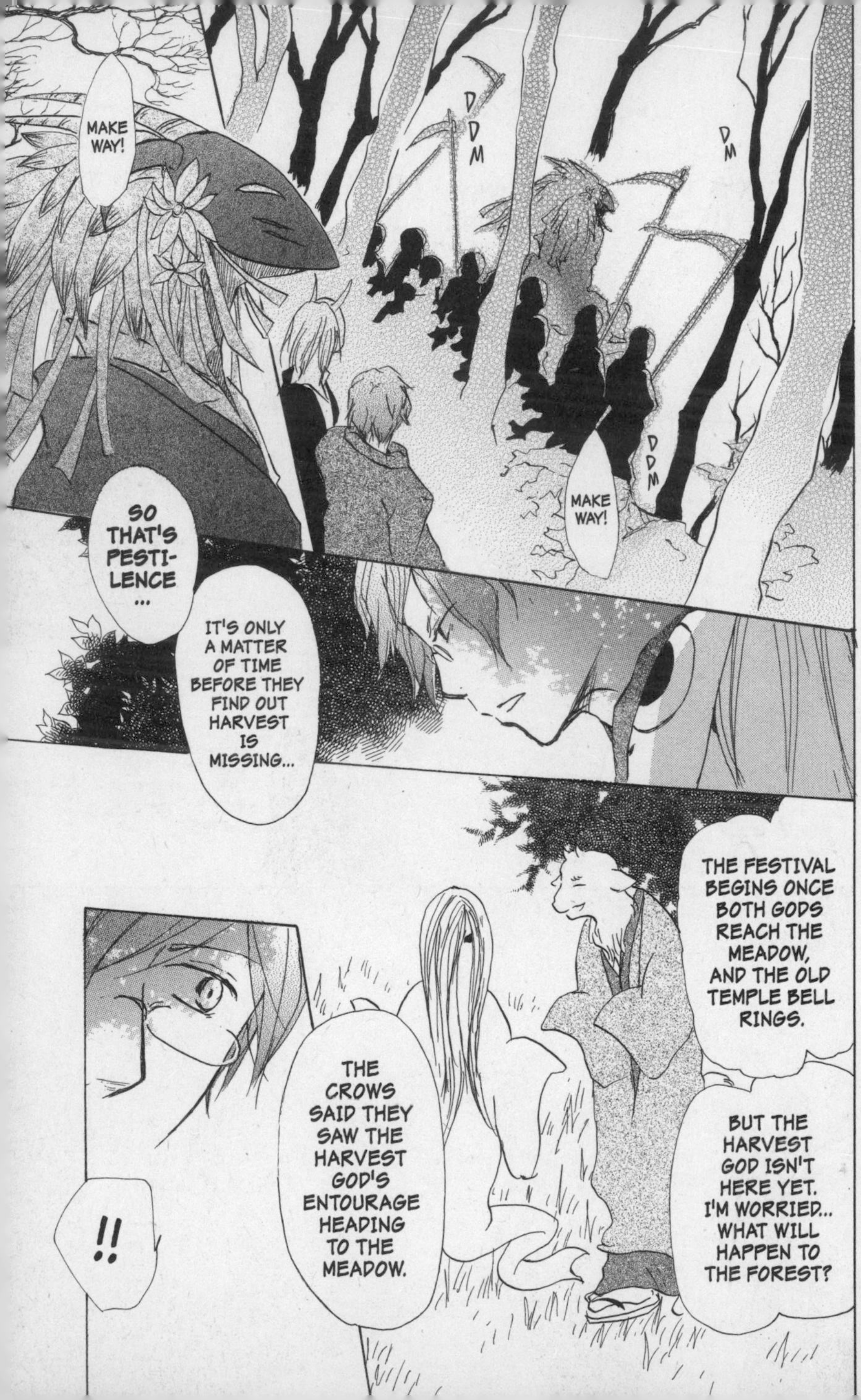
DM
DDM
MAKE WAY!
DDM
MAKE WAY!
SO THAT'S PESTI-LENCE...
IT'S ONLY A MATTER OF TIME BEFORE THEY FIND OUT HARVEST IS MISSING...
THE FESTIVAL BEGINS ONCE BOTH GODS REACH THE MEADOW, AND THE OLD TEMPLE BELL RINGS.
BUT THE HARVEST GOD ISN'T HERE YET. I'M WORRIED... WHAT WILL HAPPEN TO THE FOREST?
THE CROWS SAID THEY SAW THE HARVEST GOD'S ENTOURAGE HEADING TO THE MEADOW.
!!

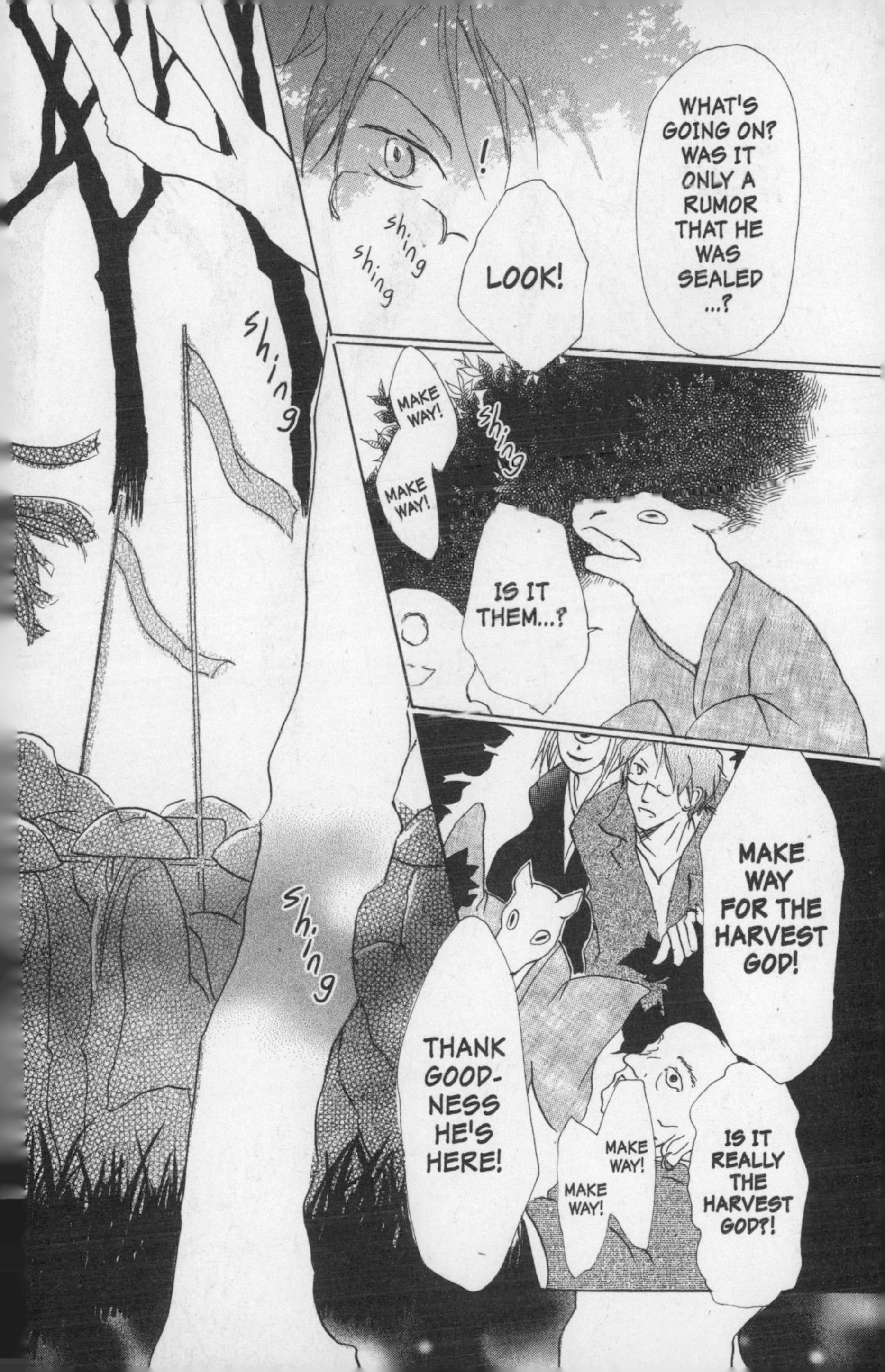
WHAT'S GOING ON? WAS IT ONLY A RUMOR THAT HE WAS SEALED ...?
!
LOOK!
shing
shing
IS IT THEM...?
shing
MAKE WAY!
MAKE WAY!
MAKE WAY FOR THE HARVEST GOD!
IS IT REALLY THE HARVEST GOD?!
MAKE WAY!
MAKE WAY!
THANK GOODNESS HE'S HERE!
shing
shing

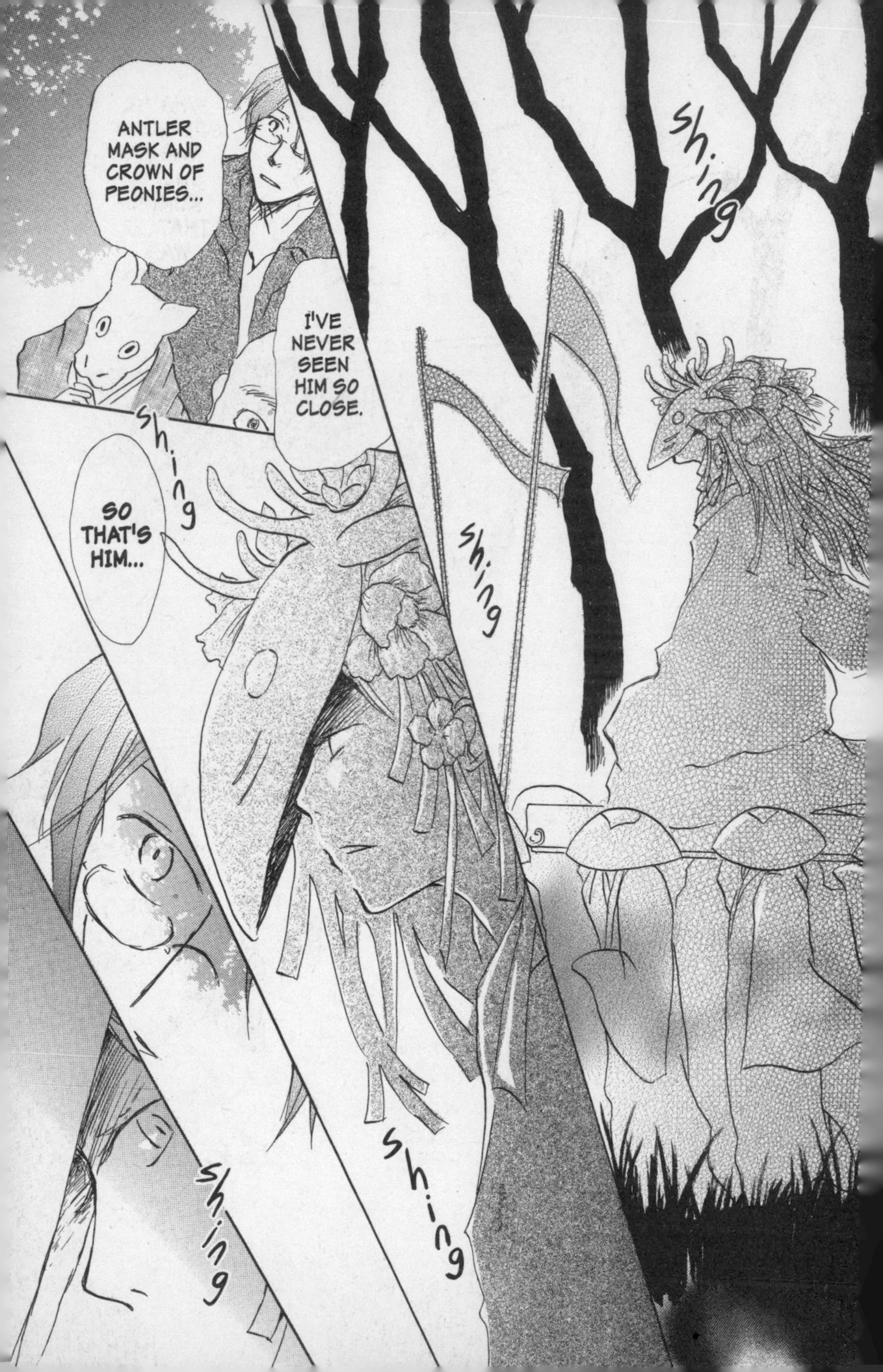
shing
shing
shing
ANTLER MASK AND CROWN OF PEONIES...
I'VE NEVER SEEN HIM SO CLOSE.
shing
SO THAT'S HIM...
shing

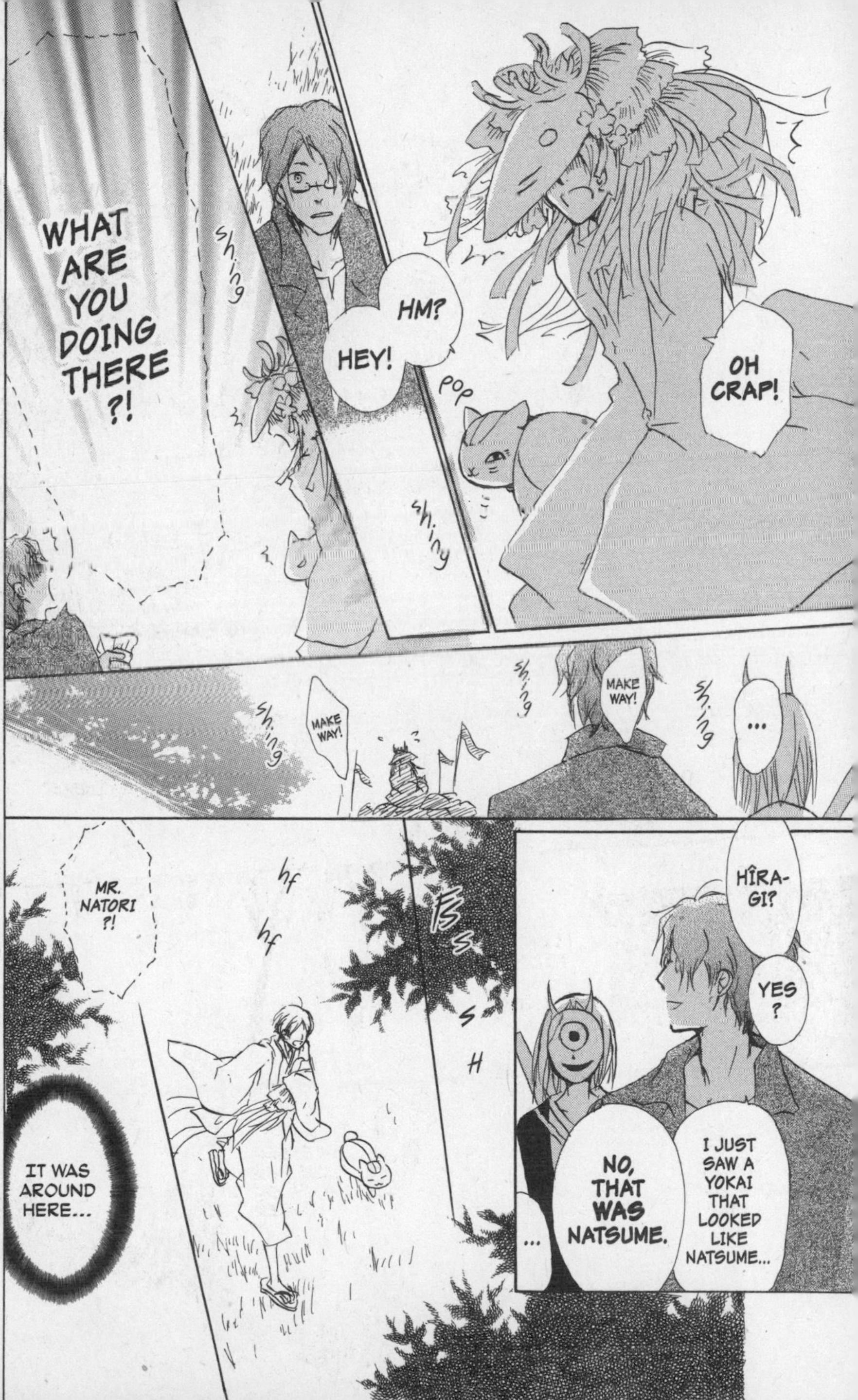
OH CRAP!
pop
shiny
HM?
HEY!
shing
WHAT ARE YOU DOING THERE?!
...
shing
MAKE WAY!
shing
MAKE WAY!
shing
HÎRA-GI?
YES?
I JUST SAW A YOKAI THAT LOOKED LIKE NATSUME...
NO, THAT WAS NATSUME.
...
S S H
hf
hf
MR. NATORI?!
IT WAS AROUND HERE...

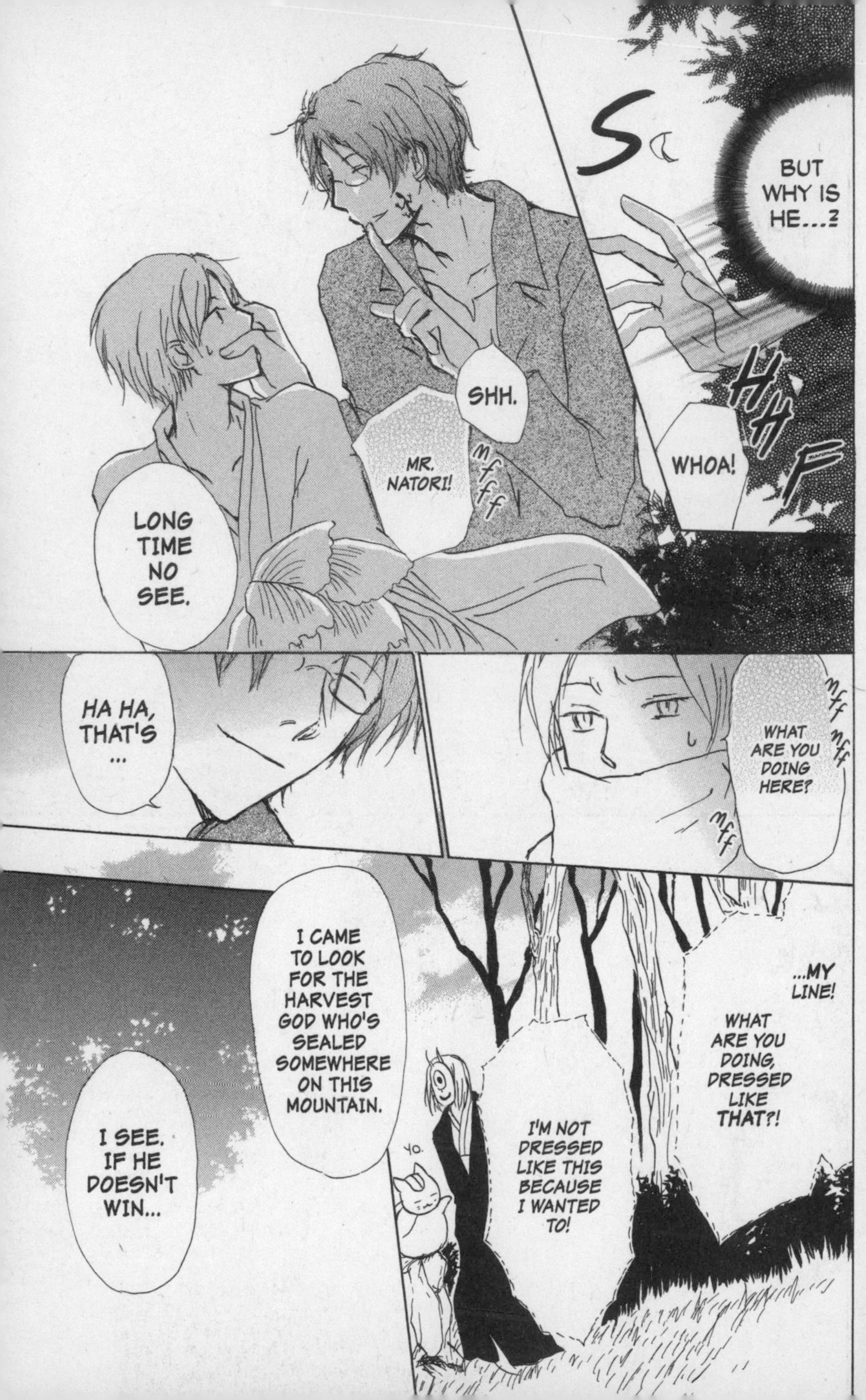
BUT WHY IS HE...?
HHF
WHOA!
SHH.
mff
MR. NATORI!
LONG TIME NO SEE.
mff
WHAT ARE YOU DOING HERE?
mff
HA HA, THAT'S ...
...MY LINE!
WHAT ARE YOU DOING, DRESSED LIKE THAT?!
I'M NOT DRESSED LIKE THIS BECAUSE I WANTED TO!
YO.
I CAME TO LOOK FOR THE HARVEST GOD WHO'S SEALED SOMEWHERE ON THIS MOUNTAIN.
I SEE. IF HE DOESN'T WIN...

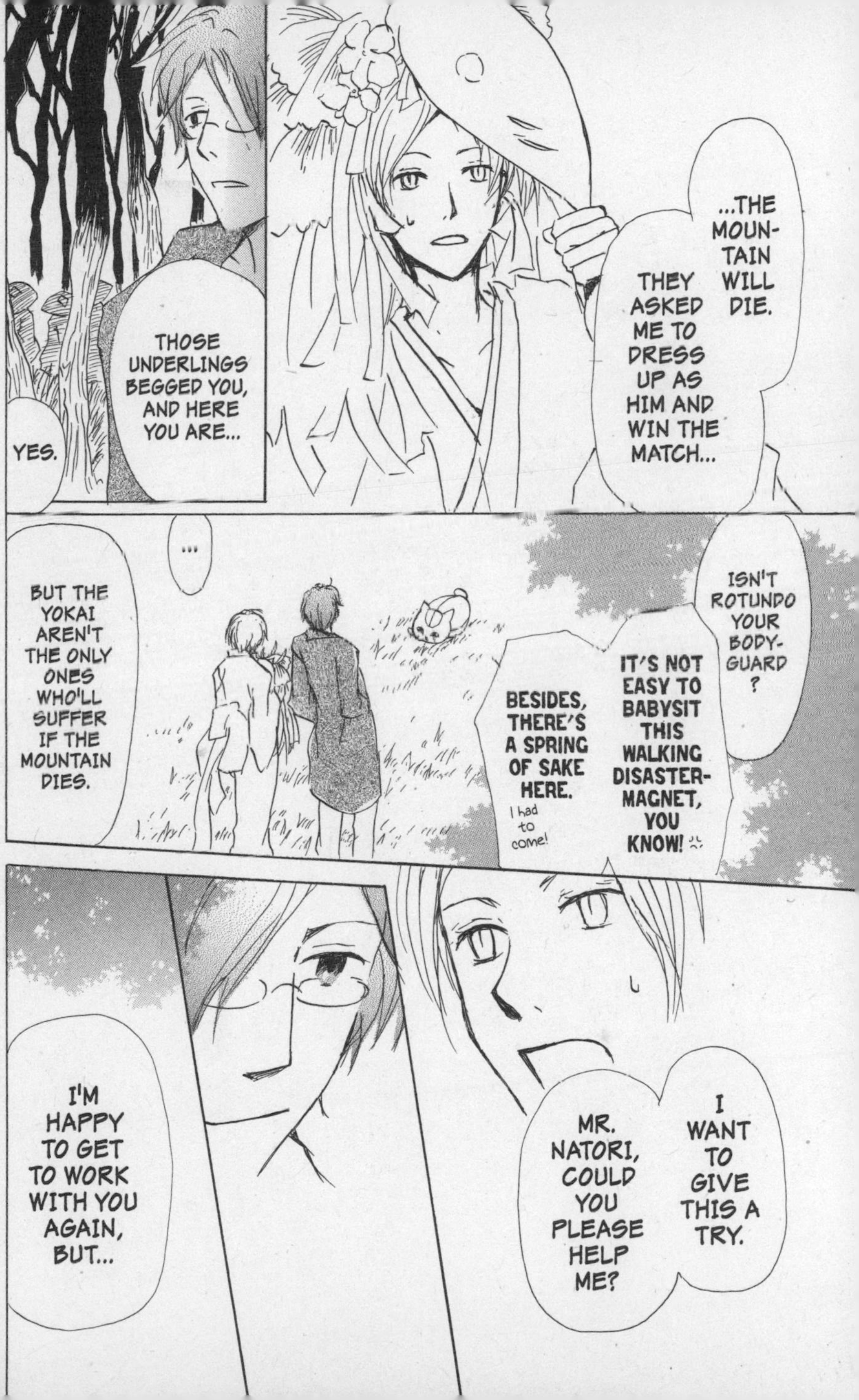
...THE MOUNTAIN WILL DIE.
THEY ASKED ME TO DRESS UP AS HIM AND WIN THE MATCH...
THOSE UNDERLINGS BEGGED YOU, AND HERE YOU ARE...
YES.
ISN'T ROTUNDO YOUR BODYGUARD?
IT'S NOT EASY TO BABYSIT THIS WALKING DISASTER-MAGNET, YOU KNOW!
BESIDES, THERE'S A SPRING OF SAKE HERE.
I had to come!
...
BUT THE YOKAI AREN'T THE ONLY ONES WHO'LL SUFFER IF THE MOUNTAIN DIES.
I WANT TO GIVE THIS A TRY.
MR. NATORI, COULD YOU PLEASE HELP ME?
I'M HAPPY TO GET TO WORK WITH YOU AGAIN, BUT...

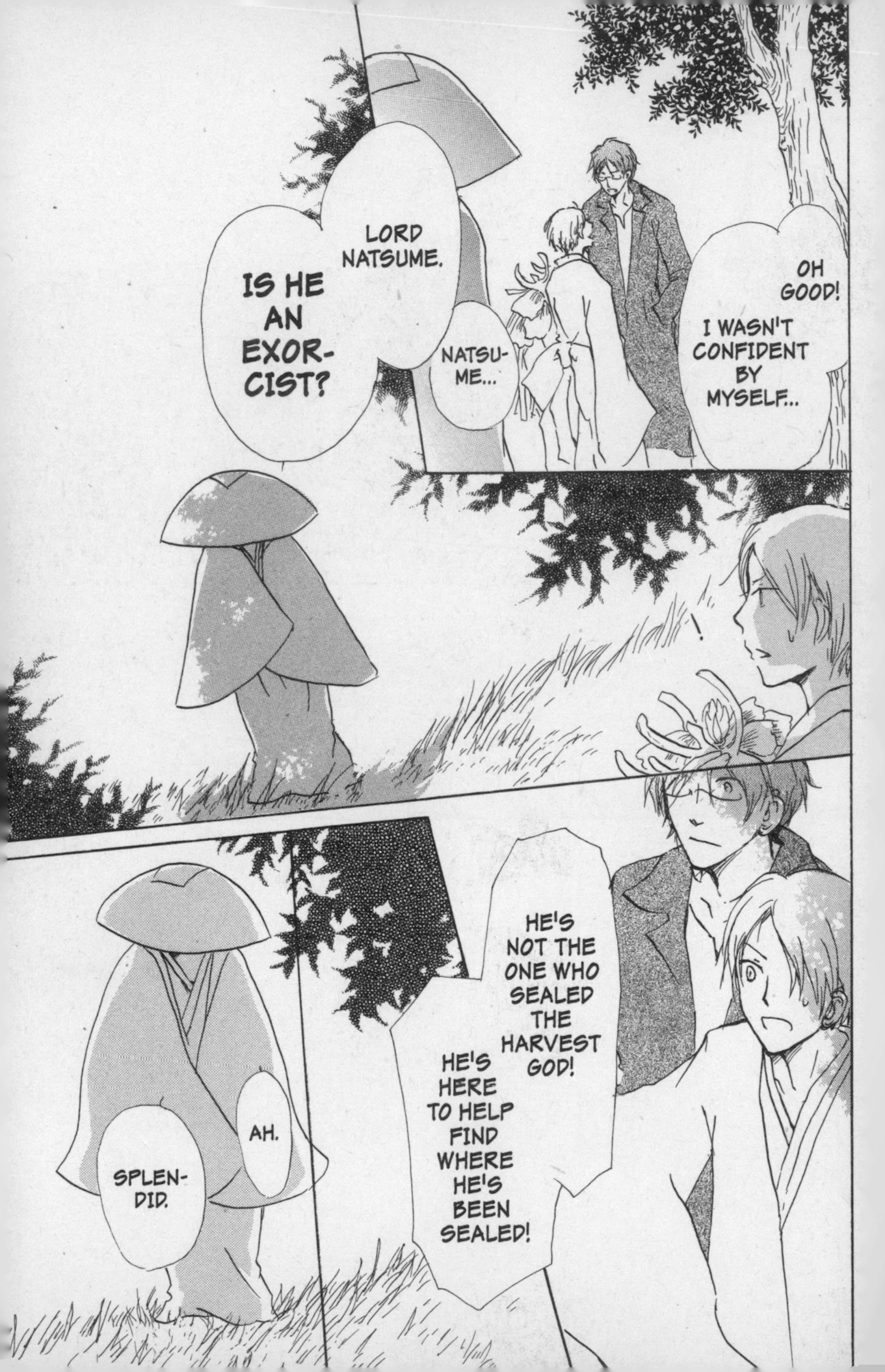
OH GOOD!
I WASN'T CONFIDENT BY MYSELF...
NATSU-ME...
LORD NATSUME.
IS HE AN EXOR-CIST?
HE'S NOT THE ONE WHO SEALED THE HARVEST GOD!
HE'S HERE TO HELP FIND WHERE HE'S BEEN SEALED!
AH.
SPLEN-DID.

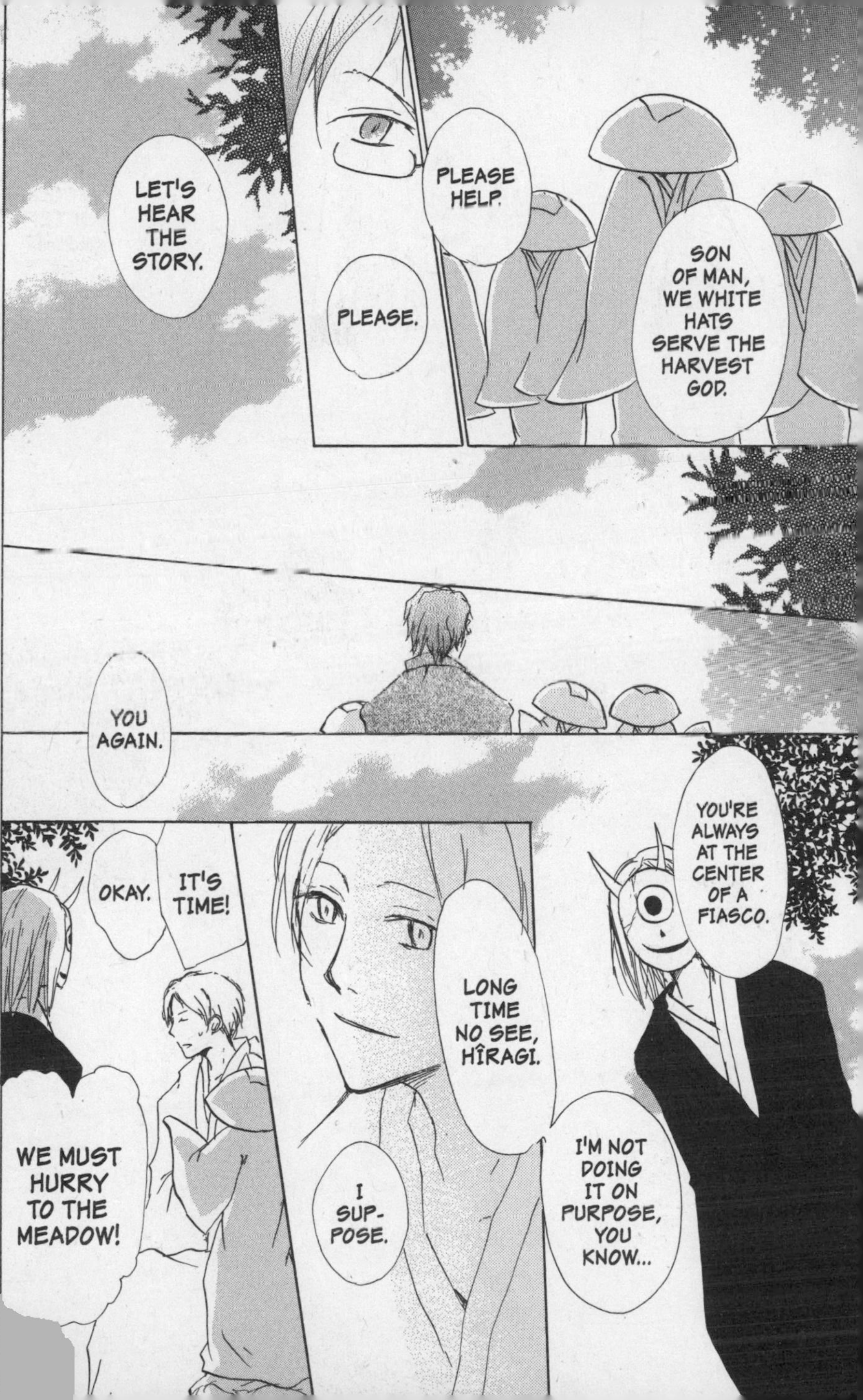
SON OF MAN, WE WHITE HATS SERVE THE HARVEST GOD.
PLEASE HELP.
PLEASE.
LET'S HEAR THE STORY.
YOU AGAIN.
YOU'RE ALWAYS AT THE CENTER OF A FIASCO.
I'M NOT DOING IT ON PURPOSE, YOU KNOW...
LONG TIME NO SEE, HÎRAGI.
I SUP-POSE.
IT'S TIME!
OKAY.
WE MUST HURRY TO THE MEADOW!

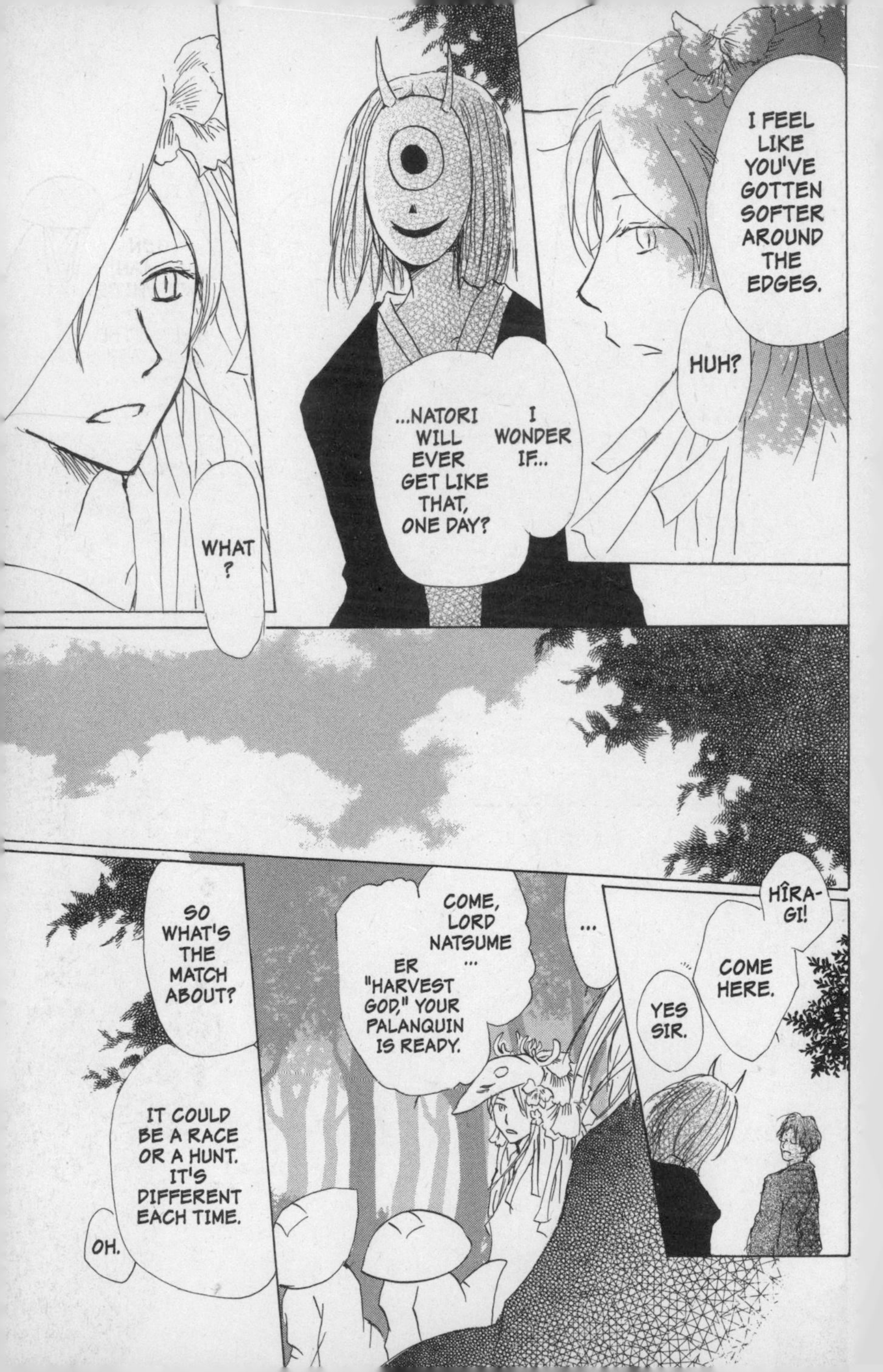
I FEEL LIKE YOU'VE GOTTEN SOFTER AROUND THE EDGES.
HUH?
I WONDER IF...
...NATORI WILL EVER GET LIKE THAT, ONE DAY?
WHAT?
HÎRA-GI!
COME HERE.
YES SIR.
...
COME, LORD NATSUME ...
ER "HARVEST GOD," YOUR PALANQUIN IS READY.
SO WHAT'S THE MATCH ABOUT?
IT COULD BE A RACE OR A HUNT. IT'S DIFFERENT EACH TIME.
OH.

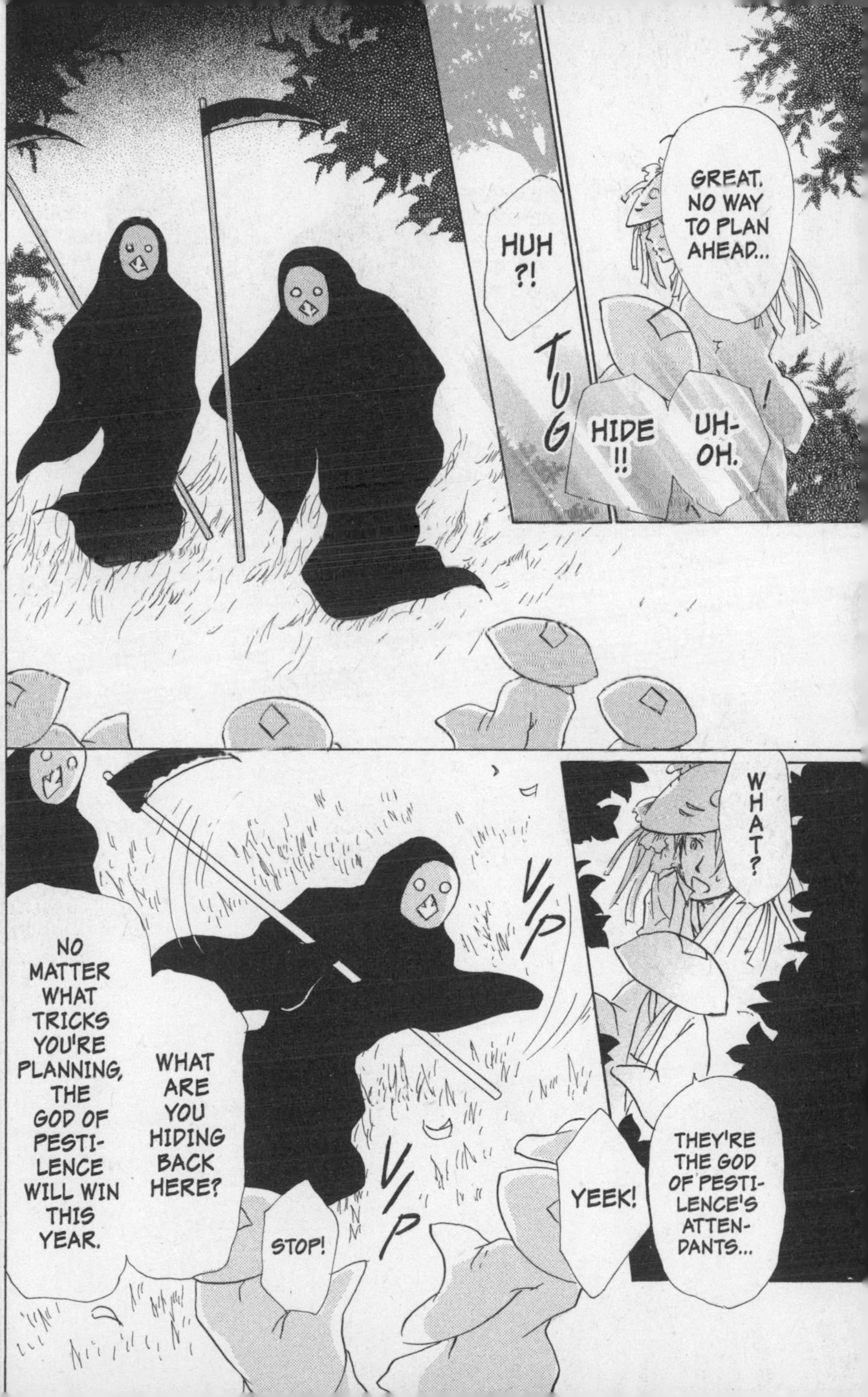
GREAT. NO WAY TO PLAN AHEAD...
HUH?!
TUG
UH-OH.
HIDE!!
WHAT?
THEY'RE THE GOD OF PESTILENCE'S ATTENDANTS...
YEEK!
VIP
VIP
STOP!
WHAT ARE YOU HIDING BACK HERE?
NO MATTER WHAT TRICKS YOU'RE PLANNING, THE GOD OF PESTILENCE WILL WIN THIS YEAR.

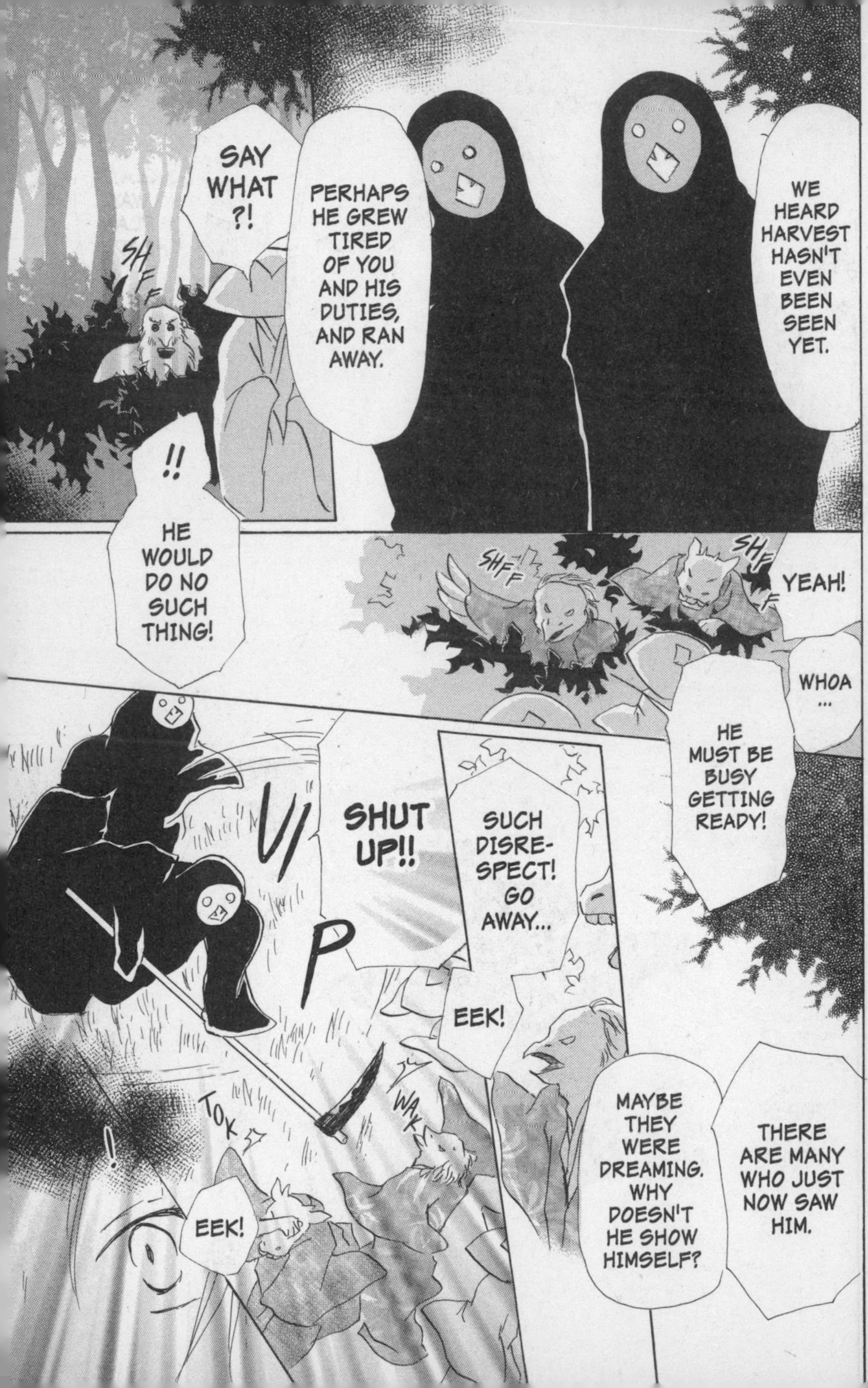
WE HEARD HARVEST HASN'T EVEN BEEN SEEN YET.
PERHAPS HE GREW TIRED OF YOU AND HIS DUTIES, AND RAN AWAY.
SAY WHAT?!
SHFF
!!
HE WOULD DO NO SUCH THING!
SHFF
SHFF
YEAH!
WHOA...
HE MUST BE BUSY GETTING READY!
THERE ARE MANY WHO JUST NOW SAW HIM.
MAYBE THEY WERE DREAMING. WHY DOESN'T HE SHOW HIMSELF?
SUCH DISRE-SPECT! GO AWAY...
SHUT UP!!
EEK!
WAK
TOK
EEK!
!

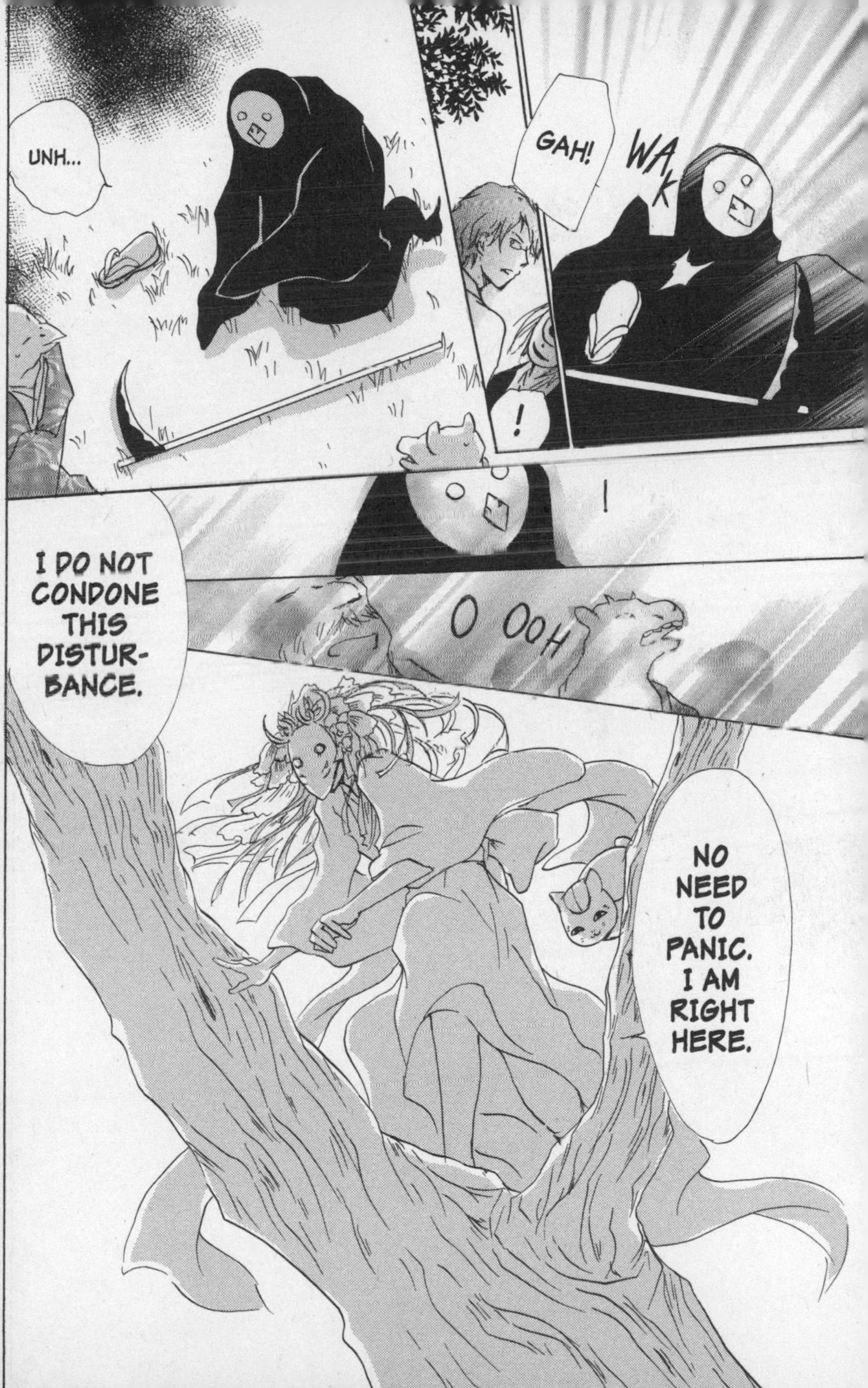
GAH!
WAK
!
UNH...
!
O OOH
I DO NOT CONDONE THIS DISTURBANCE.
NO NEED TO PANIC. I AM RIGHT HERE.

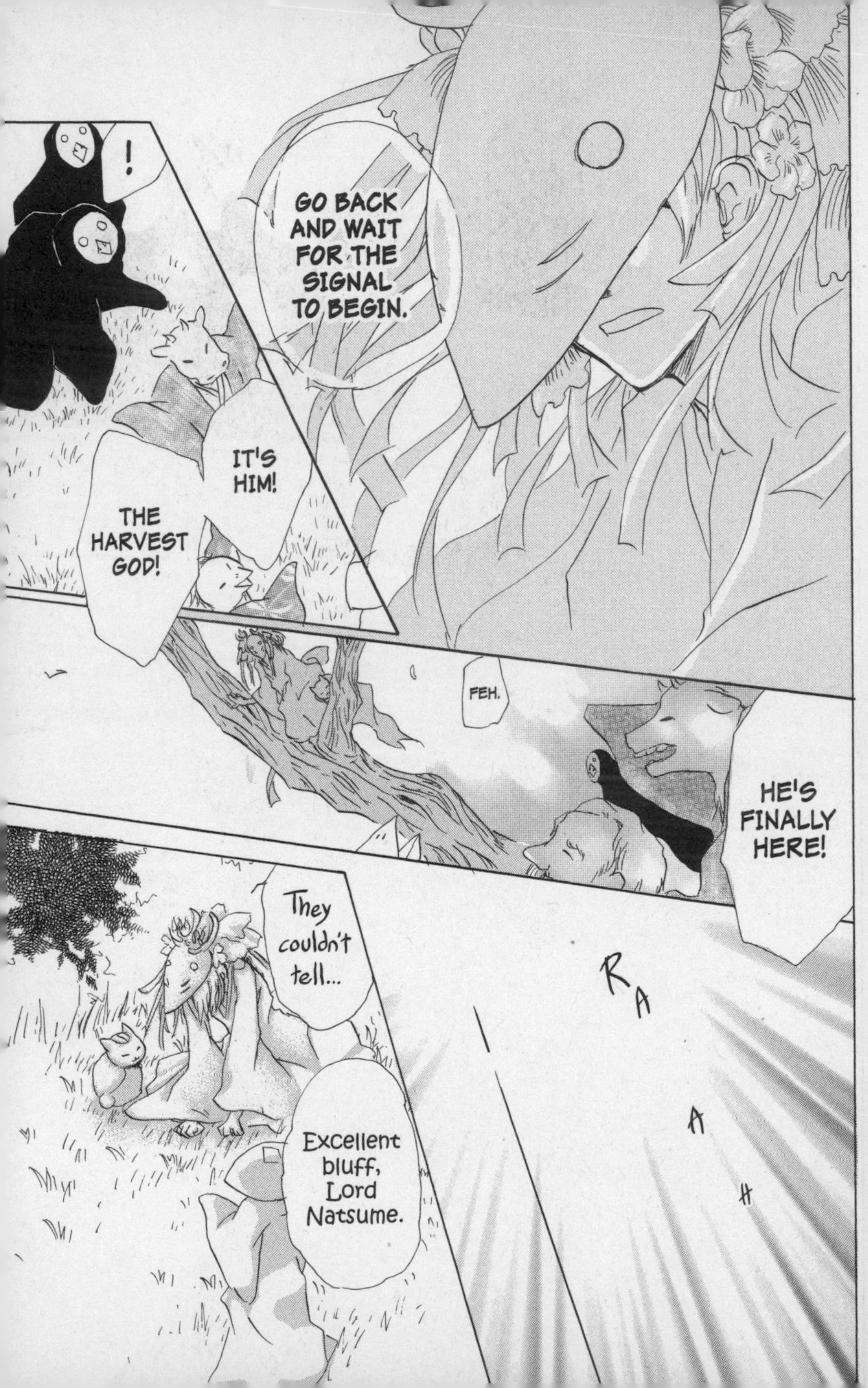
GO BACK AND WAIT FOR THE SIGNAL TO BEGIN.
!
IT'S HIM!
THE HARVEST GOD!
HE'S FINALLY HERE!
FEH.
RAAAH
They couldn't tell...
Excellent bluff, Lord Natsume.

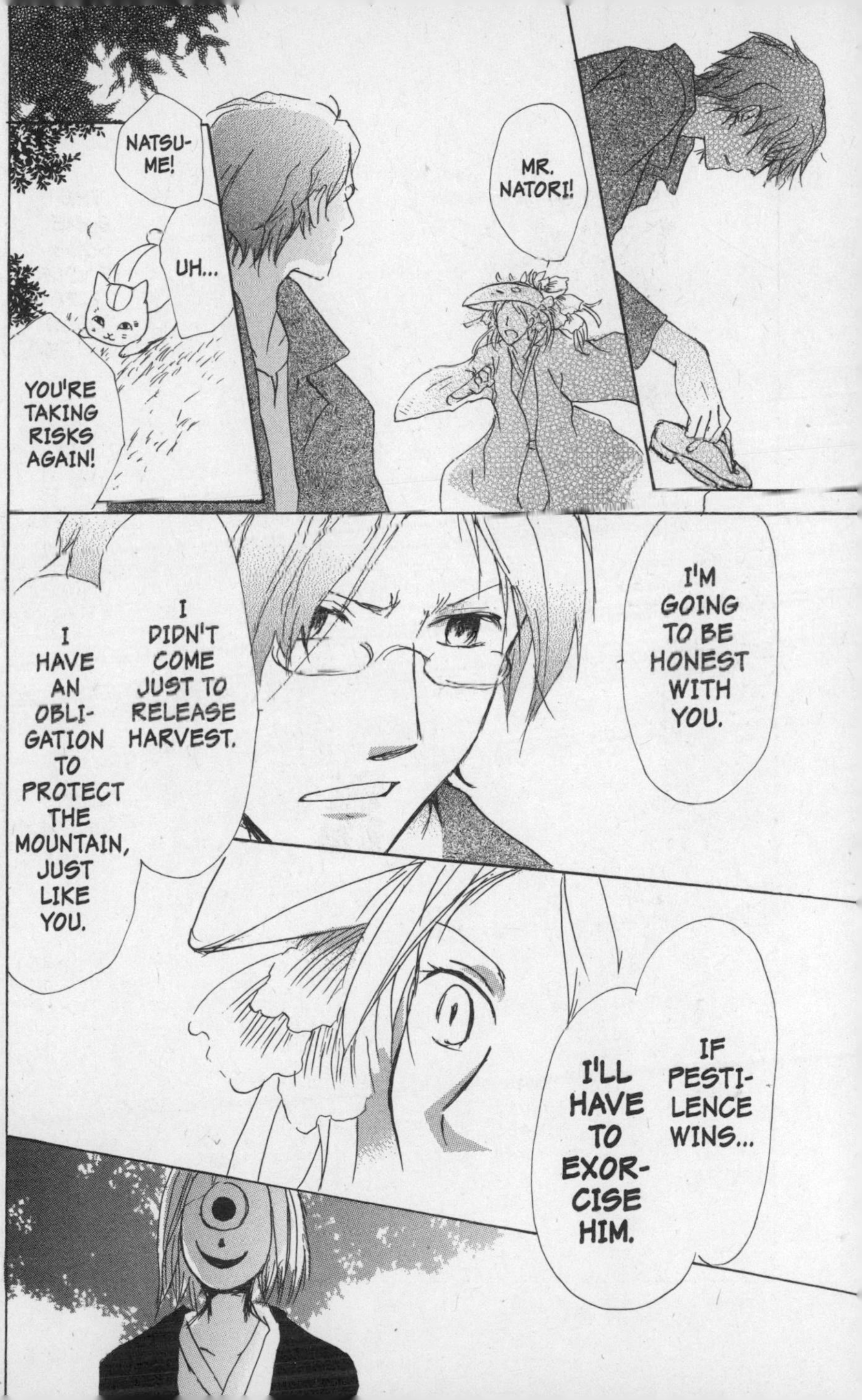
MR. NATORI!
NATSUME!
UH...
YOU'RE TAKING RISKS AGAIN!
I'M GOING TO BE HONEST WITH YOU.
I DIDN'T COME JUST TO RELEASE HARVEST.
I HAVE AN OBLIGATION TO PROTECT THE MOUNTAIN, JUST LIKE YOU.
IF PESTILENCE WINS...
I'LL HAVE TO EXORCISE HIM.

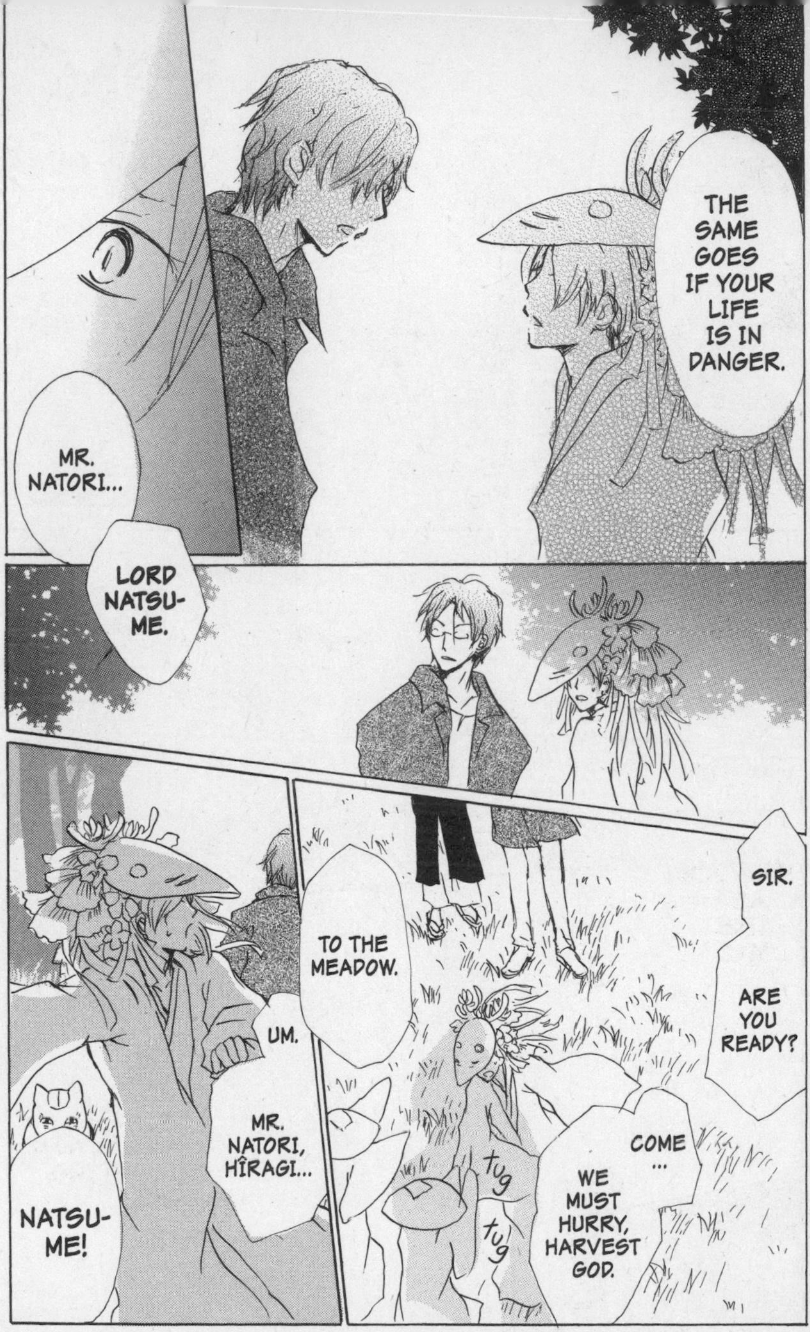
THE SAME GOES IF YOUR LIFE IS IN DANGER.
MR. NATORI...
LORD NATSUME.
SIR.
ARE YOU READY?
TO THE MEADOW.
COME...
WE MUST HURRY, HARVEST GOD.
tug
tug
UM.
MR. NATORI, HÎRAGI...
NATSUME!

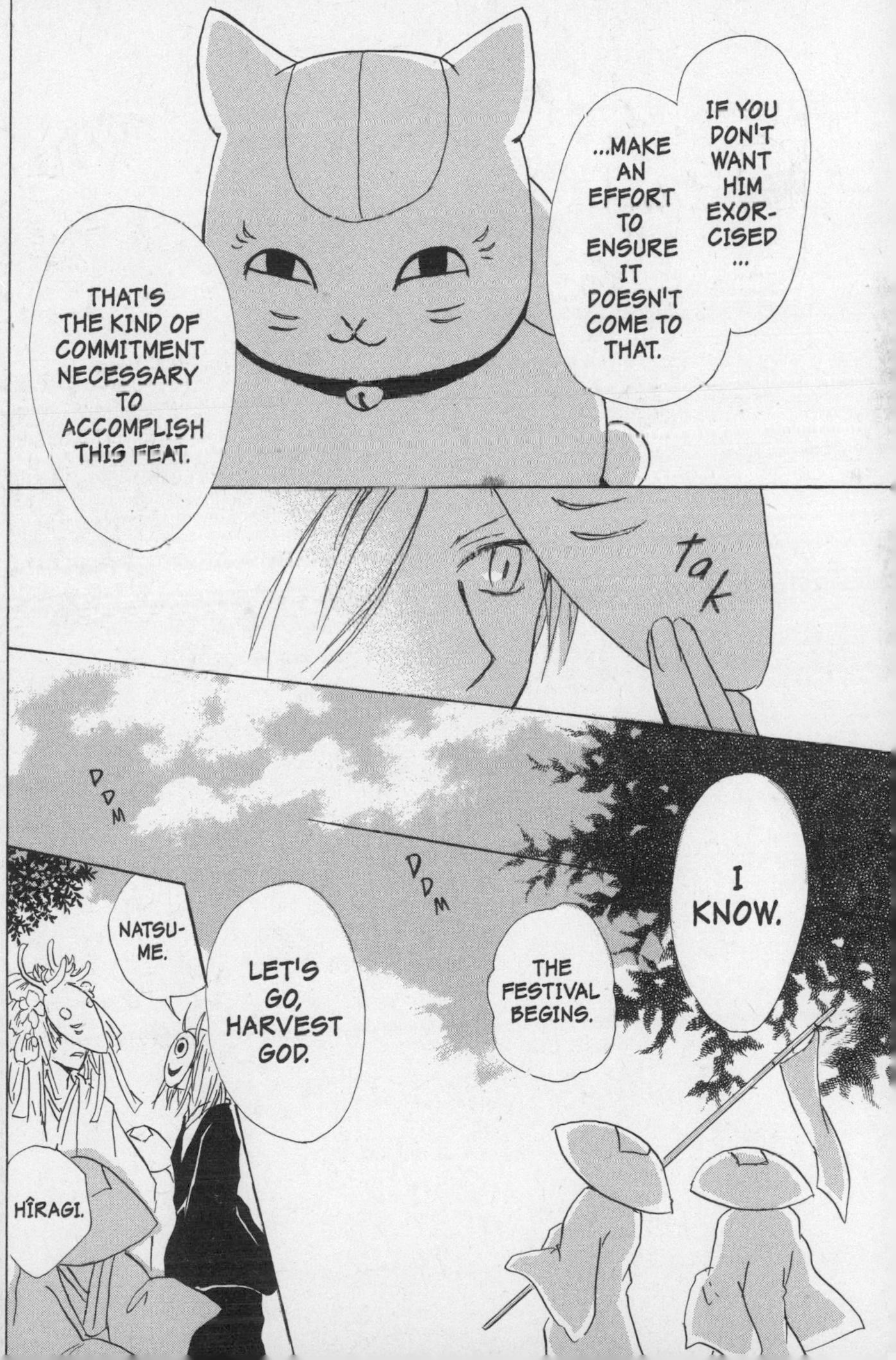
IF YOU DON'T WANT HIM EXORCISED...
...MAKE AN EFFORT TO ENSURE IT DOESN'T COME TO THAT.
THAT'S THE KIND OF COMMITMENT NECESSARY TO ACCOMPLISH THIS FEAT.
tak
I KNOW.
DOM
DOM
THE FESTIVAL BEGINS.
LET'S GO, HARVEST GOD.
NATSU-ME.
HÎRAGI.

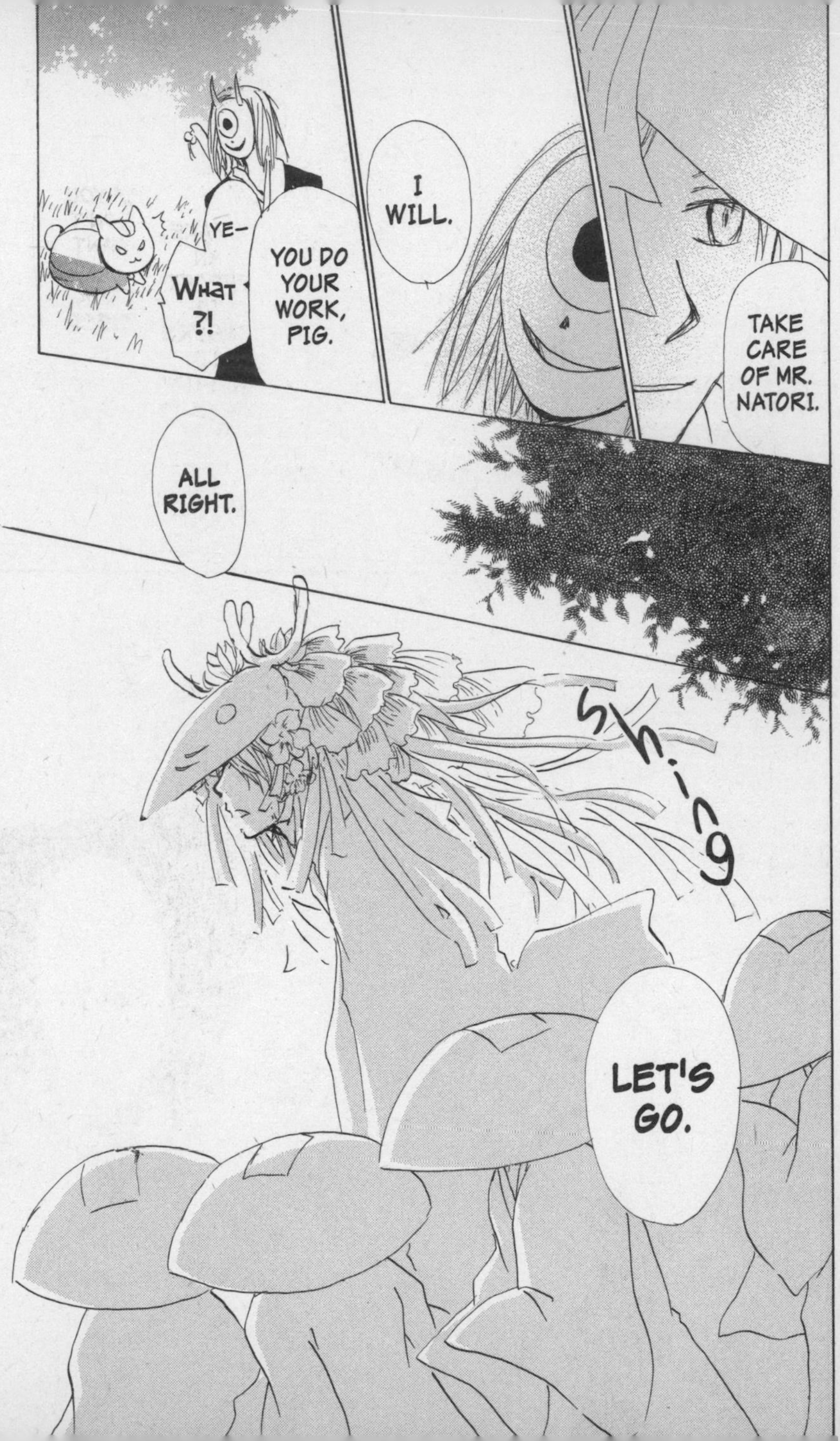
TAKE CARE OF MR. NATORI.
I WILL.
YOU DO YOUR WORK, PIG.
YE-
WHAT ?!
ALL RIGHT.
SHING
LET'S GO.

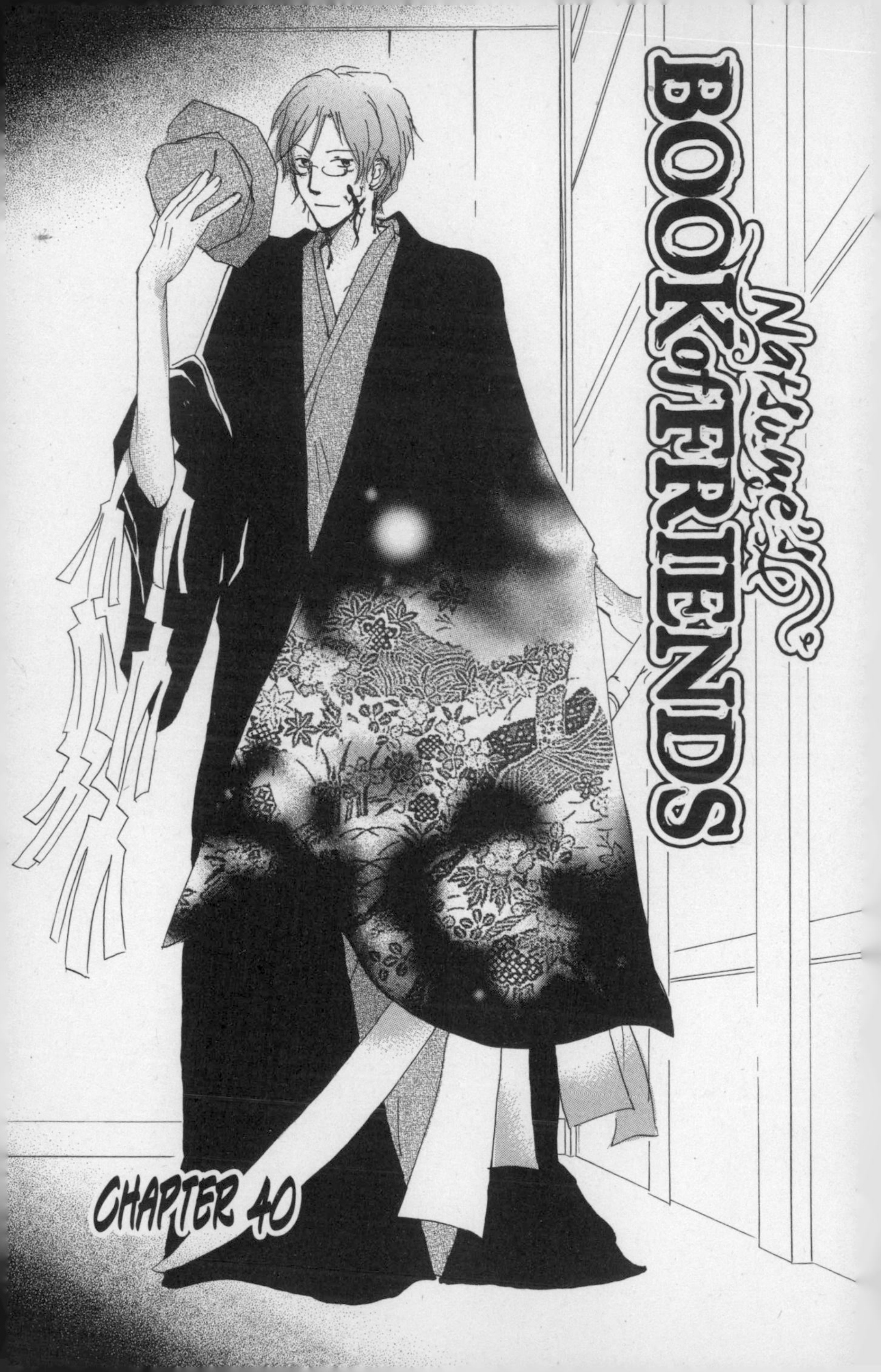
Natsume's
BOOK of FRIENDS
CHAPTER 40

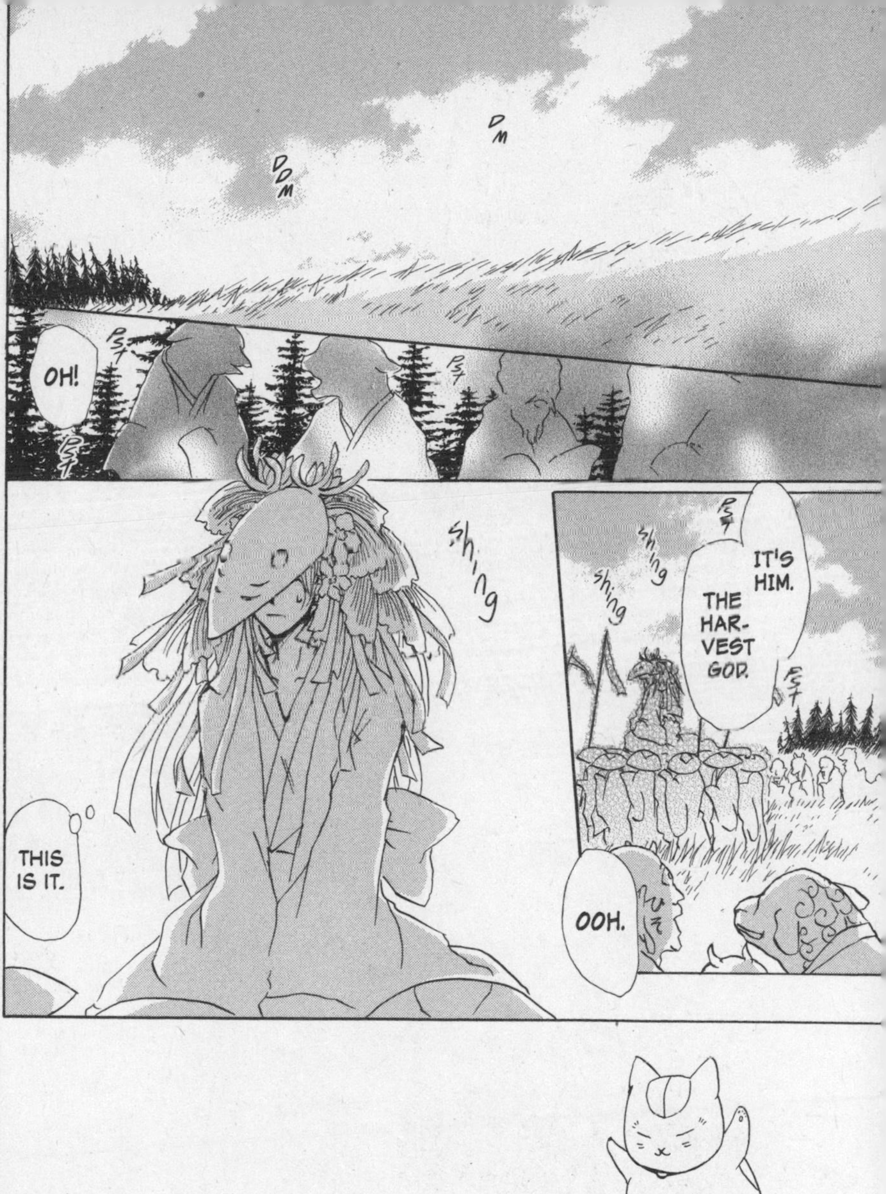
DM
DOM
PST
PST
OH!
PST
PST
IT'S HIM.
THE HAR-VEST GOD.
PST
shing
shing
OOH.
shing
THIS IS IT.

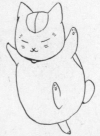

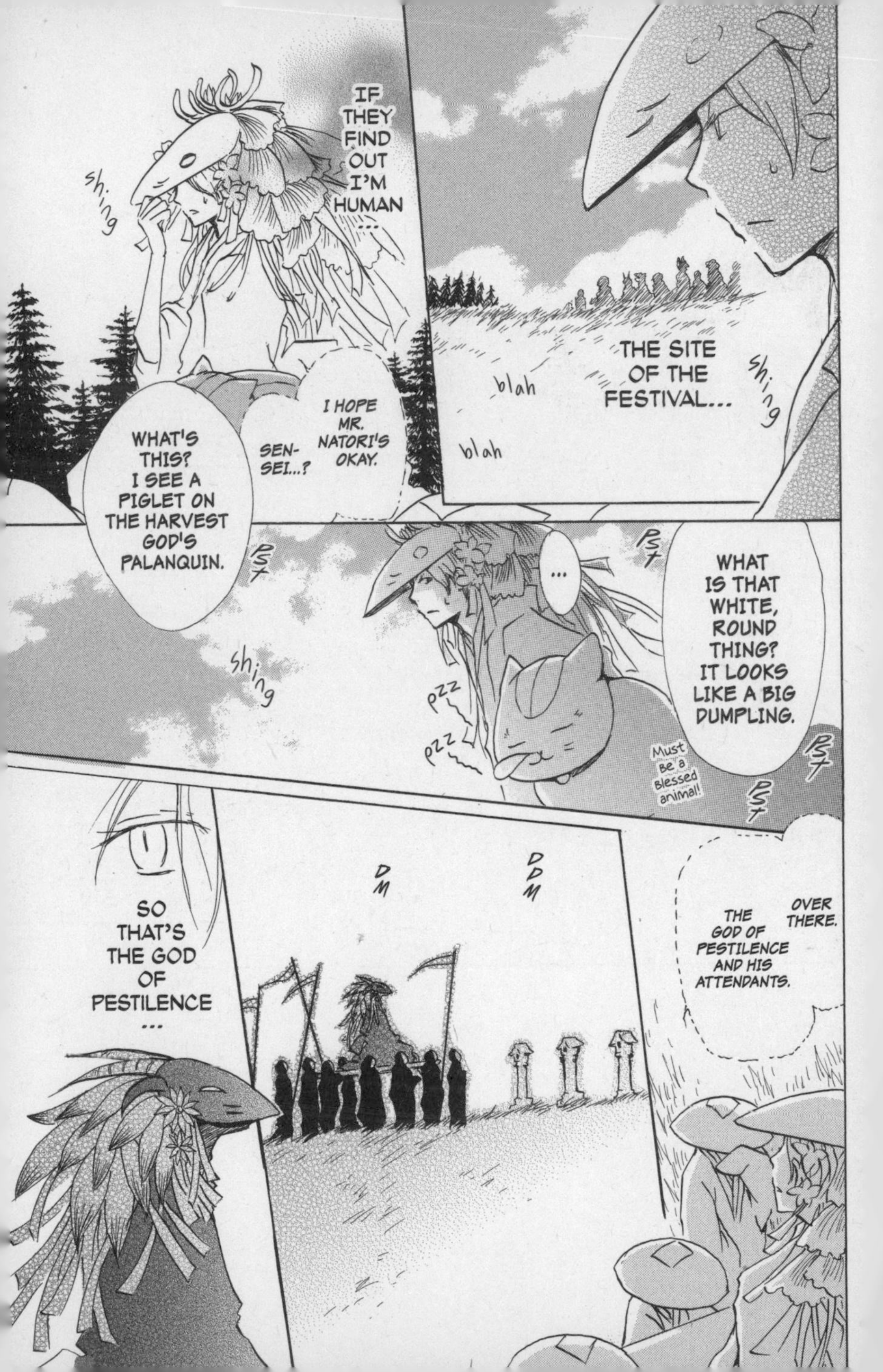
THE SITE OF THE FESTIVAL...
blah
blah
shing
IF THEY FIND OUT I'M HUMAN...
shing
I HOPE MR. NATORI'S OKAY.
SEN-SEI...?
WHAT'S THIS? I SEE A PIGLET ON THE HARVEST GOD'S PALANQUIN.
Pst
WHAT IS THAT WHITE, ROUND THING? IT LOOKS LIKE A BIG DUMPLING.
Pst
Pst
Must be a Blessed animal!
Pst
...
pzz
pzz
shing
OVER THERE.
THE GOD OF PESTILENCE AND HIS ATTENDANTS.
DDM
DM
SO THAT'S THE GOD OF PESTILENCE...

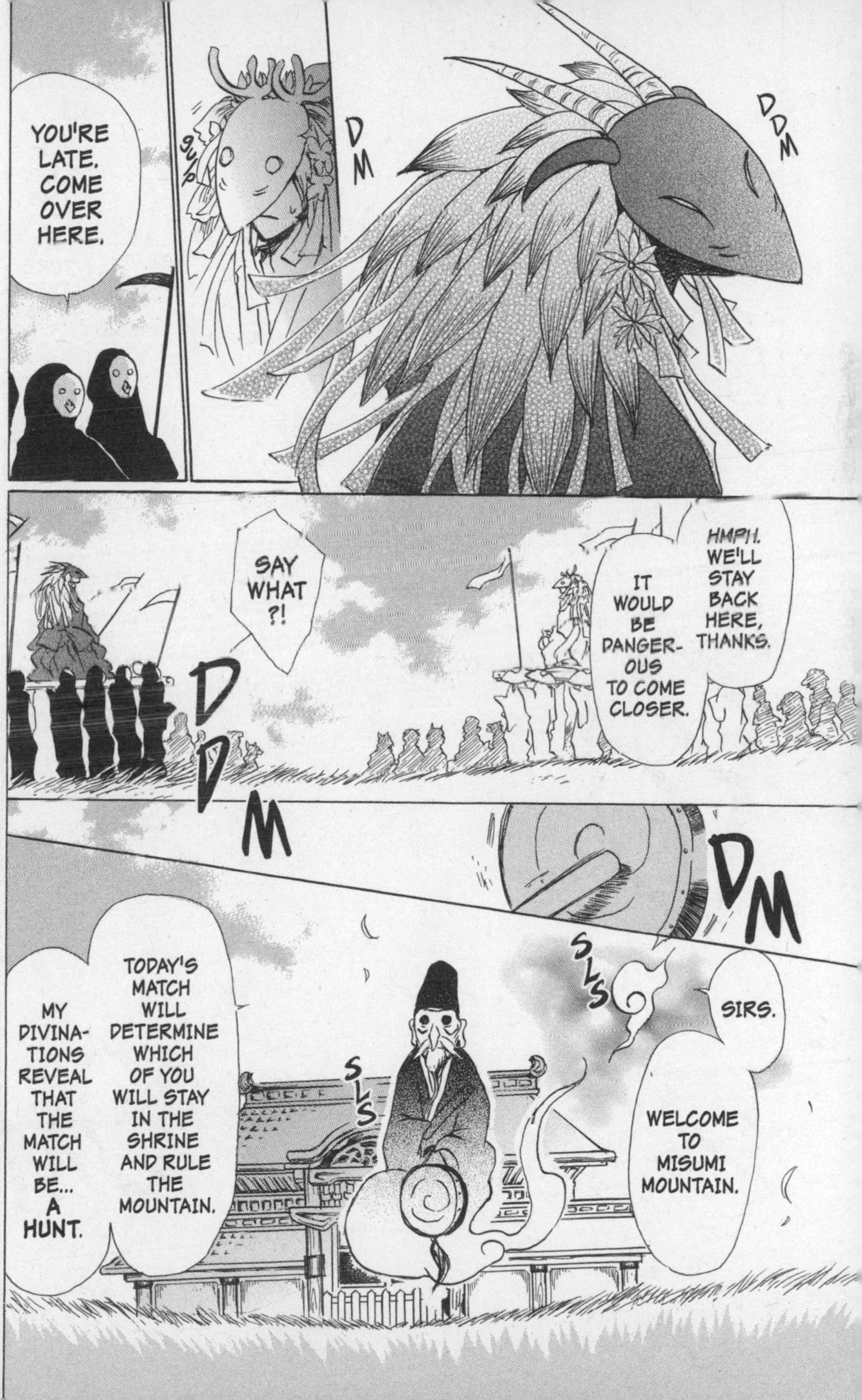
DDM
DM
gulp
YOU'RE LATE. COME OVER HERE.
HMPH. WE'LL STAY BACK HERE, THANKS.
IT WOULD BE DANGER-OUS TO COME CLOSER.
SAY WHAT?!
DDM
DM
SLS
SIRS.
WELCOME TO MISUMI MOUNTAIN.
SLS
TODAY'S MATCH WILL DETERMINE WHICH OF YOU WILL STAY IN THE SHRINE AND RULE THE MOUNTAIN.
MY DIVINA-TIONS REVEAL THAT THE MATCH WILL BE... A HUNT.

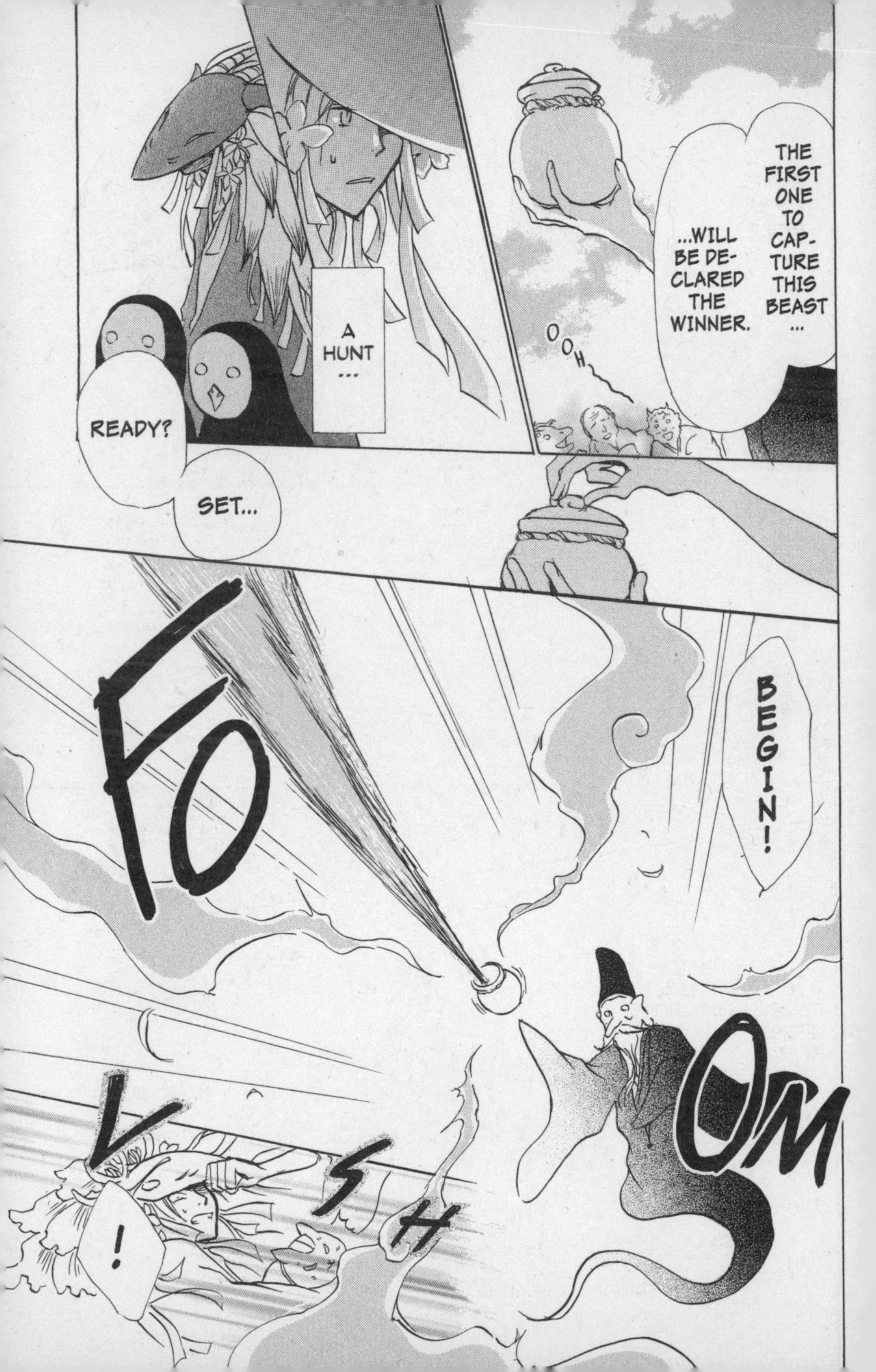
THE FIRST ONE TO CAPTURE THIS BEAST ...
...WILL BE DECLARED THE WINNER.
OOH
A HUNT ...
READY?
SET...
BEGIN!
FOOM
VSH
!

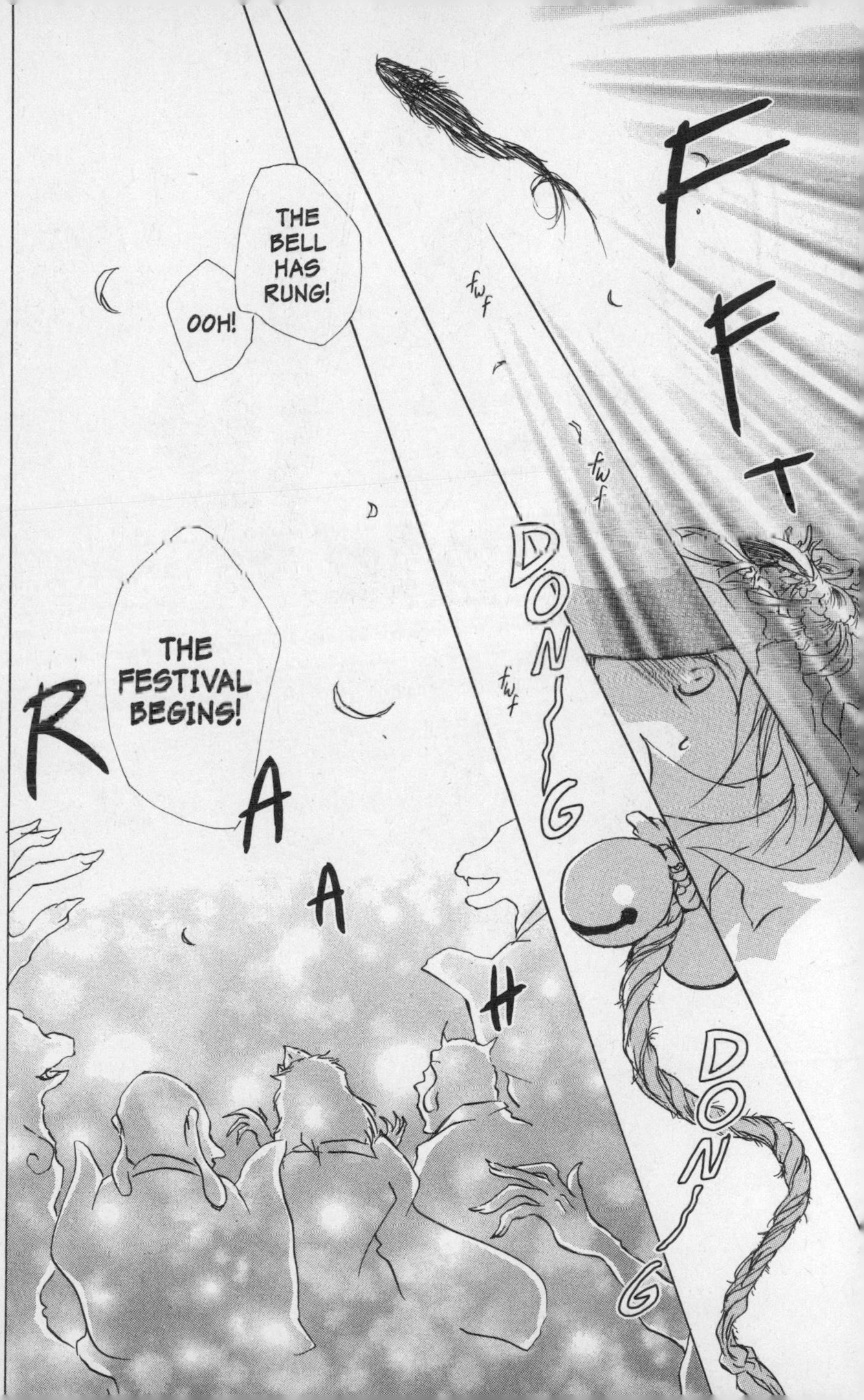
FFFT
fwf
fwf
fwf
DONG
DONG
THE BELL HAS RUNG!
OOH!
THE FESTIVAL BEGINS!
RAAH

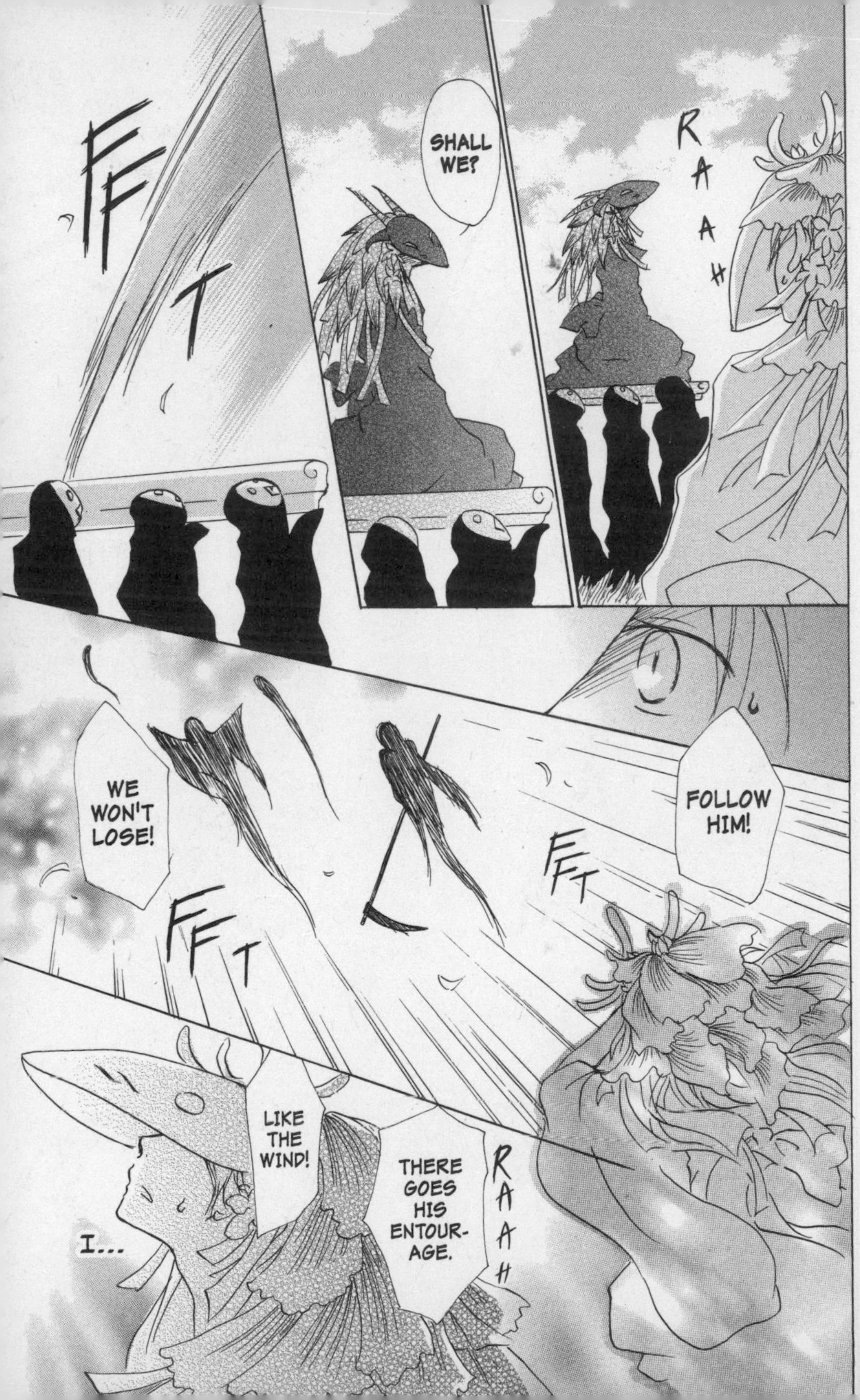
RAAH
SHALL WE?
FFT
FOLLOW HIM!
FFT
WE WON'T LOSE!
FFT
RAAH
THERE GOES HIS ENTOURAGE.
LIKE THE WIND!
I...

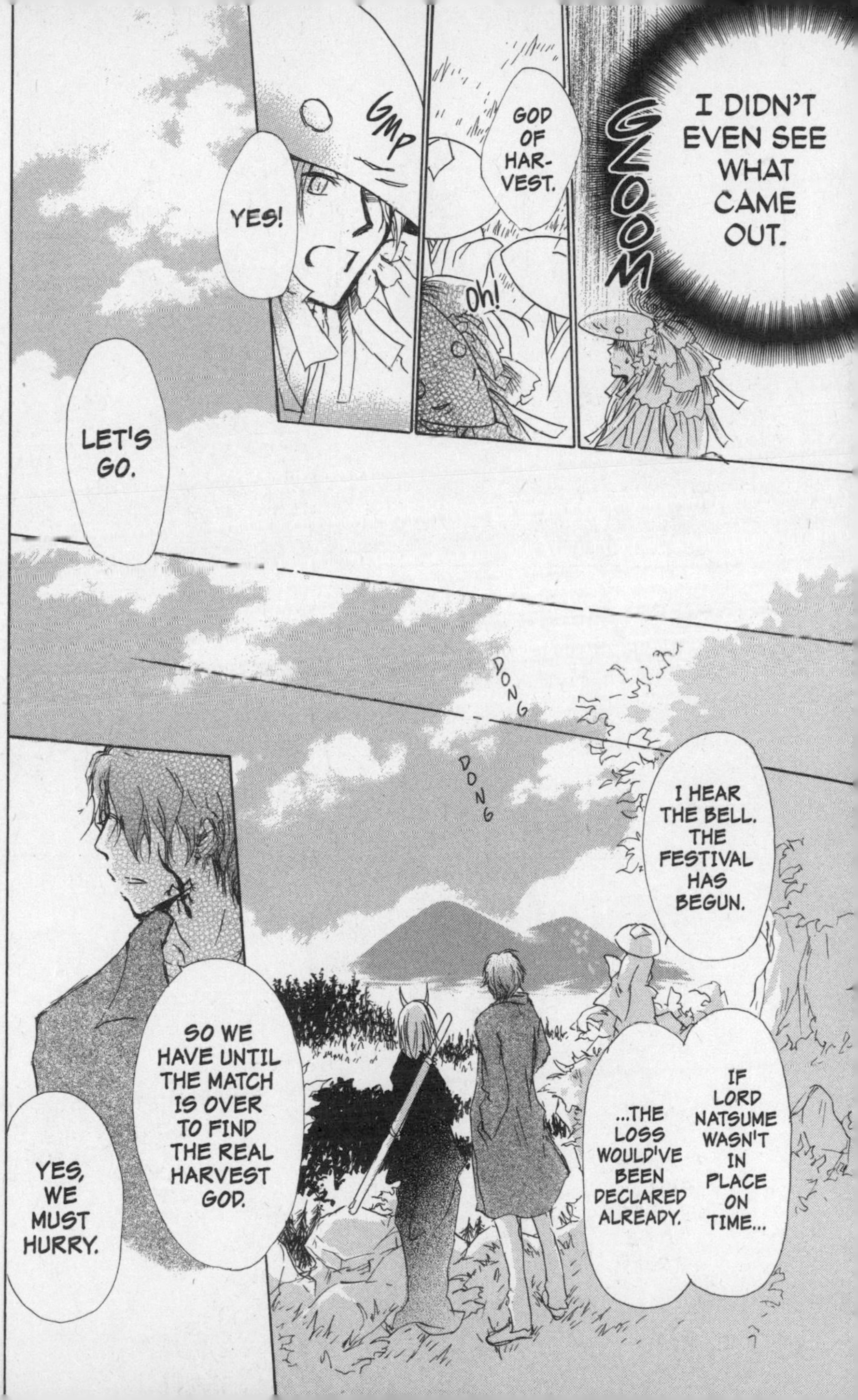
I DIDN'T EVEN SEE WHAT CAME OUT.
GLOOM
GOD OF HAR-VEST.
Oh!
GMP
YES!
LET'S GO.
DONG
DONG
I HEAR THE BELL. THE FESTIVAL HAS BEGUN.
IF LORD NATSUME WASN'T IN PLACE ON TIME...
...THE LOSS WOULD'VE BEEN DECLARED ALREADY.
SO WE HAVE UNTIL THE MATCH IS OVER TO FIND THE REAL HARVEST GOD.
YES, WE MUST HURRY.

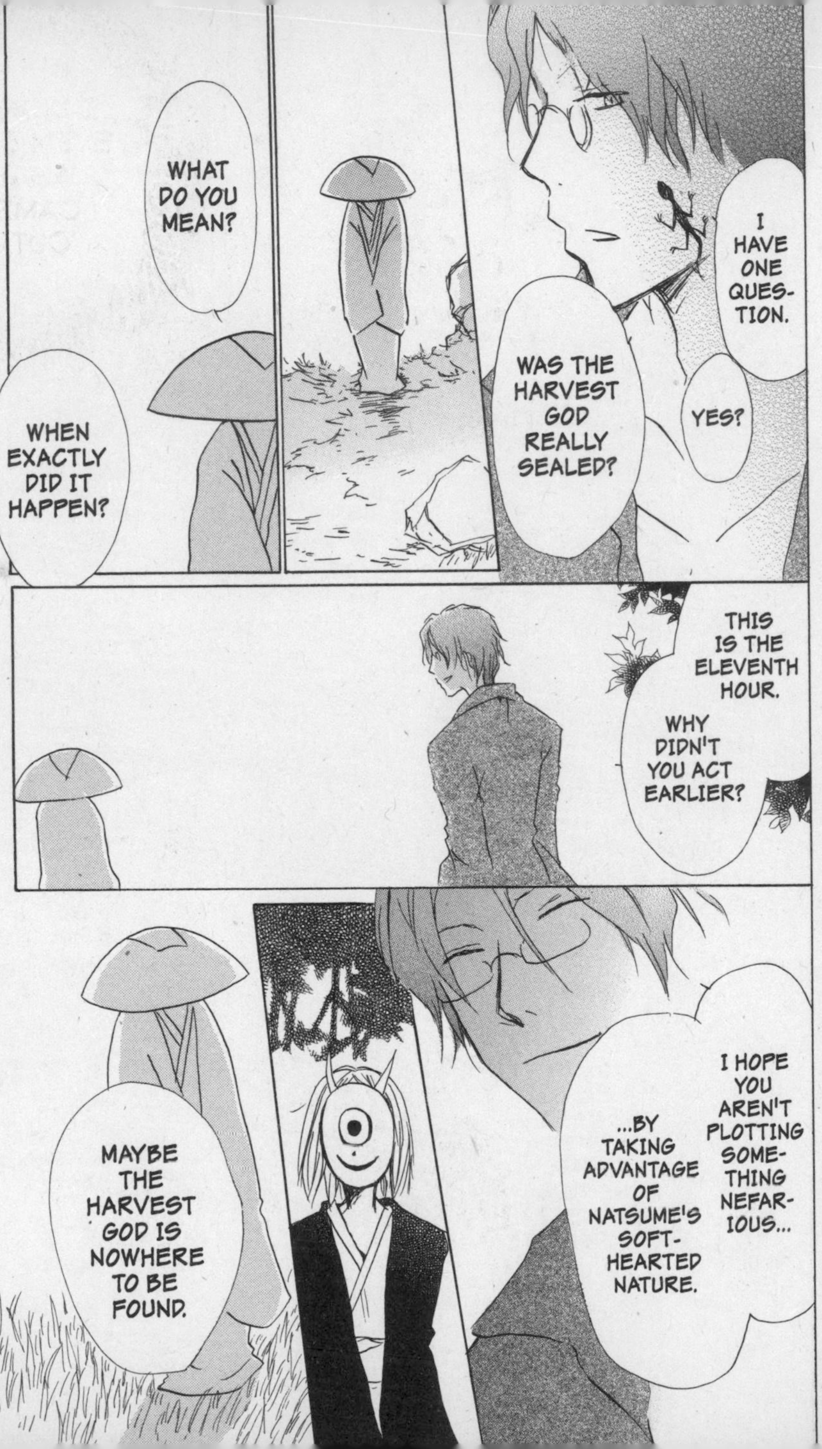
I HAVE ONE QUESTION.
YES?
WAS THE HARVEST GOD REALLY SEALED?
WHAT DO YOU MEAN?
WHEN EXACTLY DID IT HAPPEN?
THIS IS THE ELEVENTH HOUR.
WHY DIDN'T YOU ACT EARLIER?
I HOPE YOU AREN'T PLOTTING SOMETHING NEFARIOUS...
...BY TAKING ADVANTAGE OF NATSUME'S SOFT-HEARTED NATURE.
MAYBE THE HARVEST GOD IS NOWHERE TO BE FOUND.

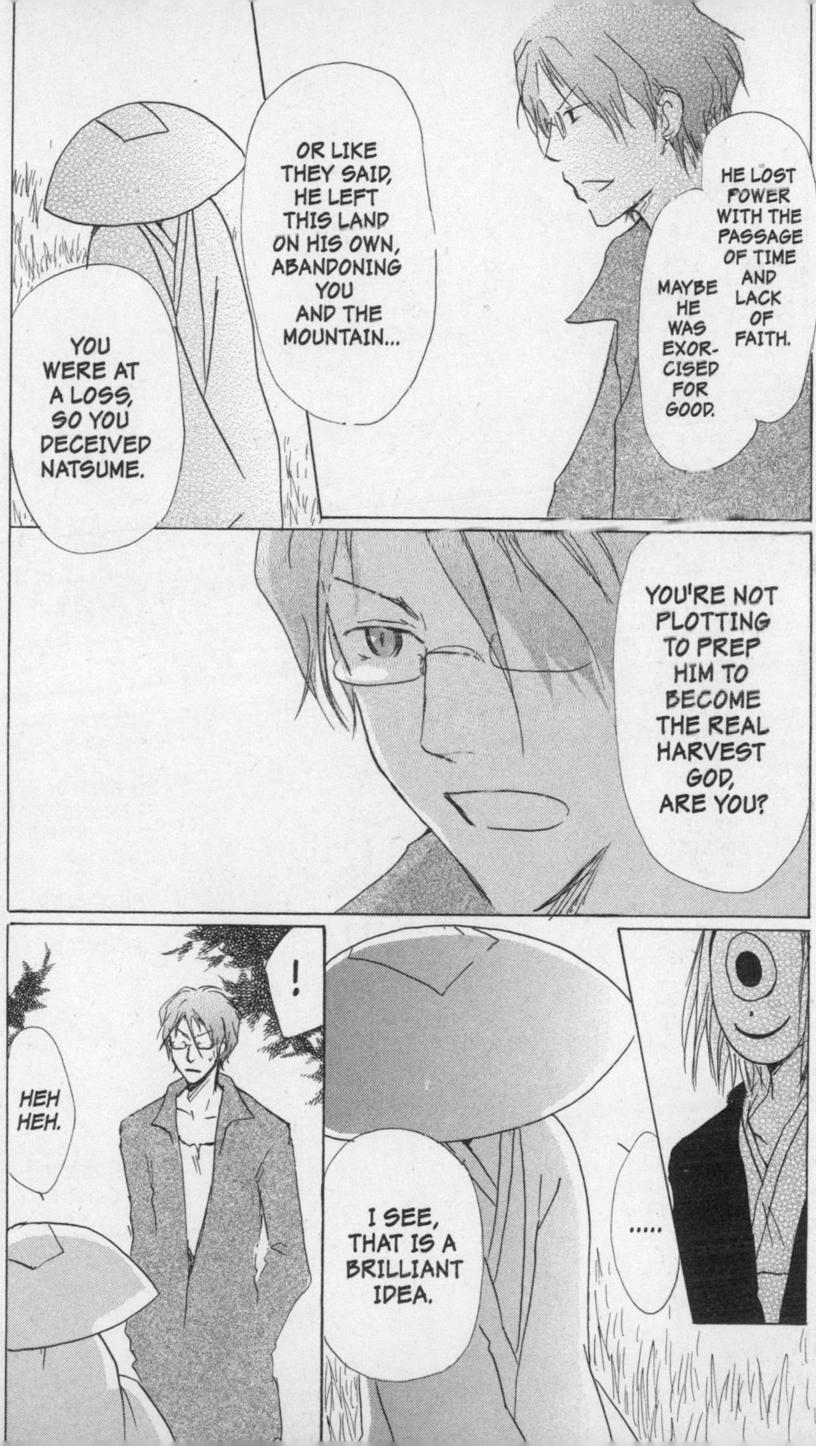
HE LOST POWER WITH THE PASSAGE OF TIME AND LACK OF FAITH.
MAYBE HE WAS EXORCISED FOR GOOD.
OR LIKE THEY SAID, HE LEFT THIS LAND ON HIS OWN, ABANDONING YOU AND THE MOUNTAIN...
YOU WERE AT A LOSS, SO YOU DECEIVED NATSUME.
YOU'RE NOT PLOTTING TO PREP HIM TO BECOME THE REAL HARVEST GOD, ARE YOU?
.....
!
I SEE, THAT IS A BRILLIANT IDEA.
HEH HEH.

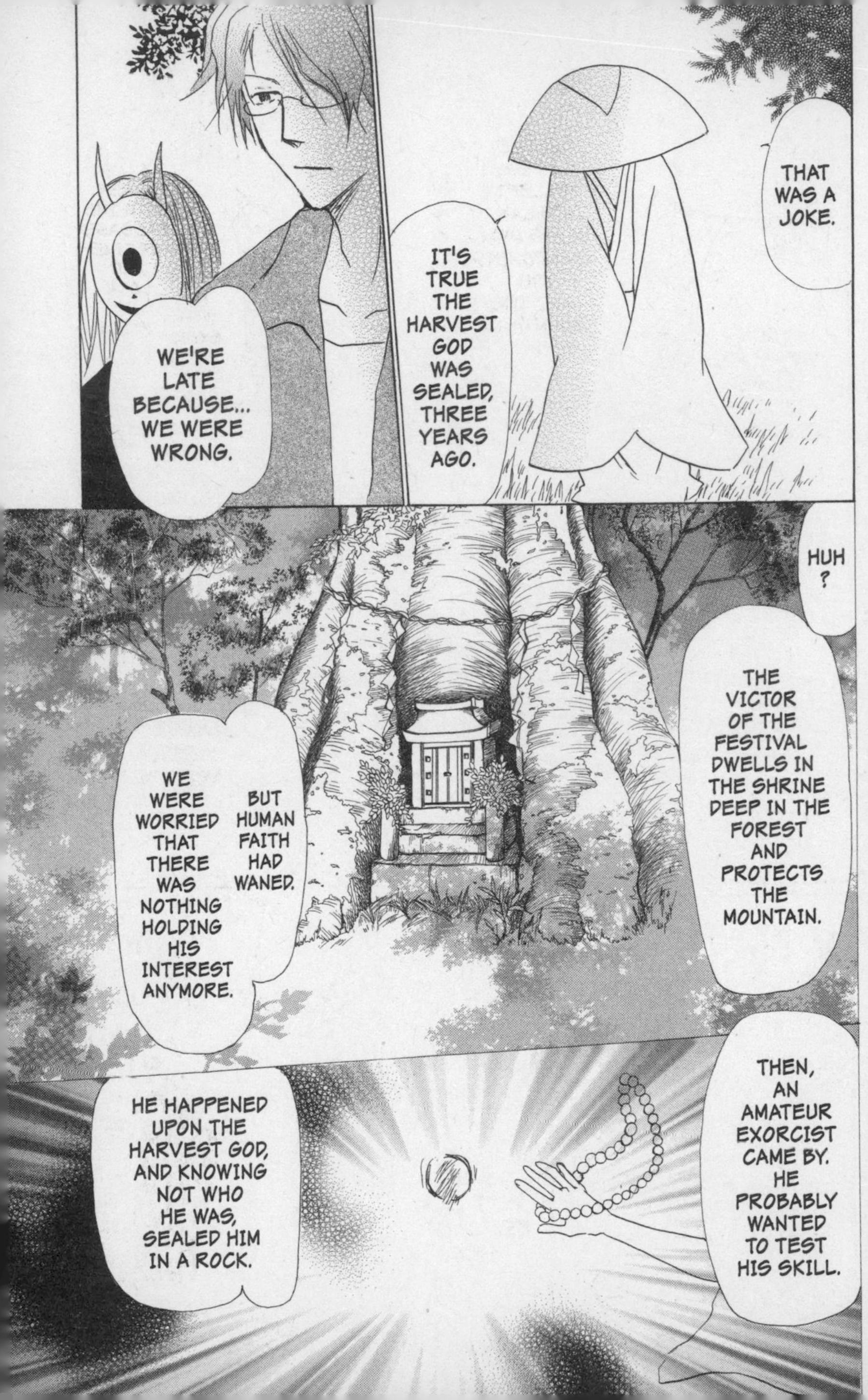
THAT WAS A JOKE.
IT'S TRUE THE HARVEST GOD WAS SEALED, THREE YEARS AGO.
WE'RE LATE BECAUSE... WE WERE WRONG.
HUH?
THE VICTOR OF THE FESTIVAL DWELLS IN THE SHRINE DEEP IN THE FOREST AND PROTECTS THE MOUNTAIN.
BUT HUMAN FAITH HAD WANED.
WE WERE WORRIED THAT THERE WAS NOTHING HOLDING HIS INTEREST ANYMORE.
THEN, AN AMATEUR EXORCIST CAME BY. HE PROBABLY WANTED TO TEST HIS SKILL.
HE HAPPENED UPON THE HARVEST GOD, AND KNOWING NOT WHO HE WAS, SEALED HIM IN A ROCK.

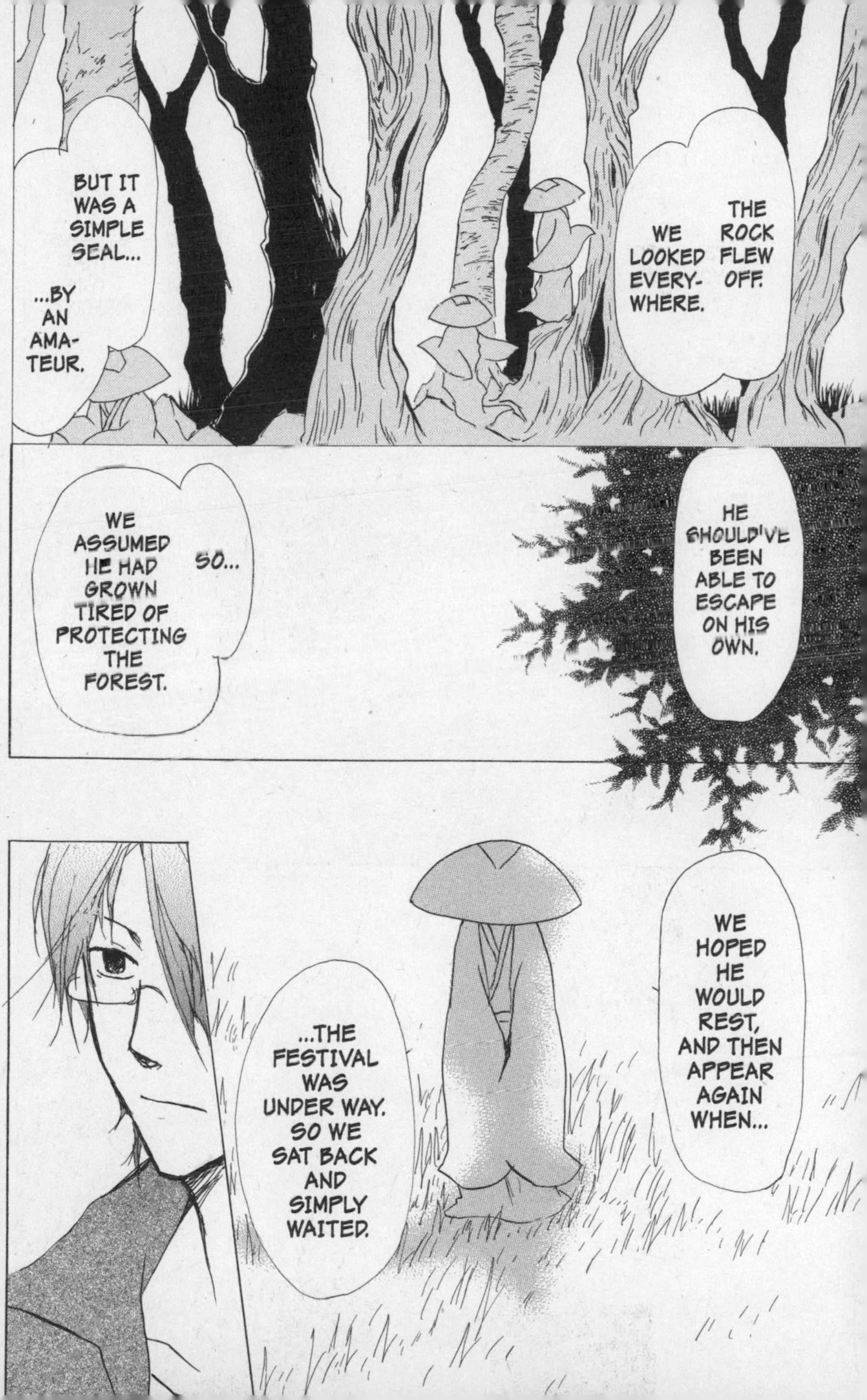
THE ROCK FLEW OFF.
WE LOOKED EVERY-WHERE.
BUT IT WAS A SIMPLE SEAL...
...BY AN AMA-TEUR.
HE SHOULD'VE BEEN ABLE TO ESCAPE ON HIS OWN.
SO...
WE ASSUMED HE HAD GROWN TIRED OF PROTECTING THE FOREST.
WE HOPED HE WOULD REST, AND THEN APPEAR AGAIN WHEN...
...THE FESTIVAL WAS UNDER WAY. SO WE SAT BACK AND SIMPLY WAITED.

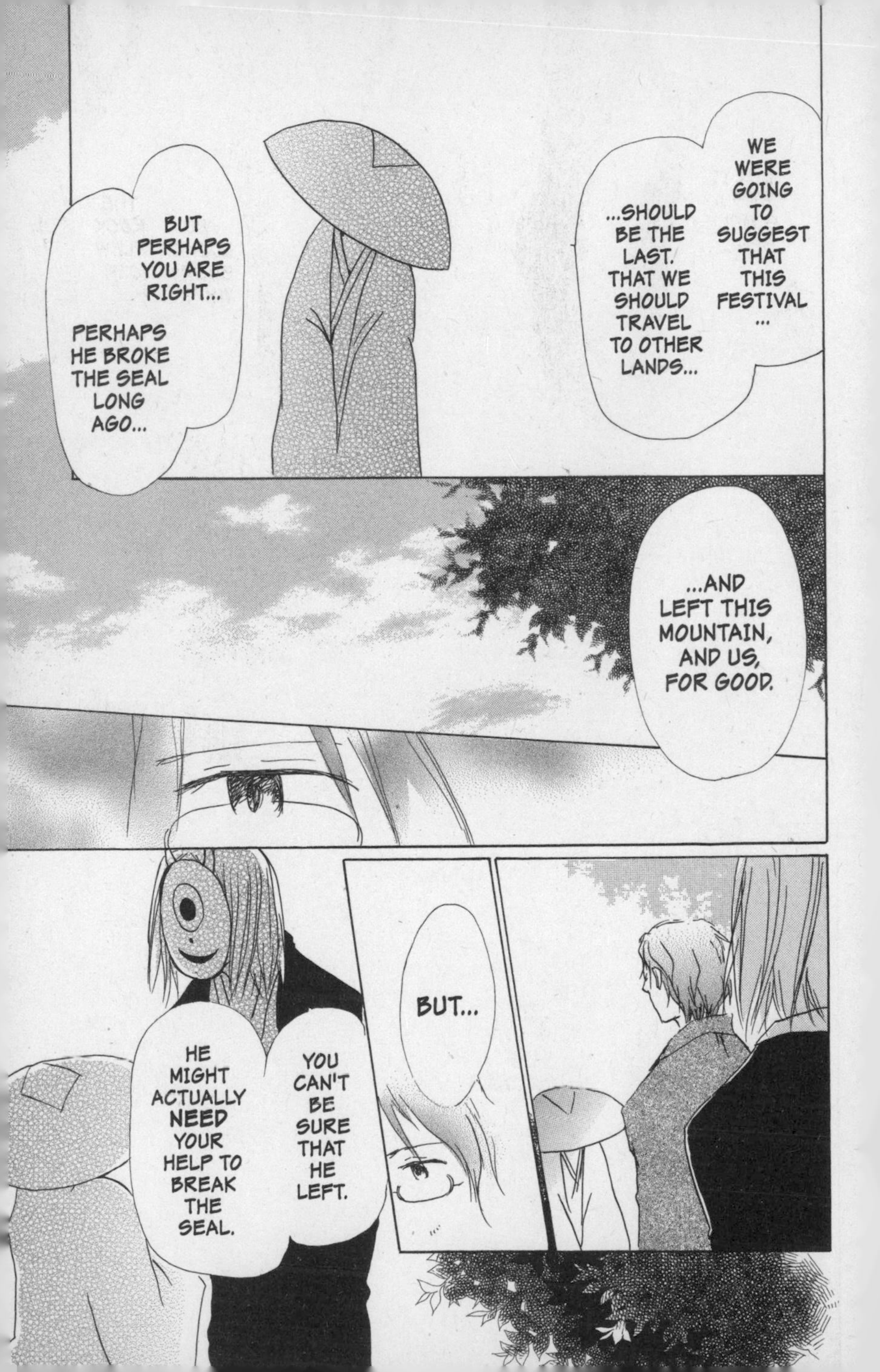
WE WERE GOING TO SUGGEST THAT THIS FESTIVAL ...
...SHOULD BE THE LAST. THAT WE SHOULD TRAVEL TO OTHER LANDS...
BUT PERHAPS YOU ARE RIGHT...
PERHAPS HE BROKE THE SEAL LONG AGO...
...AND LEFT THIS MOUNTAIN, AND US, FOR GOOD.
BUT...
YOU CAN'T BE SURE THAT HE LEFT.
HE MIGHT ACTUALLY **NEED** YOUR HELP TO BREAK THE SEAL.

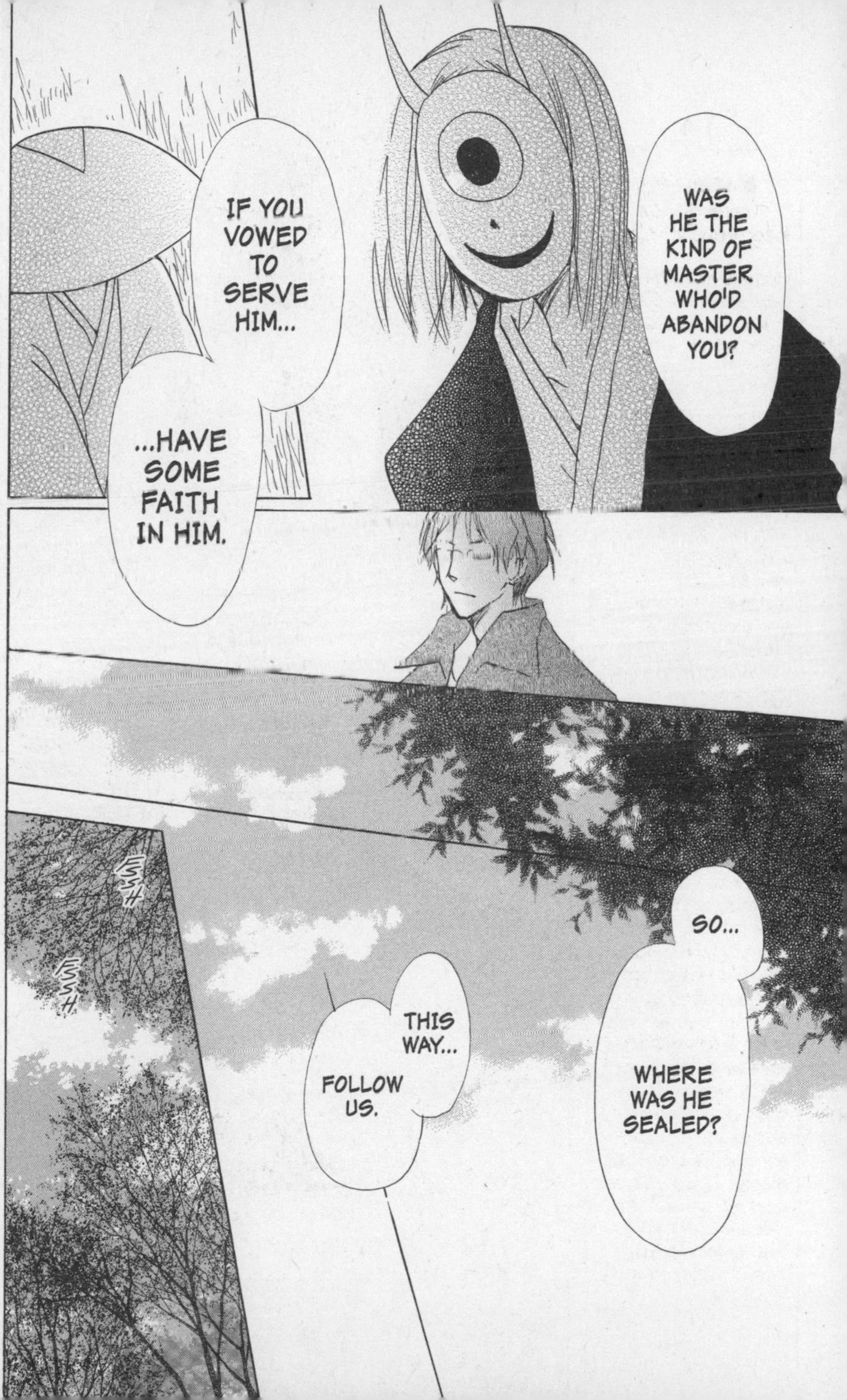
WAS HE THE KIND OF MASTER WHO'D ABANDON YOU?
IF YOU VOWED TO SERVE HIM...
...HAVE SOME FAITH IN HIM.
SO...
WHERE WAS HE SEALED?
THIS WAY...
FOLLOW US.
FSSH
FSSH

04

❋48th LMS (LaLa Manga Recruitment) Camp

I was invited to LaLa's Manga Camp in Kyushu as a guest instructor with fellow manga artist Ms. Emiko Nakano. Everyone there was so passionate about creating manga. It was lots of fun, and very invigorating. I was in awe, along with the other students, of Ms. Nakano's meticulous and delicate line work. I wasn't able to show them many techniques, but I tried to answer everyone's questions to the best of my ability, although I must've sounded quite flustered. Everyone listened very intently. I was so filled with emotion. I knew that the students were anxious and uncertain about their future, yet they put in so much effort in pursuit of an interesting story. I was touched and inspired, and eager to go back home and draw manga. I hope we can keep striving for the same goals. Thank you so much for the opportunity.

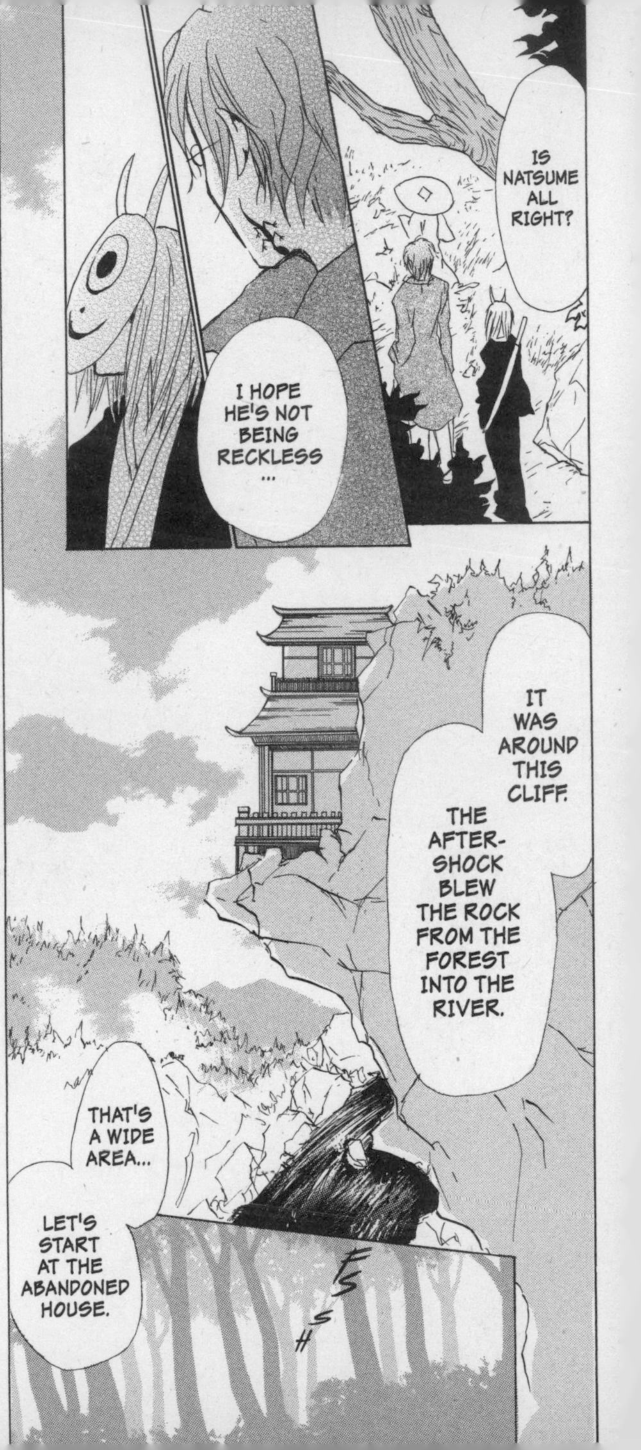
IS NATSUME ALL RIGHT?
I HOPE HE'S NOT BEING RECKLESS ...
IT WAS AROUND THIS CLIFF.
THE AFTER-SHOCK BLEW THE ROCK FROM THE FOREST INTO THE RIVER.
THAT'S A WIDE AREA...
LET'S START AT THE ABANDONED HOUSE.
FSSH

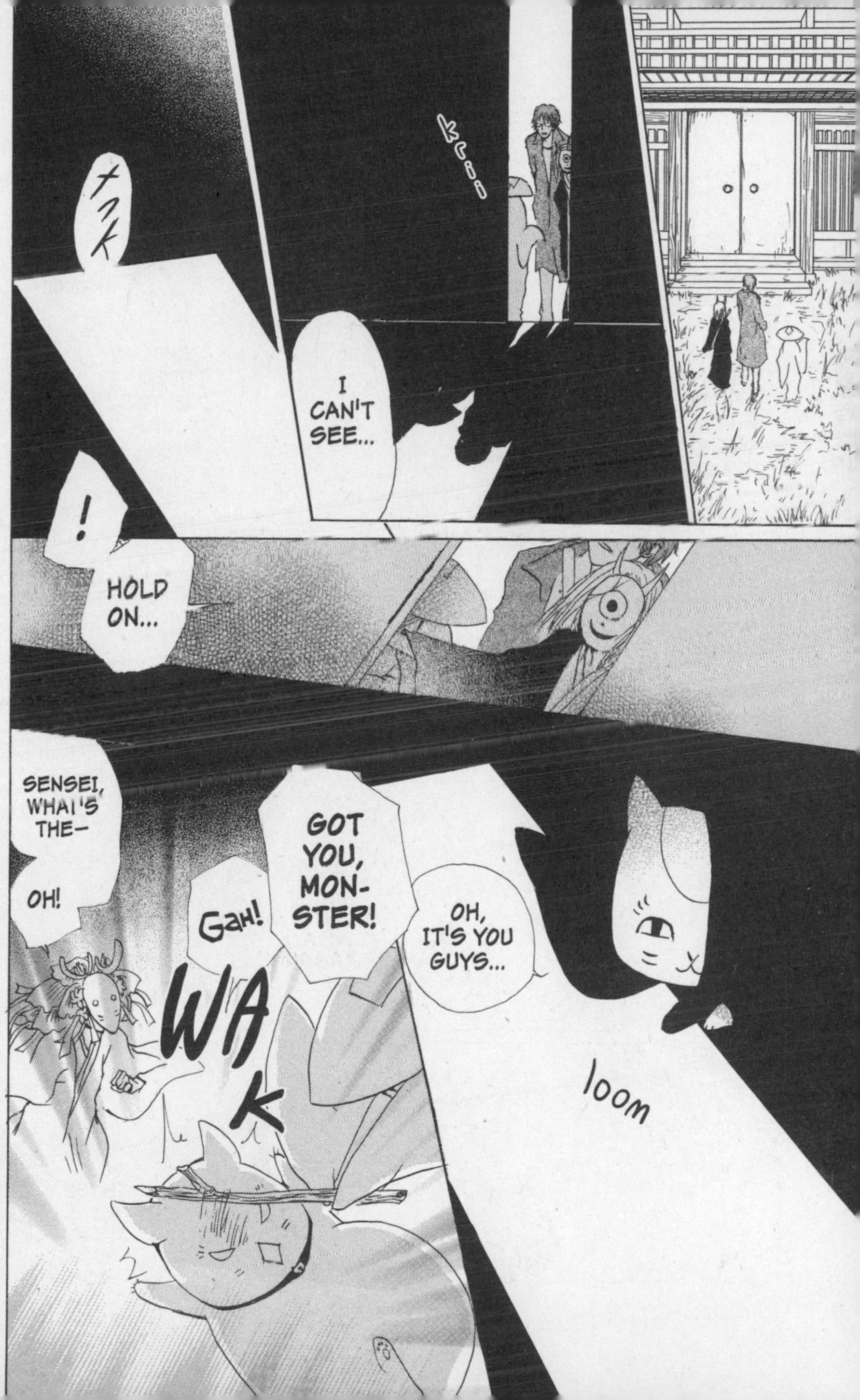
kriii
I CAN'T SEE...
!
HOLD ON...
OH, IT'S YOU GUYS...
loom
GOT YOU, MONSTER!
Gah!
SENSEI, WHAT'S THE—
OH!
WAK

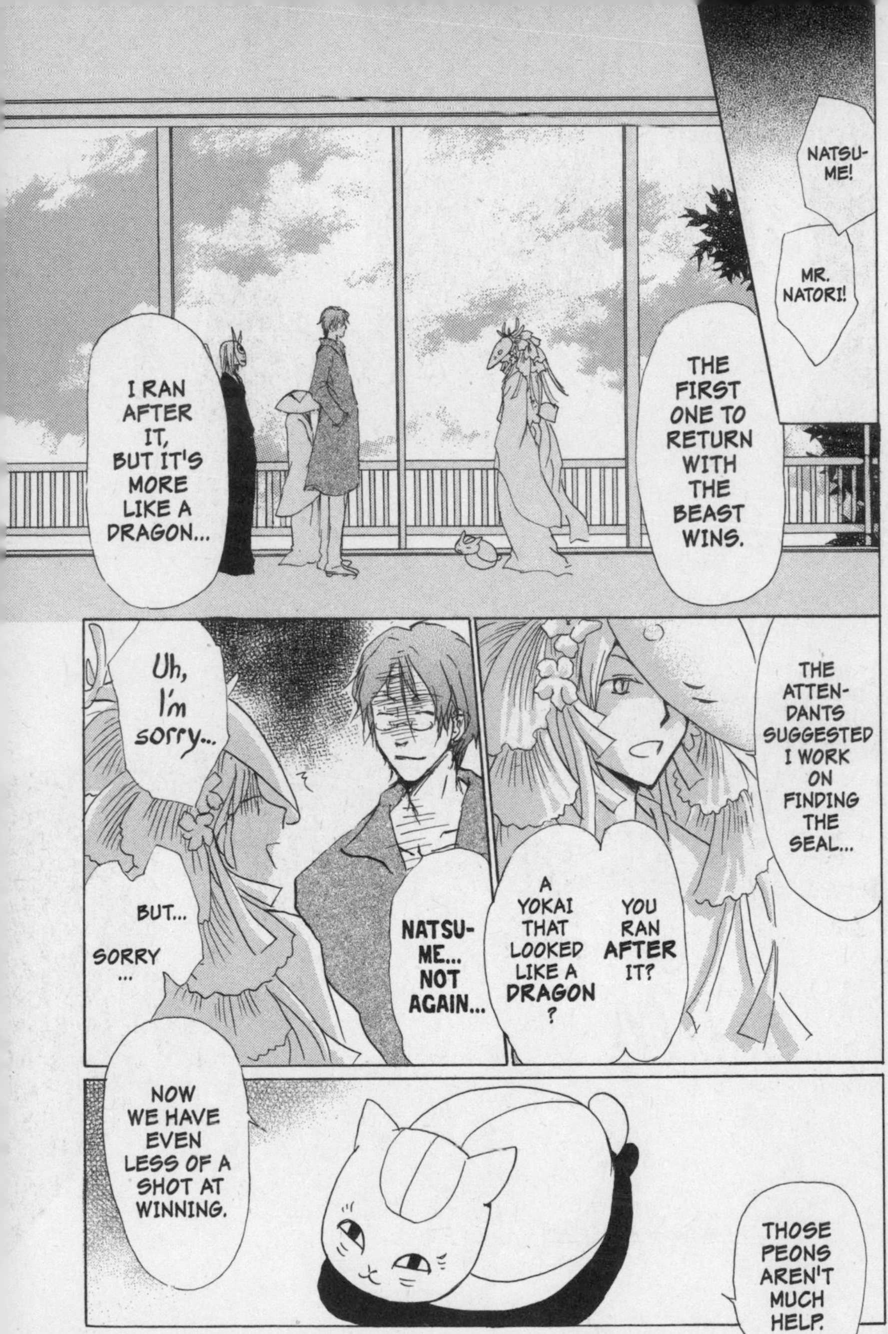
NATSU-ME!
MR. NATORI!
THE FIRST ONE TO RETURN WITH THE BEAST WINS.
I RAN AFTER IT, BUT IT'S MORE LIKE A DRAGON...
THE ATTEN-DANTS SUGGESTED I WORK ON FINDING THE SEAL...
YOU RAN AFTER IT?
A YOKAI THAT LOOKED LIKE A DRAGON?
NATSU-ME... NOT AGAIN...
Uh, I'm sorry...
BUT...
SORRY ...
THOSE PEONS AREN'T MUCH HELP.
NOW WE HAVE EVEN LESS OF A SHOT AT WINNING.

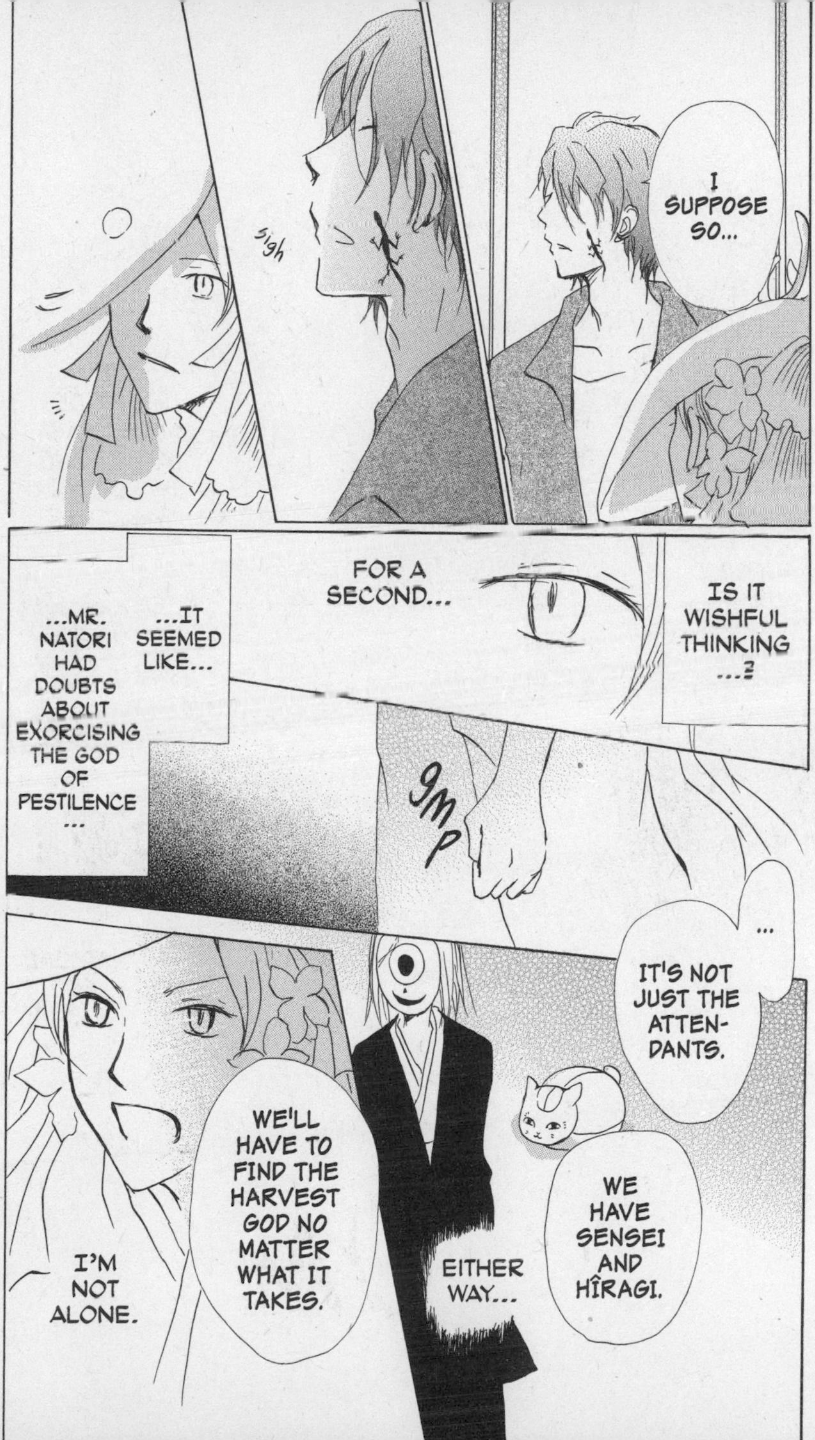
I SUPPOSE SO...
sigh
IS IT WISHFUL THINKING ...?
FOR A SECOND...
...IT SEEMED LIKE...
...MR. NATORI HAD DOUBTS ABOUT EXORCISING THE GOD OF PESTILENCE ...
gmp
...
IT'S NOT JUST THE ATTEN-DANTS.
WE HAVE SENSEI AND HÎRAGI.
EITHER WAY...
WE'LL HAVE TO FIND THE HARVEST GOD NO MATTER WHAT IT TAKES.
I'M NOT ALONE.

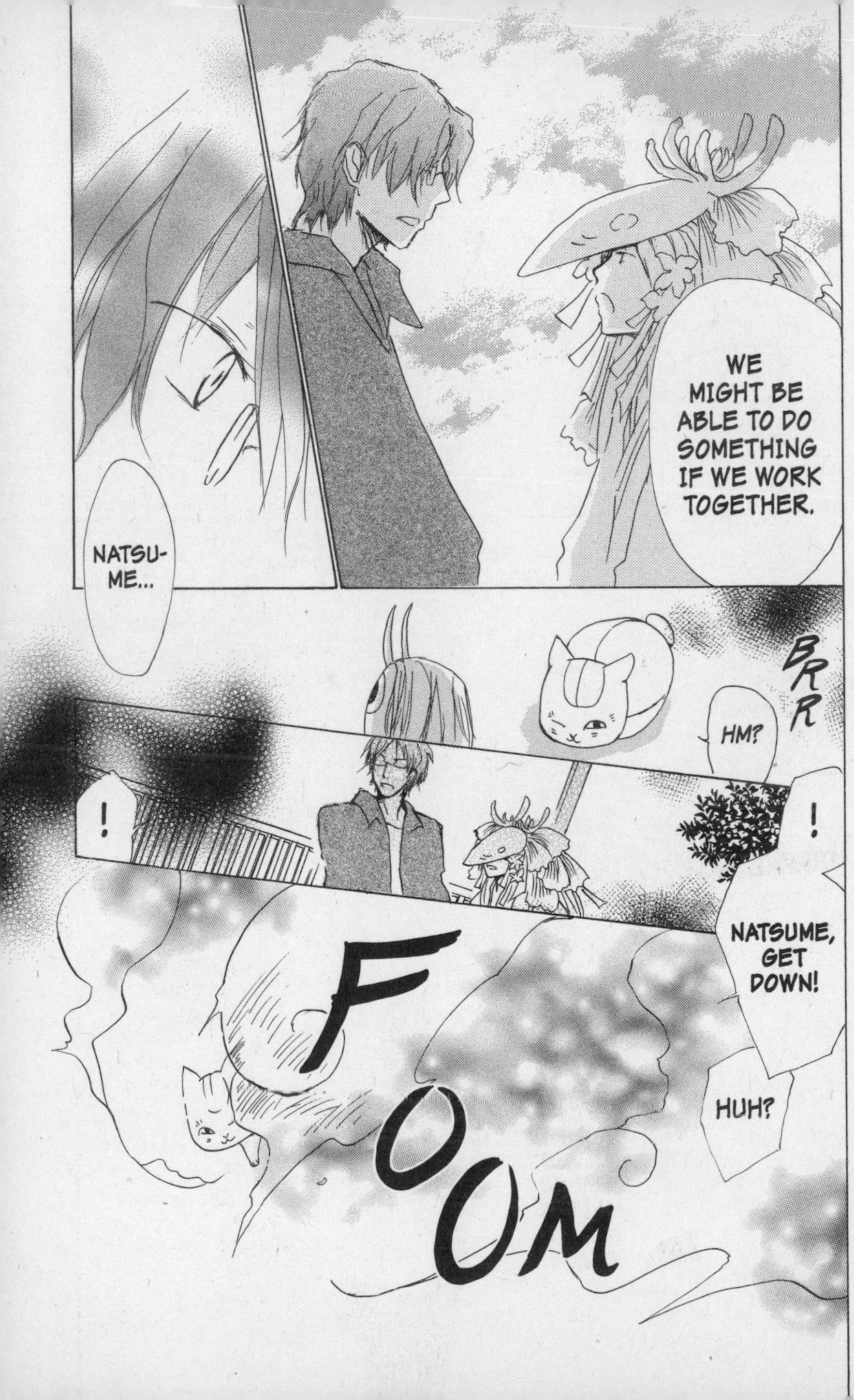
WE MIGHT BE ABLE TO DO SOMETHING IF WE WORK TOGETHER.
NATSU-ME...
BRR
HM?
!
!
NATSUME, GET DOWN!
HUH?
FOOM

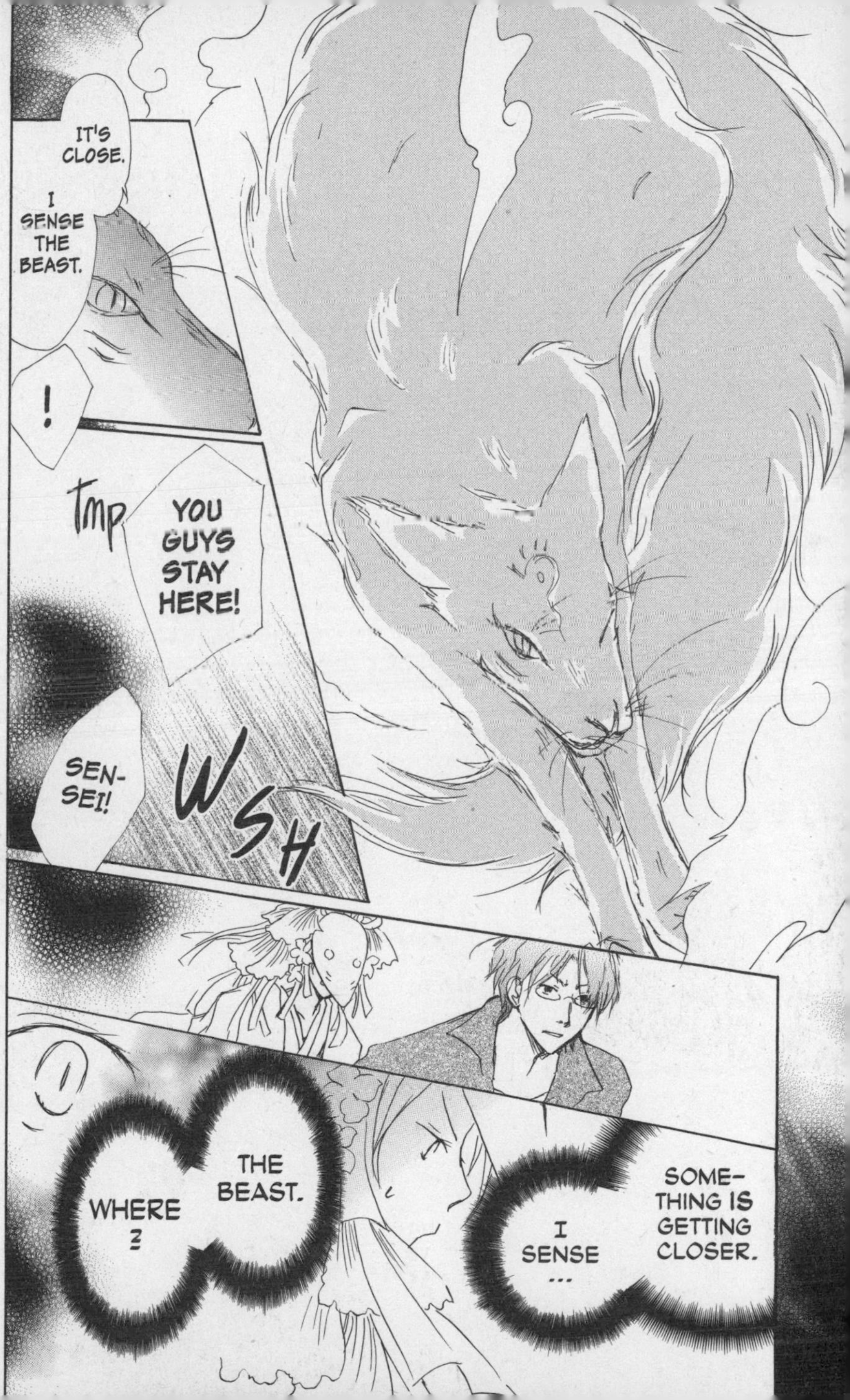
IT'S CLOSE.
I SENSE THE BEAST.
!
Tmp
YOU GUYS STAY HERE!
SEN-SEI!
WSH
SOME-THING IS GETTING CLOSER.
I SENSE...
THE BEAST.
WHERE?
!

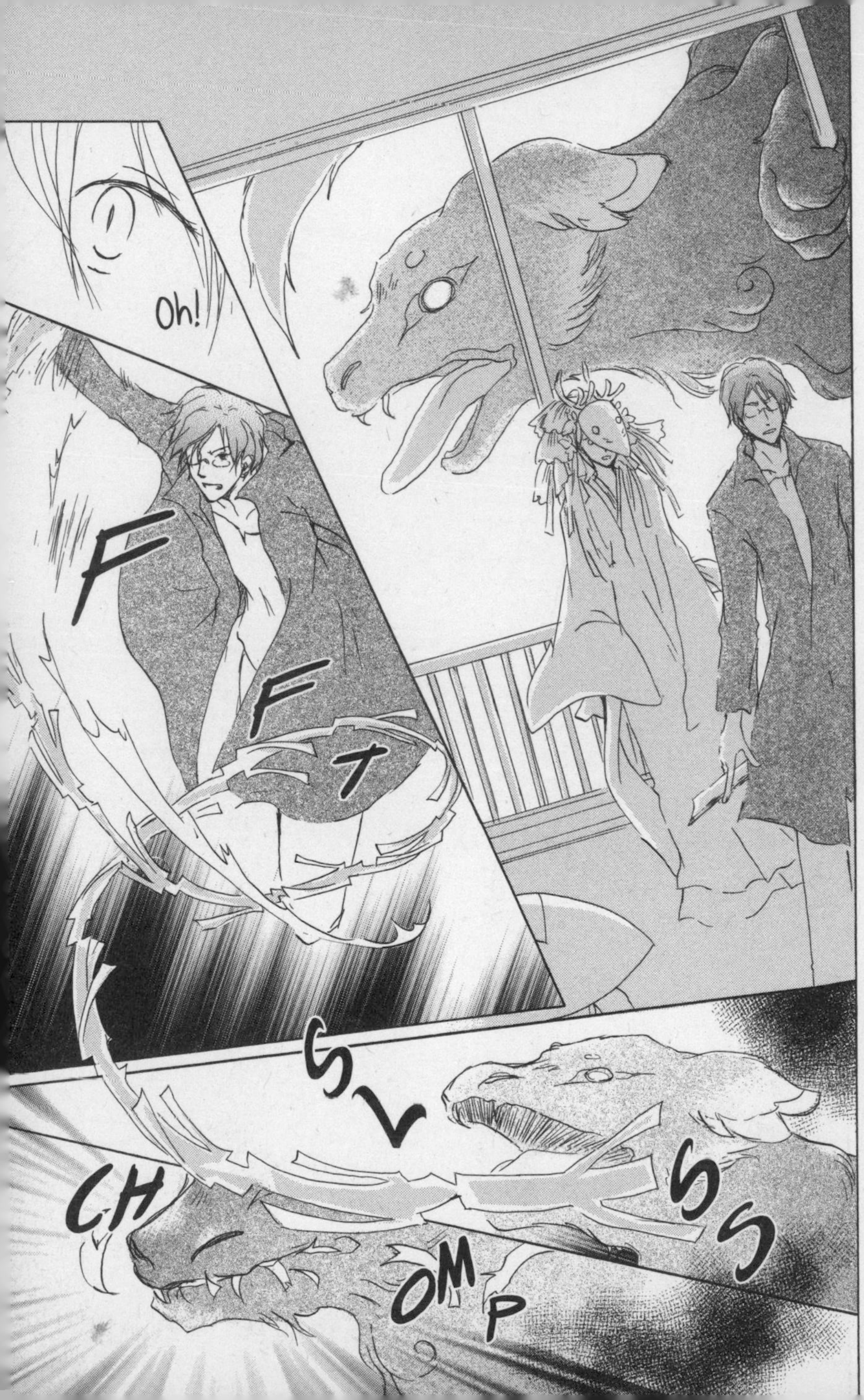
Oh!
FF
SSS
CHOMP

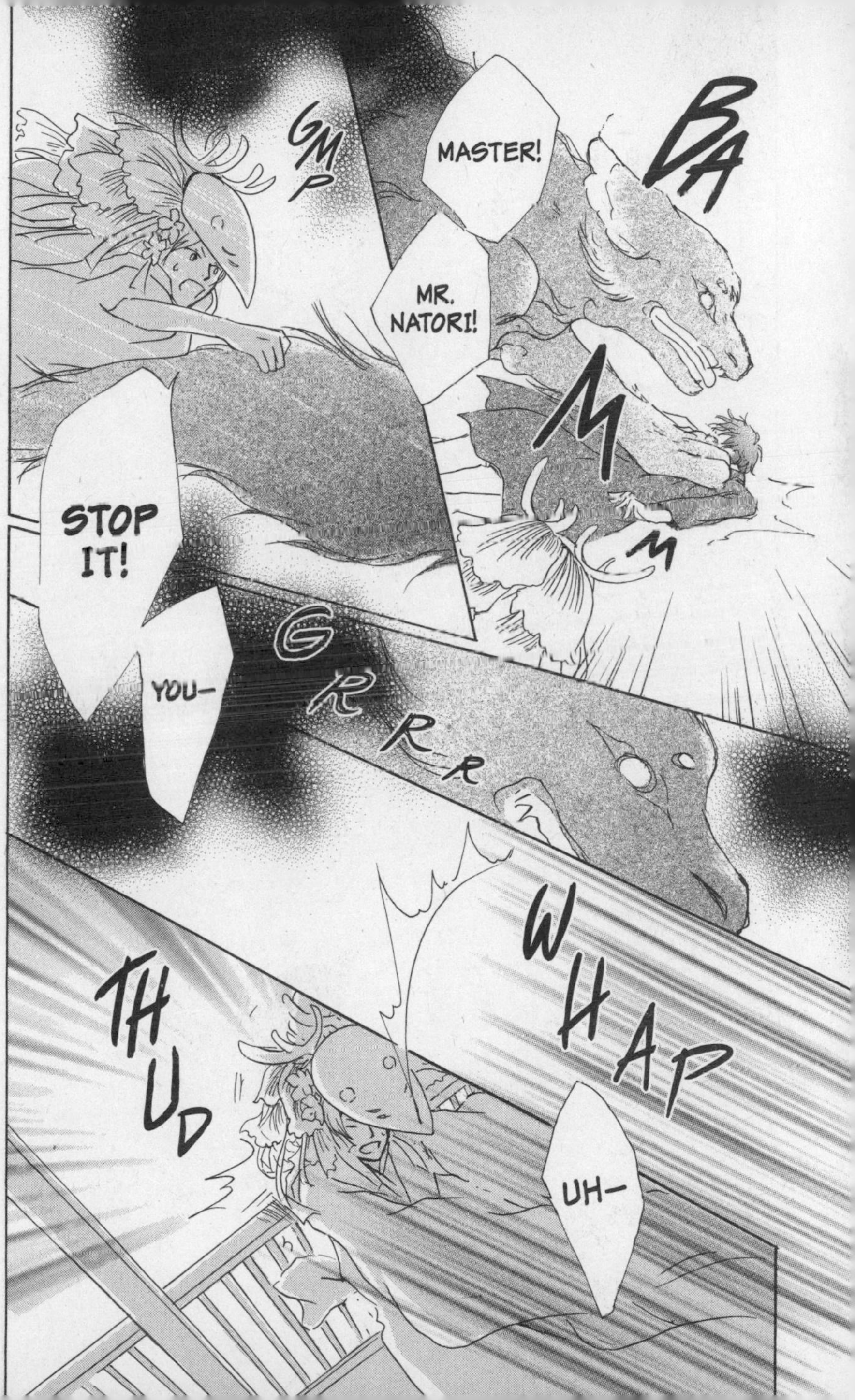
BAMM
MASTER!
MR. NATORI!
GMP
STOP IT!
YOU—
GRRR
WHAP
UH—
THUD

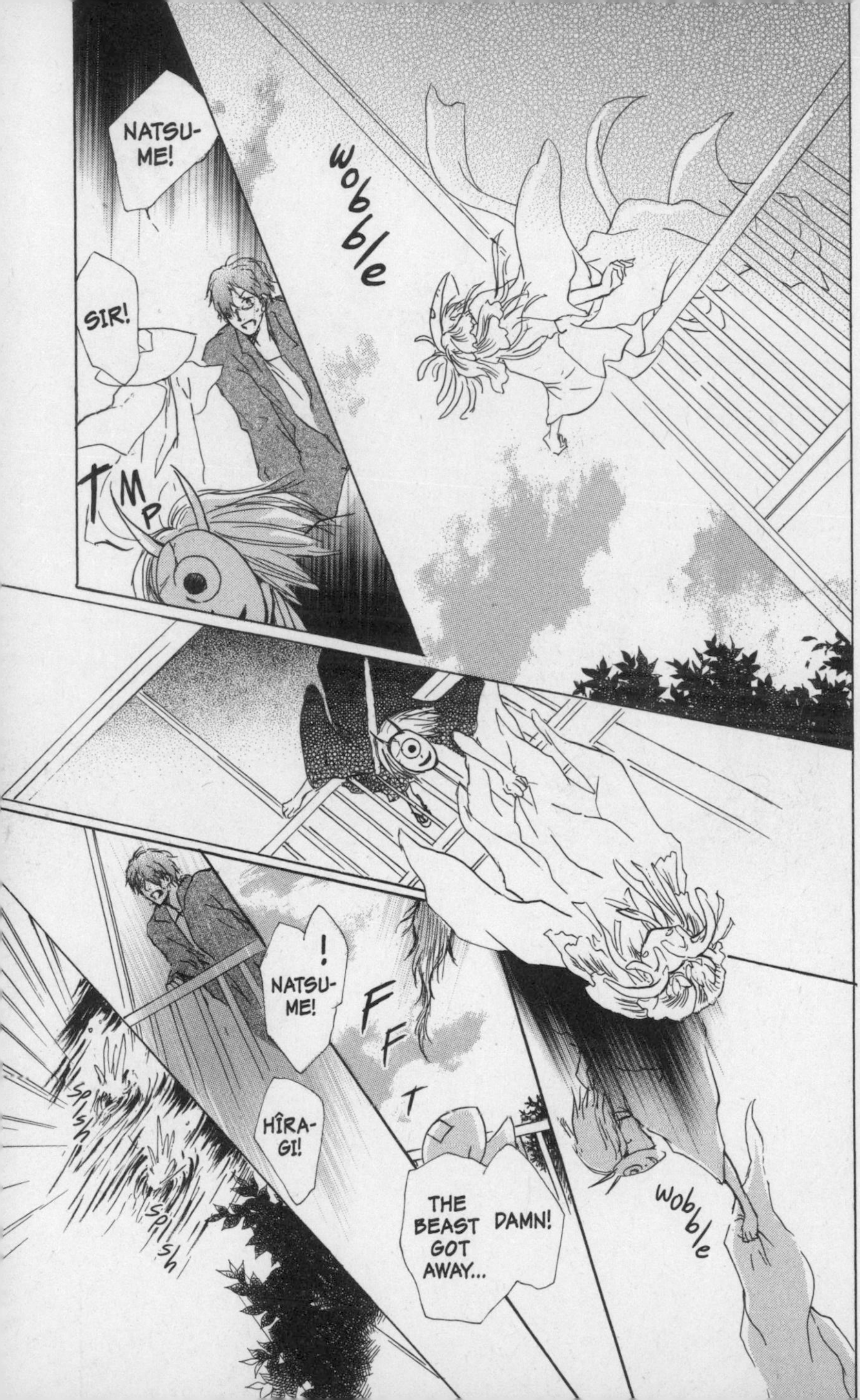
wobble
NATSU-ME!
SIR!
TMP
wobble
DAMN!
THE BEAST GOT AWAY...
FFT
!
NATSU-ME!
HÎRA-GI!
splsh
splsh

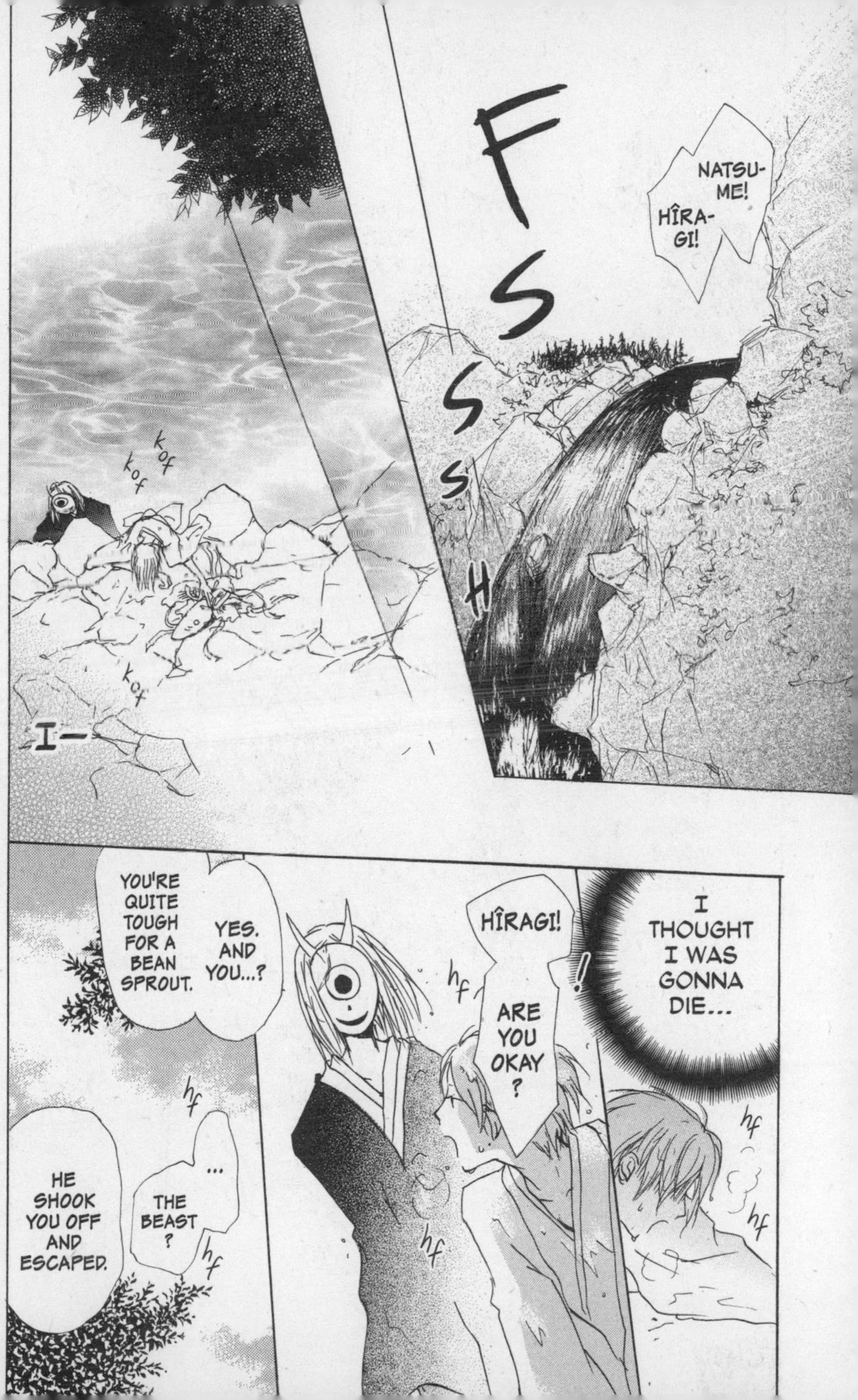
NATSU-ME! HÎRA-GI!
FSSSH
kof kof
kof
I—
I THOUGHT I WAS GONNA DIE...
!
HÎRAGI!
ARE YOU OKAY?
hf
hf
hf
YES. AND YOU...?
YOU'RE QUITE TOUGH FOR A BEAN SPROUT.
hf
hf
... THE BEAST?
hf
HE SHOOK YOU OFF AND ESCAPED.

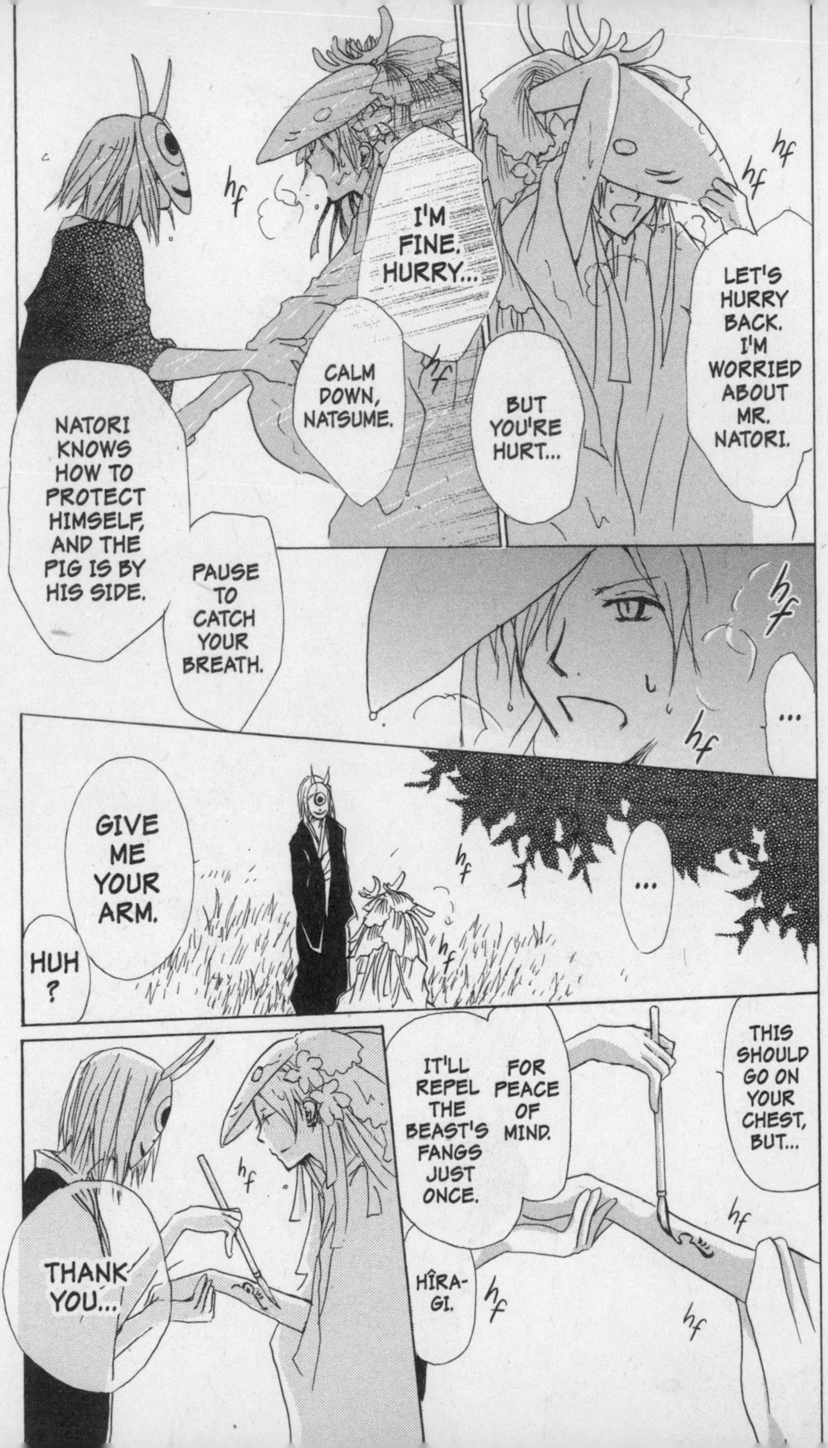
hf
hf
LET'S HURRY BACK. I'M WORRIED ABOUT MR. NATORI.
BUT YOU'RE HURT...
hf
I'M FINE. HURRY...
CALM DOWN, NATSUME.
NATORI KNOWS HOW TO PROTECT HIMSELF, AND THE PIG IS BY HIS SIDE.
PAUSE TO CATCH YOUR BREATH.
hf
hf
...
hf
...
hf
GIVE ME YOUR ARM.
HUH?
THIS SHOULD GO ON YOUR CHEST, BUT...
FOR PEACE OF MIND.
IT'LL REPEL THE BEAST'S FANGS JUST ONCE.
hf
hf
hf
HÎRAGI.
hf
THANK YOU...

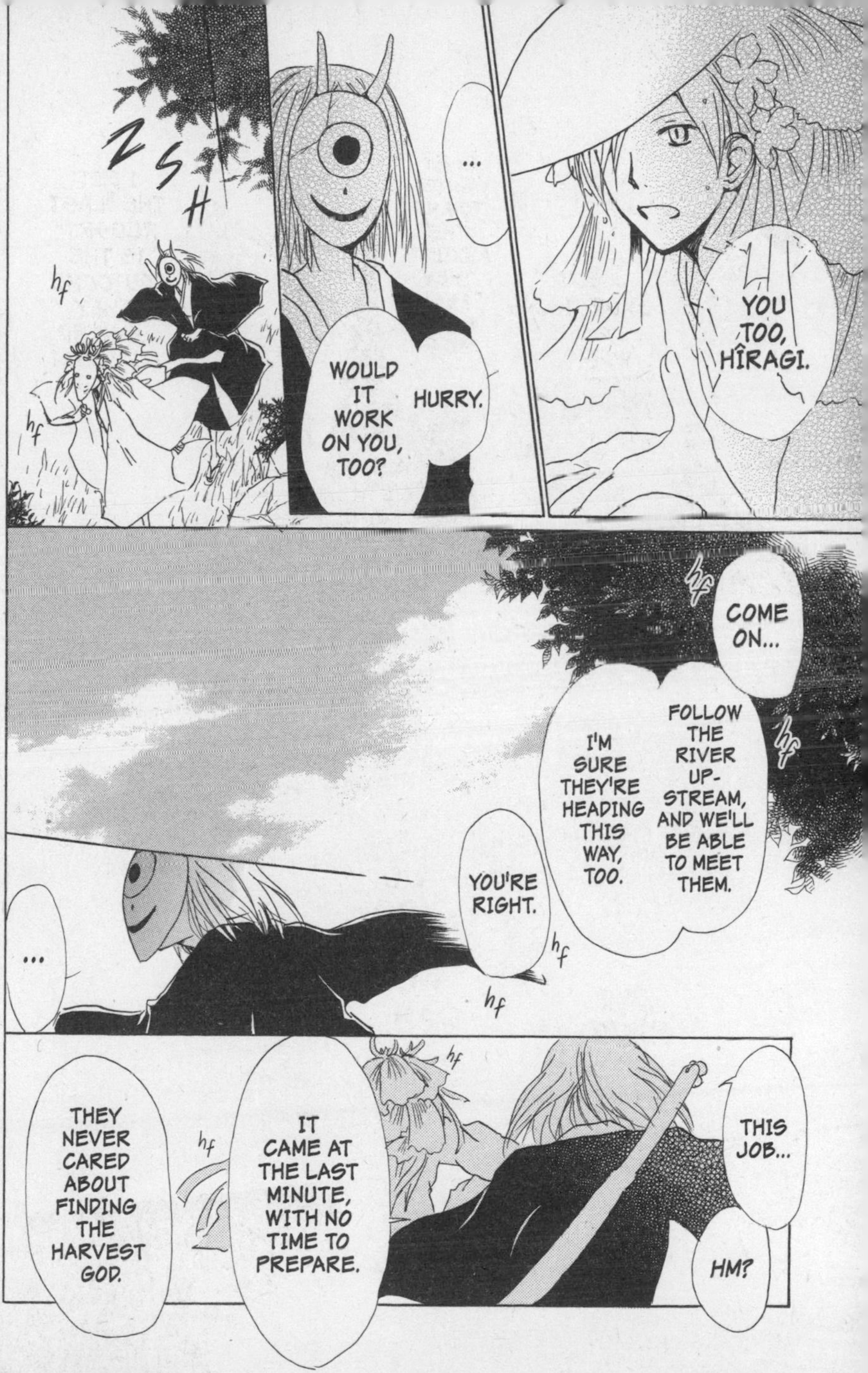

YOU TOO, HÎRAGI.
...
HURRY.
WOULD IT WORK ON YOU, TOO?
ZSH
hf
hf
hf
COME ON...
FOLLOW THE RIVER UP-STREAM, AND WE'LL BE ABLE TO MEET THEM.
hf
I'M SURE THEY'RE HEADING THIS WAY, TOO.
YOU'RE RIGHT.
hf
hf
...
THIS JOB...
HM?
hf
IT CAME AT THE LAST MINUTE, WITH NO TIME TO PREPARE.
hf
THEY NEVER CARED ABOUT FINDING THE HARVEST GOD.

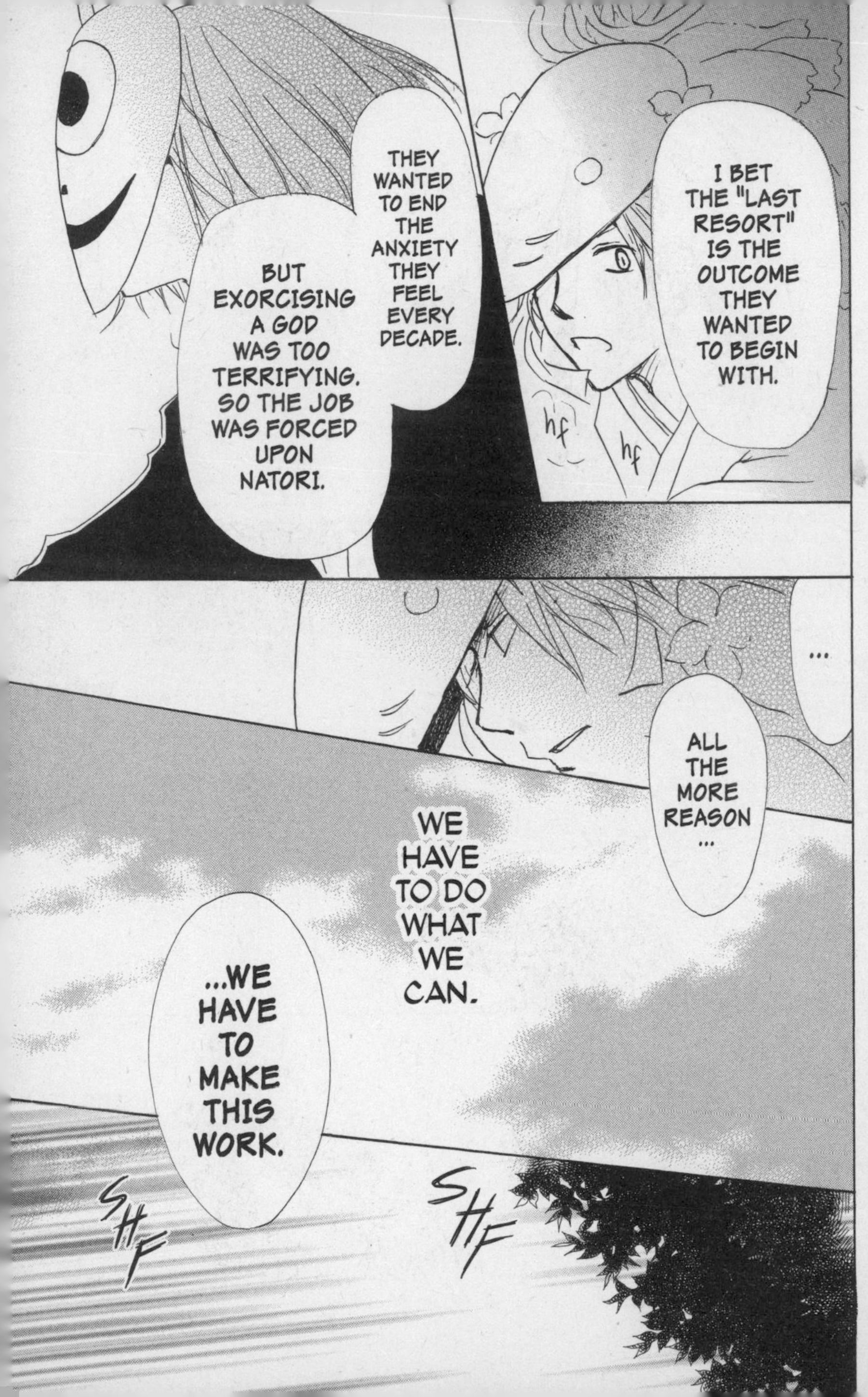
I BET THE "LAST RESORT" IS THE OUTCOME THEY WANTED TO BEGIN WITH.
hf hf
THEY WANTED TO END THE ANXIETY THEY FEEL EVERY DECADE.
BUT EXORCISING A GOD WAS TOO TERRIFYING. SO THE JOB WAS FORCED UPON NATORI.
...
ALL THE MORE REASON...
WE HAVE TO DO WHAT WE CAN.
...WE HAVE TO MAKE THIS WORK.
SHF
SHF

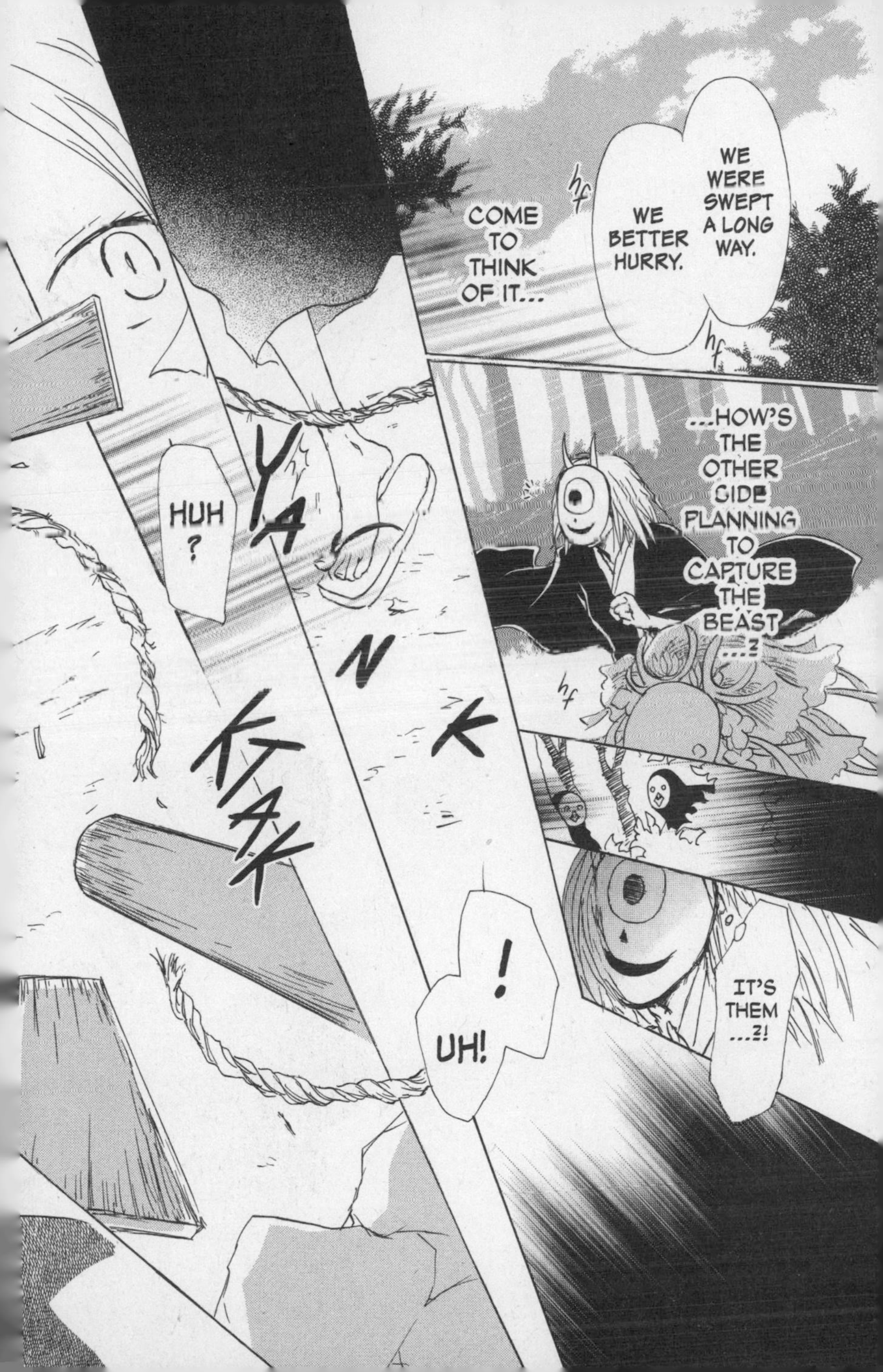
WE WERE SWEPT A LONG WAY.
WE BETTER HURRY.
hf
hf
COME TO THINK OF IT...
...HOW'S THE OTHER SIDE PLANNING TO CAPTURE THE BEAST ...?
hf
IT'S THEM ...?!
HUH?
YANK
KTAK
!
UH!

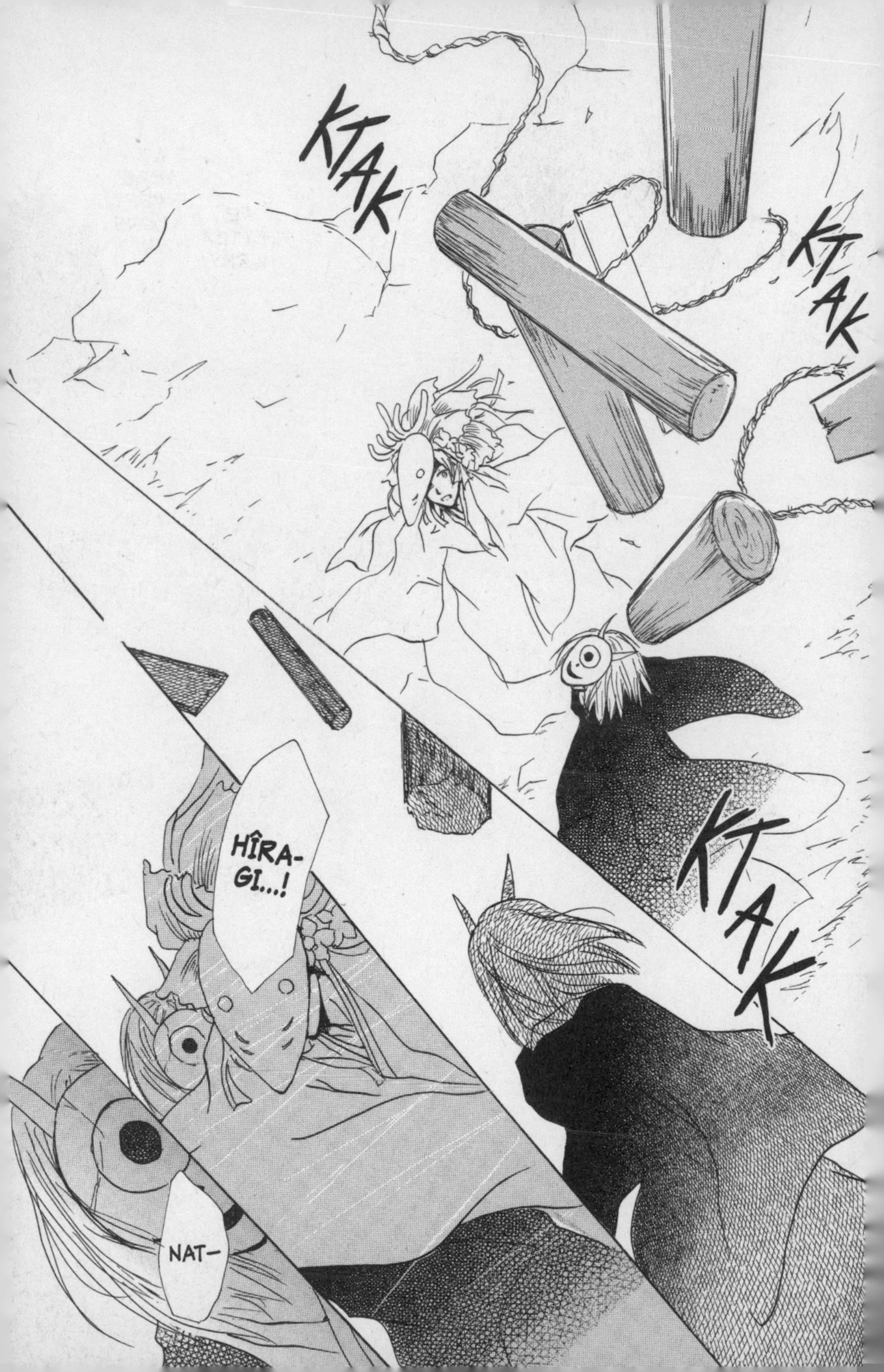
KTAK
KTAK
KTAK
HÎRA-GI...!
NAT–

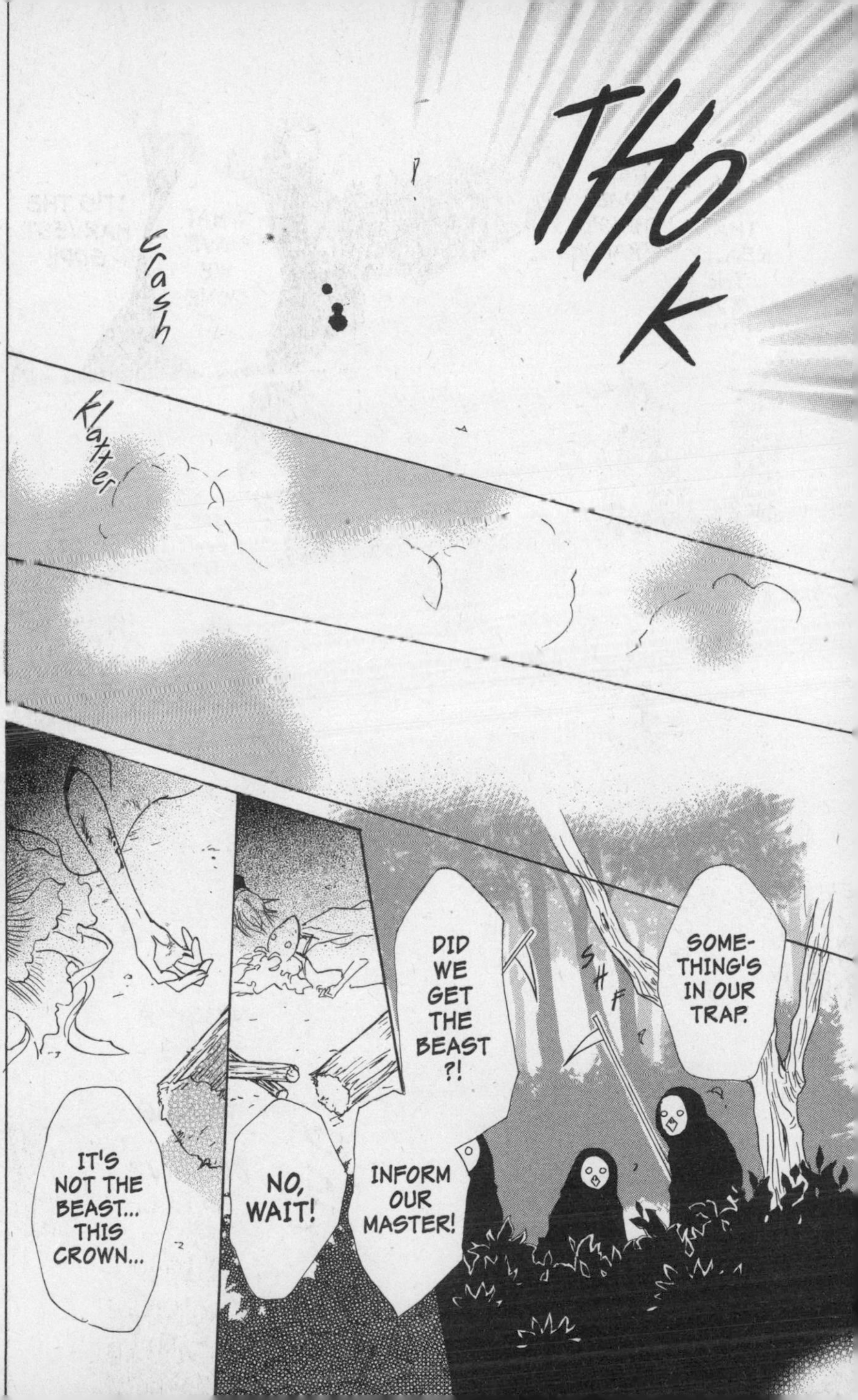
THOK
Crash
Klatter
SOME-THING'S IN OUR TRAP.
SHF
DID WE GET THE BEAST?!
INFORM OUR MASTER!
NO, WAIT!
IT'S NOT THE BEAST... THIS CROWN...

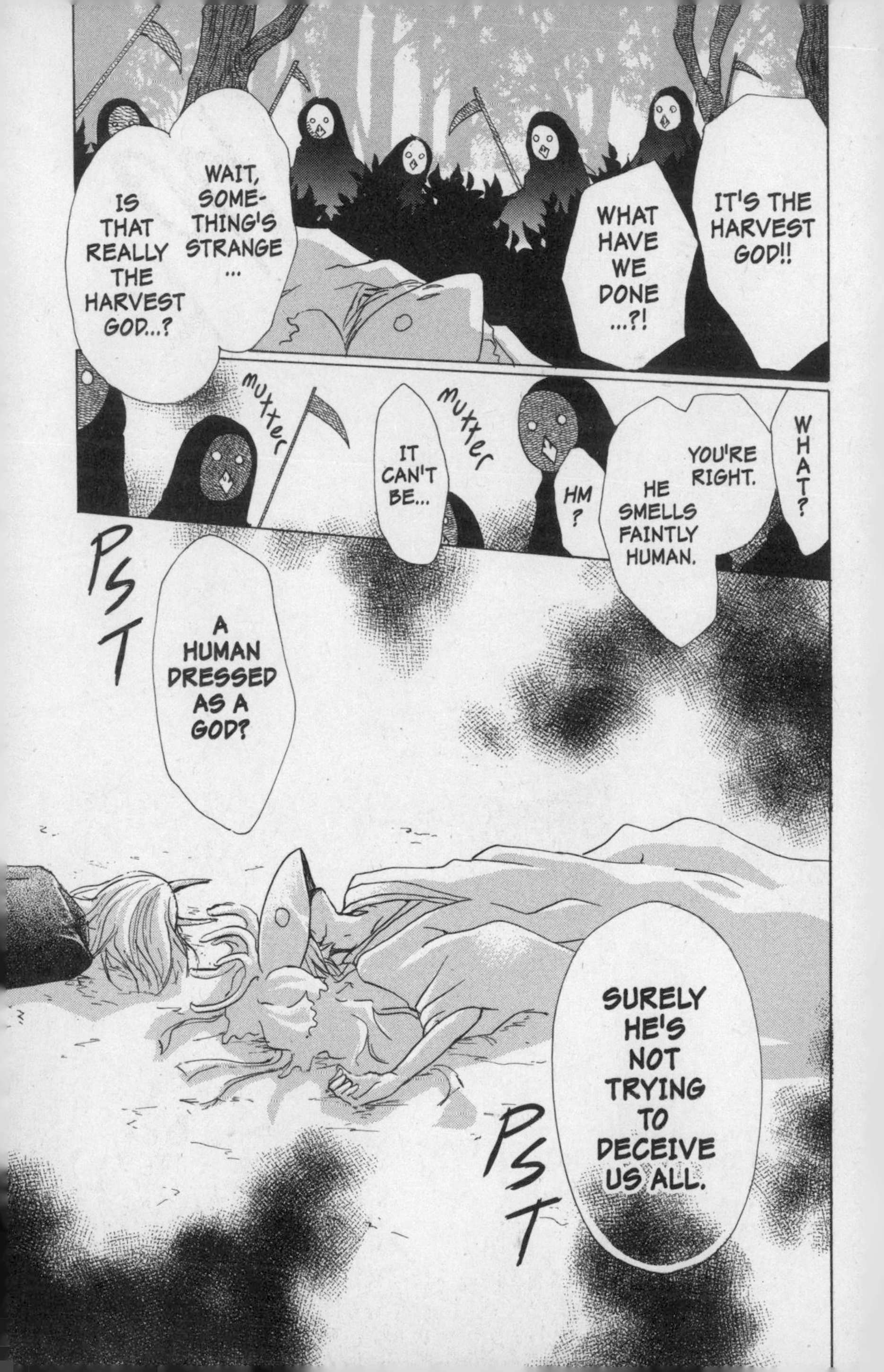
IT'S THE HARVEST GOD!!
WHAT HAVE WE DONE ...?!
WAIT, SOMETHING'S STRANGE ...
IS THAT REALLY THE HARVEST GOD...?
WHAT?
YOU'RE RIGHT.
HE SMELLS FAINTLY HUMAN.
HM?
mutter
IT CAN'T BE...
mutter
PST
A HUMAN DRESSED AS A GOD?
SURELY HE'S NOT TRYING TO DECEIVE US ALL.
PST

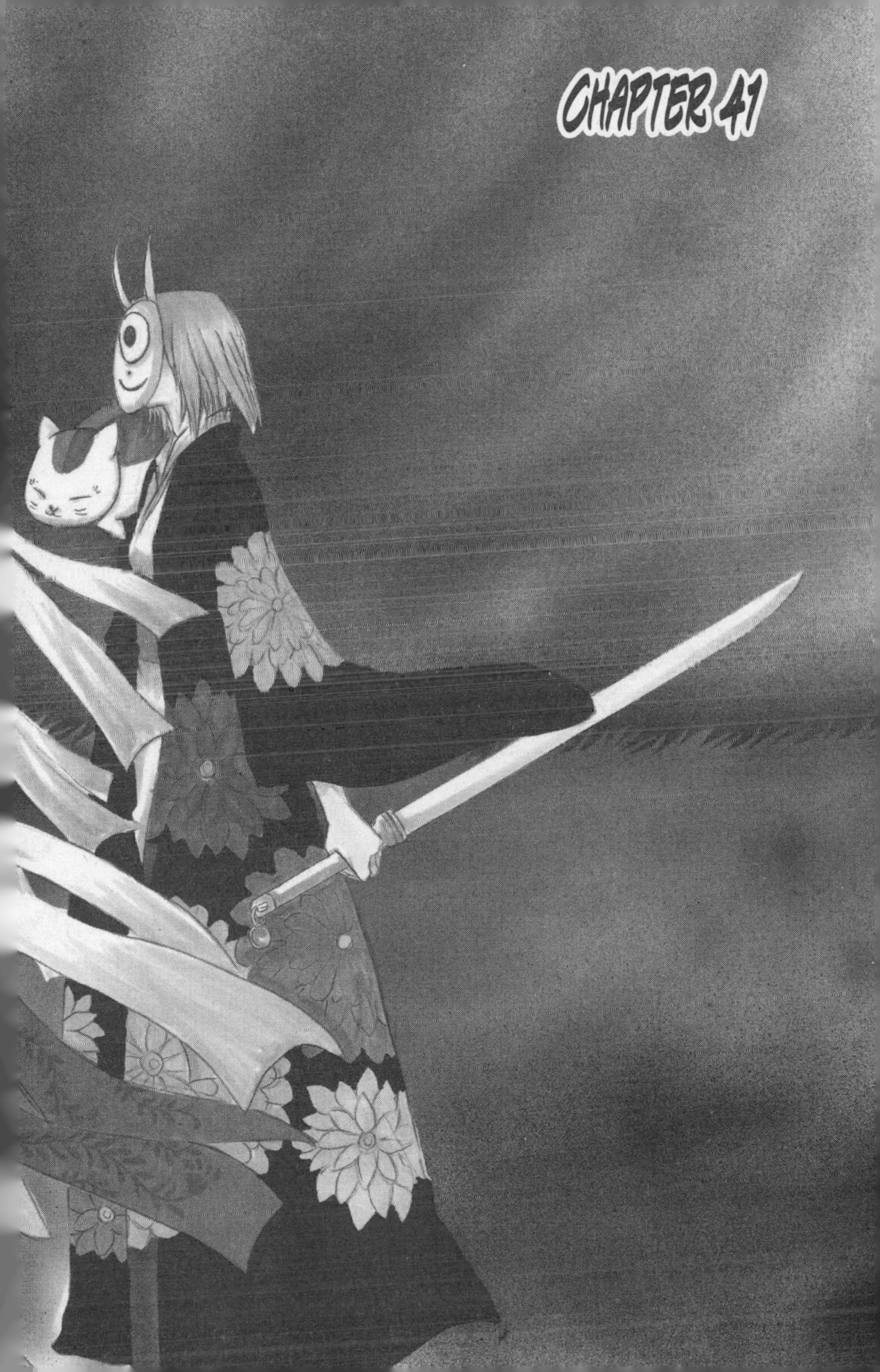
CHAPTER 41

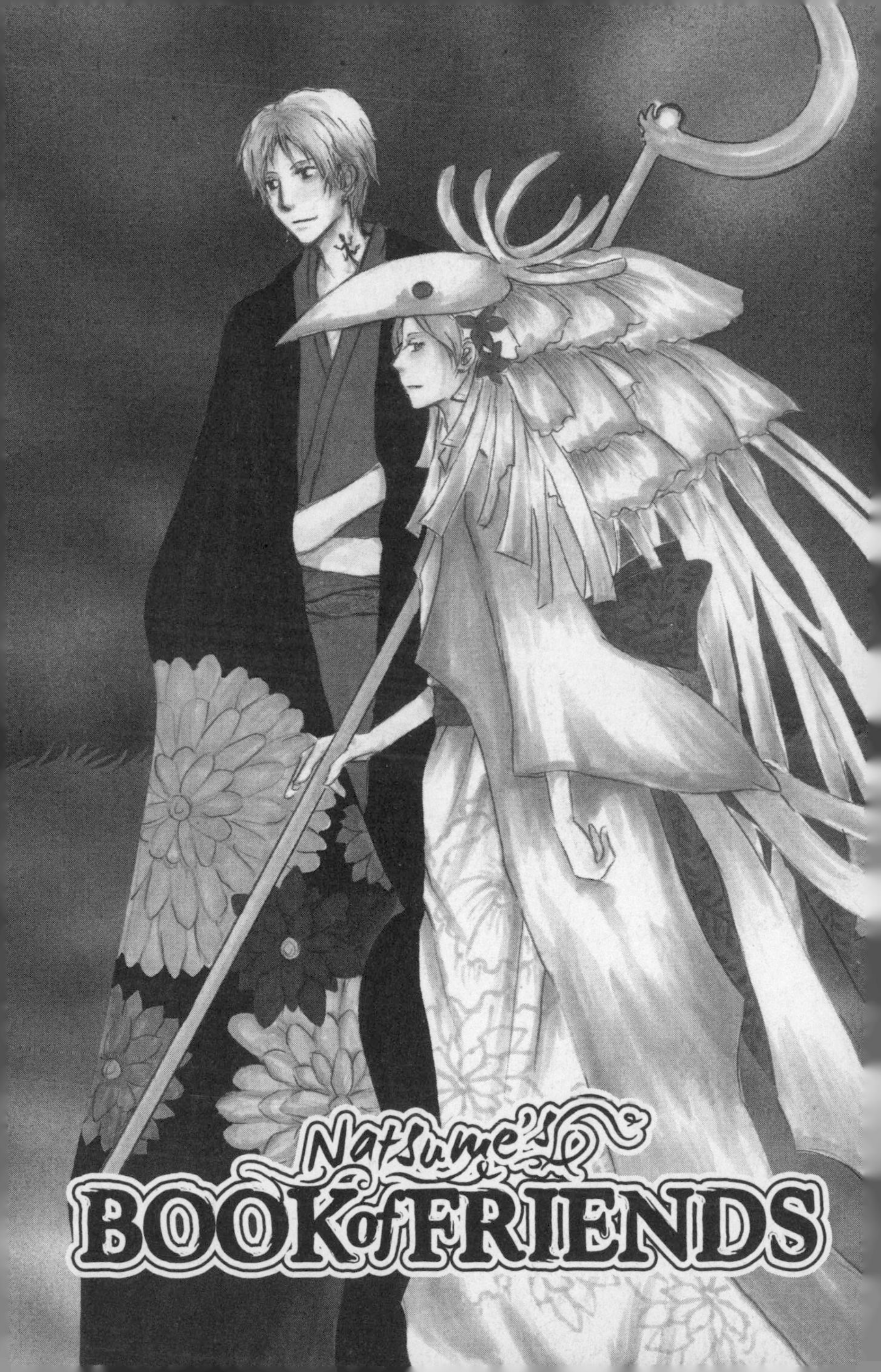
Natsume's
BOOK of FRIENDS

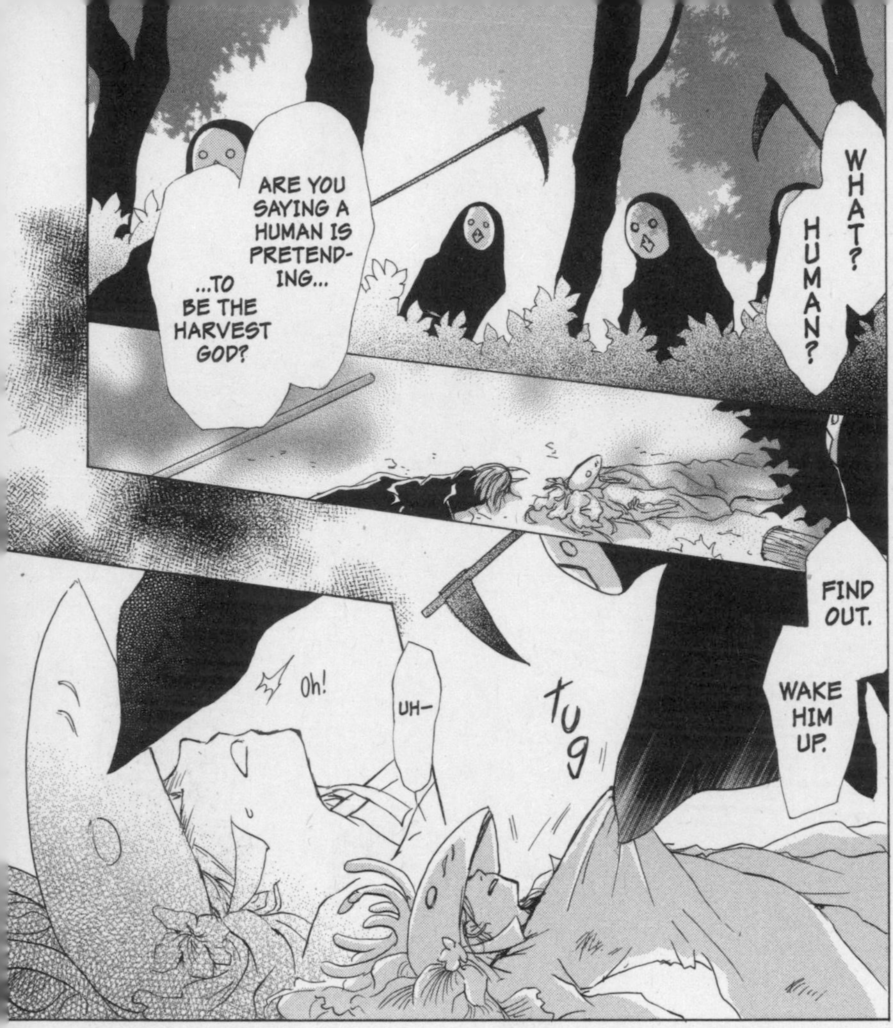
WHAT? HUMAN?
ARE YOU SAYING A HUMAN IS PRETEND-ING...
...TO BE THE HARVEST GOD?
FIND OUT.
WAKE HIM UP.
TUG
UH-
Oh!

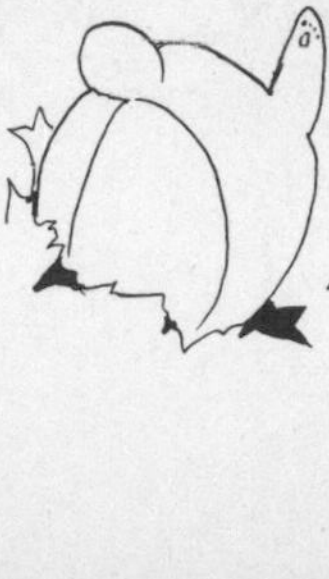

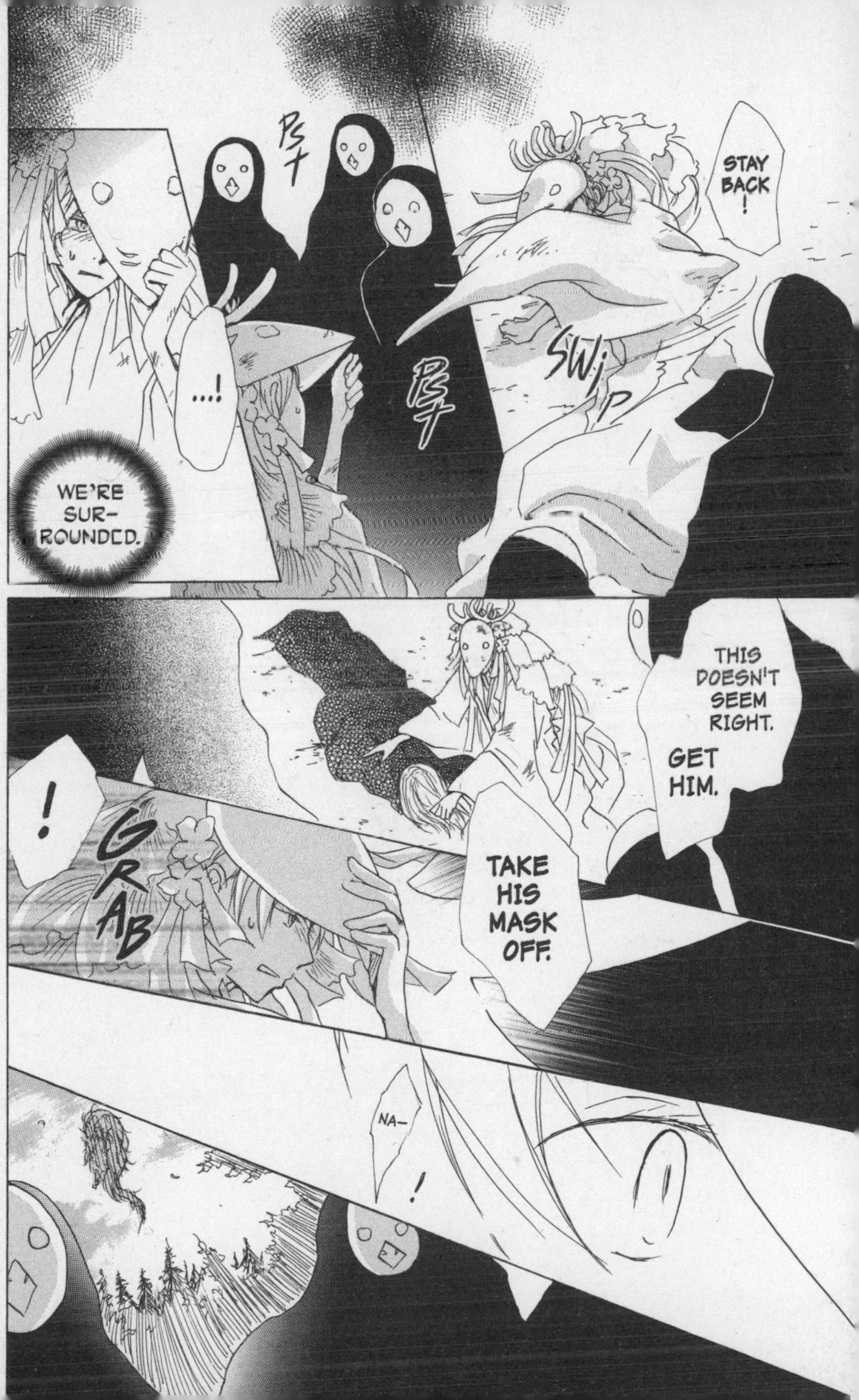
STAY BACK!
SWIP
PST
PST
...!
WE'RE SURROUNDED.
THIS DOESN'T SEEM RIGHT.
GET HIM.
TAKE HIS MASK OFF.
!
GRAB
NA-
!

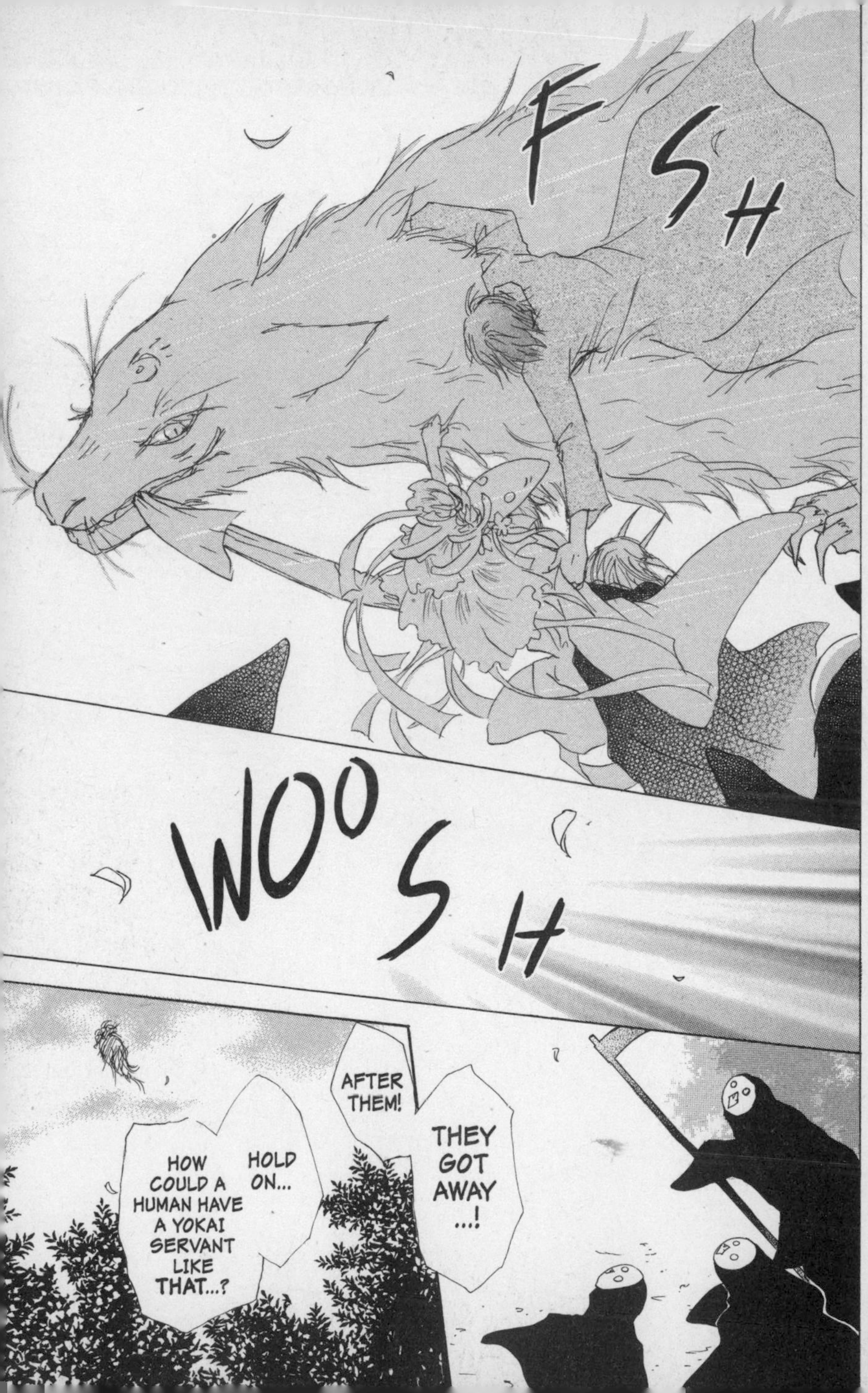
FSH
WOOSH
THEY GOT AWAY ...!
AFTER THEM!
HOLD ON...
HOW COULD A HUMAN HAVE A YOKAI SERVANT LIKE THAT...?

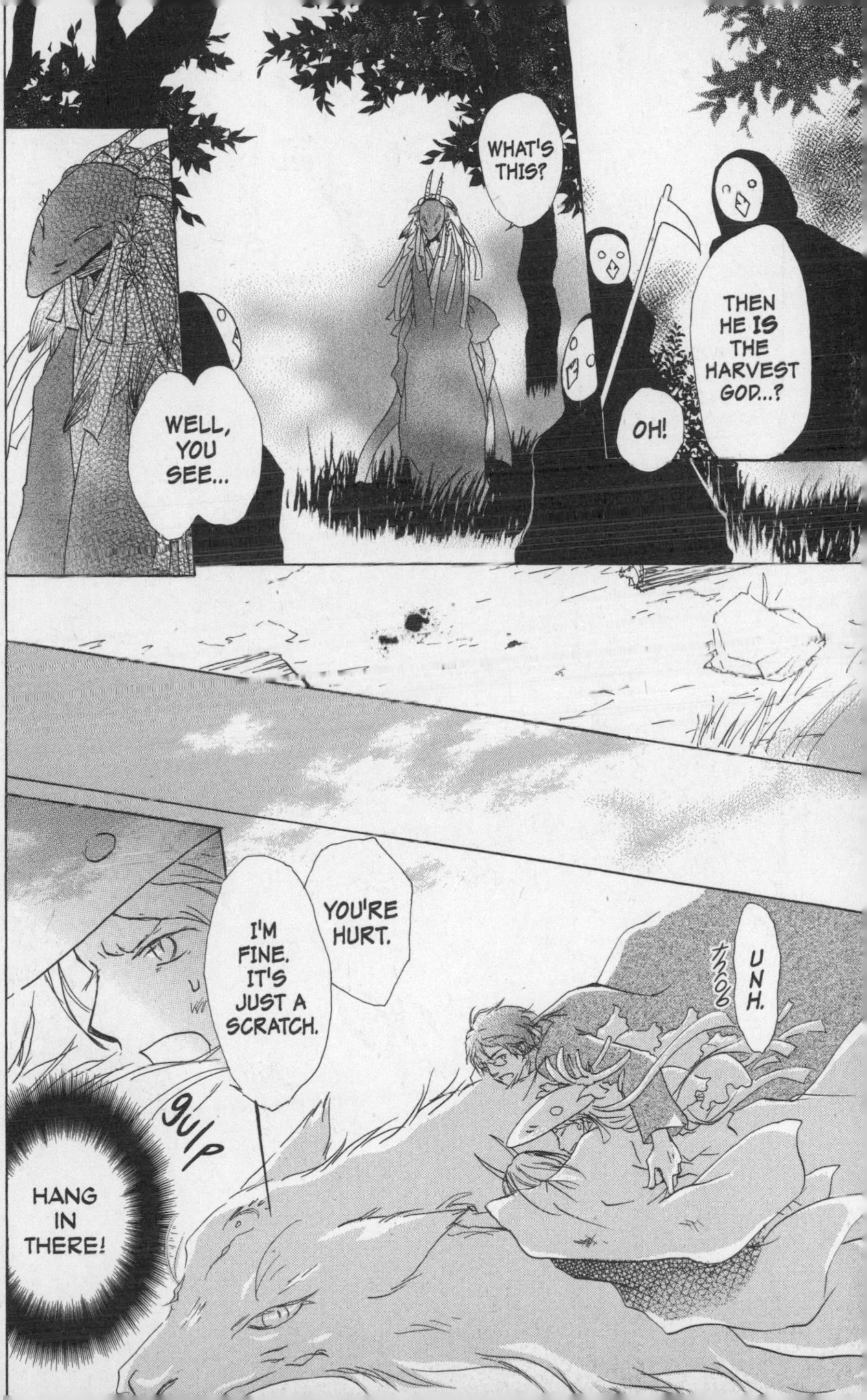
THEN HE IS THE HARVEST GOD...?
WHAT'S THIS?
OH!
WELL, YOU SEE...
UNH.
YOU'RE HURT.
I'M FINE. IT'S JUST A SCRATCH.
gulp
HANG IN THERE!

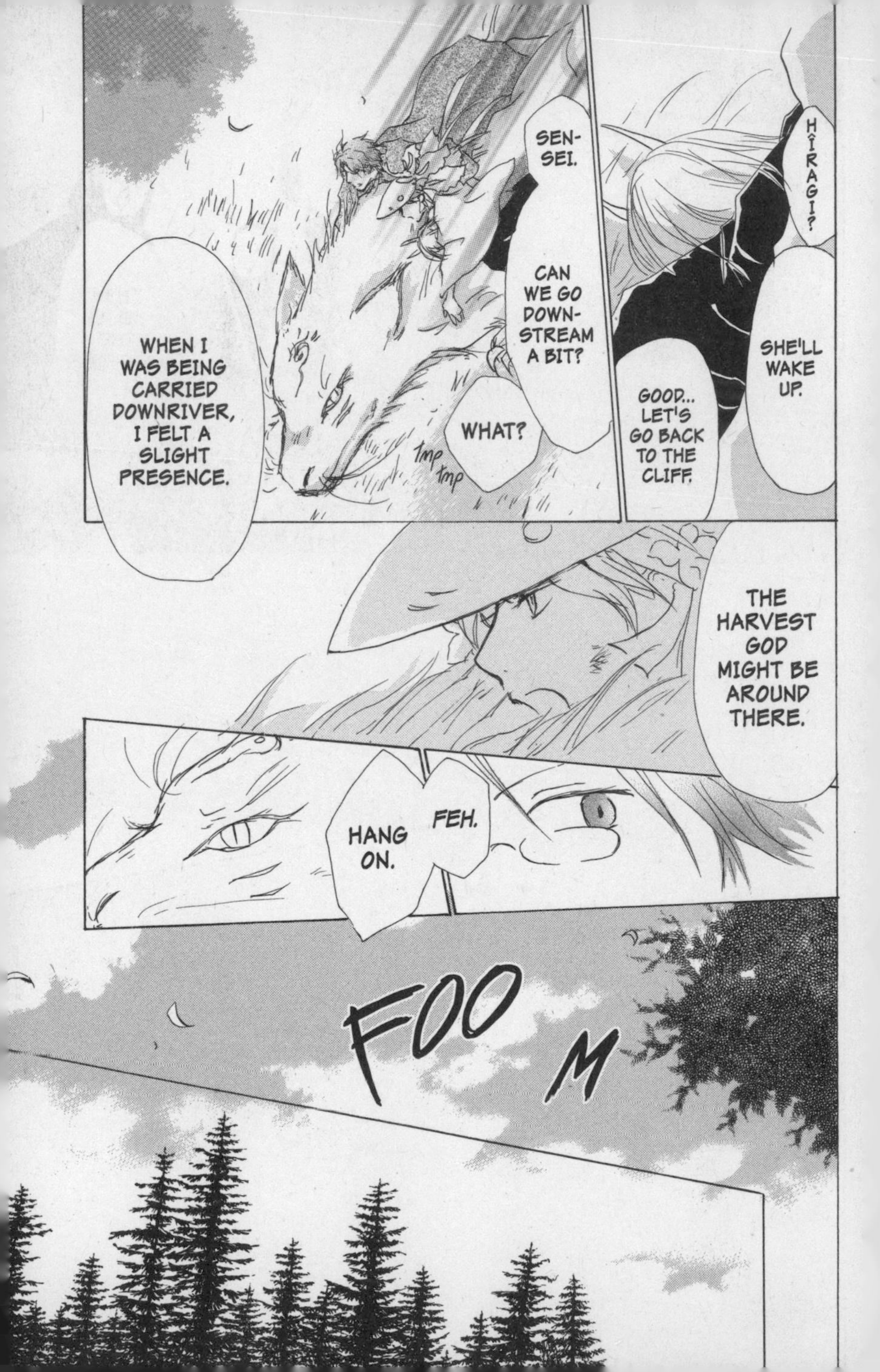
HÎRAGI?
SHE'LL WAKE UP.
GOOD... LET'S GO BACK TO THE CLIFF.
SEN-SEI.
CAN WE GO DOWN-STREAM A BIT?
WHAT?
tmp tmp
WHEN I WAS BEING CARRIED DOWNRIVER, I FELT A SLIGHT PRESENCE.
THE HARVEST GOD MIGHT BE AROUND THERE.
FEH.
HANG ON.
FOOM

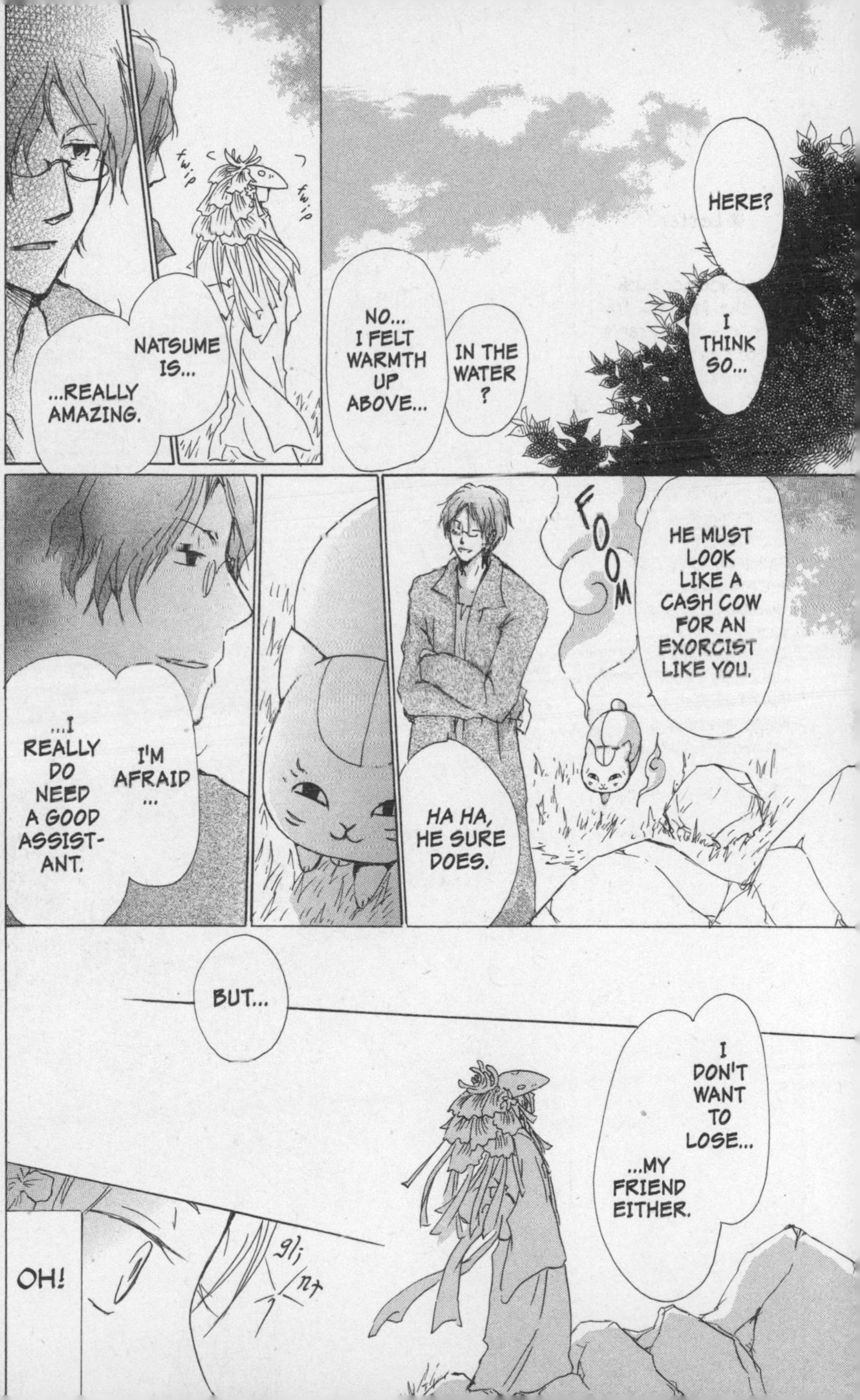
HERE?
I THINK SO...
IN THE WATER?
NO... I FELT WARMTH UP ABOVE...
twip
twip
NATSUME IS...
...REALLY AMAZING.
FOOM
HE MUST LOOK LIKE A CASH COW FOR AN EXORCIST LIKE YOU.
HA HA, HE SURE DOES.
I'M AFRAID...
...I REALLY DO NEED A GOOD ASSIST-ANT.
BUT...
I DON'T WANT TO LOSE...
...MY FRIEND EITHER.
glint
OH!

05

❋ Letters

Thank you so much for the fan mail. I'm so sorry that I can't write replies to everyone, but I read every single letter I receive. Some people reported that they visited Kumamoto after watching the anime. Others wrote kind feedback, and some people even sent their own illustrations of their favorite characters. I cherish as my treasures all the hand-made gifts and local souvenirs they send.

Thank you so much.

End of $\frac{1}{4}$ columns.

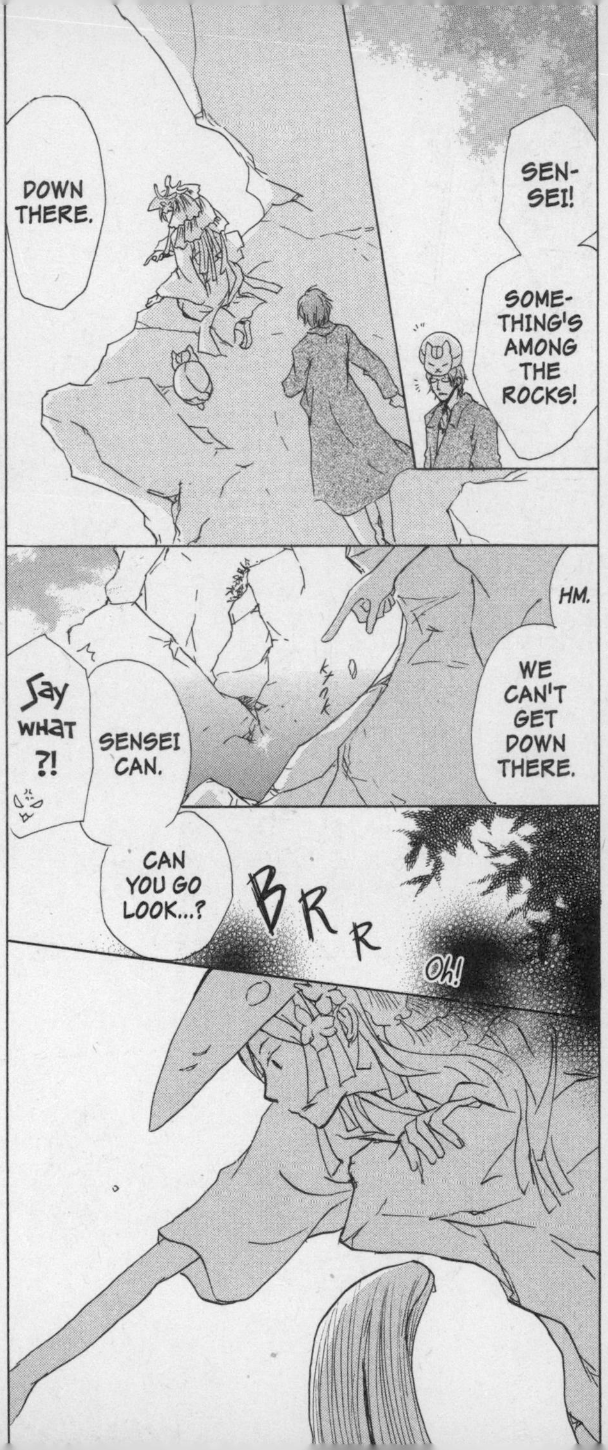
SEN-SEI!
SOME-THING'S AMONG THE ROCKS!
DOWN THERE.
HM.
WE CAN'T GET DOWN THERE.
SENSEI CAN.
Say WHAT?!
CAN YOU GO LOOK...?
BRRR
OH!

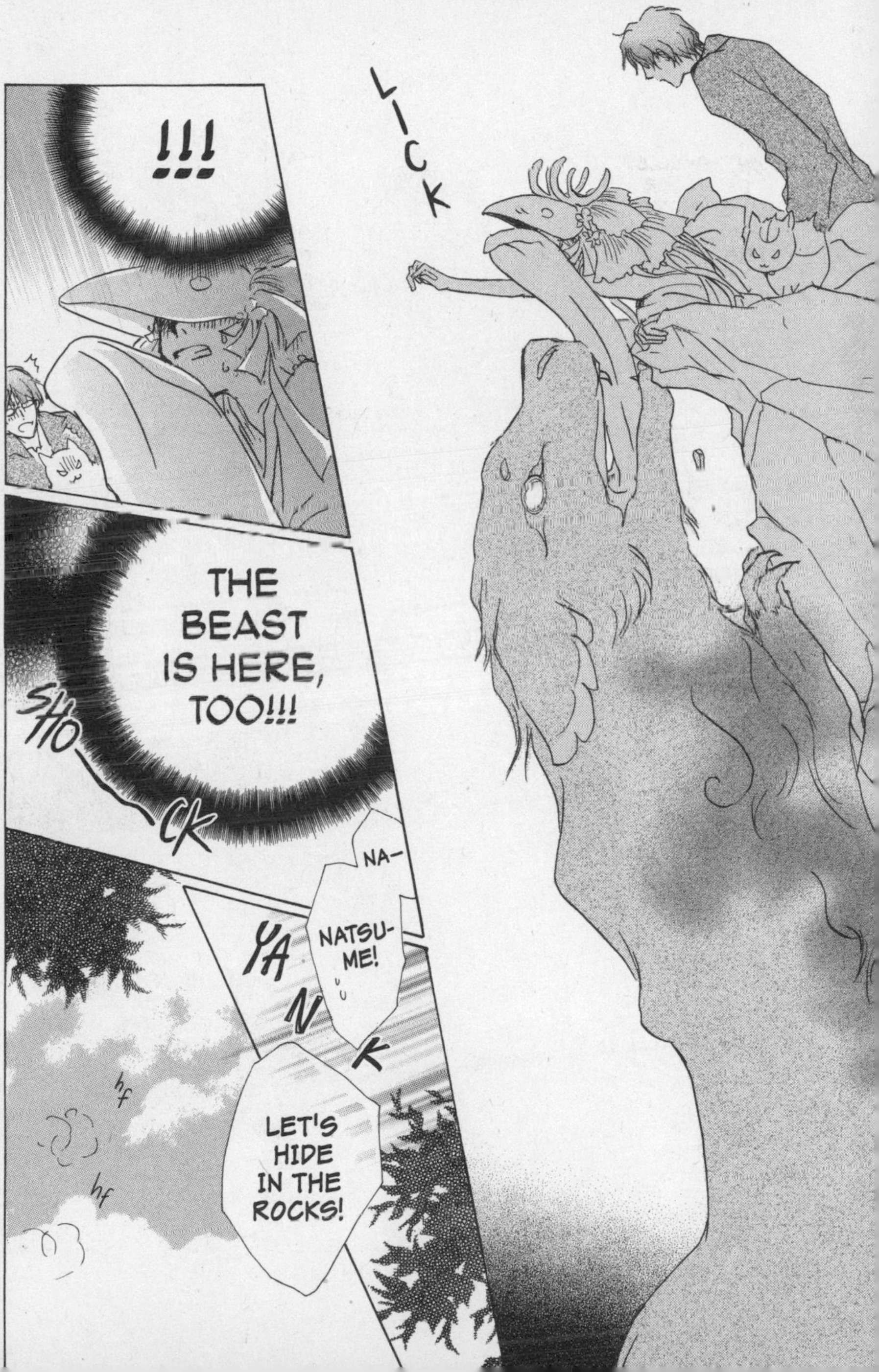
LICK
!!!
THE BEAST IS HERE, TOO!!!
SHOCK
NA-
NATSU-ME!
YANK
LET'S HIDE IN THE ROCKS!
hf
hf

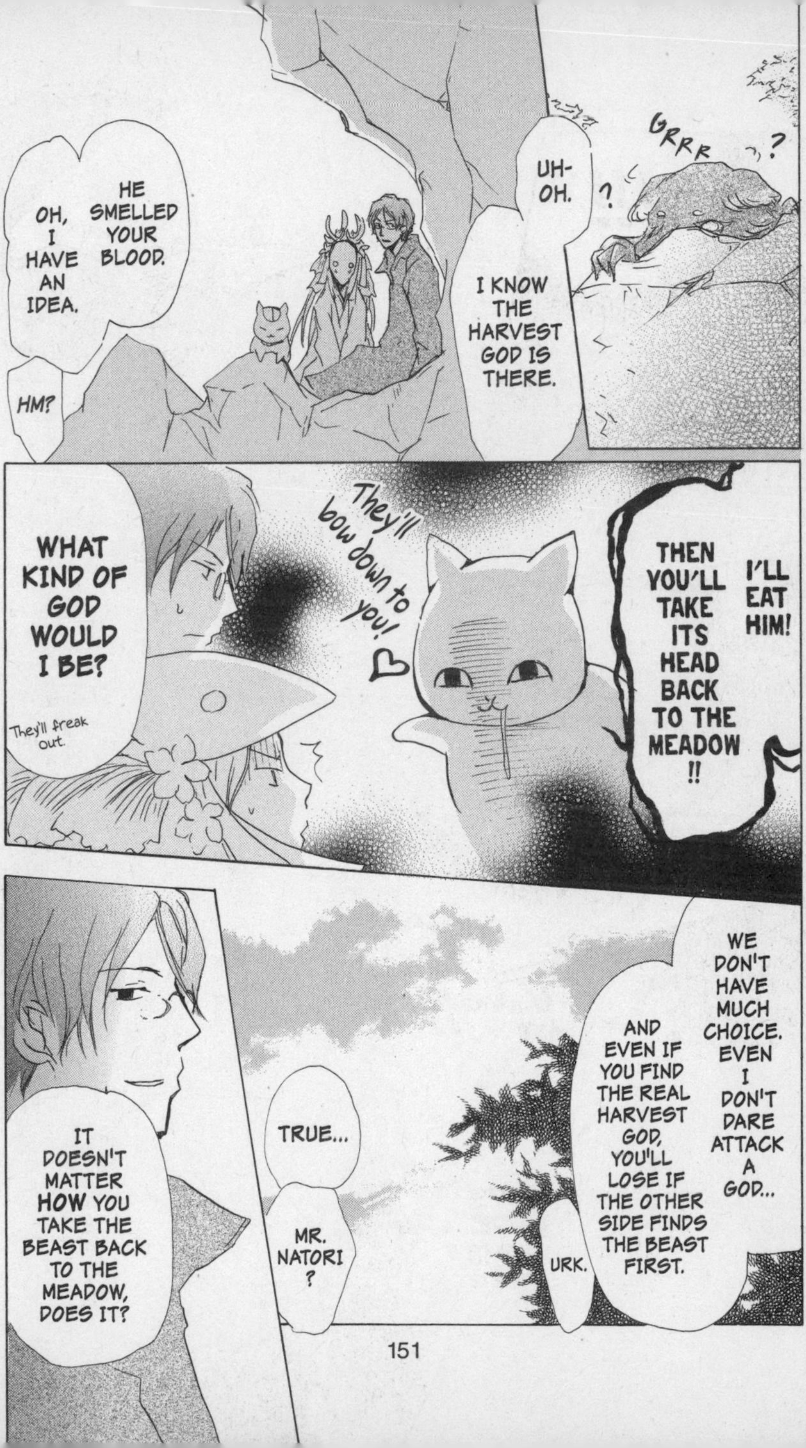
GRRR
?
?
UH-OH.
I KNOW THE HARVEST GOD IS THERE.
HE SMELLED YOUR BLOOD.
OH, I HAVE AN IDEA.
HM?
I'LL EAT HIM!
THEN YOU'LL TAKE ITS HEAD BACK TO THE MEADOW!!
They'll bow down to you!
WHAT KIND OF GOD WOULD I BE?
They'll freak out.
WE DON'T HAVE MUCH CHOICE. EVEN I DON'T DARE ATTACK A GOD...
AND EVEN IF YOU FIND THE REAL HARVEST GOD, YOU'LL LOSE IF THE OTHER SIDE FINDS THE BEAST FIRST.
URK.
TRUE...
MR. NATORI?
IT DOESN'T MATTER HOW YOU TAKE THE BEAST BACK TO THE MEADOW, DOES IT?

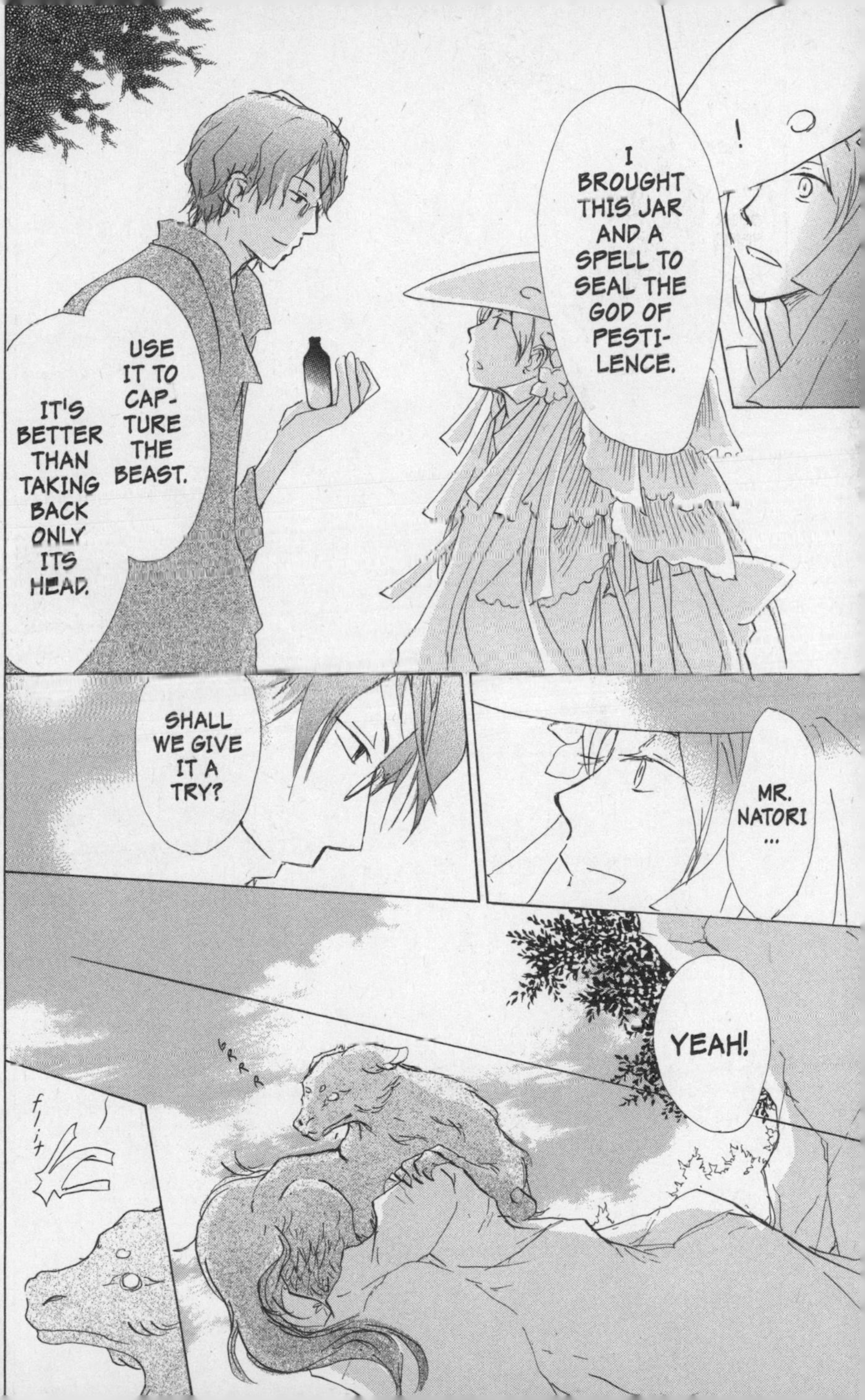
!
I BROUGHT THIS JAR AND A SPELL TO SEAL THE GOD OF PESTILENCE.
USE IT TO CAPTURE THE BEAST.
IT'S BETTER THAN TAKING BACK ONLY ITS HEAD.
MR. NATORI...
SHALL WE GIVE IT A TRY?
YEAH!
GRRR
flit

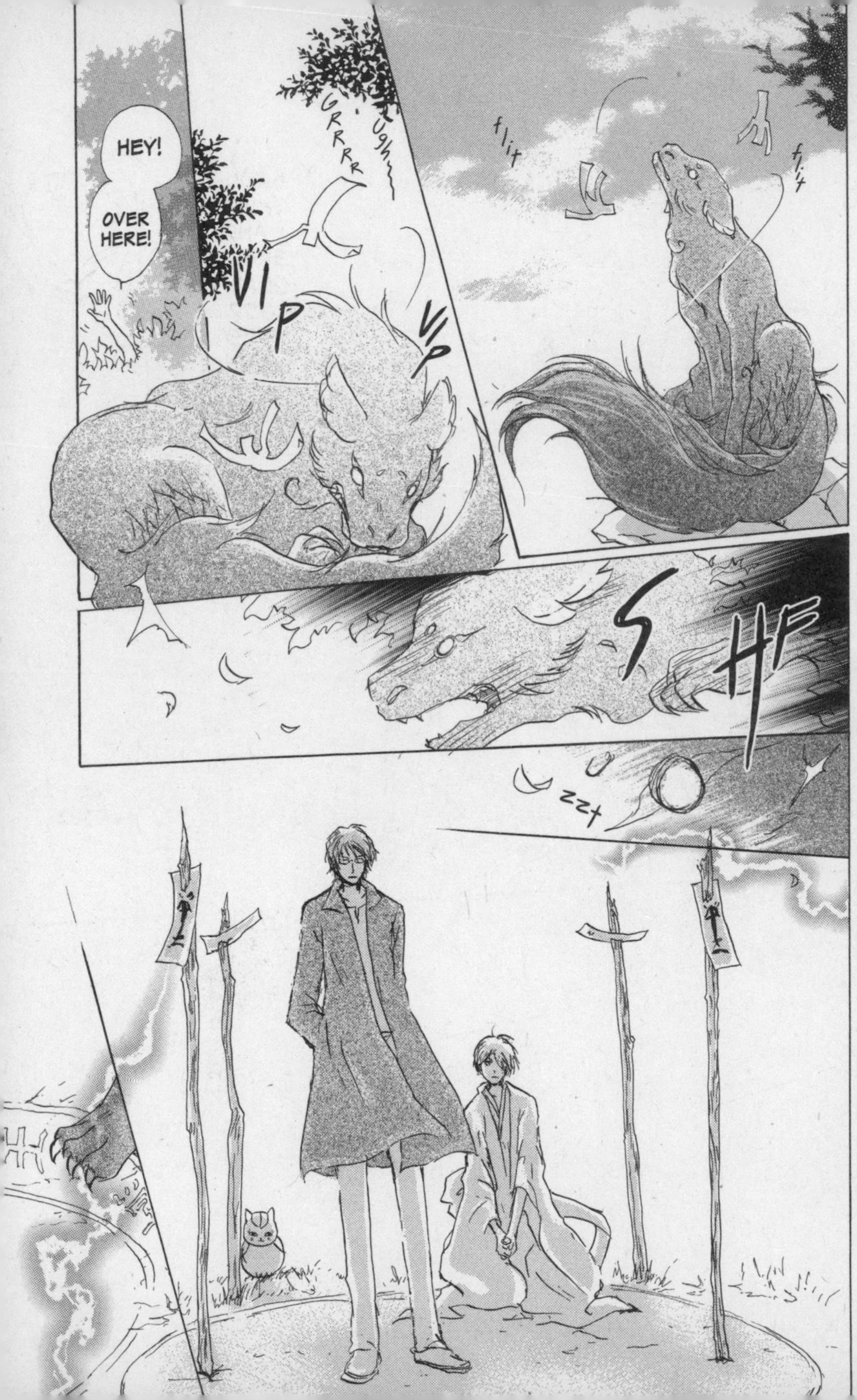
flit
flit
HEY!
OVER HERE!
GRRRR
Ugh
VIP
VIP
SHF
zzt

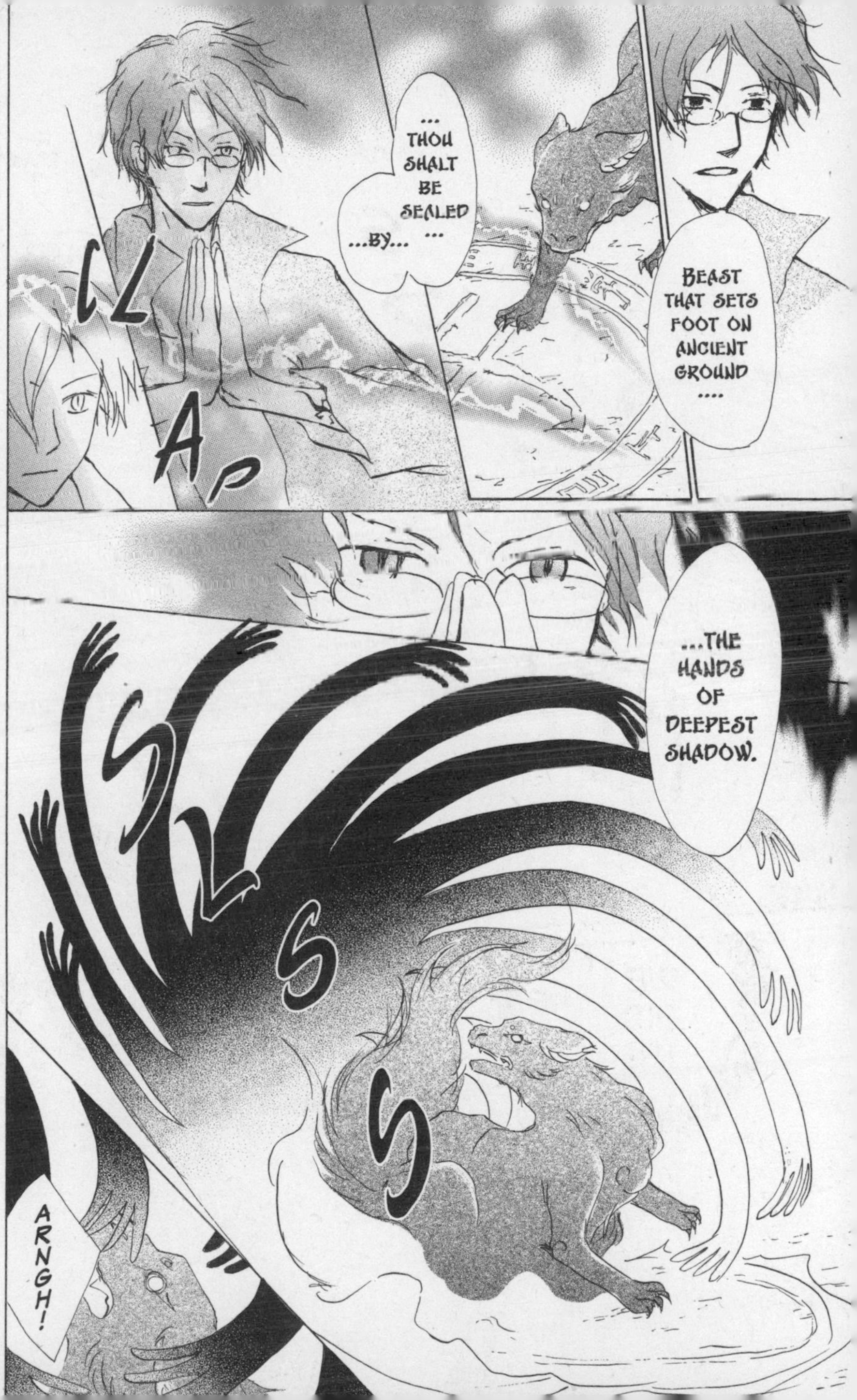
BEAST THAT SETS FOOT ON ANCIENT GROUND ....
... THOU SHALT BE SEALED ...
...BY...
CLAP
...THE HANDS OF DEEPEST SHADOW.
ARNGH!

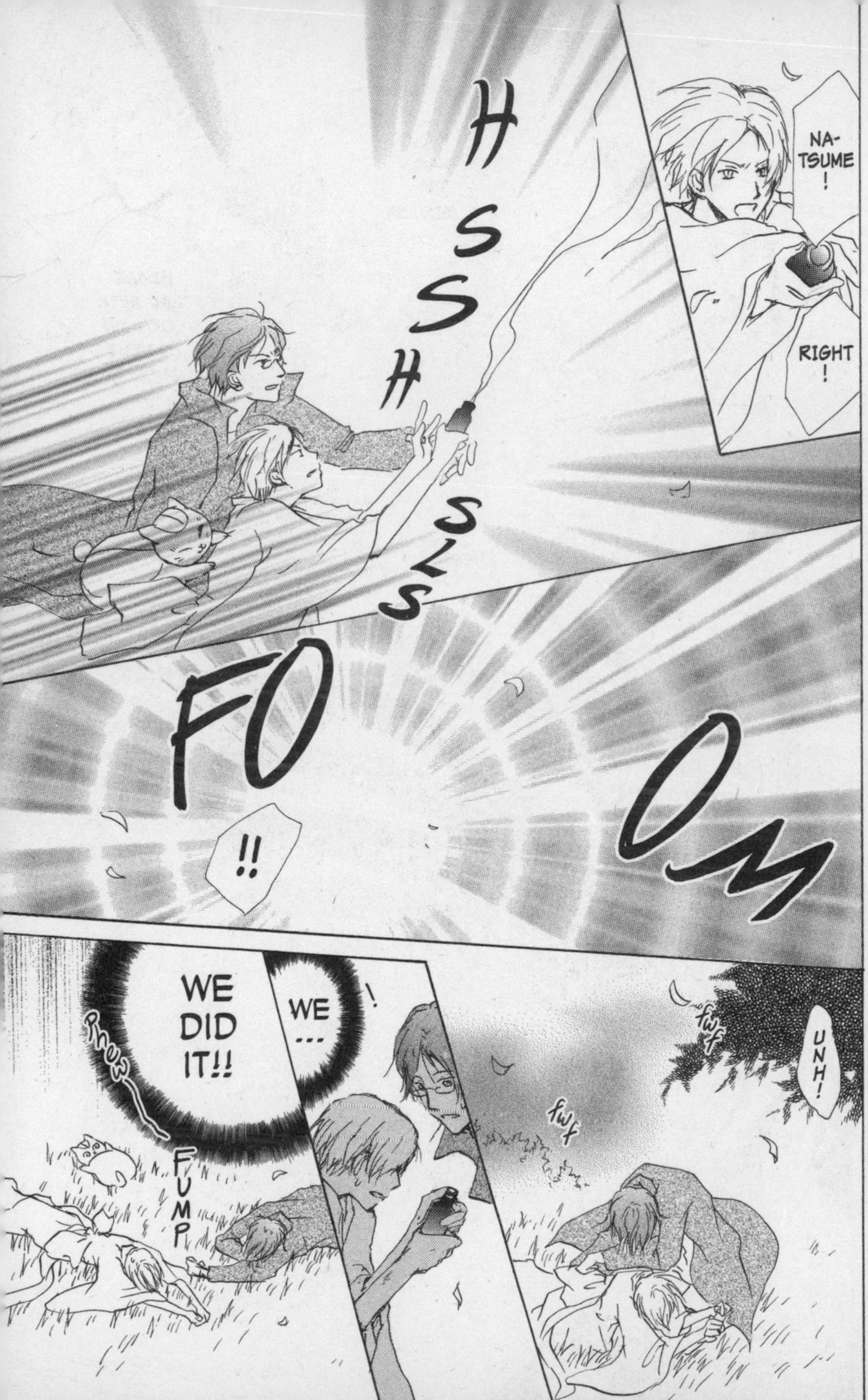
NA-TSUME!
RIGHT!
HSSH
SSS
FOOM
!!
fwf
fwf
UNH!
!
WE...
WE DID IT!!
Phew—
FUMP

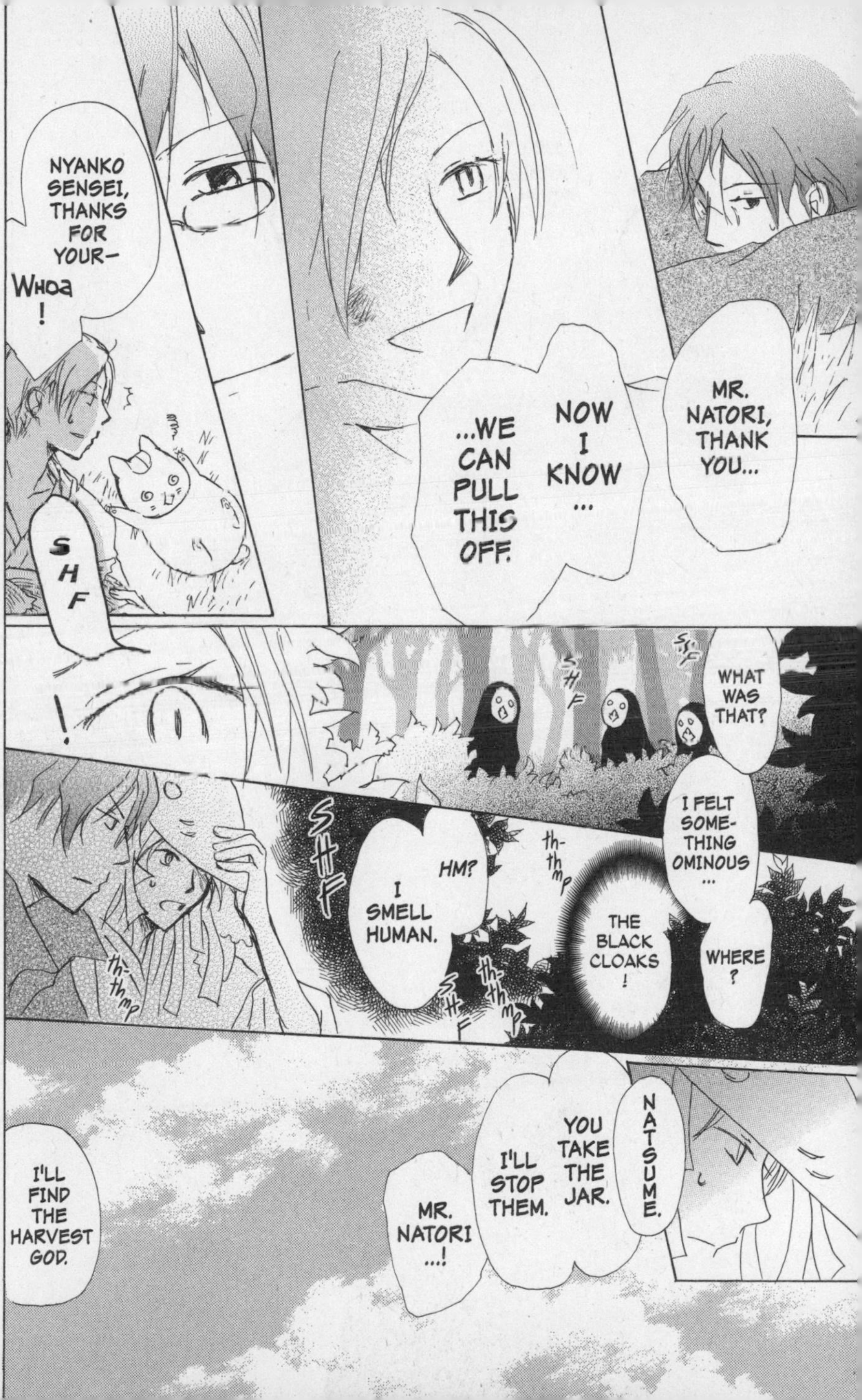
MR. NATORI, THANK YOU...
NOW I KNOW...
...WE CAN PULL THIS OFF.
NYANKO SENSEI, THANKS FOR YOUR—
Whoa !
SHF
!
SHF
SHF
WHAT WAS THAT?
I FELT SOMETHING OMINOUS...
WHERE?
THE BLACK CLOAKS!
th-thmp
th-thmp
HM?
I SMELL HUMAN.
SHF
SHF
th-thmp
NATSUME.
YOU TAKE THE JAR.
I'LL STOP THEM.
MR. NATORI...!
I'LL FIND THE HARVEST GOD.

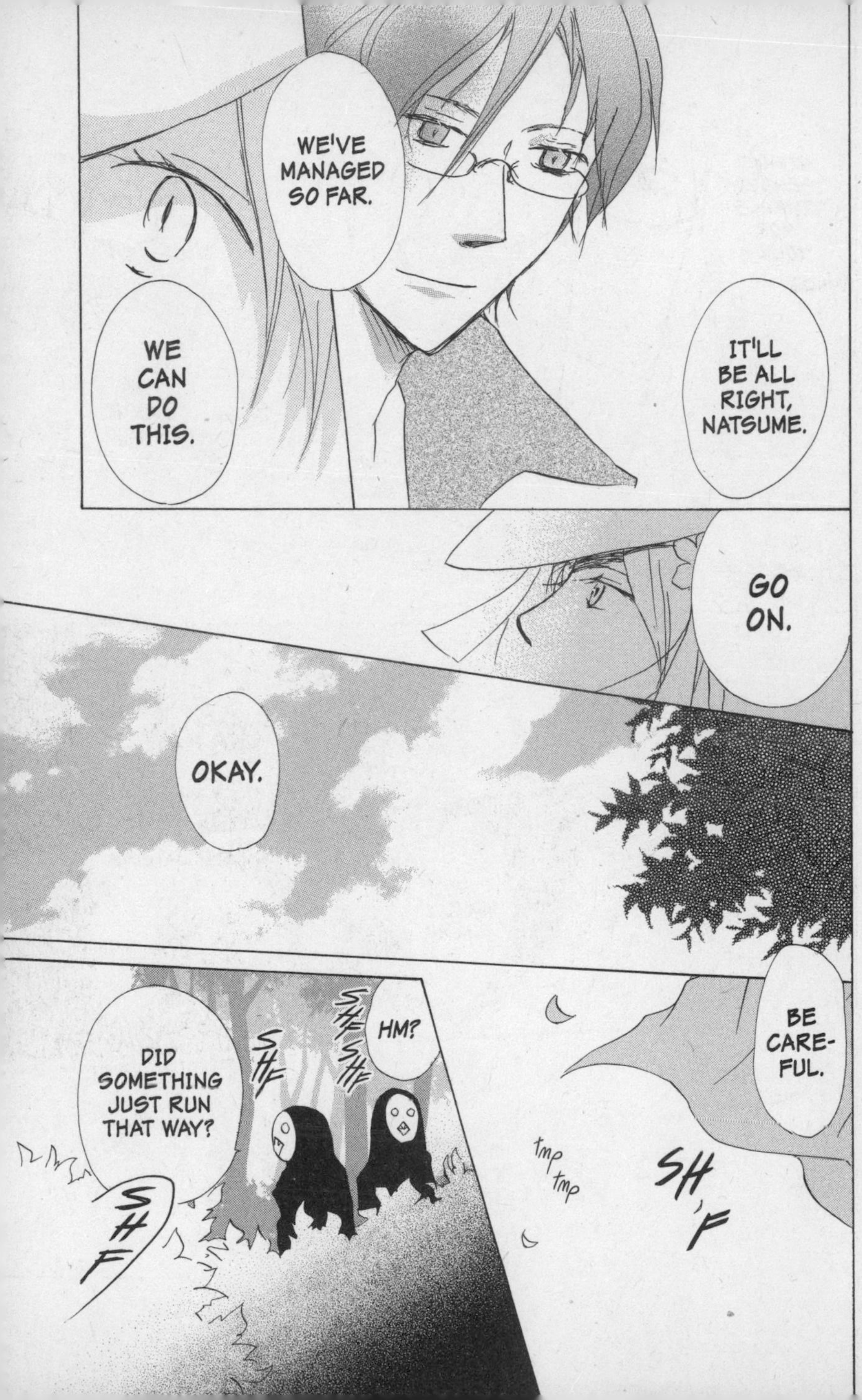
IT'LL BE ALL RIGHT, NATSUME.
WE'VE MANAGED SO FAR.
WE CAN DO THIS.
GO ON.
OKAY.
BE CARE-FUL.
SH'F
tmp tmp
HM?
SHF SHF
SHF
DID SOMETHING JUST RUN THAT WAY?
SHF

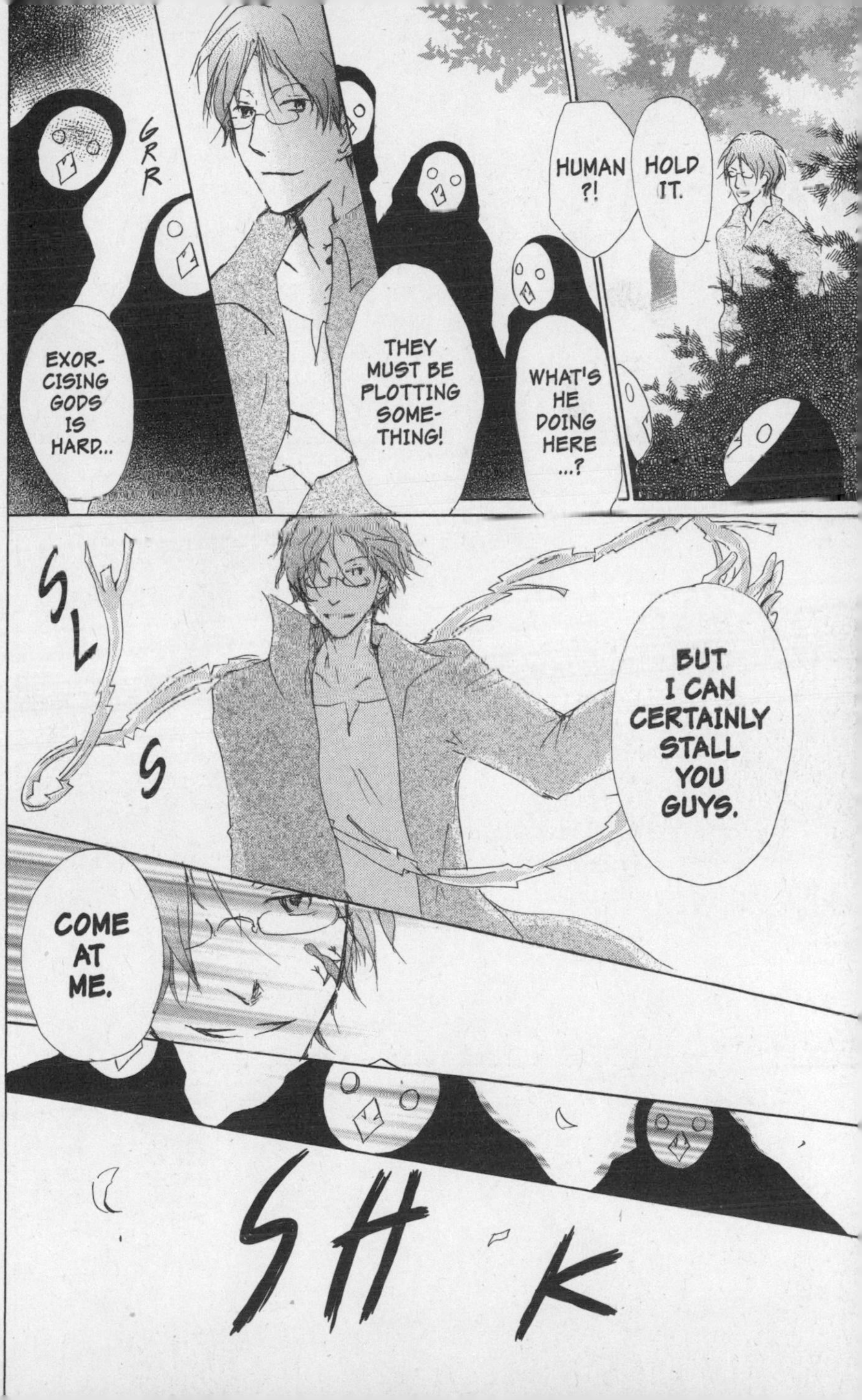
HOLD IT.
HUMAN ?!
WHAT'S HE DOING HERE ...?
THEY MUST BE PLOTTING SOME-THING!
GRR
EXOR-CISING GODS IS HARD...
S L S
BUT I CAN CERTAINLY STALL YOU GUYS.
COME AT ME.
SH K

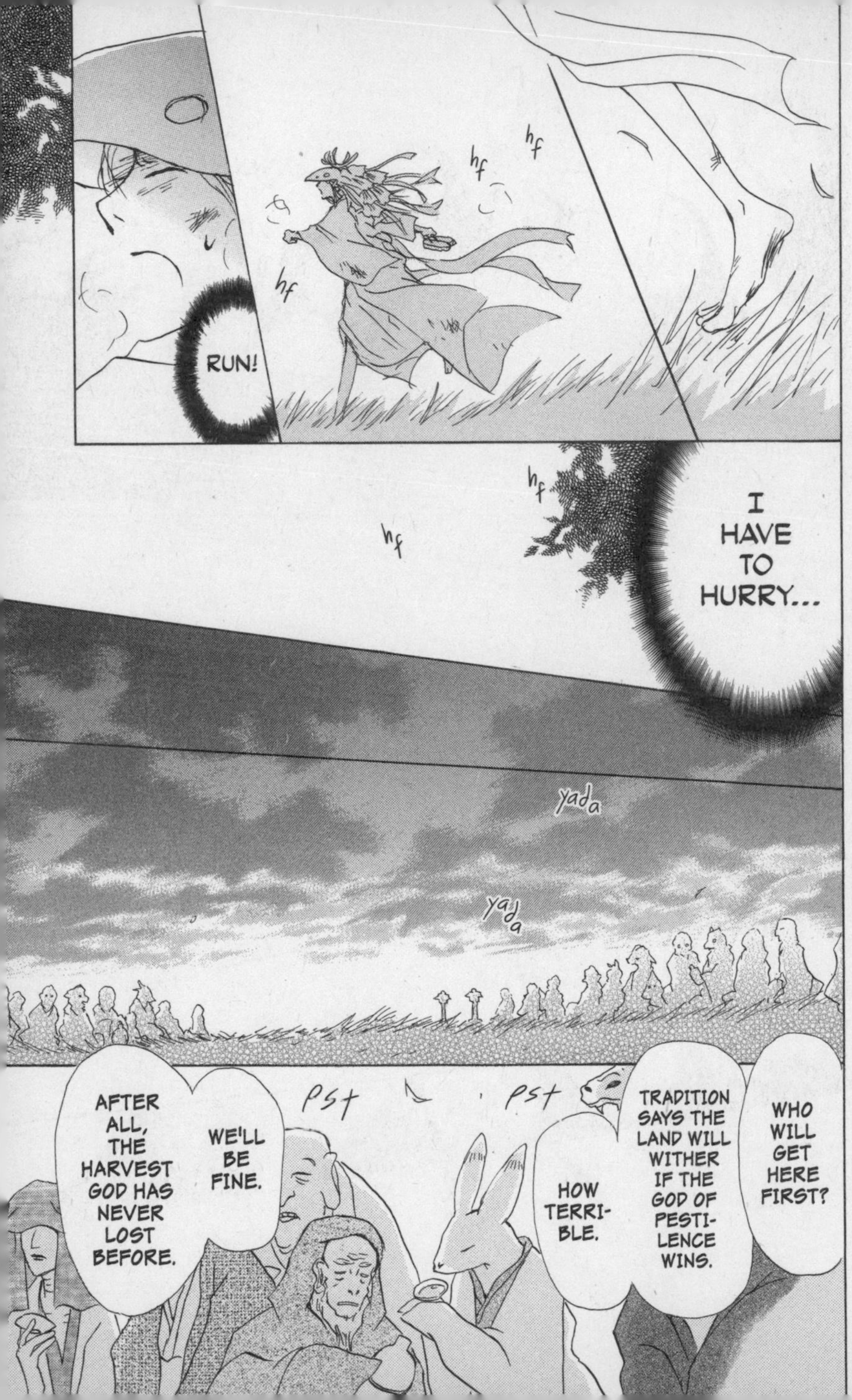
hf
hf
hf
RUN!
hf
hf
I HAVE TO HURRY...
yada
yada
WHO WILL GET HERE FIRST?
TRADITION SAYS THE LAND WILL WITHER IF THE GOD OF PESTI-LENCE WINS.
HOW TERRI-BLE.
pst
pst
WE'LL BE FINE.
AFTER ALL, THE HARVEST GOD HAS NEVER LOST BEFORE.

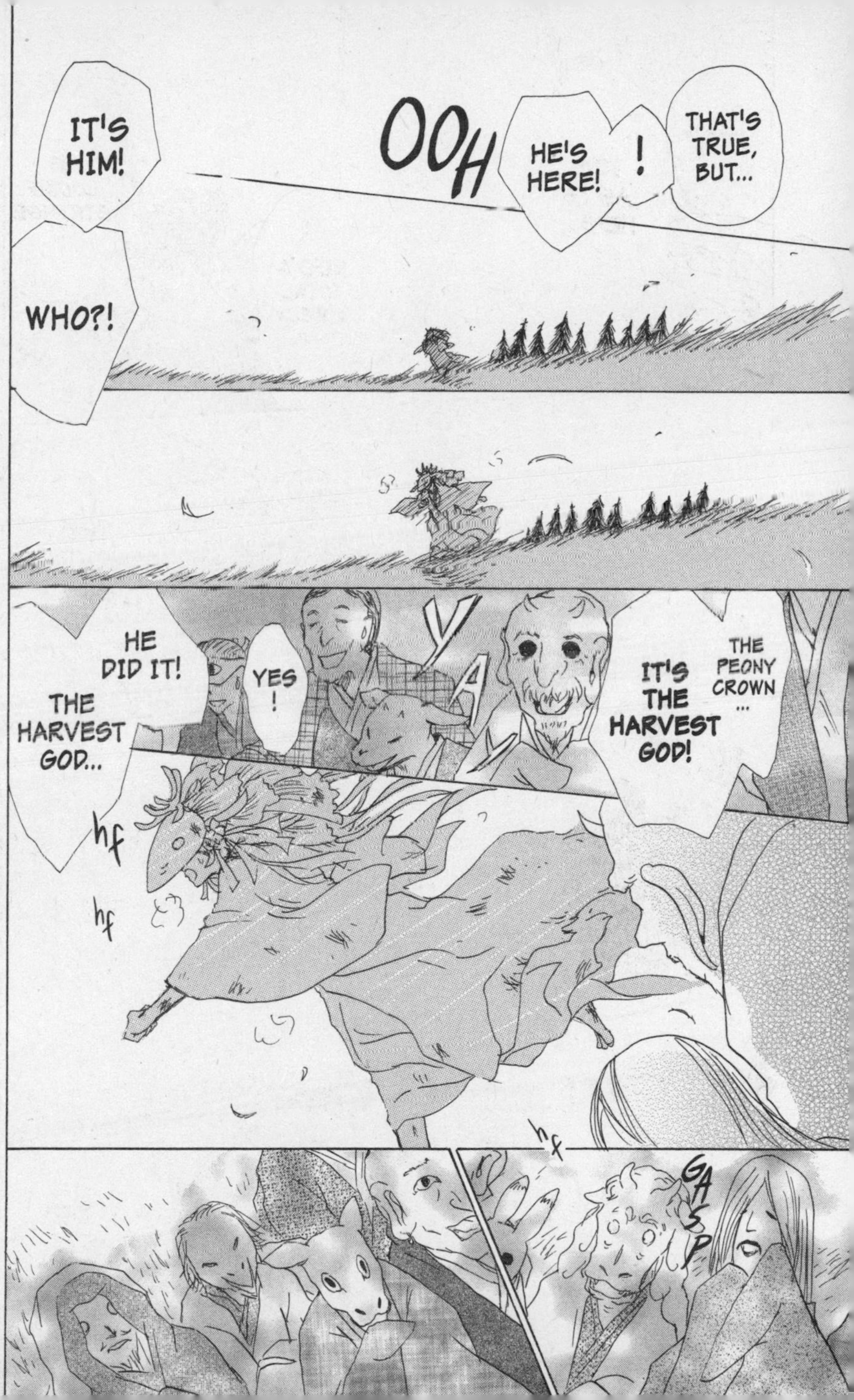
THAT'S TRUE, BUT...
!
HE'S HERE!
OOH
IT'S HIM!
WHO?!
THE PEONY CROWN...
IT'S THE HARVEST GOD!
YAY
YES!
HE DID IT!
THE HARVEST GOD...
hf
hf
hf
GASP

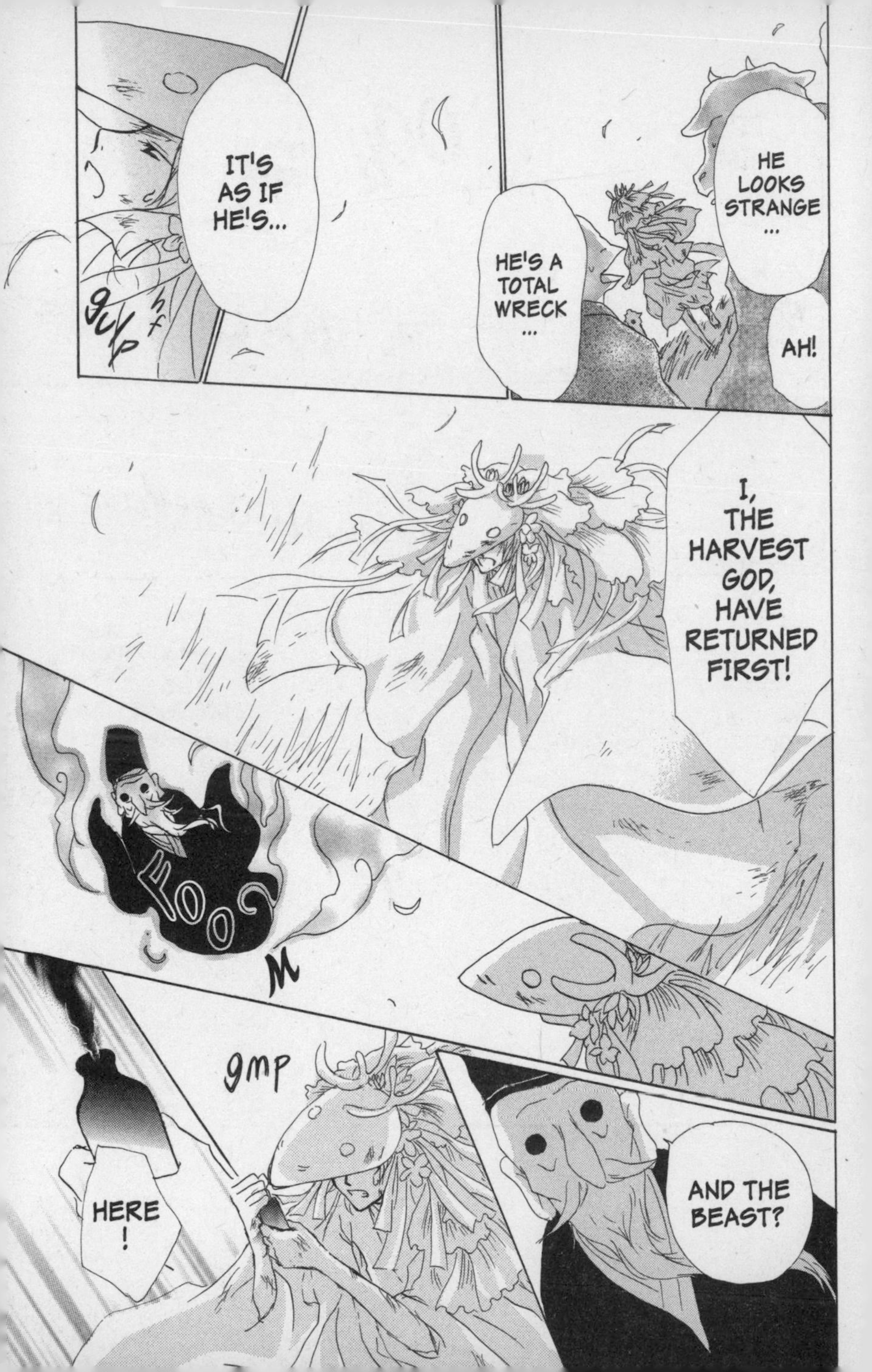
HE LOOKS STRANGE ...
AH!
HE'S A TOTAL WRECK ...
IT'S AS IF HE'S...
gulp
I, THE HARVEST GOD, HAVE RETURNED FIRST!
FOOOM
AND THE BEAST?
gmp
HERE !

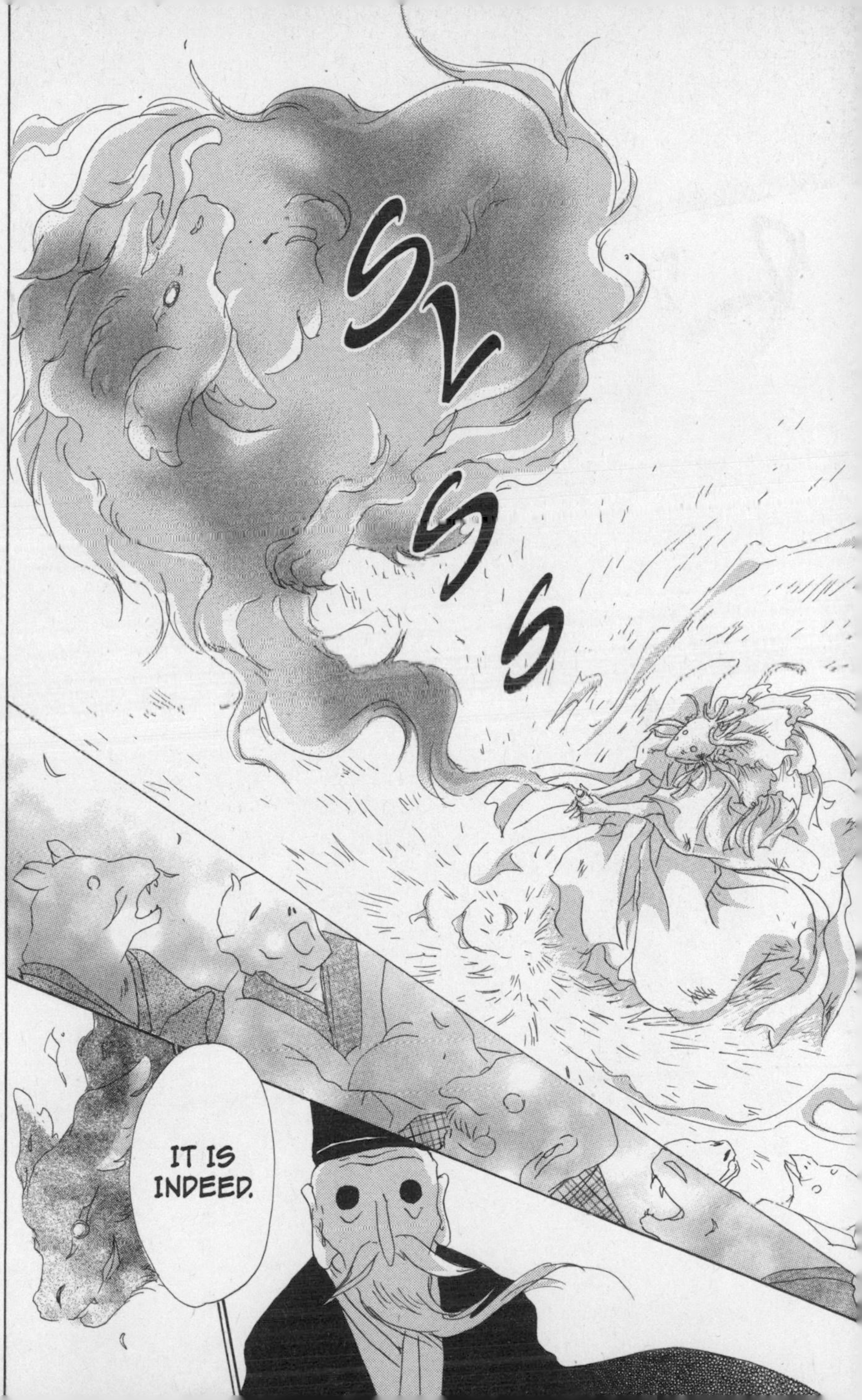
SSSS
IT IS INDEED.

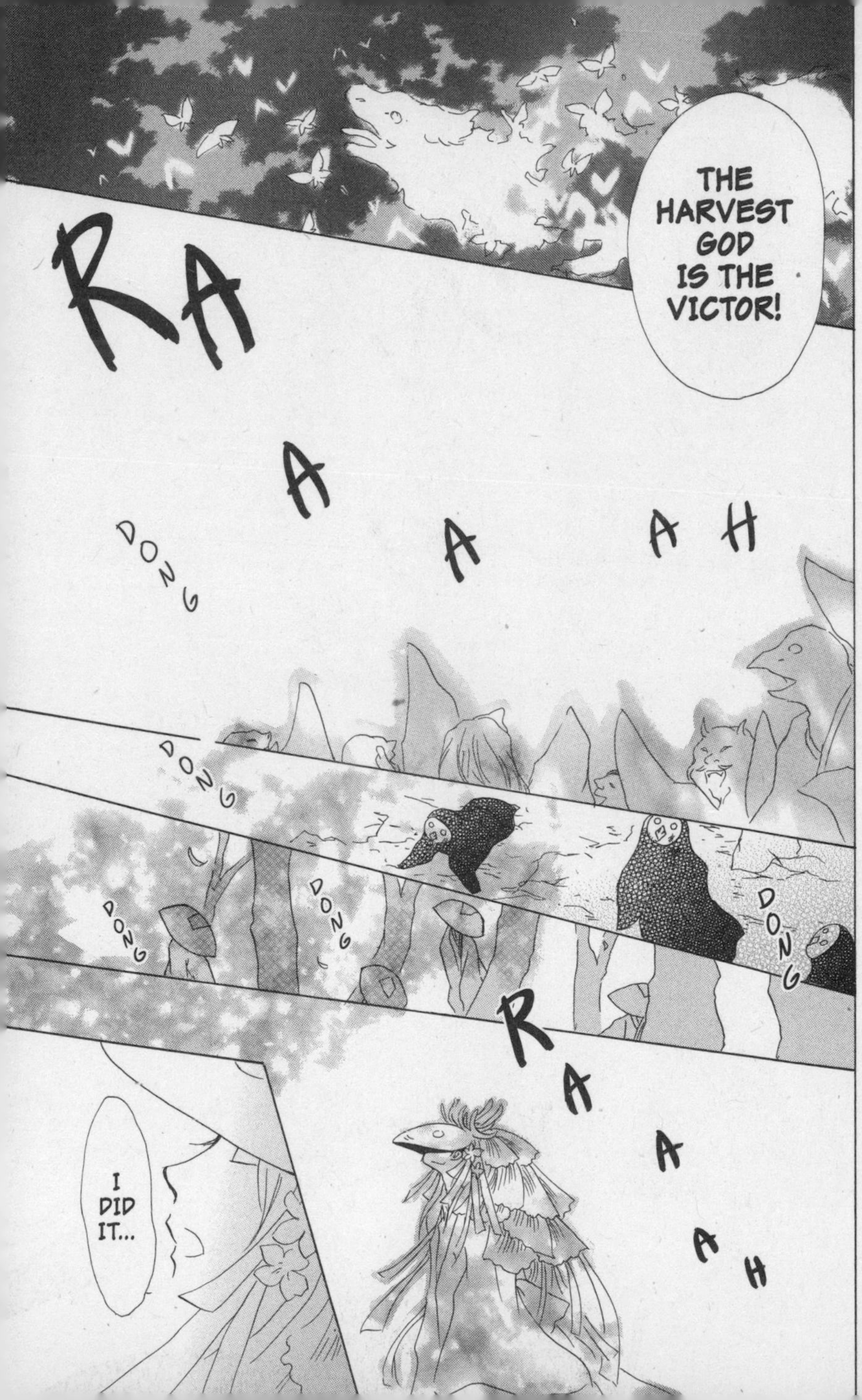
THE HARVEST GOD IS THE VICTOR!
RA A A AH
DONG
DONG
DONG
DONG
DONG
RA A A AH
I DID IT...

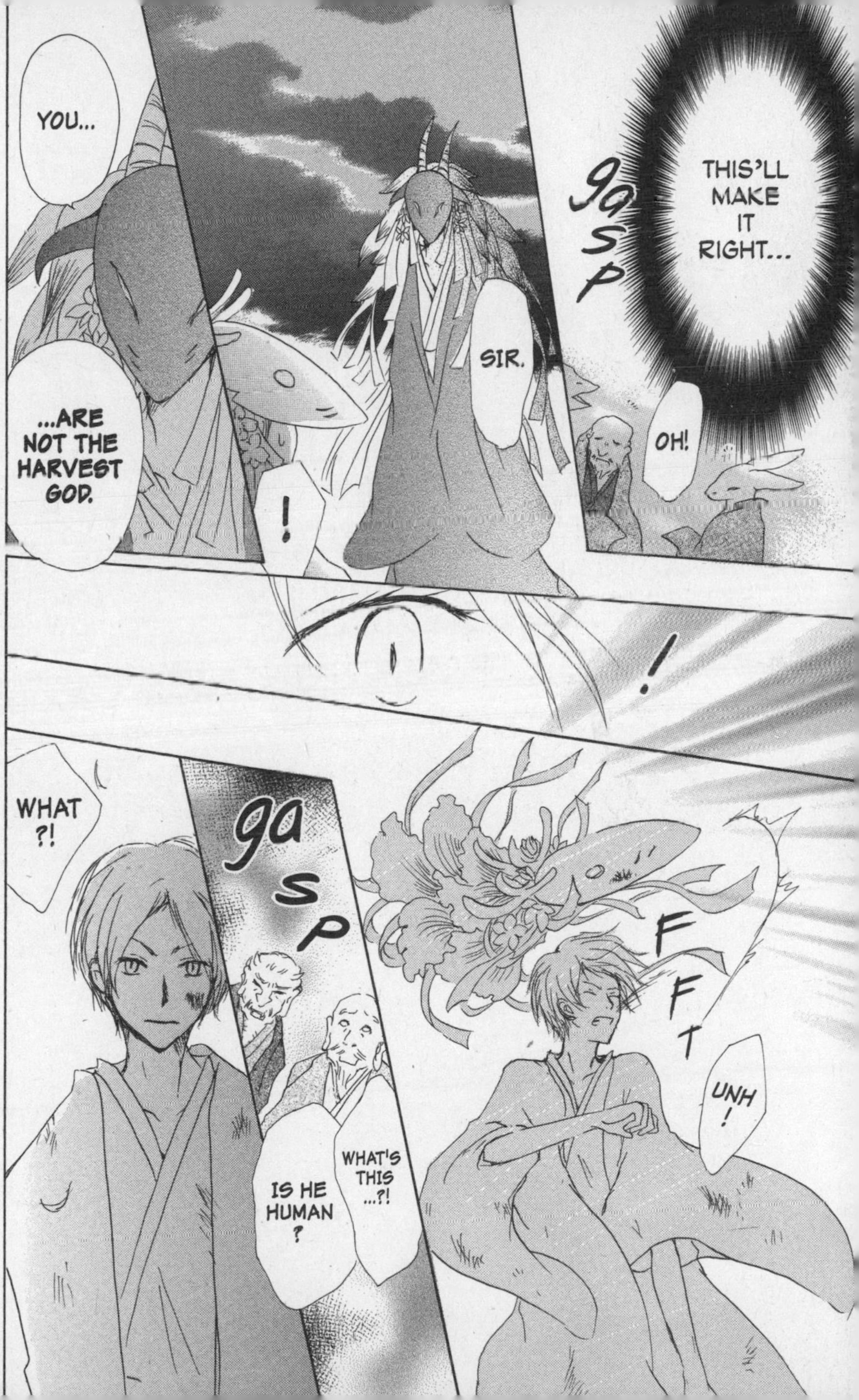
THIS'LL MAKE IT RIGHT...
gasp
OH!
SIR.
!
YOU...
...ARE NOT THE HARVEST GOD.
!
FFFT
UNH!
gasp
WHAT'S THIS ...?!
IS HE HUMAN?
WHAT ?!

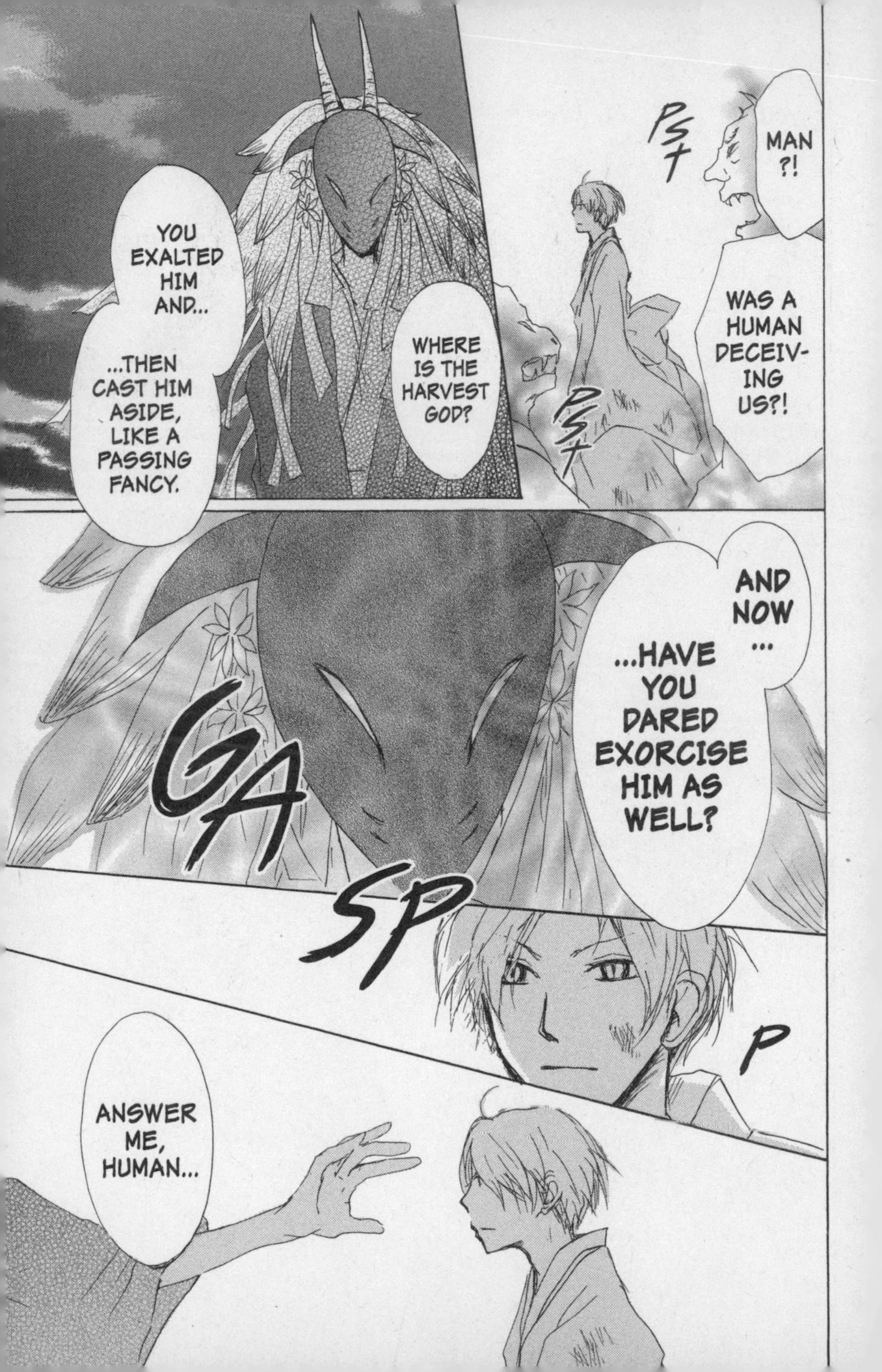
MAN ?!
PST
WAS A HUMAN DECEIV-ING US?!
PST
WHERE IS THE HARVEST GOD?
YOU EXALTED HIM AND...
...THEN CAST HIM ASIDE, LIKE A PASSING FANCY.
AND NOW ...
...HAVE YOU DARED EXORCISE HIM AS WELL?
GASP
P
ANSWER ME, HUMAN...

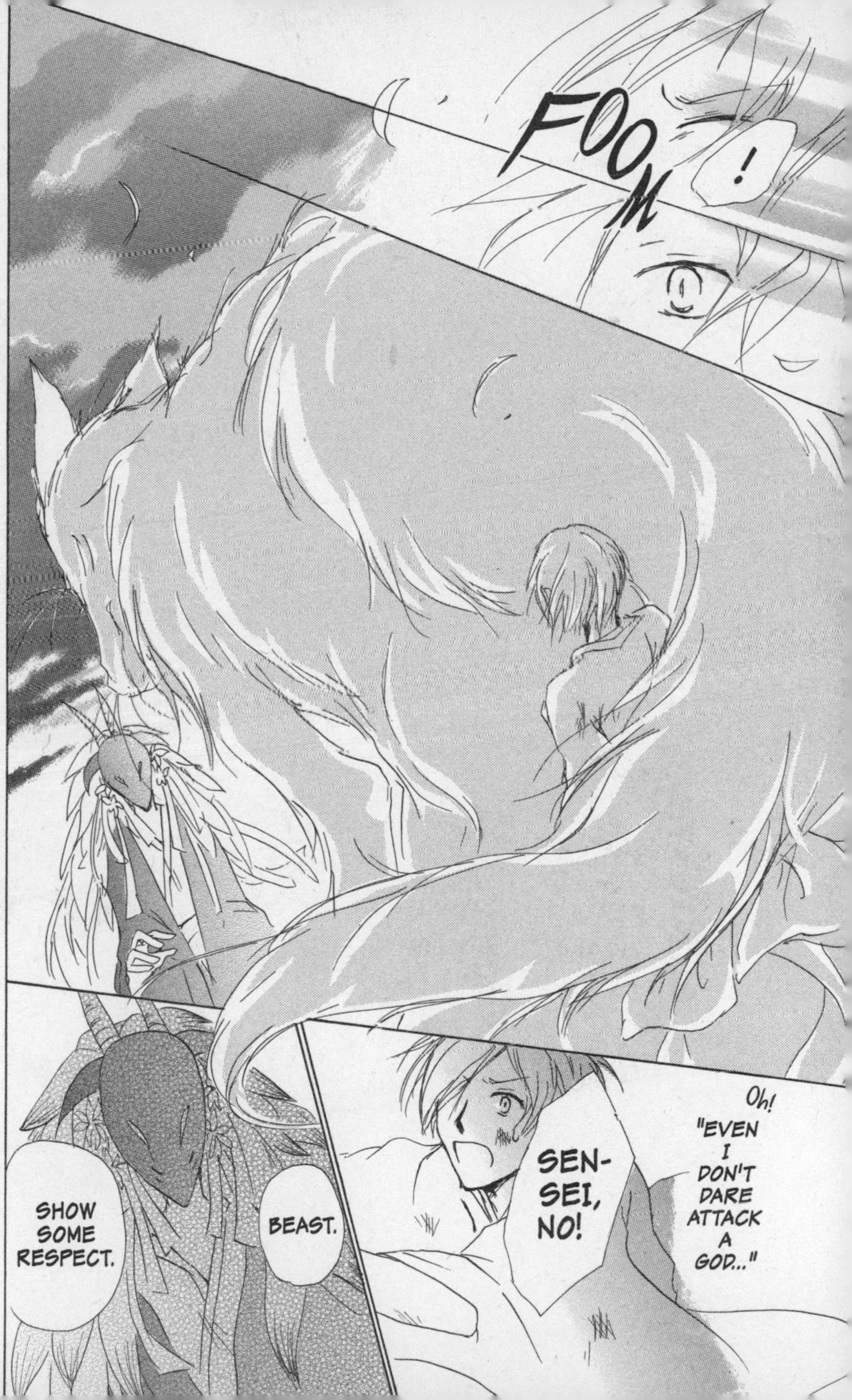
FOOM
!
Oh!
"EVEN I DON'T DARE ATTACK A GOD..."
SEN-SEI, NO!
BEAST.
SHOW SOME RESPECT.

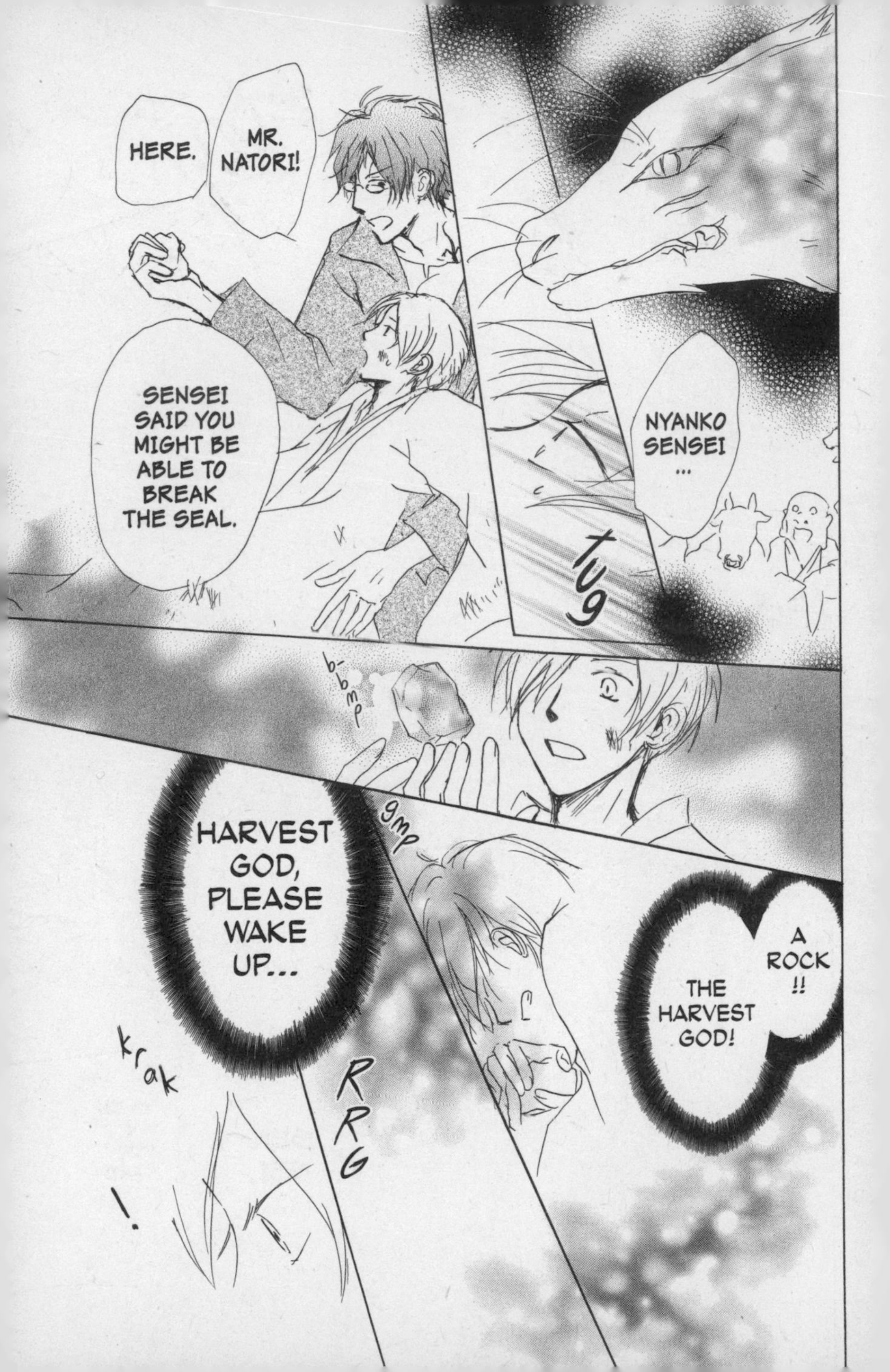
NYANKO SENSEI...
tug
MR. NATORI!
HERE.
SENSEI SAID YOU MIGHT BE ABLE TO BREAK THE SEAL.
b-bmp
gmp
A ROCK!!
THE HARVEST GOD!
HARVEST GOD, PLEASE WAKE UP...
RRG
krak
!

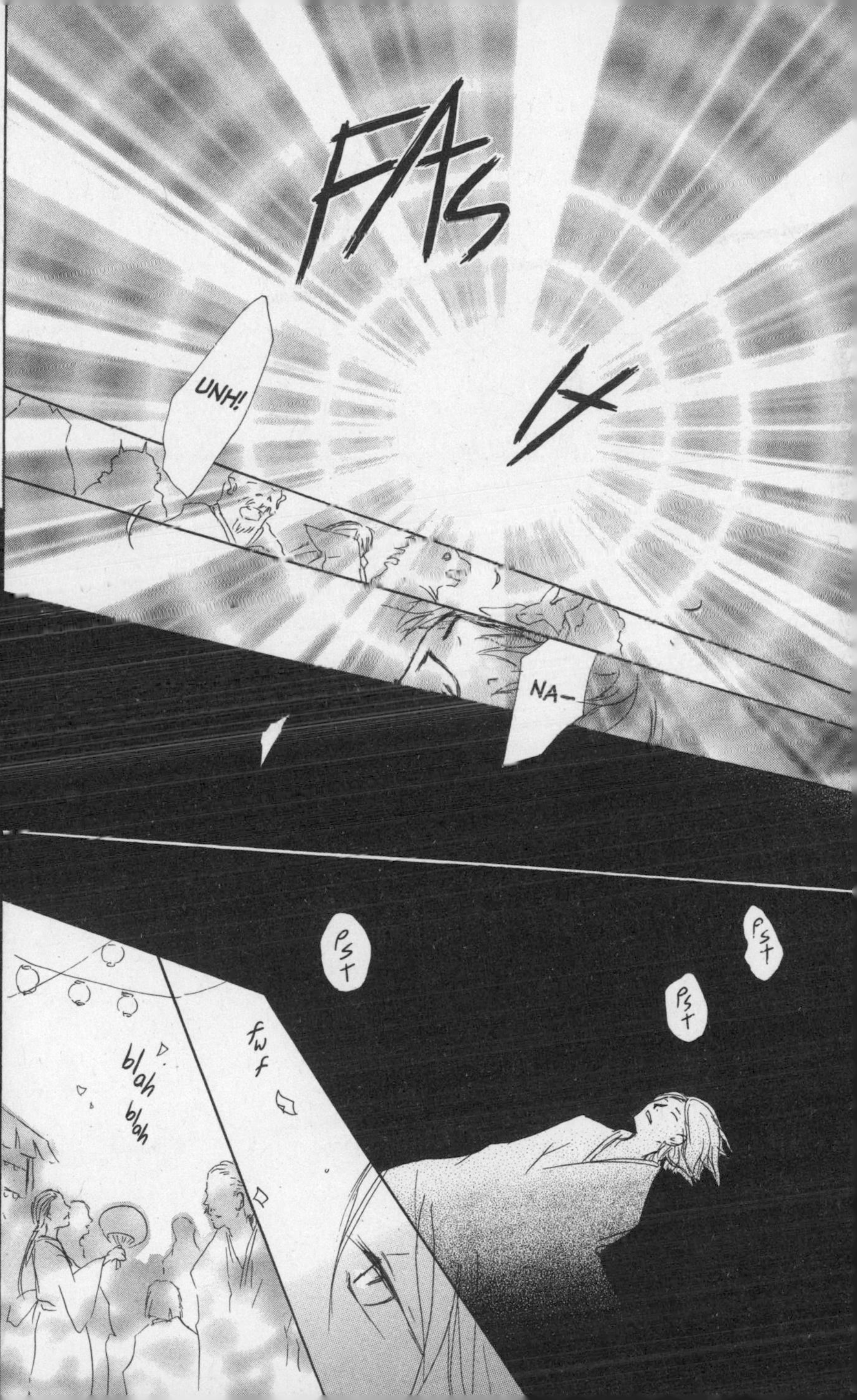
FLASH
UNH!
NA--
pst
pst
pst
fwf
blah
blah

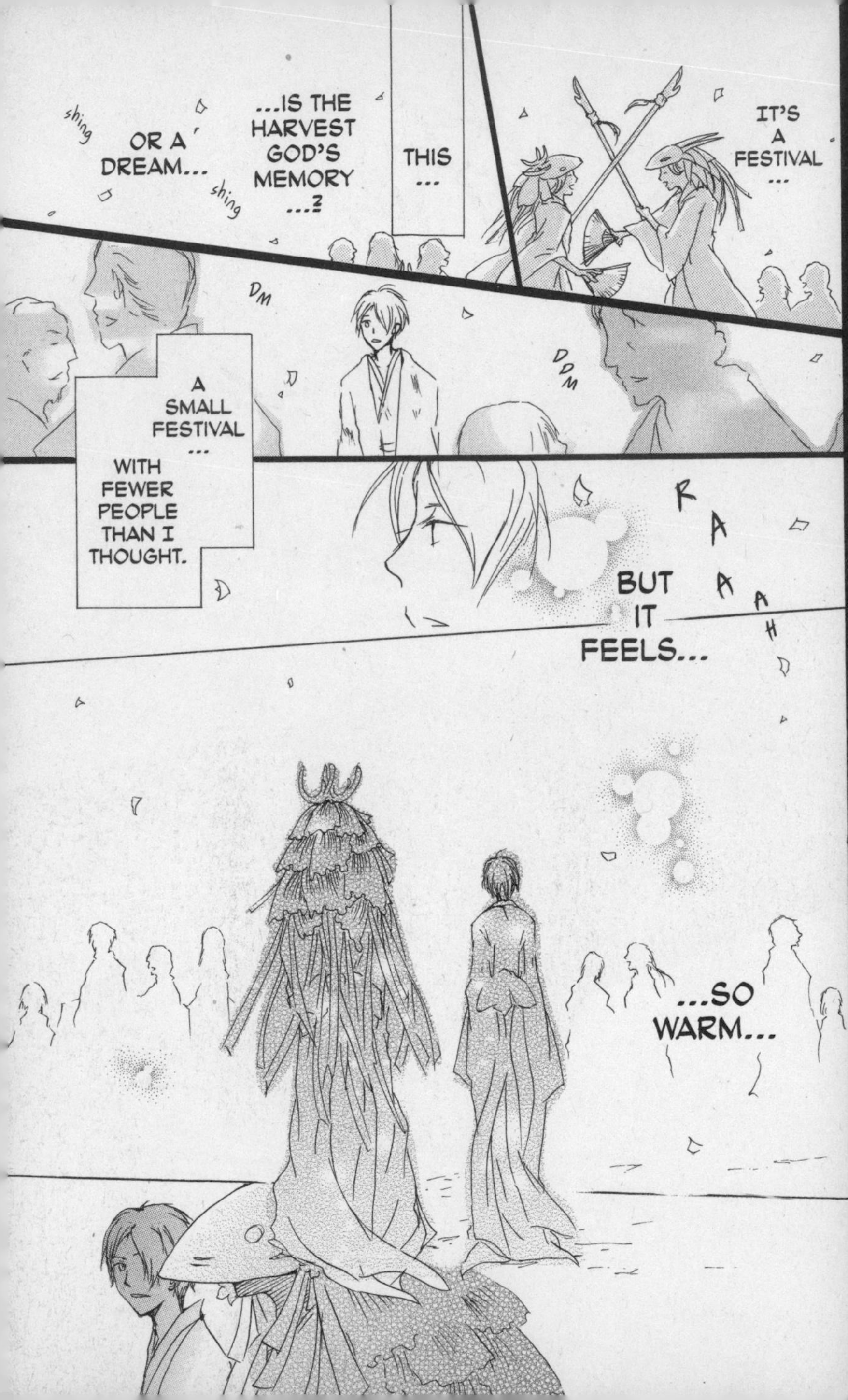
IT'S A FESTIVAL ...
THIS ...
...IS THE HARVEST GOD'S MEMORY ...?
shing
OR A DREAM...
shing
DOM
DM
A SMALL FESTIVAL ...
WITH FEWER PEOPLE THAN I THOUGHT.
RAAAH
BUT IT FEELS...
...SO WARM...

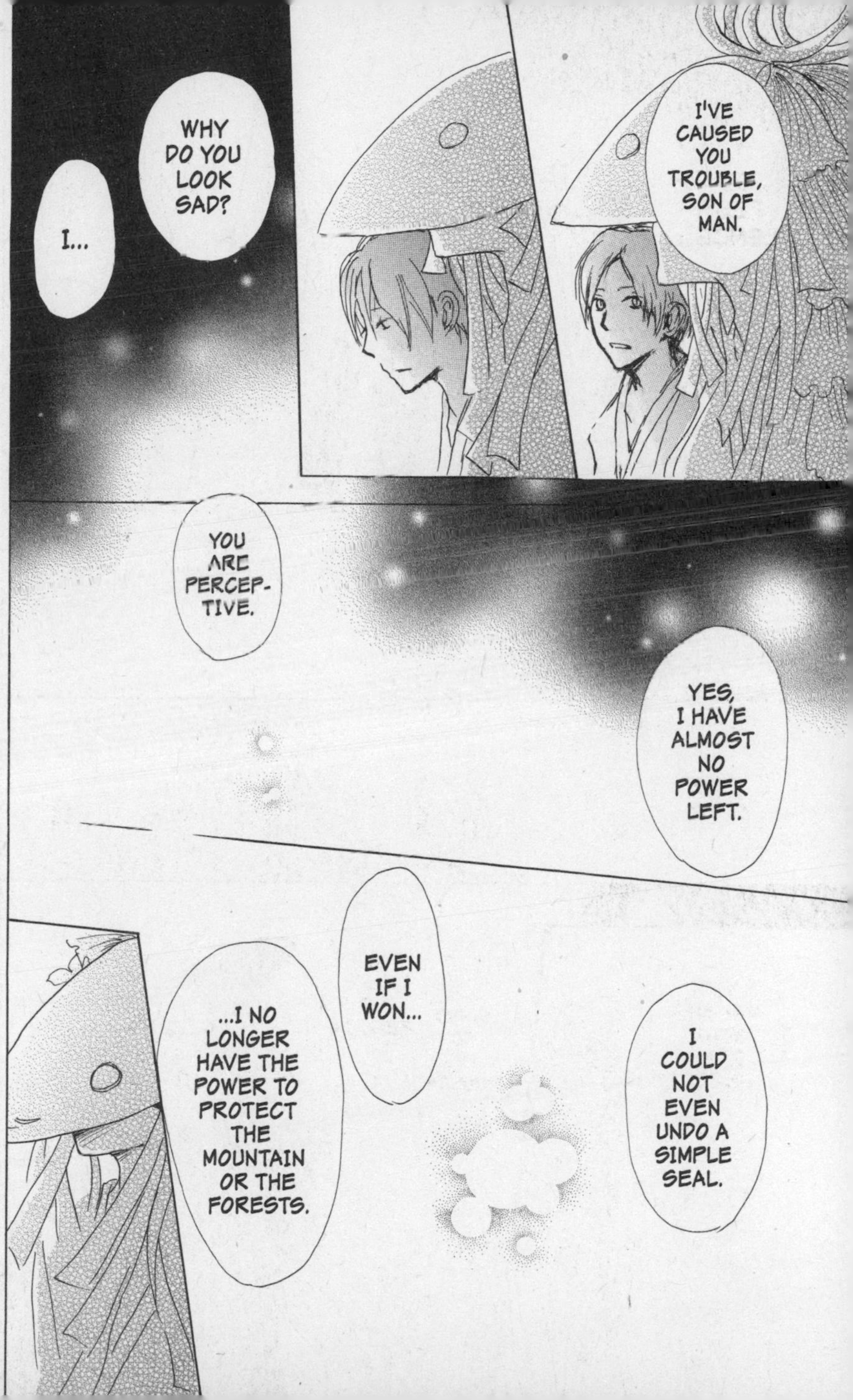
I'VE CAUSED YOU TROUBLE, SON OF MAN.
WHY DO YOU LOOK SAD?
I...
YOU ARE PERCEPTIVE.
YES, I HAVE ALMOST NO POWER LEFT.
I COULD NOT EVEN UNDO A SIMPLE SEAL.
EVEN IF I WON...
...I NO LONGER HAVE THE POWER TO PROTECT THE MOUNTAIN OR THE FORESTS.

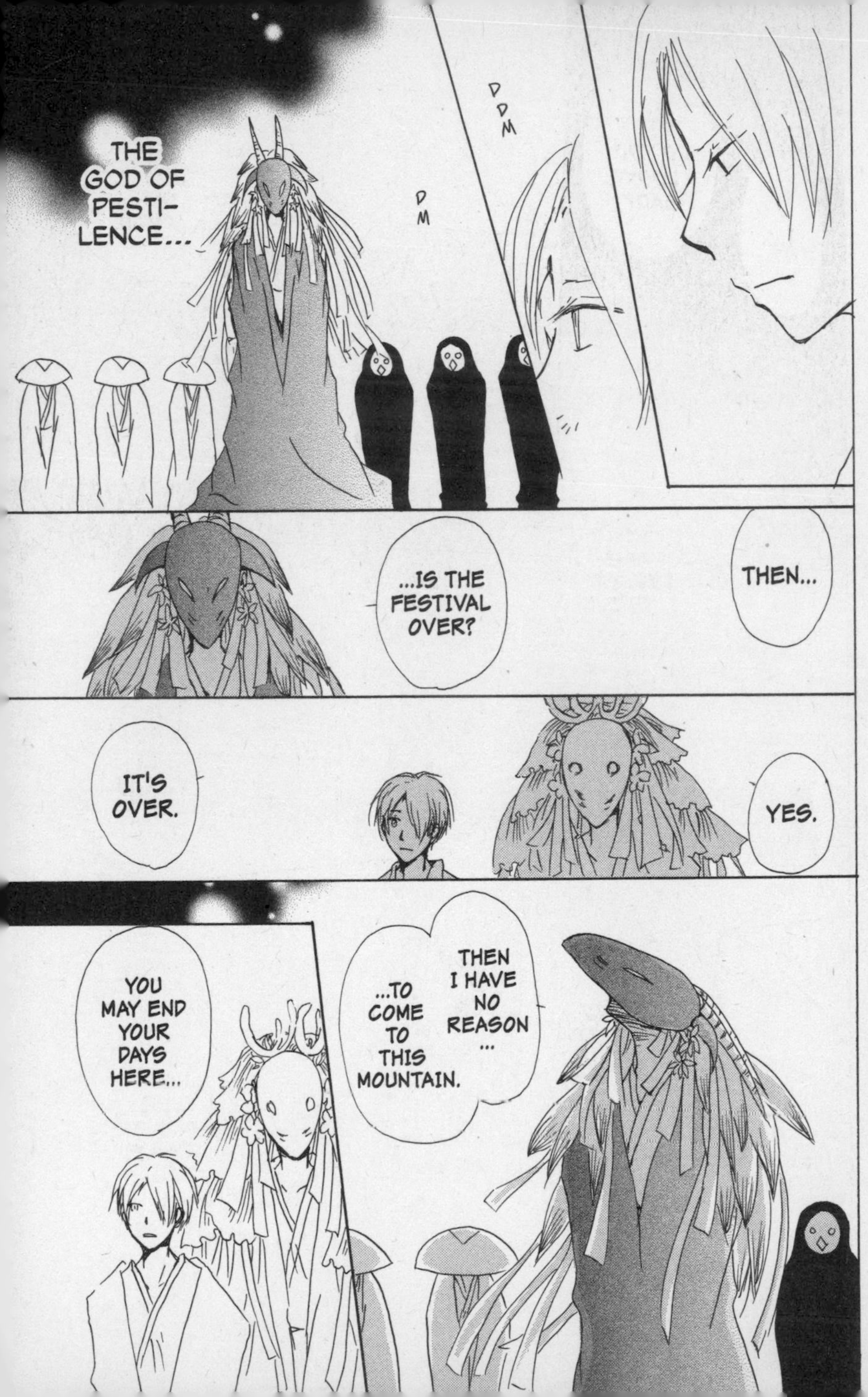
DDM
DM
THE GOD OF PESTI-LENCE...
THEN...
...IS THE FESTIVAL OVER?
YES.
IT'S OVER.
THEN I HAVE NO REASON ...
...TO COME TO THIS MOUNTAIN.
YOU MAY END YOUR DAYS HERE...

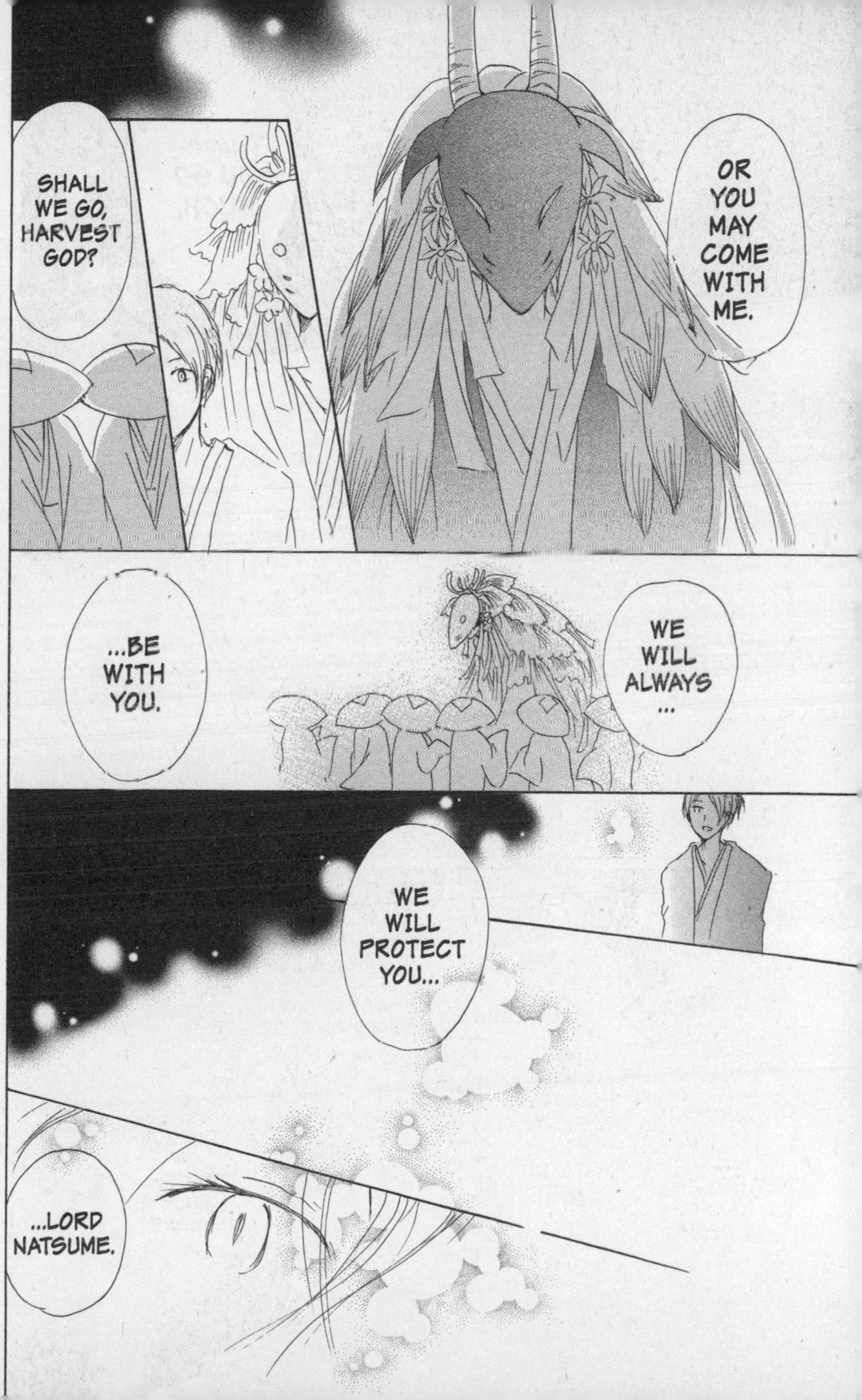
OR YOU MAY COME WITH ME.
SHALL WE GO, HARVEST GOD?
WE WILL ALWAYS...
...BE WITH YOU.
WE WILL PROTECT YOU...
...LORD NATSUME.

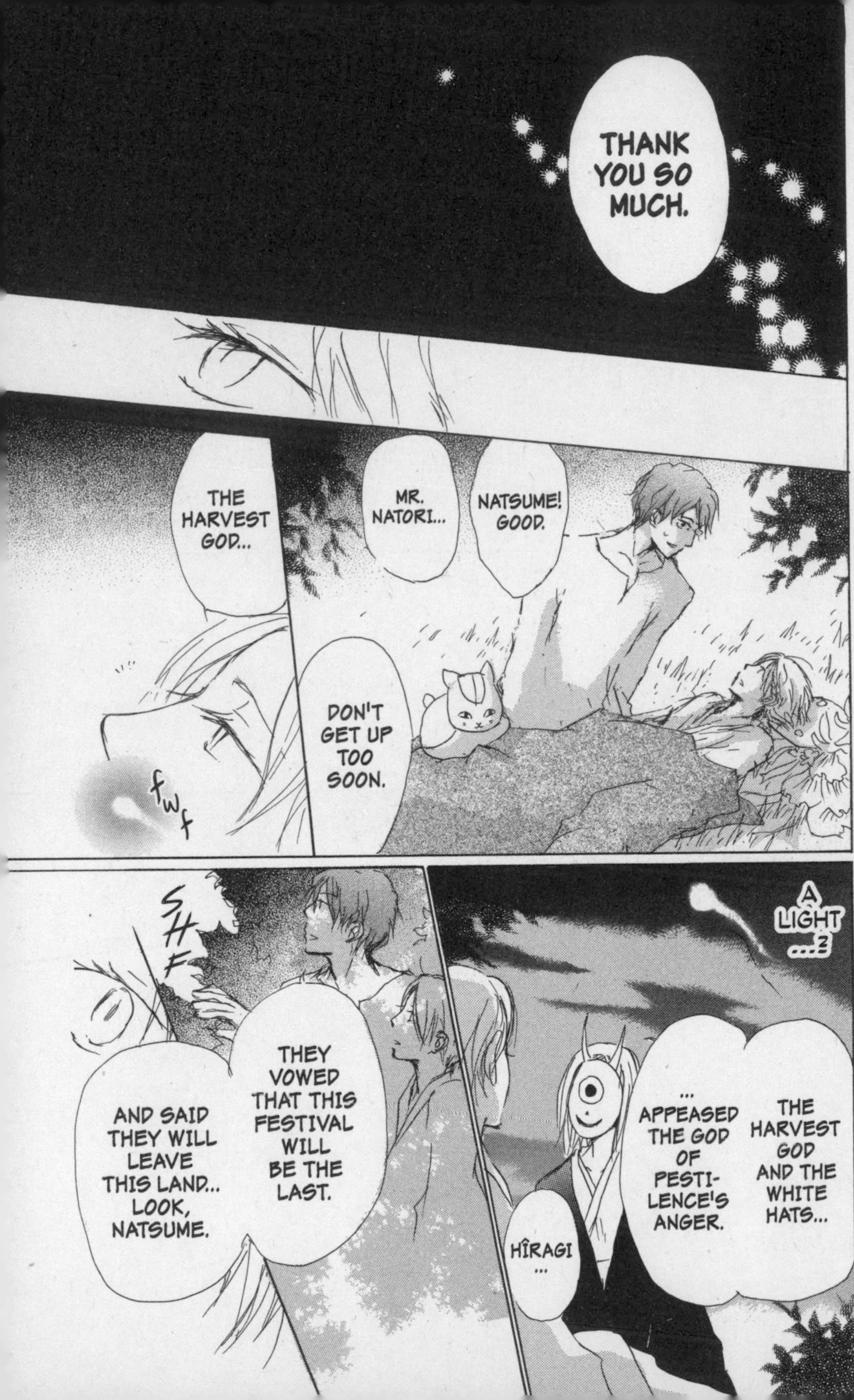
THANK YOU SO MUCH.
NATSUME! GOOD.
MR. NATORI...
DON'T GET UP TOO SOON.
THE HARVEST GOD...
fwf
A LIGHT...?
THE HARVEST GOD AND THE WHITE HATS...
...APPEASED THE GOD OF PESTILENCE'S ANGER.
HÎRAGI...
SHF
THEY VOWED THAT THIS FESTIVAL WILL BE THE LAST.
AND SAID THEY WILL LEAVE THIS LAND... LOOK, NATSUME.

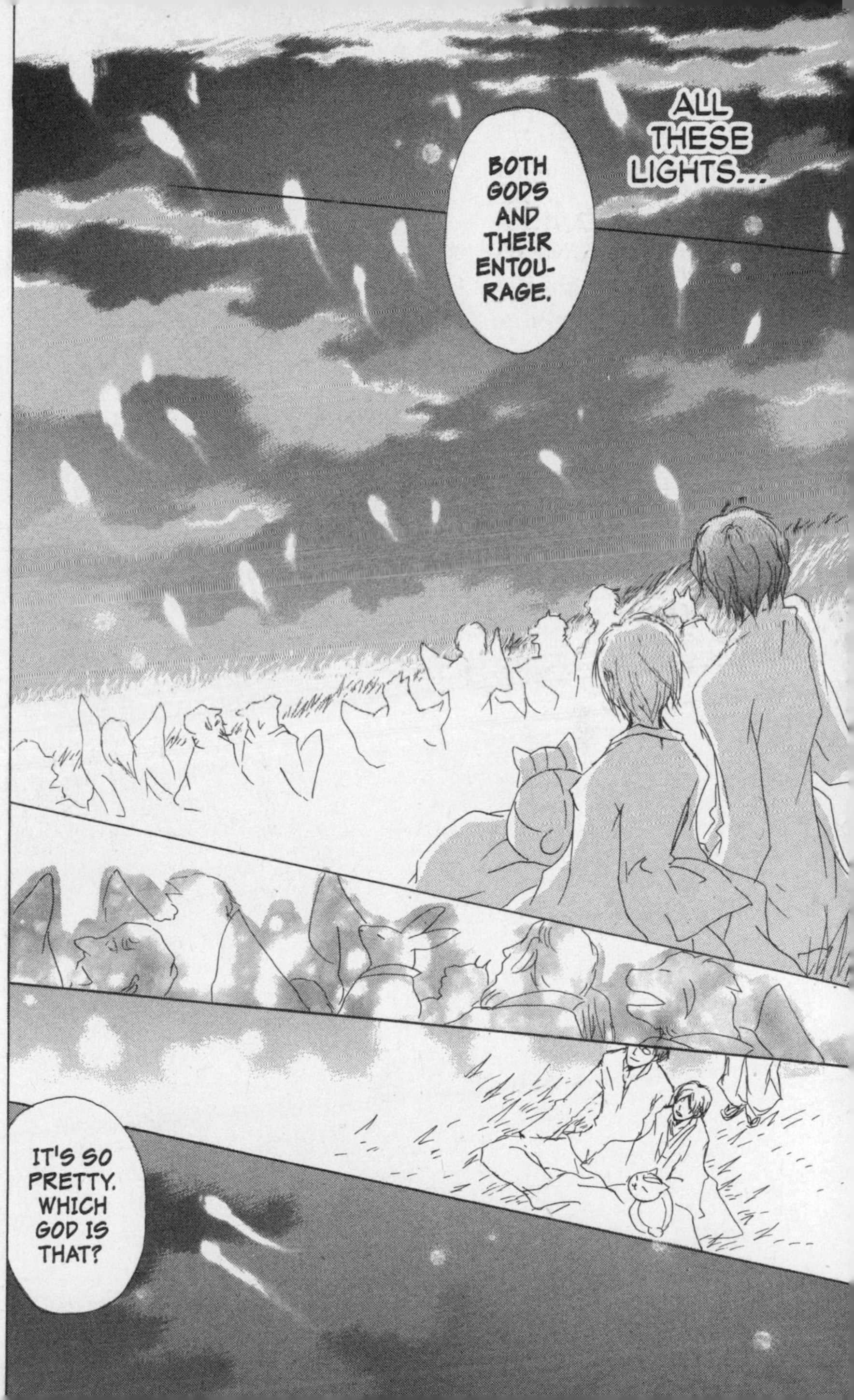
ALL THESE LIGHTS...
BOTH GODS AND THEIR ENTOURAGE.
IT'S SO PRETTY. WHICH GOD IS THAT?

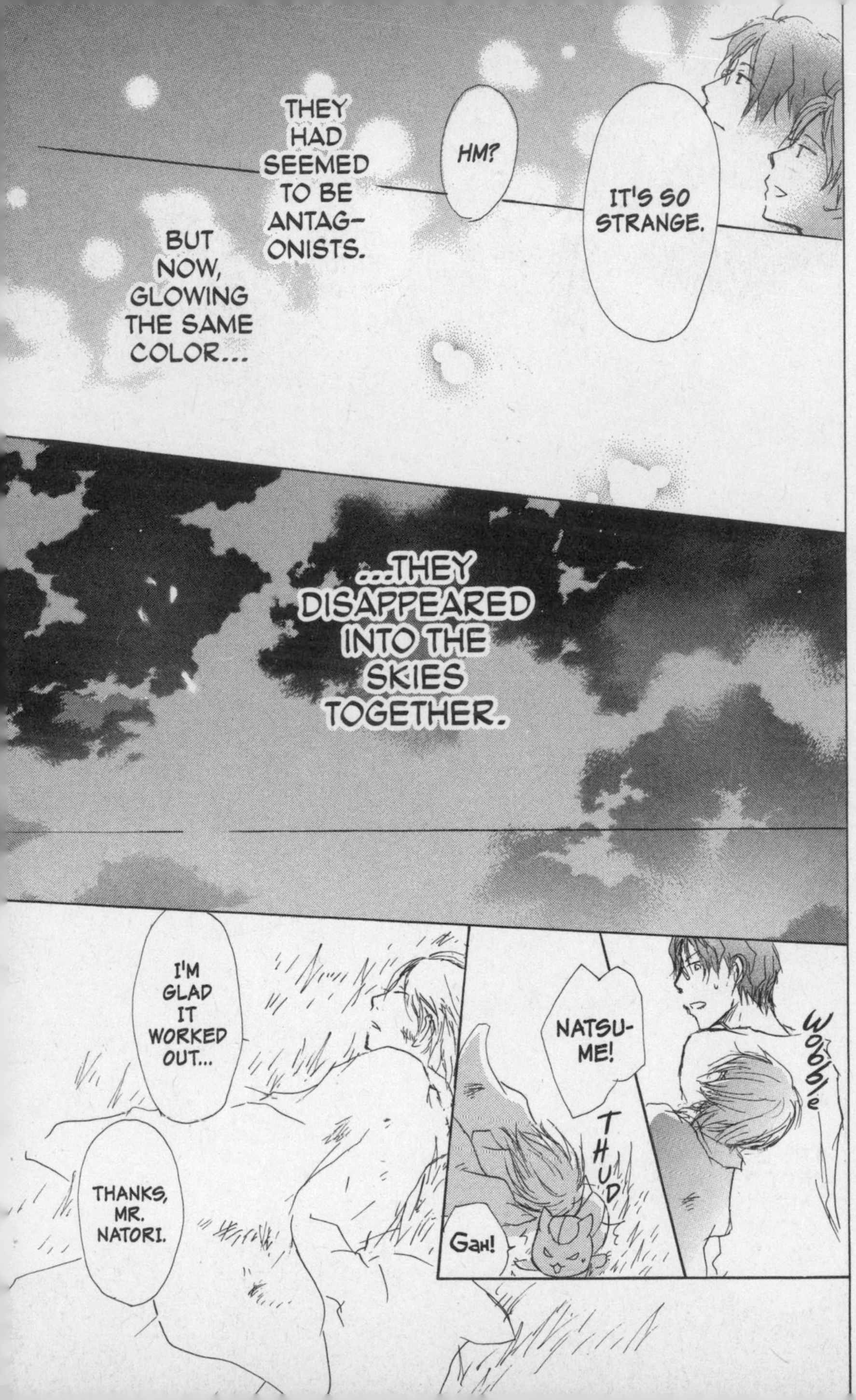
IT'S SO STRANGE.
HM?
THEY HAD SEEMED TO BE ANTAG-ONISTS.
BUT NOW, GLOWING THE SAME COLOR...
...THEY DISAPPEARED INTO THE SKIES TOGETHER.
Wobble
NATSU-ME!
THUD
Gah!
I'M GLAD IT WORKED OUT...
THANKS, MR. NATORI.

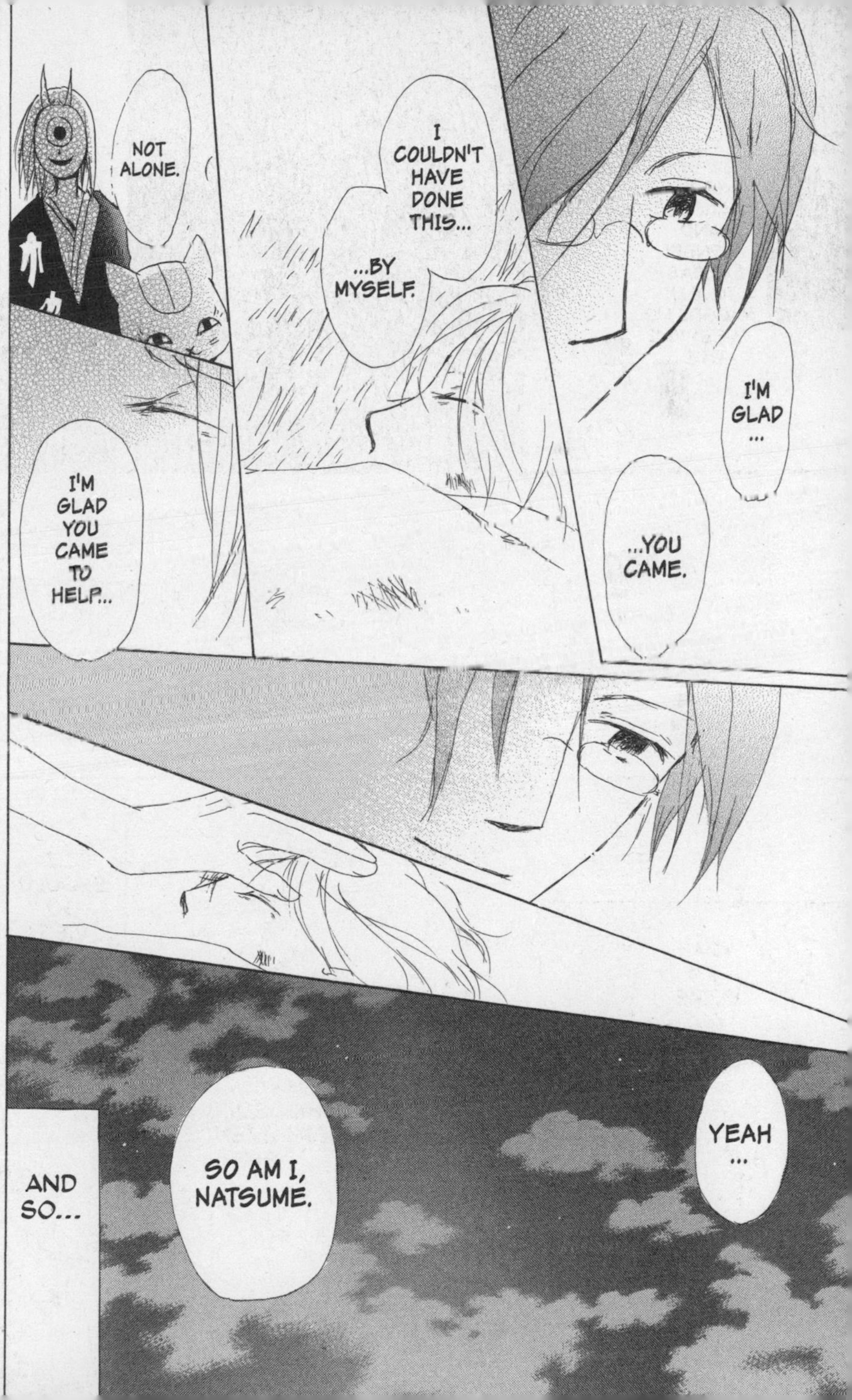
I'M GLAD...
...YOU CAME.
I COULDN'T HAVE DONE THIS...
...BY MYSELF.
NOT ALONE.
I'M GLAD YOU CAME TO HELP...
YEAH...
SO AM I, NATSUME.
AND SO...

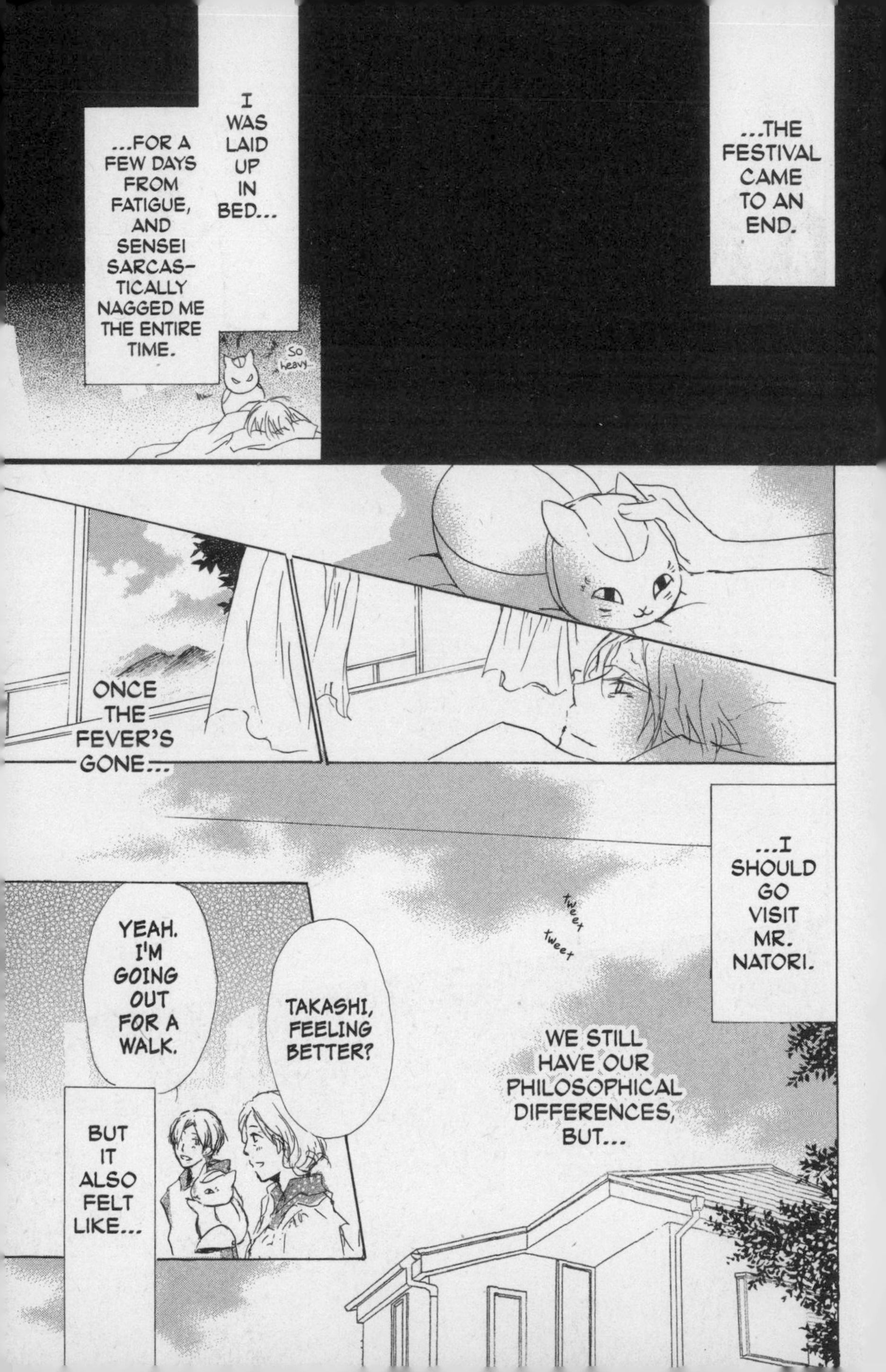
...THE FESTIVAL CAME TO AN END.
I WAS LAID UP IN BED...
...FOR A FEW DAYS FROM FATIGUE, AND SENSEI SARCAS-TICALLY NAGGED ME THE ENTIRE TIME.
So heavy...
ONCE THE FEVER'S GONE...
...I SHOULD GO VISIT MR. NATORI.
tweet
tweet
WE STILL HAVE OUR PHILOSOPHICAL DIFFERENCES, BUT...
TAKASHI, FEELING BETTER?
YEAH. I'M GOING OUT FOR A WALK.
BUT IT ALSO FELT LIKE...

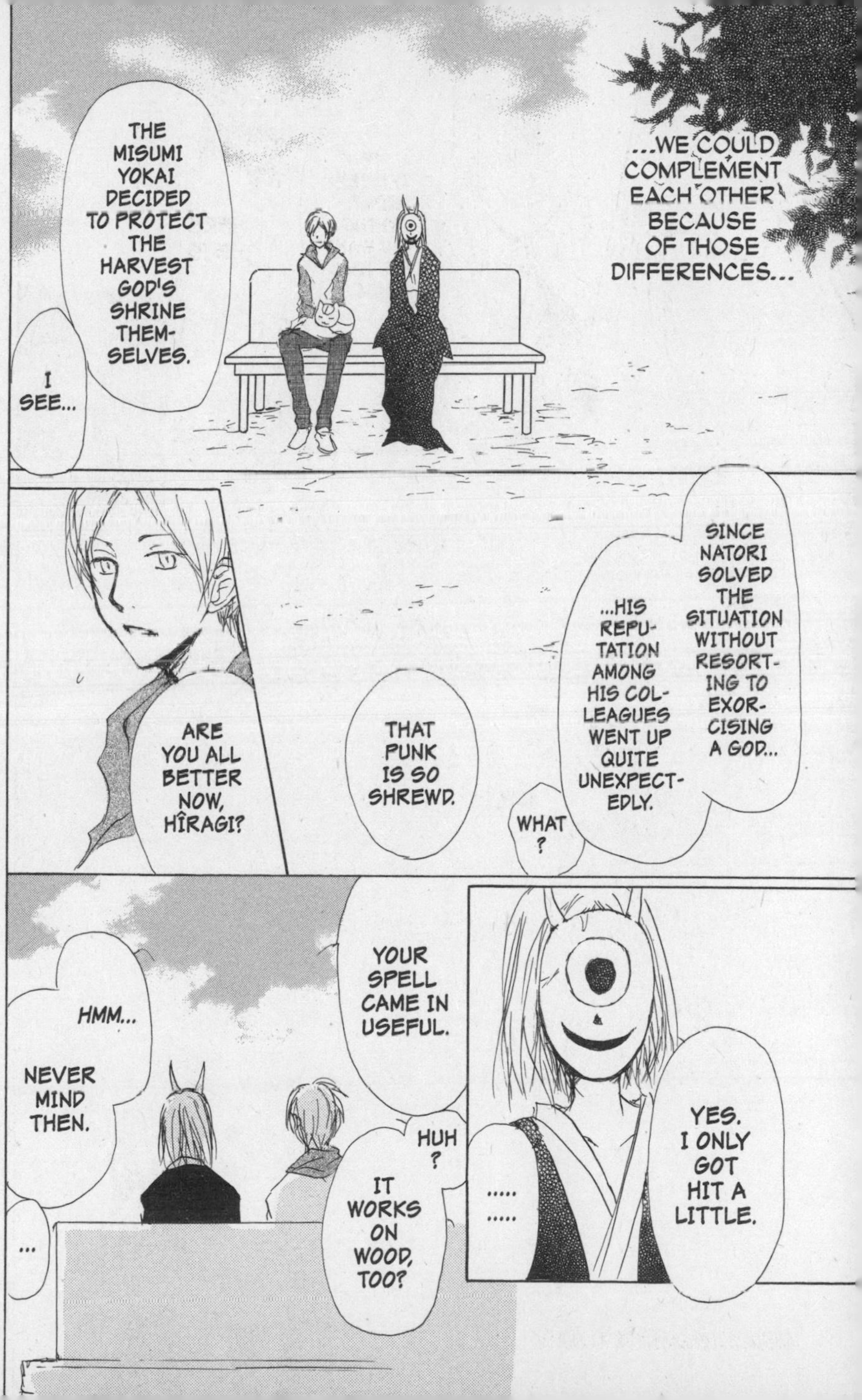
...WE COULD COMPLEMENT EACH OTHER BECAUSE OF THOSE DIFFERENCES...
THE MISUMI YOKAI DECIDED TO PROTECT THE HARVEST GOD'S SHRINE THEMSELVES.
I SEE...
SINCE NATORI SOLVED THE SITUATION WITHOUT RESORTING TO EXORCISING A GOD...
...HIS REPUTATION AMONG HIS COLLEAGUES WENT UP QUITE UNEXPECTEDLY.
WHAT?
THAT PUNK IS SO SHREWD.
ARE YOU ALL BETTER NOW, HÎRAGI?
YES. I ONLY GOT HIT A LITTLE.
.....
.....
YOUR SPELL CAME IN USEFUL.
HUH?
IT WORKS ON WOOD, TOO?
...
HMM...
NEVER MIND THEN.

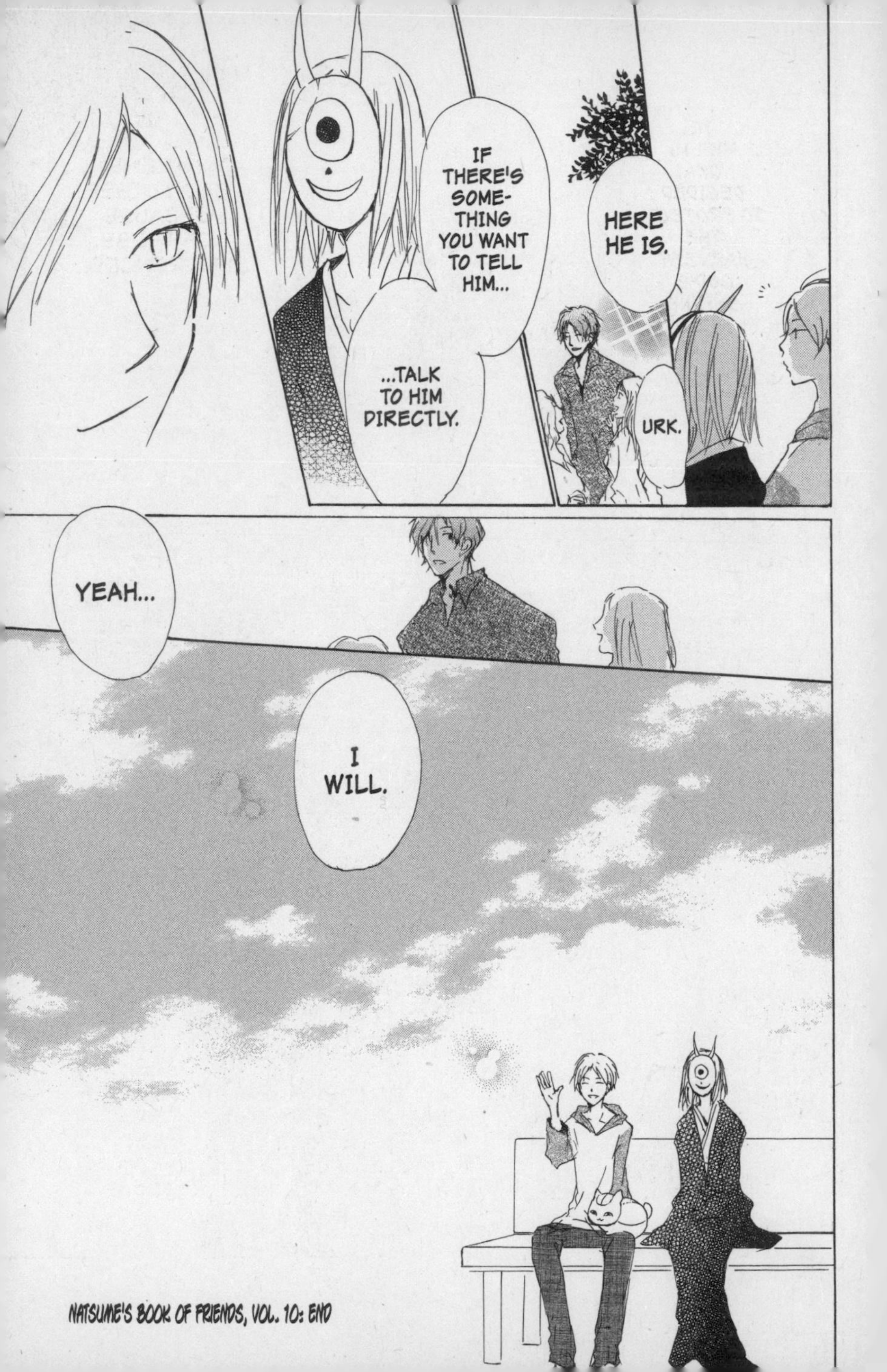
HERE HE IS.
URK.
IF THERE'S SOME-THING YOU WANT TO TELL HIM...
...TALK TO HIM DIRECTLY.
YEAH...
I WILL.
NATSUME'S BOOK OF FRIENDS, VOL. 10: END

AFTER-WORD

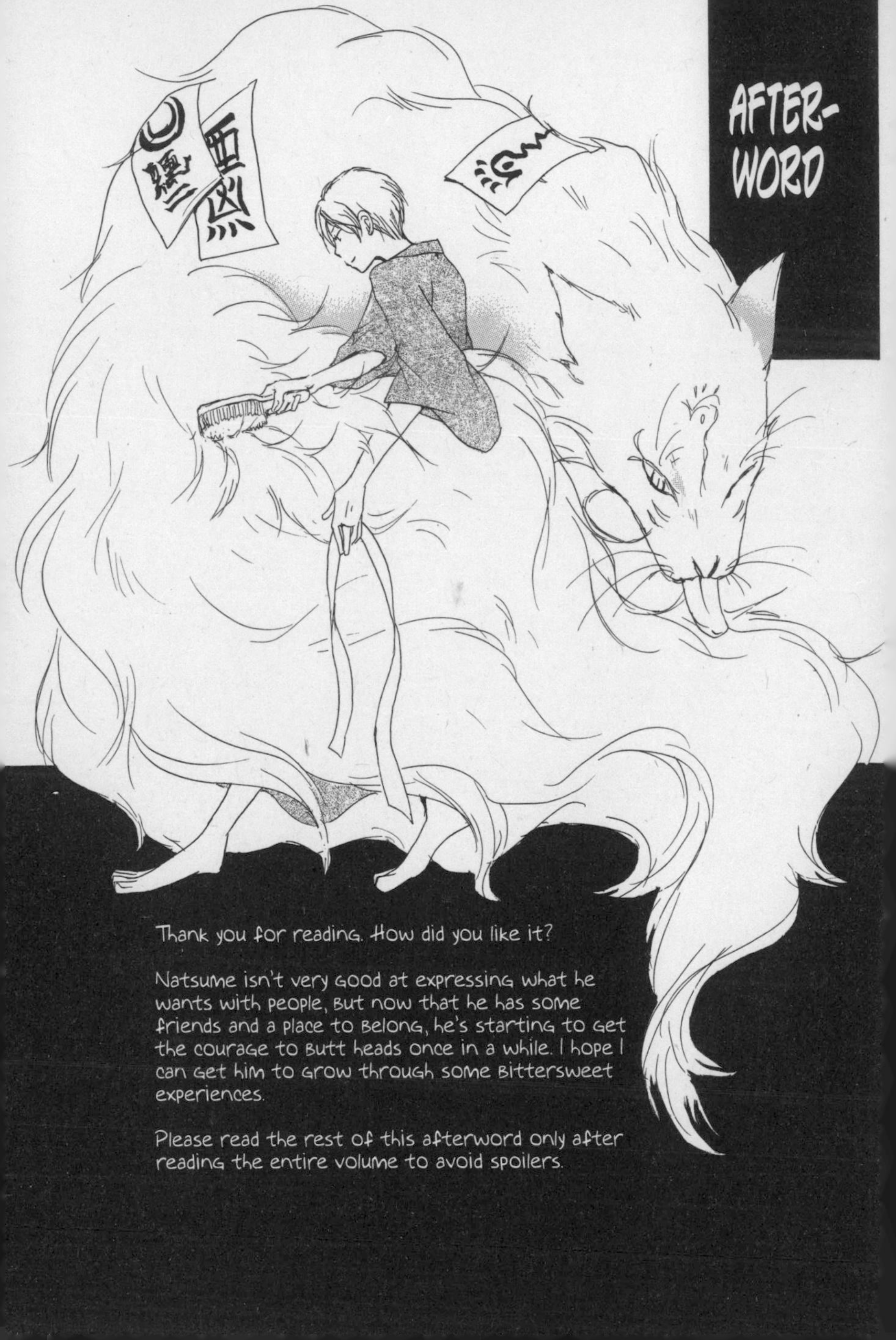

Thank you for reading. How did you like it?

Natsume isn't very good at expressing what he wants with people, but now that he has some friends and a place to belong, he's starting to get the courage to butt heads once in a while. I hope I can get him to grow through some bittersweet experiences.

Please read the rest of this afterword only after reading the entire volume to avoid spoilers.

CHAPTERS 37, 38

False Friend

Nobody believed Natsume when he talked about yokai before, so I considered this a story where he goes back and tries again. I realized it was extremely difficult to communicate a necessary message to someone without backing down, whether or not they believe you.

I was nervous about how readers would react to Shibata and what a jerk he was. Fortunately, many took pity on him and forgave him for being a poor sap in love. As for Murasaki, I gave her impossibly wavy hair so that I could have Shibata anxiously say, "No school would allow a student to get her hair permed like that!" But the scene was cut for space. I imagined her hair almost like roots that spread every which way over years of wild growth. It's so fun to draw girls. I wanted to try out all sorts of ideas. It's almost breathtaking.

Having friends used to be something Natsume could only dream about, but now they are real and an important part of his life. I'm sure he'll go to Taki and Tanuma to complain that he made a new friend, who may be a jerk sometimes, but is really not a bad guy.

CHAPTERS 39-41
The Harvest Festival

The idea was to have Natsume and Natori get asked to do conflicting sides of the same job by yokai and humans, respectively. But when you give these two the same objective, they somehow hesitate, to see how the other makes a move, and agonize over whether they're doing the right thing. They really shouldn't be so alike, but it's like they're staring into a mirror. This is how they struggle for a solution, while Nyanko Sensei and Hiragi sigh in the background, I'm sure. They take pity upon each other that they have few friends. They want to remain friends and equals even when their opinions differ, and yet they have a strange inferiority complex towards each other.

Natsume has nothing he can flourish like a girl's long hair or a skirt, so it was so fun to have him wear the Harvest God's robes for once. Come to think of it, Nyanko Sensei doesn't have much he can flourish either. Hiragi's hair is straight and short, but she's still fun to draw. I hope I can draw more of these lively and animated stories.

My heoes:
    Tamao Ohki
    Chika
    Mika
    Mr. Sato
    My sister
    Hoen Kikaku, Ltd
       Thank you.

Please send me any comments.

Yuki Midorikawa
c/o Shojo Beat
Published by VIZ Media, LLC.
P.O. Box 77010
San Francicso, CA 94107

Yuki Midorikawa

Natsume went through life suppressing his emotions because he didn't want to be affected by others. But now he's able to pick out the moments of joy and delight. However, once he experiences such emotions, he'll also be exposed to anger and fear. As he hangs out with fun, kind, cunning, fearsome yokai, he'll realize what he really needs to face.

As always, I'd like to continue drawing these calm and peaceful days that are occasionally punctuated by moving encounters and twists of fate. Reaching ten volumes is like a dream to me.

I'll keep working hard on each episode to produce manga you can enjoy. Thank you so much for reading.

May 2010